SHOOTING BLANKS

SHOOTING BLANKS
War Making That Doesn't Work

James F. Dunnigan and Albert A. Nofi

WILLIAM MORROW AND COMPANY, INC.

New York

Library of Congress Cataloging-in-Publication Data

Dunnigan, James F.
    Shooting blanks : war making that doesn't work / James F. Dunnigan
and Albert A. Nofi.
        p.   cm.
    ISBN 0-688-08947-X
    1. War. I. Nofi, Albert A. II. Title.
U21.2.D835 1991
355.02—dc20   90-26275 CIP

Printed in the United States of America

First Edition

1 2 3 4 5 6 7 8 9 10

BOOK DESIGN BY LISA STOKES

For Frank Dunnigan, who daily demonstrated that no information was trivial

ACKNOWLEDGMENTS

A large number of people gave sundry forms of assistance and support. Some provided information, others read and commented on the manuscript. Without these folks, the book would not have been possible. These people are (excluding those who did not want their names mentioned in print): Bela K. Kiraly, Brian Sullivan, Bruce Humphreys, Dan David, David C. Isby, Dennis Casey, James Dingeman, Joe Ward, John F. Prados, LTC Greg A. Rixon, Margaret Moore and the other fine folks at the NYPL, Mercedes Almodovar, Norman Friedman, Paige Eversole, Patrick Abbazia, Paul Murphy, Professor Helga Feder (CUNY), Representative Charles Rangel (Democrat of New York), Richard Jupa, Ronald Fraser (Center for Defense Information), SFC Charles Drake, Steve Zaloga, Vivian Jones (of Representative Rangel's staff), William Cruz, Austin Bay, Dan Bolger, Richard L. DiNardo, Walt Grant, Sterling Hart, Ken Hoffman, Doug MacCaskill, Mike Macedonia, Ray Macedonia, Steve Patrick, Jim Simon, Thomas J. Wisker, John Boardman, Shelby Stanton, and Mary S. Nofi and Marilyn J. Spencer for putting up with one of us.

CONTENTS

LIST OF TABLES

SHOOTING BLANKS

Why Do We Shoot Blanks?

·1·

"**S**hooting blanks" is what happens when you call out the troops and the results are not what you expected. It happens most frequently at the beginnings of wars, and even after the fighting has been under way for a while.

This is normal. It happens a lot. Shooting blanks results in the unanticipated and needless loss of men and equipment, and often a national disaster of far more political, economic, and human cost than anticipated. Nearly every war in this century involved a case of at least one side shooting blanks, and usually both.

Though different nations shoot blanks in different ways, every country commits this to a greater or lesser degree when it goes to war. The nation that shoots blanks least is likely to be the one that emerges "victorious" from a war.

In the past, the usual result of a case of shooting blanks was defeat. However much societies may have been willing to tolerate its mistakes and missteps in the past, the consequences of shooting blanks in the nuclear age are unthinkable. Today, shooting blanks can easily mean annihilation. Not just for the "loser," which did sometimes occur in the past, but also for the "winner," and even for those not involved in the quarrel at all.

Shooting blanks is inevitable in diplomacy and warfare. There are too many unknowns and variables to expect perfection in these matters. This book points out the many ways things can go wrong. If you know what the common mistakes are, you can more readily avoid them in the future.

HOW TO SHOOT BLANKS

Nations shoot blanks in many ways: socially, economically, politically, as well as militarily, but it is the latter that has the most dangerous implications.

The most obvious cause of shooting blanks is that we misunderstand our military capabilities. Miscalculating opponents' capabilities comes in as a close second. Building inappropriate military forces is a result of the first two problems that then becomes a major problem in its own right. All of these problems are the result of five basic bad habits that we identify as customary causes of shooting blanks: Intelligence Confusion, Amateurism, Media Muddle, Procurement Puzzle, and Wrong-War Syndrome.

EXPLANATIONS AND EXAMPLES

Intelligence Confusion

Military intelligence generally isn't, and leaves leaders in the dark about who has what in the way of forces and capabilities, as well as to the intentions of various powers. Even when the information is there, leaders either ignore or misuse it.

"We shall better know how to deal with them another time," said British Major General Edward Braddock, as he lay dying of wounds received from French troops and Indian warriors during "Braddock's Defeat," in 1755, near what is now Pittsburgh. Neither Braddock nor any of his troops, save some Virginians under young Lieutenant-Colonel George Washington, had ever fought in the American wilderness before, but they had assumed that the expertise that made them the finest army in Europe would work just as well in North America. A little intelligence collection on how war was waged in the New World would have changed the situation. Other British leaders of that period, such as Robert Clive in India, were more diligent in collecting information on conditions in exotic locales, and were more successful as a result.

Amateurism

Political leaders frequently don't know what to expect from the military. And the military leaders may not understand the capabilities and limitations of their forces, or those of their enemies, either.

"The English conquered us, but they are far from being our equals." Thus did Napoleon on Saint Helena try to explain his defeat by the Duke of Wellington's British and Allied troops, blaming it on anything but the enemy. In fact, at Waterloo Wellington had outmanaged him, outthought him, and outfought him, and the strategic situation was totally against him anyway, but Napoleon was never willing to admit it. While Napoleon had rewritten the book on warfare, he eventually got sloppy. His opponents kept learning, and Napoleon never acknowledged that he had lost track of who could do what to whom.

Media Muddle

The media generally give a spotty or misleading picture of military capabilities. This not only may mislead the citizenry, but also the political and military leaders as well.

"The Americans did it," charged President Gamal Abdel Nasser of Egypt of the devastating defeat his country suffered in the 1967 Arab-Israeli war, assigning it to a series of massive airstrikes by U.S. forces. Actually, it was the result of the Arabs' assumptions, constantly repeated in their media, that whatever happened, the Israelis would never strike first. This thinking ignored completely what the Israelis themselves were saying openly in their press both before and after the war. So when the Israelis did strike first, Nasser attempted to explain it away by blaming the United States. Nasser's outrageous claim was promptly dismissed in most of the world, but the Egyptian press played it up, and as a result there are still some Egyptians who believe it.

Procurement Puzzle

The large military budgets of major powers cause questionable behavior in arms development, and result in flawed weaponry that does not do the military much good.

"There's something wrong with our bloody ships today," observed British Vice Admiral Sir David Beatty at the Battle of Jutland in 1916, as he witnessed several British battle cruisers blow up upon being hit. British ship design was so seriously flawed that one German shell striking a turret would ignite the ship's ammunition supply and send the ship to the bottom. Better-designed German ships had little to fear from this problem.

Wrong-War Syndrome

There is a tendency to get ready for the wrong war.

"We goofed!" exclaimed French General Maurice Gustave Gamelin, chief of Ground Forces, after the Germans reached the English Channel on May 20, 1940, just ten days after attacking. French plans, equipment, organization, and training were based on the assumption that any new war would be much like World War I. This is commonly the best an army can do if it was victorious in the previous war. But the Germans came prepared to fight World War II.

One or more of these five factors will be found at work in any case of shooting blanks. The problem exists. We continue to be surprised when military power does not do what we think, or are told, it can do. Consider some recent examples.

UNCHARACTERISTIC BEHAVIOR

The marines getting blown up in Beirut in 1983 was the result of their not using seven standard security techniques all units in a combat zone are supposed to employ. Had the marines followed their own security procedures, the tragedy would almost certainly have been avoided. Consider the security rules that were ignored. First, the troops were all quartered in one location. Standard procedure is to disperse personnel as much as possible when in a combat zone. There was also no inner security in the form of a truck-proof barrier. Nor were the inner-zone guards provided with live ammunition for their weapons. In addition, there was no outer-zone security; the outer-zone posts were manned by Lebanese troops, with no marines present even as "observers." Moreover, there was no long-range monitoring of the outer-zone by troops with binoculars. And intelligence processing was deficient, for information on the planned truck bombing was available, but had not been passed on to the marines on the spot. Finally, the commander of the marines was at the end of so long and complex a chain of command that it was not entirely clear who was in charge.

This was not the first time the marines had been placed in a tricky diplomatic situation: Until World War II, they were referred to as "State Department troops." For more than a century, they have successfully carried out missions like Beirut many times. But this time they were let down by their numerous superiors, who gave them conflicting and dangerous instructions, forcing them to do (or not do) many of the things that made the disaster possible. Yet what the terrorists did was not unexpected. They had earlier pulled the same stunt on the U.S. embassy there and against marine installations. And even after, the embassy got hit again in 1984. Most of the security precautions that should have been taken would not have interfered with the "peacekeeping" mission assigned to the marines. You're not contributing much to peacekeeping if you get nearly 250 troops killed. If you stop such terrorist attacks, you are keeping the peace.

Yet if the marines were not the primary cause of this disaster, the commanders involved must nonetheless shoulder some of the blame. Their chief fault was in not protesting their untenable situation more vigorously. The marine commanders feared "paper bullets" more than the real ones.

WAYWARD MISSILES

That the destroyer USS *Stark* was hit by a missile or that the tanker *Bridgeton* ran into a mine in the Persian Gulf in 1987 should not have been a surprise, nor should have the tragic accidental downing of the Iranian airliner by USS *Vincennes* in

July of 1988. Peacetime armed forces expend most of their efforts on appearing combat ready, not being ready for combat. *Stark* got into trouble because certain officers on the ship came up short at a crucial moment. This happens even in wartime, but in peacetime you have less opportunity, or incentive, to weed out the officers who might not be up to the task when the shooting starts. During wartime you have plenty of opportunity to observe who can do it right and who can't. In peacetime there is another agenda, and the survivors of the peacetime selection process are not always combat ready.

The mining of the tanker *Bridgeton* demonstrated a somewhat different problem. Mines are quite effective and dangerous weapons. But they are not as, well, sexy, as aircraft, missiles, or nuclear submarines. In the U.S. Navy, mine warfare gets lip service and little else. So when eighty-year-old mines were encountered in the Persian Gulf, U.S. naval forces were ill equipped to handle them. Give credit to the U.S. naval commander on the spot when *Bridgeton* hit the mine. This officer quickly realized that *Bridgeton* was large enough to survive several mine hits. So he put *Bridgeton* at the head of his column of warships and proceeded up the Persian Gulf. What at first glance appeared an absurd decision turned out to be a wise one. This sort of quick thinking saves lives in wartime and wins battles.

The Iranian airline disaster illustrates a third important point, that men and weapons don't always work in combat the way you expect them to. *Vincennes* was a new ship embodying an innovative, highly complex weapon, the AEGIS air-defense system, with a crew that had never been in a combat zone before. Even in the best of circumstances, men make mistakes. Given the character of the weapons system, the inexperience of the crew, the eagerness of the ship's officers to strut their high-tech stuff, and the stressful conditions that prevailed in the Gulf that fateful day, a disaster was not surprising. As weapons become more sophisticated, the margin for human error will shrink, and the likelihood of accidents will increase.

THE LAND OF ILLUSIONS

The Middle East is a land of illusions when it comes to military force and what it can do. Since 1945, there have been dozens of wars, insurgencies, and "civil unrest" situations that have each demonstrated a different aspect of shooting blanks. In the late 1940s, the British found themselves in the middle of a Jewish-Arab dispute over Israeli statehood. The British had centuries of experience handling this type of colonial ethnic struggle. Actually, they did not do too badly. Their previous experience in Africa, India, Asia, and the Americas indicated that it would be a good idea to back out of this one. Compare this with the French reaction to restive colonies after 1945. Neither as perceptive nor as adroit as the British, the French found themselves embroiled in nearly twenty years of war and unrest in a futile attempt to hang on to their colonies. In the Middle East, once the British left, the first Arab-Israeli war broke out. The Arabs underestimated the resolve of the ragged-looking Israeli soldiers. The Arab armies were much better looking on paper. But it was combat performance that counted, and the Israelis had in their ranks many veterans of World War II and many others hardened by their experiences with Nazi Germany. So the Arab forces were repulsed, and Israel was established. The 1956 Arab-Israeli war was more of the same, with Egypt thinking its swell-looking forces would sweep the field. They did, in reverse. The United Nations had to bail them out. The 1967 war was a reprise of the 1956 one, except that the Egyptians thought they couldn't lose given all their fine Russian equipment and training, and with the Syrians attacking in the north and the Jordanians from the east. That didn't work either, for the same reasons.

But winning can be dangerous—we call it "Victory Disease"—and in 1973 it was Israel's turn to shoot some blanks. After a quarter century of kicking Arab armies all over the battlefield, the Israelis let reality become obscured by their vision of Arab soldiers as perpetual losers. On the other side, this time around the Egyptians had their eyes firmly fixed on reality. They recognized the fact that the Israelis were excellent soldiers and that in order to win they would have to train their butts off and develop some clever tactics. The Egyptians did just that. As a result, the 1973 war began with a series of surprising Egyptian tactical victories over the Israelis. Nevertheless, the Egyptians lost their humility too quickly, just as the Israelis embraced reality with equal alacrity. After a few days, the Egyptians cast aside their carefully thought-out tactics and got greedy, and sloppy. Meanwhile the Israelis got down to

business with a vengeance and managed to come out of the
1973 war victorious, if humbler and a lot wiser.

The Lebanese civil war began in 1975 and just went on,
and on, and on. All the participants thought they had an edge,
or eventually would. A mark of compromise—and competence—is knowing when to cut your losses. Few groups in Lebanon will do this. They continue to shoot blanks, and real bullets.
The war has also been kept going by material and psychological
encouragement from outside powers. Israel, Syria, Iran, Iraq,
and other nations all support their favorite factions. Most of the
population has adapted, as much as one can, to the horrid conditions the constant low-level conflict has created.

Shooting blanks is endemic in the Middle East. The costli-
est example began in late 1980 when Iraq invaded its larger and
more populous neighbor Iran. The Iraqi Army had never fought
a war before. For centuries a Turkish province and British colony, Iraq became a fully independent nation only after World
War II. Iraq had oil, and that gave it funds for purchasing all
the arms and military equipment it wanted. All that hardware
made the Iraqis believe what they wanted to believe, that they
had an effective military force. So they invaded Iran and initiated a nine-year bloodbath. The Iranians—the ancient Persians—had been at the soldiering business for several thousand
years. Their usual victims were adjacent Arabs, plus anyone
else in their way. But in this century Iranian soldiers had been
mostly involved fighting internal "enemies" rather than foreign
ones. At least they had some practice. In 1979, Iran underwent
one of its periodic religious revolutions, tossing out the monarchy in favor of a theocracy. The chaos in Iran appeared to
weaken the country's traditionally effective armed forces. Or
so it was perceived by the Iraqis. But once the fighting began,
it turned out that the Iranians were not so weak as the Iraqis
thought. Nor were the inexperienced Iraqi troops as efficient as
their leaders had hoped. Of course, the religious revolutionaries
in Iran believed that their country's military leadership was politically unreliable, professionally incompetent, and religiously
imperfect. But with God on their side, how could they lose? So
the war dragged on for nearly nine years, during which both
sides expended enormous numbers of courageous young men
with little skill and less result until exhaustion forced a cease-
fire at roughly where the border originally stood. While both

armies improved during the war, as is generally the case, neither improved enough to vanquish the other. It was a classic case of shooting blanks.

THE RUSSIAN DISEASE

Russia's consistent failures during the first months of any war are a subject usually avoided in discussions of the current military situation in Central Europe. Several times over the centuries, Russian armies had been mobilized and sent off to fight. In every case, the result was, at best, a mess, and at worst, a catastrophe for the Russian forces.

The twentieth-century chapter of this sorry list began in 1904 when, after Japan initiated a war in the Far East, the Russian "steamroller" went after Japanese forces in Korea and Manchuria. The Japanese not only won most of the battles, but the war as well. Actually, Russia might have eventually ground the Japanese down if rebellions had not broken out in major Russian cities in 1905. But those uprisings happened because Russia was shooting blanks politically, economically, and socially, as well as militarily. Similarly, in 1914, when Russia mobilized against Germany and Austria-Hungary, its attempt to invade East Prussia resulted in one of the most calamitous defeats ever suffered by a major army in modern history. Russia ended up losing that war too when once again unrest on the home front played a large part in the defeat.

Then, in 1939, Russia invaded Finland. The Finns not only repulsed the much larger Russian forces, but annihilated several large units and decimated many others, to inflict losses ten times those that they themselves incurred. Disregarding losses, and with no internal unrest to worry about as a result of Stalin's brutal suppression of all opposition, Russia eventually bludgeoned its way to a "victory" this time. Two years later, Germany invaded Russia. Now defense is traditionally a Russian strong point, but not this time. In one of the greatest defeats in history, Russian armies were thrown back hundreds of miles and lost millions of troops plus tens of thousands of aircraft and armored vehicles. Yet the Russians actually outnumbered the Germans in men, artillery, aircraft, and tanks. Imagine what would have happened if those Russian forces had instead been the attacker. After four years of bloody practical experience, Russian forces became first-rate practitioners of offensive combat. But after ten years of peace, 1956 found the Red Army rumbling into Hungary to put down a rebellion. The operation achieved its goal, but at great cost, with about a thousand dead within a few days. The Russians used overwhelming force against impromptu rebels without much in the way of heavy weapons or tanks. Administratively, the Russian operation was a fiasco. The mobilization of troops and equipment revealed many short-comings. Movement and supply of the invading troops was not as efficient as the Russians thought it would be. But the Russians did arrive in massive force, and the Hungarian Army decided that the odds were too great. Had the Hungarian Army assisted the irate armed citizens of Hungary, the Russians could have had a disaster on their hands: They would have "won," but at even more serious military, political, and human cost.

In 1968, twelve years after the debacle in Hungary, Russia invaded Czechoslovakia to forestall another independent-minded "ally." Though casualties were low, because the Czechs offered no resistance, this was an even bigger disaster than Hungary, with wayward Russian units firing on each other and the supply system collapsing into chaos. The next chance to exercise the offensive spirit came eleven years later in 1979, when Russian forces invaded Afghanistan. As in Czechoslovakia, the commandos and paratroopers did better than the regulars, who were quickly found to be fairly useless. A year later, while Russia was massing troops on the Polish border for a possible invasion of that restive satellite, the mobilization system just about collapsed. Over a quarter century after the Hungarian fiasco, things weren't getting better, but worse. The current *glasnost* in the Russian military media is providing ample evidence for why these problems exist, and persist.

THE PEARL HARBOR SYNDROME

People with the authority to use military forces are not stupid, at least not most of them. They are generally well-educated and have presumably studied history. Despite all this, and the realization that their armed forces may not be all they would like them to be, political and military leaders plunge into wars anyway. Regularly, they do so with a surprise attack. You could call this the Pearl Harbor (or "Preemptive Strike") Syndrome, after the 1941 Japanese surprise attack on the U.S. Pacific Fleet. The Japanese thought that if they could land a devastating blow early on, their more powerful opponent would roll over and sue for peace. It's amazing how well this illusion has endured. A casual perusal of the history of the past several thousand years finds this stratagem repeated time and again: Hit 'em hard and fast and first, and it'll all be over before the leaves fall. It rarely works, but is again and again the straw grasped by leaders going to war with slender means or for inadequate reasons. This is a classic method for shooting blanks. It's also the basic justification behind terrorist attacks, although these atrocities rarely have the desired effect either. No matter how well your surprise attack works, the effect is commonly just the opposite of what was desired. The enemy becomes angrier and more determined to achieve retribution.

ASSAULT-RIFLE DIPLOMACY

Another persistent cause of shooting blanks is mixing diplomacy and military force. While philosopher Carl von Clauswitz pointed out that warfare and politics are naturally intertwined, he did not believe that one should call out the troops as casually as one would send out for a pizza. But this is precisely what some people seem to think he said. And in this century, the proliferation of poverty-stricken nations, and of cheap and plentiful weapons, plus intrusive major powers have created a multitude of nasty "little" wars. Several years ago, it was estimated that there were more than 40 million AK-47 assault rifles in the world. There are even more around today. And most of them are in use by ill-disciplined troops or irregulars in places like Lebanon, Afghanistan, Angola, Laos, Sri Lanka, Central America, Ethiopia, Cambodia, Peru, and Colombia. The list goes on and on. One of the most enduring myths of the age is that more powerful and established nations somehow exercise control over the events in these battlegrounds. When they try to control the violent factions and events they support, these nations are frequently shooting blanks. Now let us consider the reasons why.

INTELLIGENCE CONFUSION: DO WE REALLY KNOW WHAT WE KNOW?

Information—intelligence—is power, or at least it should be. In wartime, military organizations live and die by the quality of their information. But most of the time, armed forces are not at war. In such circumstances, the effort required to obtain accurate and meaningful military intelligence is not given much consideration. In peacetime, there are more pressing matters to be attended to. Although a nation's armed forces are supposed to be designed to fight those of some other power, many armies actually exist to keep their own countrymen in line. While the appearance of conventional armed forces is maintained in terms of organization and equipment, in practice the soldiers function as heavily armed police. It follows that their information-gathering activities don't go beyond keeping an eye on their own population. Third World nations are most prone to this, but more developed powers are not immune. Communist nations, and totalitarian governments in general, prefer maintaining two separate armed forces, one for external threats and another to keep an eye on their own people. Russia, for example, has 5 million troops in the regular armed forces and another half-million, mostly organized like combat troops, to keep the Russians in line. A lot of Russian intelligence effort is spent on watching other Russians, many times to the point where the evil machinations of foreigners are ignored.

Under the best of conditions, intelligence gathering is an expensive and potentially embarrassing process. The nations on which you gather military information are not going to give up their most cherished secrets willingly. If your intelligence people get caught, you have a diplomatic crisis. There are two ways to minimize these risks. One is to recruit the best people you can for intelligence work and give them lavish budgets. This is rarely done, as good information about potential enemies must be kept secret, so you can't openly crow about your success to the people you get your money from. Unfortunately, legislators and their constituents are more willing to fund things they can see, like new weapons and equipment. One notable exception is the U.S. Congress, which is quite generous with intelligence projects. Unhappily, only the legislators get to see the results, not the taxpayers. The second approach is basically to pretend that you are diligently collecting military intelligence. This is safe, cheap, and quite common. Of course, if a war breaks out, this approach turns out to be quite dangerous and, ultimately, most expensive.

Most nations don't even have an accurate idea about what their own forces can do, and they are not much better at calculating what anyone else's can do, even when they have access to good information. While you can test-drive a new car or carefully examine a new house, there is no easy way to figure out just what your peacetime armed forces are capable of. Combat, and the "wartime atmosphere," are so removed from most people's experience that peace—and particularly a long peace—causes armed forces to drift in inappropriate directions.

Evaluating the combat capabilities of potential opponents starts with what you think your own troops can do. This is a delicate business. If your perception of your own troops' capabilities are faulty, evaluations of your opponent are likely to be even more imprecise. But the inability to understand another culture is also part of the problem. We talk of "corporate cultures" that befuddle people moving from one job to another and "culture shock" experienced by tourists. In the same way, each culture has its own military subculture. When we attempt to translate another nation's doctrine, weapons, equipment, and organization into more familiar terms, we habitually make mistakes and get it wrong. Cultural differences between nations can be great, and they are not always obvious. Thus there are enormous differences in military tradition, thought, and practice between American and Russian armed forces, some quite subtle. These are covered in greater detail throughout this book.

A further complication is that the potential enemy must be seen as strong enough to justify your own defense spending. Thus there is the tendency to portray potential battlefield opponents as larger than life. At the same time, such exaggerations can lead to potentially harmful plans and tactics. Even if this is not the case, politicians see the military as crying wolf and will sometimes deny funds when the need is real. In nations where the military is a political power in its own right, these budget battles take on political overtones and come down to outright extortion of the unarmed taxpayers by the military. Through all this, the quality of military information takes a distinct backseat.

One caveat is that you must have an enemy. Out-of-the-way nations like Australia and New Zealand have allowed their armed forces to waste away in the last few decades because there simply isn't a viable enemy nearby. Canada, for similar reasons, is having the same problem. Even in the United States, more people are beginning to think like Canadians and Australians.

Even so, there is nearly universal temptation to fudge the numbers to fit current policy. If you are at peace with your neighbors, their combat capabilities are seen as a tad lower than if there is diplomatic tension. Ideally, the military capabilities of potential threats should always be measured by the same standards. You never know when a benign neighbor might turn rabid. If that happens, you may not be able to restructure your forces and thinking quickly enough to make a difference.

To cap it all off, nations withhold valuable knowledge from their own troops in the name of national security. This practice varies from nation to nation. Russia has probably had the worst record. During arms negotiations, Soviet diplomats will find that they can get more plentiful and accurate data on Russian forces from American negotiators than they can from their own military people. While this is an extreme case, similar patterns exist in all nations and regularly cause problems.

AMATEURISM: DOES ANYBODY KNOW HOW THIS WORKS?

While politicians, and their errors in judgment, cause the troops to be called out, it is the military officers who cause things to get really fouled up. Combat experience is highly perishable. Within twenty years of your last bout of combat, most of the officers exposed to it have retired or left the service for other reasons. Thus, customarily, most armed forces rely on an intangible "military tradition" to get them through those long periods when no one in uniform remembers what it's like to get shot at. Not all "military traditions" are equally effective. Some nations never seem to get the hang of it. This is perhaps due to the fact that there are only a few officers and troops who will ever prove capable in combat. These people are not always put in charge, or even taken heed of, in peacetime. Peacetime military leaders are selected more for their administrative ability than any aptitude for leadership in combat. In peacetime, the principal business of generals is trying to seem effective at doing something they can't practice without going to war. The end result is that both the leaders and the led take it on faith that anyone knows what he is talking about in military matters. One thing you can be assured of is that when the shooting starts, many of your "best and brightest" peacetime officers will be found wanting on the battlefield. This is nothing new; it has happened throughout history, it is happening even now, and it will happen again. During both world wars, in Korea, and in Vietnam, many officers had to be relieved from combat duty because they were simply no good at leading men into battle. And this was after years of "getting ready."

And then we have the problem of professionals versus amateurs. Many nations have professional soldiers who spend decades learning what military power can, and cannot, do. But as specialists in military matters, professional soldiers are likely to be amateurs in political matters. On the other hand, political leaders and diplomats, who have responsibility for getting wars started, or avoiding them, are probably amateurs in the military department. This odd arrangement grew out of the realization that it was unwise to combine military and political authority in one person.

Partly, this is common sense. Military organizations are, of necessity, dictatorships. Orders are issued with the expectation that they will be executed promptly. Combat units require strict discipline in order to survive. Political operations are based more on compromise and consensus. There is more ambiguity and delay in politics. It is rare, though not unknown, for someone to be both an effective soldier and an able politician.

The different styles of soldiers and politicians naturally clash. Not all nations can prevent these clashes from escalating to a military takeover. These takeovers rarely work for long, simply because the military leaders are no more adept than the civilian ones. You can run a government by issuing orders and demanding discipline from uncooperative civilians for only so long. If you do keep it up, the economy will probably falter and the population become surly. In some cases, things get so bad that the soldiers hand power back and return to the relative simplicity of the military life, which is what happened several times in Latin America during the 1980s.

Those nations that do manage to keep the generals out of the presidential palace commonly end up with political leaders who are not very knowledgeable about military matters. There are cases where the military has good advice to give, but the politicians either don't ask or don't listen. American military intervention in Vietnam was ordered despite the fact that many U.S. senior military commanders advised against it. The same thing happened with the Russians in Afghanistan: The military leaders thought it was a bad idea, but the political leaders went ahead anyway. Argentina's attack on the Falklands and Iraq's invasion of Iran were both instances where the military leadership and the civilian governments were intertwined. There may have been military leaders in each case who thought war was not a good idea. But under such circumstances, it was more a matter of one group of generals outvoting another. Underscoring the debacles in Argentina and Iraq was the low level of military professionalism. It was the blind leading the blind down a road strewn with mines.

But even where the political leadership is willing to listen, and the military leadership is competent, there are apt to be problems. Senior military leaders are expert at what they believe war is like, but their training and experience are likely to be a generation out of date. This is where professionalism comes in handy, since a professional force will have a better chance of recognizing what's changed and what hasn't once the bullets start flying.

So long as generals can't govern nations and politicians can't run armies, there's always going to be some amateurism in military affairs. Because declaring war is a political act, the troops who are going to be sent off into combat often find themselves in impossible situations.

MEDIA MUDDLE: THERE ARE EXPERTS WHO CAN EXPLAIN IT ALL

Because most of the time there is not much in the way of tangible major combat experience available for study, most information on military affairs is based on extrapolation and speculation. Even when there is combat, the information coming out is scrambled by censorship or bad reporting. It frequently takes several years for the "fog of war" to clear and a more accurate picture of what happened to emerge. Often this may not happen until the war is long over.

Most people do not fully realize the major role played by the civilian media in distributing military information to the military, as well as to the civilian sector. The military tends to view much of its information as secret. Even if it wanted to circulate information freely, civilian media organizations are much more efficient at it. As a consequence, even military people get much of their information on military matters from the press, notably so with regard to information dealing with other branches of the service. Newspapers, magazines, TV, and radio all saturate their audiences with information. Nonetheless, most of what is said about military affairs is the same brief summary of events repeated over and over again. This alone distorts the situation, particularly for an audience that has little experience of military activity. At least when the media talk about the weather, business, sports, crime, or education, many in the audience have personal experience to draw upon. This makes such news easier to understand, and keeps those who gather information for the media on their toes. These conditions generally do not apply when reporting military affairs. There is also a certain wicked glamour attached to military affairs, making it even easier to embellish military reporting with imaginative details and hysterical implications. The military and civilian consumers of this information can only take it all in and try to make the best of it.

While the print media—newspapers, books, and magazines—do a decent job, what passes for military information in the electronic media—television and radio—is frequently erroneous, habitually misinterpreted, and occasionally distorted, though rarely with any deliberate intent. While there is an antimilitary bias in the media, this can be traced to the traditional attitude toward the military of the American people as a whole.

Generally, the military reporting in the electronic media is so misleading that it's dangerous. Part of the distortion arises from the format of television news, which tends toward brevity, headlines, and emphasis on visual items at the expense of sober examination and evaluation. Complex matters are reduced to a level of simplicity that clouds the issues. The print media can go into more detail, but detail usually puts off most readers, who are inclined to fall back on the headlines and visuals they more easily obtain from TV. Radio news also relies on the headline approach, but lacks the visuals. Television and radio do have a perverse advantage in that they get their message across very effectively, or at least quickly. For most people, some distortion in TV military reporting is no big thing. But for the military professionals who absorb the same lessons, the distortions can eventually prove fatal.

As bad as this situation is, current commentary on military affairs is getting worse, because a new generation of reporters is coming up that has almost no exposure to the military. While military experience is not essential for understanding and reporting on military affairs, it is extremely useful. Yet, combined with a generation of senior government officials, and voters in general, lacking military experience, there is more potential for myths and illusions to thrive. It is in these conditions that warlike attitudes can take root.

When many readers have no way of separating accurate from fanciful military reporting, it is possible for some fairly outrageous attitudes to become established. Be alert when confronted with military reporting. Yes, even this book is the sort of thing we are warning the reader about.

PROCUREMENT PUZZLE: GUNS AND BUTTER AND ANYTHING GOES

One of the more lucrative commercial enterprises around is selling weapons and equipment to the armed forces. Because the military has a difficult time determining what it will need in the next war, it's possible, and frequently the case, that an adroit sales representative from a commercial firm can sell the military items that are not needed, or that won't work, or both. For a military officer to work in the procurement side of things is not considered a very glamorous way for a warrior to spend his time. As a result, the commercial sales reps are likely to be more talented, experienced, and effective than their military counterparts. You can imagine who controls the business of determining what will be purchased. Caught up in this system, the military is reluctant to admit errors in judgment and generally tries to make the best of the situation. A cycle of errors, self-deception, and outright lies begins that is rarely broken until the fighting starts, and perhaps not even then.

Another problem is that without a real war to determine what works and what doesn't, everyone's an expert, particularly everyone of high rank. Rarely does anyone possess sufficient stature to effectively resolve disputes over how the money should be spent.

No nation is immune to this disease. Of all the items in a government budget, defense funds are most vulnerable to misappropriation. It is understood that these funds can be tampered with without much chance of retribution. This happens in nearly every nation. The abuses range from outright embezzlement to steering contracts away from the best source and toward the most politically suitable contractor.

WRONG-WAR SYNDROME: WHO (OR HOW) ARE WE SUPPOSED TO FIGHT VERSUS WHO (OR HOW) ARE WE PREPARED TO FIGHT

The people you are preparing to fight are rarely the ones you end up fighting. This is nothing new, but the cost of these mistakes is rising. Misinformation and misperceptions create and perpetuate these bad habits. The United States began gearing up for a war with Russia in 1948. Since then, America has fought a number of opponents, none of them Russian. Meanwhile Russia was getting ready for "the Big One" with the United States for the same length of time while itself indulging in several small wars, none of which have been with the United States. Each power has had some unpleasant experiences in these "little" wars, usually involving opponents trained and equipped by the other power. There's a perverse logic to this, which would make this subject interesting and entertaining were the results not so tragic. The solution is to solve as many of the problems surveyed above as one can before the shooting starts. This is not easy, and realizing that it is not easy is the first step toward solving some of these puzzles.

SYMPTOMS

There are several symptoms of the shooting-blanks disease. Like most afflictions, shooting blanks expresses itself in familiar and easily recognizable ways. A sampler of the more common symptoms follows:

The Best Damned Army

We are the best, and our enemies are neither warlike nor bright. The media love to jump on this one, often with the encouragement of a bloodthirsty government. "We are the best" is a shared characteristic of most armed forces, at least officially. Of course, most soldiers keep tabs on the other fellow's track record and generally know the score, even if they won't admit it publicly. After the Argentines seized the Falkland Islands in 1982, they thought Britain would not bother to try to recapture them. Then Britain announced that the Royal Navy was on the way and that the Royal Marines, Commandos, Guards, and Gurkhas would soon be storming the Islands. At that point, most Argentine soldiers knew, even without saying it out loud, that they were in big trouble. These "We Are the Best" attitudes often backfire, as Americans learned in Vietnam, Russians discovered in Afghanistan, and Israelis learned against Egypt in 1973.

Martial Race

We are the warrior people, and the other guys are just a bunch of shopkeepers, peasants, or lily-livered scum. Also a media favorite. Another way of putting this would be to say "unworthy opponents," but that depends on the opponent of the moment. A martial race believes it will wipe the floor with any opponent. The Afghans used this attitude to sustain them through their ordeal with the Russian Army in the 1980s. The Japanese did less well with these beliefs when they went up against American marines and GIs in the 1940s; nor has this attitude helped the Pakistanis against India or the Arabs against Israel.

The Perfect Plan

If we do things precisely this way, we cannot but win. This is a somewhat recent conceit, the result of an explosion in military technology and theory in the last two centuries. Unlike in the past, you can now get on the radio and keep after the poor wretches desperately trying to carry out the "plan." Military professionals who think very highly of themselves are prone to "perfect plans." The disastrous results usually reveal an underlying amateurism and failure of intelligence. Respect for the "perfect plan" reached a peak during World War I. Then a lot of people got killed carrying out perfect plans that turned out to be fatally flawed, or just plain fatal, although only for the troops and not for the planners. World War II still used a lot of plans, but with a great deal of more circumspection. This phenomenon cropped up again in the postwar era, with the result that the United States fell flat on its numerous and ever-changing perfect plans in Vietnam, as did Russia in Afghanistan. Perfect plans will continue to crop up whenever military commanders (or, more frequently, their political masters) believe overly much in their own abilities, or those of their ever-growing staffs.

Science of War

War is a predictable science, reducible to a few simple laws of universal application. This is not an extension of the perfect plan, but rather a general faith in *all* your planning to the point that you believe you can predict any situation and act accordingly. This is gold-plated amateurism growing out of the nineteenth-century notion that human affairs are susceptible to logical analysis. Academics and defense consultants still favor these fictions. Anyone who's been a soldier for a while takes a jaundiced view of this one.

Technology Will Out

Black boxes and high-tech weaponry will overcome all obstacles. This particular curse, which began about a century ago, is presently in full flower. It's a manifestation of fighting the wrong war, although in this case the conflict is a future one that is only dimly perceived. But technology is more fixed and substantial. The reality is more fixed and substantial. The reality is that future wars and existing gadgets are rarely a perfect fit. Many of the people who actually use the high-tech equipment know this, but the stuff costs so much that it's difficult to admit that all that expenditure won't produce some kind of miracle. Another secondary problem is calculating how much less quantity you can get away with once you have paid for greater quality. You can't have both, and the formula is rarely calculated correctly except in combat. The B-2 bomber is an excellent example of the "triumph of technology," and demonstrates another area where the United States leads the way.

The Intelligence Advantage

You can't fool us, we know everything, we're reading the other guy's secret codes, understand his mind, and have reliable spies over there, with "perfect" security of our own, and anyway, we're in general on to every trick in the book. The reality is that you never can know for sure. The Allies broke German and Japanese codes in World War II while keeping their own secure. They had had similar success in World War I. But that didn't prevent the enemy from coming up with a few surprises anyway. And there have been many indications since 1945 that it's been getting easier, not more difficult, to penetrate veils of security. Deception is coming back into favor, but not quickly enough for many major powers. The Russians retain a lead here, treating deception as a minor religion.

Air Power

No need to fool around on the ground, just bomb them back to the Stone Age. This goes beyond mere technology; if it has wings, it can perform miracles. This myth dies hard. The Gospel of Air Power was first preached during the 1920s and 1930s. Even strong evidence of the serious limitations of air power during World War II and subsequent conflicts has not dulled the enthusiasm for ever more complex and expensive air weapons. It just goes to show you how far you can get with diligent self-promotion. The United States leads the way in this area too. Maybe it's the glamour of it all. Who knows?

More Is Better

More troops, more guns, more firepower, will always win. Another variation of the "intelligence failure." You've got to get the right combination of quantity and quality. The "More Is Better" approach led us to nuclear weapons, which were so effective in producing "more firepower" that nations are fearful of using them. Thus everyone falls back on massive quantities of troops and conventional weapons. The human factor is ignored in this pursuit of quantity, much to the battlefield grief of those who do so.

Victory Disease

We've been winning so long, how can we lose? Especially against those yo-yos. This fallacy is a combination of media-muddle euphoria, intelligence confusion, and amateurism. Victory Disease (which is not to be confused with the perfect plan or the best damned army) may be rooted in a number of errors, but the primary reason for it is that your forces actually *are* better and have demonstrated this by winning regularly, particularly against a specific enemy. There may be many reasons for your success, such as superior numbers or technology or training. These reasons include psychological and diplomatic ones. Basically, you convince yourself that you can't lose. The problem is that a good track record may lead you to overextend yourself, to assume that your incompetent opponent will continue to be so, or to take on other folks who may not be so inept. One of the better examples of this was the war plans the Japanese made after their success in the first six months of World War II. The planners believed their own press releases and proceeded to overextend the slender Japanese resources. A year after Japan went to war with America, the tide had changed, and Japan had, essentially, lost the war.

Citizen-Soldier

Large standing armed forces are not necessary, because our citizens will spring to arms on a moment's notice in such numbers and ferocity that the enemy will be stopped cold. A lot of media assistance is needed to perpetuate this one. The United States, Russia, and China have successfully relied on this approach many times in the past. However, this solution is very expensive in terms of citizen-soldier lives. Because of this, the aforementioned nations more recently favor permanent, large, professional armed forces. The citizen-soldiers are still there if you need them. Meanwhile, nations like Switzerland, Sweden, and Israel still rely on the citizen-soldier almost exclusively.

Military Solution

Political problems can be resolved by military action. Some philosophers have been espousing this logic for thousands of years. Its most recent manifestation was in Beijing in June of 1989. Save for a few exceptions, like Socrates and Marcus Aurelius, most philosophers have not had to personally participate to the fullest in their violent extensions of diplomacy: Frederick the Great of Prussia, who initially advocated "military solutions" to sticky problems, personally experienced the consequences and became very interested in more peaceful methods thereafter. This approach is a favorite of large nations having disputes with smaller ones, or of nations having internal problems. Using the troops to bring in the crops or chase smugglers or drug runners are common examples. One could call it moral laziness; it is also very amateurish.

Surprise

Hit 'em hard and fast, or, to put it another way, "Scare them to death." This tactic is not much different than any other ambush, except for scale. It is also a form of amateurism that requires constant media reinforcement. This approach provides short-term benefits and long-term grief. For example, even though the United States was victorious against Japan in World War II, "Remember Pearl Harbor" can still get the juices flowing. The Japanese really believed that their surprise attack on Pearl Harbor would scare the United States into submission. While surprise is a situation much sought after, it is not easily accomplished. In times of crisis, the defender generally becomes quite wary. Moreover, once you have gotten away with a surprise attack, the victim is going to be very upset and burning for vengeance. Unless you can really put the screws to the other side, you will have a bitter feud going until someone is obliterated. As you are one of these sides, there is a certain amount of risk involved.

Treachery

We didn't lose, we were the victims of double-dealing. This is a form of shooting blanks that appears after a defeat. Don't take the heat for failure, blame somebody else. It's been heard many times: Americans accusing President Roosevelt of complicity in the Pearl Harbor disaster or the "peaceniks" for defeat in Vietnam, or the "fifth columnists" and "traitors" who aided Hitler in overrunning France. It's easier this way, as you then don't have to effect reforms in your defense establishment, just conduct a witch-hunt or two. That will only set you up for another fall, the next time there's a war.

THE SHOOTING-BLANKS GUIDE

This book is designed as a guide to the phenomenon of shooting blanks. Our method is to examine the principal components of shooting blanks so that the reader will be able to develop a clearer understanding of the problem of evaluating military power, its strengths, and its limitations. Most of the chapters that follow deal with specific aspects of the phenomenon of shooting blanks as it affects modern armed forces, with particular reference to those of the United States and Russia, though without neglecting other nations. Our approach will necessitate some repetition, because, although there are literally hundreds of instances of shooting blanks from which to draw examples, we have chosen to select most of ours from a small number of particularly notable and relatively recent cases, such as the Falklands War, Lebanon, the Iran-Iraq War, and so on, on the theory that the reader is most likely to have some familiarity with these.

What follows first is a summary survey of some notable disasters in recent military history, with some observations on the reasons why they occurred. Several of these will also reappear in later chapters, although from different angles. (For example, Chapter 4 will look at things from the point of view of intelligence.) The chart is terse, as charts must be. Each of the disasters mentioned contains a rich background of material.

SHOOTING BLANKS AND GREAT WARTIME DISASTERS

(NOTE: Under Cause, I = Intelligence Confusion, A = Amateurism, M = Media Muddle, P = Procurement Puzzle, and W = Wrong-War Syndome.)

SHOOTING BLANKS DISASTER (YEAR)	VICTIM	VICTOR	CAUSE
The Guns of August (1914)	France	Germany	I A M W
The Marne (1914)	Germany	France	I A
Tannenburg (1914)	Russia	Germany	I A M P
The Western Front (1915–18)	Allies	Germany	I A M W P
The Fall of France (1940)	France	Germany	I A M W P
Dunkirk (1940)	Germany	Britain	I A M P
Battle of Britain (1940)	Germany	Britain	I A M W P
Barbarossa (1941)	U.S.S.R.	Germany	I M P A
Pearl Harbor (1941)	U.S.	Japan	I W M P
Midway (1942)	Japan	U.S.	I M W
Stalingrad (1942)	Germany	U.S.S.R.	I M P
D-Day (1944)	Germany	U.S., Britain	I M
The Bulge (1944)	U.S.	Germany	I M
Indo-Pak War I (1947)	Pakistan	India	M
Arab-Israeli War I (1948–49)	Arabs	Israel	M I
Korea, General (1950)	N. Korea	U.S.	M I
Korea, Phase I (Mid-1950)	U.S.	N. Korea	I P M
Korea, Phase II (Late 1950)	U.S.	China	I M W
Korea, Phase III (1951–53)	All	None	M W
Sinai (1956)	Egypt	Israel	M I A
Bay of Pigs (1961)	U.S.	Cuba	I M
Vietnam (1964–73)	U.S.	Vietnam	I W A
Indo-Pak War II (1965)	Pakistan	India	M
Six-Day War (1967)	Arabs	Israel	M I A
Indo-Pak III (1971)	Pakistan	India	M
October War, Phase I (1973)	Israel	Arabs	I M P
October War, Phase II (1973)	Arabs	Israel	M I
Afghanistan (1979–89)	U.S.S.R.	Afghan	I W
Iran/Iraq I (1980–86)	Iraq	Iran	I M A
Falkland Islands (1982)	Argentina	Britain	I A
Lebanon (1982)	Israel	No one	I M
Iran/Iraq II (1987–88)	Iran	Iraq	W A P
Panama (1989–90)	Panama	U.S.	I A M
Kuwait (1990)	Kuwait	Iraq	I A
Iraq (1990–91)	Iraq	U.N.	I M W

The Guns of August (1914)

French defeats in opening stages of World War I. France had been spoiling for a war with the Germans since they beat her in 1871 and took the provinces of Alsace and Lorraine. Had the French paid more attention to their intelligence on the German Army, they would have realized they were seriously outclassed by 1914. Among other errors, the French grossly miscalculated the number of troops the Germans could deploy against them. To make matters worse, they decided that the best way to defeat Germany was to launch an immediate offensive into Lorraine. They then compounded their errors by developing a body of tactics based on throwing masses of inspired French infantry at the Germans. The idea was that French élan would overcome whatever puny weapons the Germans had. The French media got behind all these fairy tales because the army promoted them with such enthusiasm. The Germans, on the other hand, had decided that a direct confrontation would be too costly, so they planned a surprise offensive into the French rear through Belgium, and brought with them lots of machine guns, rapid-firing artillery, and more realistic tactics. In combination, these shot to pieces the French theories, not to mention their infantry, and brought the Germans to the gates of Paris. France avoided a replay of 1871 largely because of German errors.

The Marne (1914)

The Germans almost won World War I in the first month, but were ultimately halted in front of Paris on the river Marne. While most of the French Army was getting itself slaughtered attacking a few entrenched Germans in Alsace and Lorraine, the bulk of the German Army had marched rapidly through lightly defended Belgium, in a right hook aimed at Paris. This was the German "perfect plan." It almost worked. Overlooked was the desperation of the French when confronted by a threat to their capital, plus the fact that the Germans had to march, while the French could use their railroads. The Germans literally marched their troops into a state of exhaustion. For "perfect plans" to work, one side has to be perfectly right, and the other inept, or at least willing to perform exactly according to the perfect plan's concepts. The other side is rarely so obliging. Desperation is a staunch ally of the defender. Finally, the Germans simply misjudged their situation when they reached the Marne and snatched defeat from the jaws of victory.

Tannenburg (1914)

Russia's catastrophic defeat by Germany in 1914. While the French managed to recover from the debacles of 1914, their Russian allies were not so fortunate. The Russians were not really eager to go after Germany. Through most of the late 1800s, Russia and Germany had been allies. But the French took advantage of German errors and got Russia to sign a mutual-defense pact. Russia was a dubious ally. Whatever military shortcomings the French had, the Russians had in greater quantity. Compared to the Germans, the Russians were essentially amateurs. Russian intelligence was woefully inadequate; Russian procurement left their troops poorly armed and equipped, and the media kept most Russians from realizing how bad things were. All was revealed during the Battle of Tannenburg, when a Russian invasion of East Prussia was chopped to pieces by a smaller German army. This defeat established a pattern that the Russian Army was never able to break.

The Western Front (1915–18)

After World War I's hectic opening months, the Western front settled down to a steady grind, a slaughter actually. The Germans were outnumbered and fighting on two fronts, as the Russians kept trying despite their debacle at Tannenburg. This gave the Western Allies (Britain and France) an advantage, which they proceeded to squander. Just about every mistake that could be made was. It was a blood-drenched orgy of shooting blanks. There was an intelligence failure in analyzing German intentions and plans. Tactics and training tended to increase friendly casualties. Procurement obtained few items that improved the infantryman's chances. In effect, the Western Allies were fighting the wrong war. Most of the innovations came from the German side. The performance of the Western Allies has become a model of how not to do it.

The Fall of France (1940)

Twenty-six years after the Germans came through Belgium toward Paris, they did it again, cutting through the Ardennes this time. The French had learned a lot the last time around, and the Germans knew just what to do to fool them into making new mistakes, like not launching an offensive when they should have. The French once more believed that they had found a perfect solution to the problem of defense. This time there was no "Miracle of the Marne." The Germans sent many of their troops in on tanks and trucks, thus eliminating the fatigue factor. The French made every possible mistake to abet this German victory. On paper, the French and their allies were superior. On the battlefield, nonetheless, the French were shooting blanks big time. And ironically, even in victory the Germans were still shooting blanks. In 1914, the Germans came anticipating complete victory, and so were seriously handicapped when they failed to get one. In 1940, they anticipated a partial victory, and as a result the collapse of France left them at a loss as to how to continue the war: Short of an invasion, the only way to bring Britain to the negotiating table would have been to bleed the British in France as they had tried in 1914–18. This error led to many bad strategic decisions in 1940–42.

Dunkirk (1940)

One bright spot in the campaign that took France out of the war in 1940 was the "Miracle of Dunkirk," where the bulk of the British forces escaped the victorious German armies. When the French forces began to collapse, it left their British allies nearly surrounded by Germans. The British had no choice but to attempt a withdrawal to the seacoast, although there were a few Germans and the English Channel in the way. The victorious Germans were not unaware of this British attempt to steal away to fight another day. If the Germans had made the effort, they could have sent sufficient mechanized forces after the British and halted or interrupted the evacuation. But the German Air Force *(Luftwaffe)* commander insisted that his fighters and bombers could stop the British evacuation without any help from the ground forces. The British and their allies begged to differ.

The Germans were held off in a desperate rear-guard action, while the Royal Air Force (RAF) committed everything that could fly, and a hastily mobilized fleet of ships and boats came over the Channel to pick up a third of a million British, French, and Belgian troops. This was the first, but not the last, time the fly-boys boasted they could do it all by themselves. It didn't work. It rarely has.

Battle of Britain (1940)

Germany loses the first major air campaign in history. Fresh from their failure to stop the British evacuation at Dunkirk, the *Luftwaffe* proposed an air offensive against Britain. The *Luftwaffe* would bring Britain to its knees before the Germany Navy began to ferry the German Army across the English Channel. The Germans went all the way in shooting blanks. Their intelligence ignored the British radar and early-warning systems. Their high command (led by a World War I fighter ace named Hermann Göring) was amateurish in its response to initial difficulties. German media kept nearly everyone in the dark about all the problems until it was too late. The German failure to use intelligence correctly caused the Nazis to miss knowing how close they were coming to defeating the British. The German Air Force was basically fighting the wrong war, and not even doing that very well. It was several years before they fully admitted that new techniques, and the procurement of different weapons and equipment, would be needed.

Barbarossa (1941)

The German invasion of Russia. In 1939, Stalin had signed a mutual-security pact with Hitler in which each agreed not to attack the other, and on who could steal what in Europe. By early 1941, Hitler was beginning to move enormous forces into Eastern Europe. Some of this movement was due to the necessity of subduing Yugoslavia and Greece. But the forces massing near the Russian borders were much too large for that. Meanwhile British and American intelligence, not to mention Russian agents, learned that Hitler planned to invade Russia in late spring. Although Stalin was repeatedly apprised of this, and although German reconnaissance flights over Russian territory increased markedly in the last weeks of spring, he continued to claim that any evidence of a German invasion was "imperialist provocation" designed to get Russia to help Britain. Besides, Russia had an enormous military, the largest and most heavily equipped in the world. But he was wrong on both accounts. As a result, when Hitler did invade Russia, on June 22, 1941, the Russian armies disintegrated. This was partially because of the surprise, and partially because they were overburdened with enormous amounts of obsolete heavy equipment, organization, and doctrine. But another important reason for the defeat was inept leadership, Stalin having shot most of the experienced officers in a prewar purge. It was a massive case of shooting blanks, made worse by the fact that the flaws in the Russian Army had been revealed in the brief "Winter War" of 1939, when the Red Army took ten times as many casualties as it inflicted in overcoming tiny Finland. On the plus side, the Russians demonstrated impressive recuperative powers and the ability to learn from their mistakes.

Pearl Harbor (1941)

The disaster that struck the U.S. armed forces at Pearl Harbor on December 7, 1941, is a classic example of shooting blanks. Although aware of Japan's aggressive intentions in East Asia and the Pacific, the United States was certain that when Japan went to war, it would launch its initial attacks against Malaya, the Philippines, and Indonesia. U.S. forces in the Philippines were considered strong enough hold out for six months or so until the U.S. Navy's battleships fought their way across the Pacific from Pearl Harbor to relieve the garrison. The common U.S. view was perhaps best expressed by an article that was published in *PM* magazine a few weeks before December 7, "How We Can Lick Japan in 60 Days." In the event, the Japanese *did* launch the offensive we anticipated, but even as they did so, they also struck a devastating air-raid blow against the U.S. battlefleet at Pearl Harbor, demonstrating considerable technical and tactical skill. So unwilling were many Americans—including some of the officers responsible—to believe that we had been shooting blanks, that there persist to this day accusations of treachery in the highest places. Such delusions are also a form of shooting blanks.

Midway (1942)

Japan loses the initiative in the Pacific. The six months after
Pearl Harbor saw an unbroken string of Japanese victories. Then
the Japanese decided to seize the island of Midway, in the Central Pacific, preparatory to an eventual invasion of Hawaii. They
amassed an enormous armada to accomplish this goal, including five aircraft carriers, seven battleships, and dozens of cruisers, destroyers, and submarines, plus a large invasion force.
They planned to lure the remnants of the U.S. fleet into a decisive battle for the tiny atoll and there destroy America's remaining naval forces. Considering the sorry state of U.S. naval
forces in the Pacific at the time, the Japanese should have had
a sure thing. But victory had inflated Japanese confidence to an
extraordinary degree, and they were very contemptuous of the
possibility that the U.S. Navy could put up much of a fight.
Moreover, despite evidence that battleships were no longer the
weapon of decision—an issue that they themselves had demonstrated—the Japanese believed that the critical action would
be a slugout between surface forces, after a preparatory air battle. And they ignored certain indications that the United States
was reading codes that they considered unbreakable. The result
was a spectacular disaster in which they lost most of their carriers and any chance they might have had to force a negotiated
peace. It was a combination of Japanese arrogance, and U.S.
skill at code-breaking, ship handling, and dive-bombing, plus
some luck.

Stalingrad (1942)

The decisive German defeat in Russia. Although the German offensive of 1941 had come close to destroying Stalin's
Russia, it had ground to a halt before Moscow as a result of
fierce resistance and the onset of winter. In the spring of 1942,
Hitler decided to finish off Russia with a massive offensive in
the Ukraine. Initially, all went well, but late in the campaigning
season resistance began to stiffen markedly before Stalingrad.
Believing his own propaganda—"The German soldier can do
anything!"—Hitler insisted on turning the struggle for Stalingrad into a test of wills and resources. The city could easily

have been bypassed, which was the correct "military solution." As Hitler poured men and equipment into the fight, he ignored increasing evidence that the Russians were about to undertake a massive counteroffensive. This was a significant failure to effectively use intelligence. When the attack came, the Russians managed to surround an entire Germany army, and numerous satellite troops as well. Hitler insisted that these forces hold out at all costs, convinced that his air force could supply it from the air. The result was a devastating defeat. It was the turning point of the war in Russia, and of World War II. Stalingrad also demonstrates that it takes many errors of judgment to create spectacular cases of shooting blanks.

D-Day (1944)

The Allied amphibious invasion of German occupied France. During World War II, the only way for the Western Allies to carry the war to Germany was to effect a massive landing in France. Their preparations for this included an elaborate deception plan designed to confuse the Germans as to the probable location of the invasion. The plan was enormously successful, convincing Hitler that the landings would come at the Pas de Calais, considerably north of the actual site in Normandy. Moreover, Hitler also fooled himself as to the strength of the German defenses, which were actually much less effective than he—or the Allies—believed, with the result that the landings were far less costly than anticipated.

The Bulge (1944)

The last major German offensive in the West. By late 1944, the Allied drive that had liberated most of France in the early autumn had ground to a halt. The pause was largely attributed to a lack of logistical support, but was equally due to stiffening German resistance. With the "campaigning season" at an end, Allied forces settled in for the winter, confident that the Germans were on the ropes, certain that their mastery of German secret codes would keep them informed of any surprise maneuvers, and assured by their belief that the German Army hadn't undertaken a winter offensive in 200 years. They were wrong on all three counts, as Hitler marshaled the last men, tanks, and shells for one final throw at victory, using secure telephone and telegraph lines instead of radios to communicate his orders. The result was the "Battle of the Bulge," which gave Allied, and particularly U.S., forces a healthy dose of intelligence reality.

Indo-Pakistan War I (1947)

The first war between India and Pakistan wasn't even declared, although over a hundred thousand troops were involved for over a year with thousands of casualties. The issue was which of the two newly minted nations the border state of Kashmir would join. Kashmir had a Muslim population (as did Pakistan) and a Hindu ruler (as did India). The ruler opted for joining India, causing his Muslim subjects to rebel. Pakistan sent undeclared aid in the form of troops and arms. Kashmir's ruler called for assistance from India, which was forthcoming. When India saw that the fighting could go on forever, she played the media angle, offering concessions and calling for mediation. The fighting died down, India reneged and eventually secured control of Kashmir. Pakistan was shooting blanks in her belief that she could win such a lopsided confrontation. The militarily weaker Pakistan did not forget.

Arab-Israeli War I (1948–49)

Long-simmering tensions between Arabs and Jews in Palestine, coupled with a Jewish insurgency against continued British rule, led the United Nations to partition the territory between the two peoples. This didn't sit right by the Arab nations. Confident that their nicely uniformed, well-equipped armies could easily defeat a bunch of unwarlike Jewish farmers, the Arabs subjected the nascent Israel to an invasion on all fronts. And were defeated on all fronts. They had failed to notice that the "unwarlike Jewish farmers" had adequate, if old, stocks of weaponry, with thousands of World War II veterans in their ranks, and were extraordinarily well motivated, while the Arab forces were equipped mostly for parades and police work, had virtually no seasoned personnel, and were largely disinterested in the issue at hand. This war set a pattern that was to be repeated, with minor variations, in 1956 and 1967. A massive sequence of shooting blanks.

Korea, General (1950)

The partition of Korea after World War II led to the establishment of mutually hostile regimes in the North and South. Soon both were arming. By 1950, North Korea had resolved upon a military solution to the country's division. North Korea was the primary loser of the Korean War, and its decision to invade South Korea in June of 1950 was based on any number of misconceptions. To begin with, partially as a result of a lack of clarity in the U.S. strategic position, it misread America's probable reaction to an invasion, a serious intelligence failure. In addition, largely raised on the propaganda of their Russian mentors, which denigrated the role of the United States in World War II and stressed the imminence of revolution in America, the North Korean Communists firmly believed that the United States was a "paper tiger," and lacked any sense of the enormous military resources that the Americans were capable of bringing to bear, given some time to prepare. Curiously, this bit of self-delusion was similar in many particulars to the reasoning that caused Japan to attack the United States only nine years earlier.

Korea, Phase I (Mid-1950)

The Republic of South Korea (ROK), backed by the United States, was being prepared for counterinsurgency operations, given that pro-North guerrillas were active there. The ROKs proved fairly capable in this work, and when the United States pulled its own troops out in 1949, America optimistically declared that the ROK Army was "the best damned army in Asia." Although cross-border incursions, guerrilla attacks, and similar activities increased markedly during the spring of 1950, both South Korean and U.S. intelligence continued to assume any threat would largely be posed by an insurgency. Unfortunately, this was not what the North Koreans had in mind. U.S. and South Korean intelligence experts were way off base in their estimate of what North Korea was up to. In mid-June, North Korean troops stormed across the demarcation line in a Russian-style offensive spearheaded by tanks and battle-hardened troops who'd spent World War II in the Red Army. Though the

ROKs tried to fight, they were neither trained nor equipped for such warfare and rapidly disintegrated. A similar fate befell ill-prepared U.S. occupation troops sent in from Japan to impress the natives. The result was one of the most serious defeats in American history, and one that could easily have been much worse but for air and naval superiority. With their backs to the sea, U.S. troops fought an heroic and successful battle against unfavorable odds and their own plunging morale.

Korea, Phase II (Late 1950)

In the autumn of 1950, the U.S. Navy turned an impending disaster in Korea into a spectacular victory by landing two divisions in the enemy rear. The result was a near-total collapse of the North Koreans and a spectacular drive northward. Now it was North Korea's chance to shoot blanks, as it was believed that the United States would not support South Korea. But as U.S., South Korean, and other UN troops drove closer and closer to Manchuria, Red China began to send signals about being uncomfortable with non-Korean forces on its frontier. The U.S. command, in the person of Douglas MacArthur, chose to ignore these signals, arguing that the war would be over shortly, and that even if the Chinese intervened, they could only do so with a small number of troops, who would be unable to cope with the massive firepower of an American army. Within days, hundreds of thousands of Chinese troops launched offensives all along the front and, using efficient light-infantry tactics that stressed their strengths and UN weaknesses, threw the UN forces back in a bloody reverse, at a time when the United States was beginning to realize that Korea was less than vital to American interests. The American-led forces had indeed set up their own defeat.

Korea, Phase III (1951–53)

The Chinese entry into the Korean War led to a protracted stalemate, in which U.S., South Korean, and UN forces were essentially held hostage for nearly two years, while deluding themselves that they had the upper hand. Eventually, both sides realized that neither could achieve a victory at a political cost they could afford. A cease-fire resulted, but the war has never ended and the two armies glare at each other across the 1953 battle lines to this day. While many nations will not accept a defeat, here was a case where for two years neither side was willing to accept the absence of victory.

Sinai (1956)

Arab-Israeli tensions came to a head again in 1956, sparked by the Egyptian seizure of the Suez Canal. This time the Egyptians thought they had the Israeli farmers where they wanted them, what with their larger army equipped with masses of new Soviet equipment. But the Israelis did it again, mildly aided by the fact that the Egyptians had also got themselves into a war with Britain and France. It was a massive disaster for the Egyptians, who had managed to fool themselves into believing their own propaganda. But if the Egyptians came up short, so did the British and French, as they did not receive the diplomatic support they expected from the United States. This was particularly irksome to the French, and contributed to their withdrawal from NATO in the 1960s.

Bay of Pigs (1961)

Castro's increasingly Communist dictatorship in Cuba was proving so troubling to U.S. sensibilities that the CIA convinced President Eisenhower that he had to do something. Based on intelligence supplied by Cuban exiles, it appeared that Castro was extremely unpopular and that his regime would collapse if a small revolutionary force managed to secure a foothold in the country. Although the Joint Chiefs of Staff objected to the plan, their expert advice was ignored. In early 1961, President Kennedy, despite misgivings, gave the CIA the go-ahead lest he be thought to be "soft" on communism. The operation was not as carefully planned as it might have been, with the landing site being changed at the last minute. Kennedy's lack of enthusiasm led to his refusing to supply air support. The result was an overwhelming defeat for the invasion force, an enormous outburst of support for Castro, and a political humiliation for the United States, which had believed what it chose to believe.

Vietnam (1964–73)

For the United States, military involvement in Vietnam was a result of poor use of intelligence, domestic political pressure, and fighting the wrong type of war, in the wrong place, at the wrong time. The first problem was the internal situation in Vietnam. For nearly a century, it had been a French colony. The French had picked up control of the area by initially offering aid to one or another warring faction and eventually taking over themselves. During World War II, President Roosevelt had been inclined to let the Vietnamese become independent because they had fought a guerrilla war against the Japanese while many of the French had collaborated. But Roosevelt died before the war ended, and the State Department counseled noninterference with French policy toward France's wayward colony. The attempted reconquest of Vietnam dragged on until 1954, when the French finally gave up. A compromise was reached whereby the Communist-led rebels got control of North Vietnam while various anti-Communist and pro-French factions moved into South Vietnam. There was a major political problem with this arrangement that few Americans paid much attention to. First, North and South Vietnam had rarely been united as an independent nation. The northerners and southerners did not like each other very much, and the ideological divisions created by Communism in the North and anti- (or simply non-) Communism in the South did not help matters much. Then there was nationalism. The northerners, Communist or otherwise, were indisputably Vietnamese national heroes. They had fought to free the nation from foreigners. Many of those in the South had collaborated with the French or the Japanese, sometimes both. These groups controlled the South Vietnamese government, and many in the South Vietnamese population resented it. Not much effort was required by the North to get a southern rebel movement, the Viet Cong, going. Yet, the United States saw that many in the North and South were repelled by communism, and this attitude eventually proved to be well-founded. But while the United States was pouring economic and military aid into South Vietnam through the late 1950s and early 1960s, South Vietnamese officialdom was pocketing most of it and this corruption was antagonizing the population and swelling the ranks of the Viet Cong. By 1963, the situation was becoming desperate. The United States finally recognized the role government corruption was playing in supporting Viet Cong recruiting and began pushing less corrupt leaders to take over. This didn't work out. Now American domestic politics came into play. President Lyndon B. Johnson feared that "losing" Vietnam to the Communists would damage his extensive program of social reform. Rather than take the heat, he chose the easy solution. U.S. combat troops landed in 1964. So the Vietnamese again had a foreign enemy on whom to focus their hatred. This was the second major problem—the United States was never able to disassociate itself from the role of a foreign "invader." Most Vietnamese saw little difference between French or American troops shooting up their homes and fields. Although the eventual Communist takeover of the entire country proved to be a social and economic disaster, Vietnamese nationalism was a primary factor in keeping the struggle going. American military forces never really came to grips with the nationalism problem, making all their battlefield victories empty ones. The solution to the Vietnam civil war was more political than military, but the United States ended up putting more effort into battlefield operations. There are many ways to shoot blanks, and neglecting the political aspect of a conflict is one of the more common ones.

Indo-Pakistan War II (1965)

Ill feeling over disputed border areas, many of them containing Muslims ruled by India, festered from the initial creation of Muslim Pakistan and Hindu India in 1947. But India was much larger than Pakistan, and although the Pakistanis considered themselves better soldiers, there were simply too many Indians. This is a typical shooting-blanks error. Hope appeared when India's border disputes with China erupted into a shooting war in 1962. It wasn't much of a war, as the battlefield was high in the mountains. Nevertheless, in two battles a thousand miles apart, Chinese troops were victorious. The Pakistanis decided that India's armed forces were even worse off than their propaganda had proclaimed. Better still, Pakistan saw China as a potential ally in another war with India. As it turned out, China was pursuing purely local goals in its mountain battles with India and was very vague when it came to wartime alliances with Pakistan. In 1965, fighting broke out between India and Pakistan, sparked by a border dispute in a desert area that had never known marked borders because there was nothing there that anyone wanted. This went on for a few weeks and died down in May. In August, India staged a large raid across the border in the Kashmir area. The UN truce observers negotiated a cease-fire, but in September Pakistan retaliated with a full-scale invasion of Kashmir. China made threatening noises, but was dissuaded from anything more meaningful by American and British warnings. By the end of September, there was another cease-fire, and everyone pulled back to his original position. Nothing was gained, much was lost. All that remained was the echo of shooting blanks.

Six-Day War (1967)

In early 1967, the Arabs again decided it was time to settle with Israel once and for all. Stimulated by their many new Soviet arms, their enormous armies, and Russian support in the United Nations, they calculated that Israel would be helpless to do anything. And they were wrong once more, for the third time. Rather than await the Arab onslaught, the Israelis decided to strike first, in an extraordinary blitzkrieg that saw them victorious on all fronts within days. The Arabs, who had already demonstrated a remarkable ability to believe their own press releases, then compounded their humiliating defeat by concocting a tale that U.S. naval aircraft had actually conducted the initial air strikes, only to be caught short again when Israeli intelligence, which had been monitoring high-level communications among Arab leaders, released tape recordings in which two of them agreed on this tale. Classic shooting blanks.

Indo-Pakistan War III (1971)

While Pakistan supported insurgency among the Muslims in Kashmir, India eventually found a Muslim separatist movement in East Pakistan to support. When India and Pakistan were created in 1947, Pakistan was in two portions, separated by a thousand miles of Indian territory. The only thing the two populations had in common was their Muslim religion. East Pakistan would soon become Bangladesh, but not before yet another war between India and Pakistan. This time it was the Pakistanis who were caught short all round. India had increased and improved its armed forces since the 1960s. India took advantage of the situation, constantly goading Pakistan while massing troops to defend Kashmir and invade East Pakistan. The media became a principal weapon in this. It worked; Pakistan eventually attacked with only modest success, India invaded East Pakistan with great effect, and Bangladesh was created. This war did not improve long-term relations between India and Pakistan, and both began to develop nuclear weapons. These three wars, and the arrival of nuclear weapons, appear to have made both nations aware of the escalating cost of shooting blanks.

October War, Phase I (1973)

The 1973 Arab-Israeli war was actually two wars. The first one, lasting about a week, was won by the Arabs, who staged a surprise attack in which Egypt crossed the Suez Canal while Syria nearly ran the Israelis out of the Golan Heights. There were three primary reasons for these Arab successes. First, there had been the element of surprise, as the Arabs used the media to profess peaceful intentions and to explain away troop movements. While this was ultimately an intelligence failure on the part of the Israelis, there was also a political aspect to it as the Israeli civilian leadership decided not to act on intelligence reports that the Arabs "might" be ready to launch an attack. There were also equipment-procurement problems, as the Arabs had loaded up on air-defense and antitank weapons that Israel was not adequately prepared to handle. As a consequence, Israeli forces took an uncharacteristic beating during the opening stages of the war. In a reversal of past experience, Israel was shooting blanks more than the Arabs. It was a sobering experience, which taught the Israelis some very quick lessons.

October War, Phase II (1973)

After the first week or so of success, the Arabs began to catch "Victory Disease." The Arab press was quick to trumpet the success of Arab armies, and Arab intelligence was slow to notice Israel's quick response to these new situations. Israeli forces quickly reversed the situation, although at substantial cost, and won their fourth war with the Arabs.

Afghanistan (1979–89)

Even the Russians now admit that the war in Afghanistan was a mistake. This is easier to state in hindsight, but at the time of the invasion there were apparently a number of senior officers who took a dubious view of the prospects. The decision to enter Afghanistan with the army was apparently largely a political one. Aside from being the wrong war for the Red Army to fight, Russian intelligence work was lacking, and the struggle got off to a shakier start than expected. The situation never improved appreciably, and the Russians spent most of the conflict shooting blanks. They did definitely learn about the shortcomings in their armed forces, lessons that could not have been learned any other way. The Russian ground and air forces will be digesting these lessons for many years to come.

Iran/Iraq I (1980–86)

Bad intelligence, believing what they read in their tamed papers, and a lack of professionalism in their military combined to hand the Iraqis a shocking defeat. Invading Iran while civil disorder raged there did not weaken that nation sufficiently to enable Iraq to grab a contested border area. It's an old story of which this is just the latest chapter.

Falkland Islands (1982)

By 1982, Argentina had been ruled by a bloodthirsty military dictatorship for nearly six years. The economy was in a shambles, an estimated 9,000 civilians had been abducted and murdered, and the generals and admirals were looking for a way to retire gracefully—and safely. The solution was to make a grab for the Falkland Islands, held by Britain for 150 years but consistently claimed by Argentina. They reasoned that the islands would fall easily to their forces, that Britain would not fight, that even if the British did fight, the Argentine armed forces were tough enough to deal with them, particularly given the distances over which the British would have to come, and, moreover, that the international community would back them in their claims to be decolonializing a portion of their national territory. A victory would leave them smelling so sweet that they would not have to face the music for their years of misrule. The islands were captured. But the British did fight, and their troops were tougher than any that Argentina had, although the Royal Navy ran into a few surprises. Moreover, the international community—including most of Latin America—was more upset about aggression than about the Argentine claims.

Lebanon (1982)

This was a war that nobody won. Even many senior Israeli Army officers look upon the enterprise as a "lost war." The primary goal of the operation, to get the PLO out of the area, was successful for only a short time. The Israeli invasion had no apparent effect on settling the Lebanese civil war. Worse, the conflict created divisions in the Israeli forces. Many Israelis performed their reserve duty under protest over the wisdom of the operation. There was even dissension in the higher ranks about taking the troops into Beirut street fighting, one brigade commander reportedly resigning in protest over being ordered to do so. The Israeli media were sharply divided on the operation, which reflected the mixed feelings of many of the troops. Israeli intelligence also came up short, which isn't surprising considering the chaotic state of affairs in Lebanon.

Iran/Iraq II (1987–88)

While the Iranians stopped the Iraqis cold in 1980, after about a year the Iraqis calmed down and began to rebuild their armed forces. They had access to a lot more money and, fearing for their very existence, adopted a very sober attitude. Not so the religiously inspired Iranians, who slighted training and procurement for too long and depended instead on the fervor of their teenaged infantry. By the time the Iranians realized that training and equipment were the key to success, it was too late. Iraq had got too large a lead in the bloodbath. Iran then did what it had vowed never to do: ask for a cease-fire and peace negotiations.

Panama (1989–90)

In a move that's got to rank right up there with Adolf Hitler declaring war on the United States after Japan's Pearl Harbor attack, Panamanian dictator Manuel Noriega declared war on the United States in mid-December 1989. This was accompanied by assaults on U.S. military and civilian personnel in Panama. Less than a week later, American forces moved against Noriega and replaced him with the last elected government (which Noriega had kept out of power). While Noriega can take most of the blame for this situation, which resulted in several thousand U.S. and Panamanian casualties (dead and wounded), the United States also underestimated Noriega's ability to sidestep attempts to seize him and the fragility of civil order in Panama. Aside from Noriega's ill-advised interpretation of American intentions and capabilities, it was a classic civil-war situation. Once the United States came in, those Panamanians exploited by Noriega supported the action while Noriega followers kept the fighting going for over a week. The international opinion was against the United States, but what else is new?

Kuwait (1990)

For several centuries, tiny Kuwait had survived as an independent state by astute diplomacy with its larger neighbors. Iraq has made claims to Kuwait ever since Iraq was created in the 1930s and pressed these claims as Kuwait's oil wealth grew in the subsequent decades. Iraq threatened an invasion in 1961, only to be deterred by the presence of British troops. Through the Iran-Iraq War of the 1980s, Kuwait was a generous supporter of Iraq, to the tune of tens of billions of dollars in loans and gifts. This merely whetted Iraq's appetite for Kuwait's wealth. In the summer of 1990, Iraq found itself broke and its credit exhausted. Iraq asked Kuwait and Saudi Arabia (another generous supporter during the war with Iran) for $30 billion and forgiveness of many other loans. These demands were not met and Iraq threatened invasion. Kuwait miscalculated Iraq's desperation (or greed) and chose to not "provoke" Iraq by mobilizing Kuwaiti armed forces. Iraq needed no provocation and came across the border before dawn on August 2, 1990. Kuwait's armed forces were swamped, with only part of the air force and most of the tiny navy getting away to Saudi Arabia.

Iraq (1990–91)

After devouring (and pillaging) Kuwait, Iraq found that it was the uncomfortable focus of world attention and outrage. Just as in its 1980 invasion of Iran, Iraq found it had seriously underestimated the risks involved and was facing yet another threat to its national existence. This is an exceptional record of disastrous adventurism. Twice in ten years, Iraq attacked a neighbor who, at the moment of attack, appeared a pushover, but turned out to be a much more formidable foe. Iran was larger than Iraq to begin with, and Kuwait had numerous powerful and reliable allies. Never underestimate the propensity for shooting blanks big time.

What Is Military Power?

·2·

*H*ow do we measure military power? What are the proper functions of the military? How can we determine what are the best armed forces for our needs? Why do national "styles" affect military power? What happens to the warriors in peacetime?

Military power is what works on the battlefield; anything else is just a dangerous illusion. Armed forces spend very little of their time in combat. As a result, it is difficult for anyone to separate the reality of military power from its appearance. There are techniques for calculating military power, but for various political and organizational reasons these techniques are not used, or if they are, the public rarely sees the results. Put simply, it is more convenient for all concerned to say military power is whatever they want it to be. For example, most of the time a government will assert that its military power is quite adequate. Still, if some official—or political candidate—suddenly decides that more troops or weapons are necessary, then your military power magically dissolves to something quite a bit less than what it was a short while ago. On the other hand, another official—or political candidate—might decide that you have too much military power and that a cut here and there will no impair "national security" and may even enhance it, while providing other advantages as well. Sometimes the very same person will take both stances at different times. In the early 1970s, Caspar Weinberger was known as "Cap the Knife" for the glee with which he slashed away at military—and other—appropriations as President Richard Nixon's budget director. But less than a decade later, he presided over the largest peacetime expansion of the defense budget in history, as defense secretary to Ronald Reagan, who had come to power partially by criticizing America's alleged lack of readiness for war. This particular skit has been played out for as long as there have been organized governments and organized military forces, and knows no limits of party or political beliefs. Despite centuries of experience with organizing, maintaining, and using armed forces, there does not exist a simple, rational, and commonly accepted basis for determining what constitutes an adequate military establishment.

Recent unpleasant reverses—Vietnam and Afghanistan—have not been good for popular perception of the military capacities of the Superpowers, or for the self-image of their armed forces. Both countries entered these wars with an excessive degree of confidence in their troops, their doctrine, and their technology. Each found itself mired in an ongoing conflict that the other, while wisely keeping out of direct involvement, willingly supported with arms, propaganda, and in other ways. In both cases, but particularly that of the United States, the war proved increasingly difficult to sustain politically. And both powers ended their involvement by a more or less ignominious abandonment of the faction that they had gone to war to sustain. The Afghan experience appears to be at least partially connected to the changes that are being effected in the Russian armed forces and to demands for a smaller, more professional force. Vietnam led the United States toward very much the same changes, with the abolition, after twenty-five years, of conscription, the introduction of more realistic training, and a greater reliance on historical precedent. Although they went on to win, the British suffered a similar salutary reverse in the 1899–1902

Boer War, which resulted in a major reorganization of their army so that by 1914 it was one of the best in the world. But that didn't mean it was well-prepared for the horrors of World War I.

REAL MILITARY POWER

So what is the reality of military power? Real military power is military power that gets the job done, and somehow does so without agonizing months or years of battlefield losses. Real military power is made up of tradition, training, technique, and technology, in that order. Tradition is combat experience remembered. Training is spending money on something you can't see but need very much, that is, getting the troops ready for war. Technique is developing procedures that are in sync with reality. Technology is equipment that does what needs to be done.

TRADITION

Military tradition is a collection of habits that make armed forces effective in combat. These habits are commonly viewed as bizarre, dangerous, or otherwise undesirable in peacetime. Military tradition is not easy to sustain in a peacetime environment. Part of the tradition is the parades, the uniforms, the saluting, and all the other ceremonial trappings of military life. These are not the most important traditions, but they are the easiest to maintain and do provide a basis for the more useful traditions. The more difficult items involve training methods, personnel selection, and spirit. It's such things as the confidence of a British or American sailor, who puts to sea secure in the knowledge that an English-speaking nation has not lost a naval war in over three centuries. Tradition is the relationship of mutual trust and respect that exists between officers and enlisted personnel. A strong military tradition is difficult to detect and measure. An intangible, perhaps, but its impact shows up in combat. For many nations, and their troops, that's too late.

TRAINING

Well-thought-out, strenuous, and dangerous training is a major factor in creating superior armed forces. Yet good, arduous training gets diluted because it's expensive and troops are injured or killed during these exercises. Especially in democracies, these injuries generate opposition from civilian groups and politicians, who demand less perilous training.

Frequently, officers and troops themselves avoid the hard training. After all, who wants to get mutilated or killed in peacetime? And besides, it's tiring and there won't be a war anytime soon anyway. Only seemingly mindless devotion to military tradition keeps the troops at it when there's not a war on.

The historical record is unequivocal—as the Romans put it, "The more you sweat in peace, the less you bleed in war." But these days, the exertions are also financial. Becoming proficient with modern weapons requires using them, and this is what breaks the budget.

For example: A modern jet fighter is not expected to last for more than 5,000–10,000 hours of flight time spread over twenty or so years. In combat, it might last only a few dozen hours. How long these expensive aircraft last in war or peace depends on the training of the pilots. Most pilots will never see combat. But if they do, they must be prepared. The better prepared pilots last longer in combat and the better prepared air forces win battles and wars. A $30 million Western jet is going to cost $5,000–$20,000 an hour to fly just for training. That covers the cost of the aircraft, spare parts, fuel, and other support. If you use the missiles and bombs these aircraft carry, you can easily burn up several hundred thousand additional dollars per training mission. Flying combat aircraft, even in training, is also dangerous. Many nations avoid the expense of adequate training for pilots. However, in all the air battles since 1939, the most effective pilots have been those who spent the most time in the air before they entered combat.

A navy has a similar problem with its equally expensive ships and weapons. Russia is a case in point. As Russia felt the effects of its faltering economy in the late 1980s, money was saved by keeping warships in port most of the time: Soviet ships are at sea as few as 30 days a year, U.S. ones 120–200. Warships that don't spend a lot of time at sea are simply expensive targets for those warships that do train hard. Most Western navies have long naval traditions. Their sailors know that the only way to prevail in wartime is to work the ships heavily in times of peace. This, more than anything else, gives the U.S. fleet its unquestioned combat superiority.

Ground forces are most prone to avoid strenuous training in peacetime. Modern ground forces have a lot of costly weapons and equipment. It's expensive and exhausting just keeping all of the vehicles and gadgets operational. Taking all that gear out for lengthy exercises is horrendously expensive, and most nations avoid it as much as possible. The ground forces also have a lot of missiles that should be practiced with regularly. This is rarely done. Even lowly, and inexpensive, artillery and tank shells are not always lavishly expended in training. The Russians allow their tank and artillery crews to fire only a fraction of the shells their Western counterparts fire each year. The Russians are aware of this disparity, but part of their military tradition is placing quantity ahead of quality, believing that whatever accuracy is lost as a result of parsimony in training during peace will be more than compensated for by massive expenditures of ammunition in war. Western observers generally do not absorb the full import of this attitude.

Inadequate training is often the fault of a tightfisted legislature, although imaginative commanders can work around this. Politicians are usually reluctant to spend money on something they cannot touch or feel. Many times the military is at fault, having allowed the quality of their noncommissioned officers (NCOs) and officers to decline to a dangerously low level. When an army has the money but cannot get the right candidates for leadership jobs, the usual solution is to promote people who previously would not have been promoted. This happened to the U.S. Army during the latter years of the Vietnam War and into the late 1970s. Few people realized how much the quality of all troops had fallen because inept leaders were unable to adequately train their subordinates.

A common decision of low-quality military leadership is to cut back on training. After all, training is expensive and dangerous, and the results can't be seen, while drill is cheap and makes the troops look good, and they're much less likely to get hurt, which could really ruin a man's career. Peacetime leaders, both civilian and military, tend to lose sight of their priorities. The reality is that when war comes, it's better to have a small number of well-trained troops than to have a large number of less well prepared but perhaps more heavily equipped ones. Despite this historical truth, the price of training appears too high when there isn't a war going on.

Training is complicated by technological factors. Modern warfare is dominated by complex equipment. Nations that have a tradition of diligence do well with military training in general. If the nation is also industrialized, it has a head start in mastering complicated modern weapons and instilling discipline. Thus you have two extremes. On the high end of the scale, you have hardworking, highly industrialized nations doing quite well with training. At the other extreme, we have less diligent nations with no industrial establishment doing it poorly. There are exceptions. An outstanding leader can whip a lackluster nation's troops into a high state of training. A national emergency can do the same. This is what happened to the Iraqis while they were being hammered by Iran during the early 1980s. Iraq suddenly became much more industrious and effective in its training methods. The Iranians neglected serious training efforts. Their attitude was that religious fervor would do the job. Unfortunately, in battle God favors the well-trained.

TECHNIQUE

Technique is tricky. Technique is the collection of habits, routines, drills, and leadership styles that make a military organization more than a collection of armed and uniformed individuals. Technique is all those things that you do with your weapons and equipment on the battlefield.

Techniques vary greatly, even though their total effect may be similar. Not all armed forces are the same, even if they appear to be identical in terms of weapons and organization. What differentiates them is the techniques they employ. The extent of these differences is stark when you compare client states adopting Superpower weapons and organization. During the Vietnam War, South Vietnamese forces were organized and equipped like their American mentors. But in the field, there was a considerable divergence in effectiveness between U.S. and South Vietnamese troops. What made the difference was the combination of traditional Vietnamese attitudes toward warfare and the effect of nearly a century of French colonial influence. The same phenomenon could be seen in Afghanistan. Not only were Russian-equipped and Russian-trained Afghan troops much less effective than Russian soldiers, but there were also considerable differences in effectiveness between the various Russian army units.

Quite often, the failure of Third World soldiers to use effectively the weapons and techniques of Superpower mentors has simply been due to the use of inappropriate techniques. In Vietnam, the North Vietnamese used Russian weapons and organization but developed their own techniques, which enabled them to eventually defeat the South Vietnamese and American forces. In Chad during the 1980s, the Libyans were weighted down with Russian equipment and ideas about conventional warfare. Their opponents, once they got their political act together, relied heavily on lighter, cheaper equipment, wielded by well-motivated troops using locally developed, and highly innovative, tactics that practically made a virtue of their poverty. The equipment-bound Libyans lost as the Chadians danced around them in light trucks armed with antitank guided missiles and machine guns.

Even within the same nation, there are considerable differences between similar units that use different techniques. It's widely known that U.S. Marine infantry and U.S. Army infantry differ in their effectiveness and that this is largely due to the unique techniques each force uses. In wartime, identically organized and equipped battalions in the same infantry division will differ greatly in effectiveness because leaders in some units have developed more effective techniques, or managed to use the existing ones more efficiently. This was demonstrated in the U.S. Army as recently as the Vietnam War. During the Falklands, Afghan, and Iran-Iraq wars, the same thing happened.

Troops are accused of always being ready to fight the last war and not the next one. There's a reason for that. You are fairly certain which techniques worked in the last war. You know much less about exactly what the next war will be like. Besides, if the next war happens soon after the last one, the old techniques will probably work. Despite appearances, wars are relatively rare events in the experience of a military force. During the Vietnam War, senior U.S. commanders with World War II experience kept promoting the attitude that combat there was similar to the jungle fighting American troops had experienced during World War II. They passed this erroneous attitude on to their South Vietnamese allies. The Viet Cong and North Vietnamese were also fighting the last war, the one against the French that had ended in 1954. But they were more correct in their approach, for the French had insisted on using inappropriate World War II techniques against Vietnamese guerrilla forces. As far as the Vietnamese were concerned, the American troops were just like the French, only there were more of them and they spoke English. U.S. innovations like helicopters and massive firepower forced the Viet Cong and North Vietnamese forces to develop new techniques. The U.S. forces were much slower in adapting new and more effective techniques. In the end, the side with superior techniques had the edge.

Developing techniques, tactics, and doctrine that will be more in touch with the reality of the next war requires a lot of effort and a modicum of luck. During long periods of peace, the techniques most likely to be accepted are those put forward by the most powerful, or persuasive, advocates, such as the "heroes" of the last war. These "heroes" are not always those who were successful on the battlefield, but officers who were more adept at turning their wartime experience into rapid peacetime promotions. It's the guy skillful at getting promoted, not the guy who can fight effectively, who decides how the troops will conduct themselves in the next war.

Prolonged periods of peace delay acceptance of the most effective new techniques, largely because without any war in which to test them, no one recognizes what the best future combat techniques will be. More common is the development of less effective techniques that appear more likely to be successful, or simply have a more effective patron. Two examples, several centuries apart, demonstrate how tricky it is to develop new techniques for the next war. During the mid-1700s, Frederick the Great of Prussia rewrote the book on infantry tactics, developing a number of innovative winning techniques (superior combat formations and maneuvers). After his death in 1786, his successors captured the form, but not the substance, of his innovations. Twenty years later, the Prussian Army was wiped out by the superior techniques of Napoleon's French Army. One item noted at the time was that the Prussians, intent on retaining the advantages of Frederick's tactics, had seized upon his fastidious insistence that the troops maintain their formations on the battlefield. So in the years prior to their defeat by Napoleon, Frederick's successors were wont to use surveying instruments to line up the troop formations during training.

In 1945, the Russian Army emerged triumphant after defeating the German Army in a bloody four-year war. During this conflict, the Russians had developed a number of effective techniques. Some they copied from their German opponents, and after the war they adopted even more German techniques. But as the decades of peace rolled on, form began to gain over substance. By the 1980s some Russian officers were complaining about the use of surveying instruments to line up formations on the battlefield during training.

Fortunately, combat techniques do not change rapidly, so the damage caused by bad ones takes a while to become serious. But after a decade or two, you can be in real trouble. This has been demonstrated in every major war in this century. It will be demonstrated again in future wars.

TECHNOLOGY

Technology frequently gets a bad rap, but the right technology can be a lifesaver. In peacetime, however, technology falls victim to the same problems as technique. Who is to decide which technology will do the best job? Some technologies can do more harm than good. Nearly all technologies have a deleterious effect before all the bugs are worked out. A classic example is found in the case of antiaircraft guided missiles. First proposed in the 1940s, such missiles were developed in the 1950s. Both the ground-launched and air-launched versions caused embarrassment all around when they were given a combat workout during the 1960s. While these missiles eventually became effective, and the principal means of bringing down aircraft in the 1970s, their early use was unimpressive. After several decades of heavy use, reality and technology finally came together.

Some weapons take even longer. The self-propelled torpedo, introduced in the late 1860s, was around for almost twenty-five years before it was first successfully used in combat, in the early 1890s, and the U.S. Navy still did not have an effective torpedo going into World War II due to a number of technical "improvements" that failed in combat.

All armed forces use technology, and some are dependent on it to the exclusion of other factors. The U.S. armed forces have been accused of this. But, in fact, the American advantage historically has mostly been larger quantities of technologically inferior weapons. It was only after World War II, and particularly after the Korean and Vietnam wars, that the United States adopted the idea of an outnumbered but technologically superior American Army defeating Communist (or any other) hordes. In Korea, the key factor in the lopsided casualty figures was the greater quantities of artillery ammunition available to U.S. troops. As far as weapons technology went, there was not much difference between Communist and U.S. troops. In some cases, as, for example, in infantry weapons, American technology was inferior. There have been cases where the technology was too complex for the troops, who were then defeated by forces using lower technology weapons, which happened in tank battles between India and Pakistan in the 1960s. It's also been a problem with Third World armed forces in general. It's not technology that counts, but appropriate technology. What is appropriate is rarely revealed until the shooting starts.

NATIONAL DIFFERENCES

Peacetime forces depart from reality by degrees, depending on a nation's attitudes about warfare. In some nations, the most capable people avoid service; in others, the military is seen as a prestigious career and attracts very capable candidates. Affection is frequently fueled by need. Most nations respect their military more if the country is surrounded by potential enemies. The military is even more respected when the troops have recently defended the nation against a foreign invader. Consider the following survey of national attitudes toward the military, and the people in it.

UNITED STATES: ORGANIC DEFENSES

Historically, the principal defenses of the United States have been two broad oceans, weak neighbors, a strong fleet, and a numerous militia. Not much has changed over the years except that after World War II large forces were uncharacteristically stationed overseas. This has led to the largest peacetime army

in American history and a navy equal in combat power to all
the rest of the world's fleets combined. In 1940, the United
States had 458,000 men in uniform and a defense budget (in
1990 dollars) of $14 billion. This was only 1.5 percent of GNP.
After demobilizing in 1947, there were 1.6 million troops and a
defense budget of $77 billion (5.6 percent of GNP). Histori-
cally, Americans have been ambivalent about their "boys" in
uniform, alternating periods of virtual contempt with moments
of high regard, the latter mostly during wartime. The need to
maintain large forces after World War II has not altered this
basic pattern.

RUSSIA: THE STEAMROLLER LIVES ON, OR MORE IS BETTER

The Russian concept of military power has always revolved around huge ground forces and enormous expanses of
territory. Traditionally, being in the armed forces has not been
very well regarded or brought much prestige or reward, unless
one happens to be an officer. Nothing much has changed as a
result of the Revolution and nearly seventy-five years of communism. The Russian armed forces are larger today (on a per
capita basis) than they were a century ago. This growth is partially attributable to the addition of new weapons, particularly
lots of tanks, and to the uncharacteristic growth of the Russian
Navy. Also, unlike a century ago, there is now an air force, a
large air-defense establishment, and a separate Strategic Rocket
Force. Unmarried women still consider an officer "a good
catch." Bigger may not be better, but if you're a Russian, it is
reassuring.

BRITAIN: THE TIGHT LITTLE ISLAND

Britain has not suffered a successful invasion by foreign
troops for over 900 years, something of a world record. A lot
of this has to do with Britain being a rather out-of-the-way island. This does not mean that its military has been idle and
useless. Britain's military has developed a tradition of being
armed diplomats. Basically a small, somewhat elite force, the
army does its fighting on foreign soil. Under these conditions,
supported by a strong navy, British troops have developed a

winning tradition. Even their losses are tempered by the fact that the victorious enemy does not then proceed to rampage about the British countryside. The British genuinely like their soldiers and sailors, particularly because they are out of the way most of the time, and the queen's service is seen as a fine career. The British military tradition is what many nations would like to have, if only they were also a heavily industrialized island off the coast of Europe. . . .

FRANCE: A LITTLE "GLOIRE" GOES A LONG WAY

France has been invaded regularly through the ages. As a result, the French are a bit cynical about their military. In the last century or so, most of their military victories have been in colonial wars against peoples not likely to invade France. In that same period, France lost two out of three wars against German invaders. The one victory, World War I, was a very costly triumph and required substantial assistance from allies. The French are not bad soldiers, but the Germans they faced in three wars were simply better. The colonial experience, from the 1700s to the 1960s, taught the French the advantages of small numbers of well-trained troops, and French volunteers or conscripts take well to good training by competent officers. Although there has been an influx of Eastern Europeans since the collapse of the Soviet bloc in late 1989, even the Foreign Legion, the classic band of hardened mercenary professionals, is nearly two thirds French: French citizens who want to join simply lie about their nationality, and the Legion recruiters look the other way. France has a long military tradition, even if the success record is a bit mixed. Of all the nations in Europe, France has fought the most wars over the last few centuries. Europeans have long memories, and the glories of the past are never forgotten. More recent embarrassments are rarely kept in proper perspective. Current French military professionals are more intent on emulating past victories, not more recent defeats. They also go out of their way, more than most nations, to do things differently. This applies to weapons design, tactics, and organization, even to uniforms. The quirk does not seem to have adversely affected French military power.

GERMANY: IN THE MIDDLE

With the brief exception of Frederick the Great's Prussia in the mid-1700s, until about 120 years ago Germany was something of a long-standing joke in the military-affairs department. For centuries, Germany was the favorite battleground of other nations, primarily because the Germans were not united and could not keep foreign armies out. Most German troops were considered good, and frequently served as mercenaries: The Hessians used by the British during the American Revolution were typical of this. But the Germans as a nation were not regarded as militarily potent, except to the Slavs who were continually being harried by one German prince or another. Yet these things are subject to change, and the Germans, especially the Prussians, were diligent and, with unification, in the period 1864–71 finally came into their own as proficient practitioners of the military arts. Losing two world wars was not a bad reflection on German military abilities, as they outperformed more numerous opponents on a man-for-man basis, and, indeed, the German people still have a good deal of respect for their soldiers, even after its armies' defeats and the Nazi horror. The typical German qualities of thoroughness and assiduousness are particularly well suited to preparing troops for combat, and these traditions are still practiced in Germany.

POLAND: TOO MANY STRONG ENEMIES

Historically, Poland has always been surrounded by potential enemies. Unfortunately, two of these are Germany and Russia, so as a rule Poland has been strong and influential only when these two powers have been weak. This has not occurred very often in recent centuries. Poland was a united nation long before either Russia or Germany. Its political weakness in early modern times was enormous and, as a result of being partitioned several times, Poland has spent most of the last 200 years ruled by Germany, Russia, and Austria. After World War I, Austria was destroyed, Russia and Germany were weak, and Poland was independent. But in 1939, Nazi Germany and Communist Russia put aside their differences and carved up Poland once again. There followed years of war and German occupation and more war. After 1944, Poland was occupied by Russian troops and dominated by Russian foreign policy until the general collapse of the Soviet empire in late 1989. Thus, the last two centuries have provided abundant opportunities for Poles to fight for other nations, but little experience in defining a purely national defense policy. Nevertheless, even during the primacy of the Communist party, the Polish armed forces still maintained a decidedly nationalist tradition. The name of the Warsaw Pact is an indication of how important Poland was to Russia, not the other way around. As a consequence, however, the Communist government paid more attention to political reliability in senior officers than to military ability. The junior officers, and particularly the NCOs, maintained the useful military traditions and make it easy to support the armed forces even though these forces, in theory, propped up an unpopular Communist dictatorship. The government was reluctant to rely on these nationalistic professional soldiers to fight their countrymen. Their fears were well-founded, as the Romanian Revolution demonstrated, with the army siding with the people against the party and secret police. As Poland enters a new era of democratic rule, the relationship between the army and the government will have to be redefined.

ISRAEL: URGENT BUSINESS

Israel is, like Russia, an army with a nation attached. The Israeli military traditions are unique in several ways. First, the traditions are of very recent origin; they go back only to the 1930s and 1940s. Second, these traditions are very effective and have been tested regularly in combat. Third, the traditions are perpetuated and sustained largely by civilians who turn into soldiers for only a few months each year. The Israeli armed forces are among the most effective in the world not because of popular support. The Arab and extremely religious Jewish portions of the population do not care much for the armed forces. What has made Israeli forces effective has been fear, fear that if they were defeated, everything would be destroyed. Thus most Israelis support and serve in the armed forces, giving an all-out effort to make the system work.

ARGENTINA: PRETTY UNIFORMS AND POLICE WORK

Argentina is typical of nations that lack external threats but not internal ones. This situation is particularly prevalent in Latin America, and among Third World nations in general. In these nations, the illusion is maintained that the armed forces exist to defend the fatherland. But long periods of repression at the hands of the troops dissipates any goodwill civilians might have had for the military. If the troops subsequently go up against a foreign opponent and make a bad showing, the population can turn quite nasty. This happened in Argentina after the armed forces seized the disputed Malvinas/Falkland Islands from the British in 1982. Britain soon came back and ejected the Argentine troops. Even with the generals and admirals replaced by civilians as government leaders, the population continues to cast a wary eye on the military. In a situation like this, the military sustains itself through force, or the threat of force. Basically, the military extorts money from the government and takes care of its cadre of officers and NCOs. The troops are largely conscripts, who are treated well enough to keep them loyal until they are discharged.

KOREA: SPLIT ACROSS THE MIDDLE

Korea has developed two different attitudes toward its military because of the division of the nation in 1945. The Communist North developed into a military dictatorship, very much on the model of Stalinist Russia. The big difference in North Korea is that the military overshadows national life, even more so than in Russia. The conscript army takes in men for five to six years, far in excess of the one to three years common in most nations. Almost everything revolves around a citizen's relationship with the military. North Korea is a closed society and very much a police state. There is even a version of the "thought police," whose officials can make life miserable for anyone suspected of incorrect thinking. Attitudes toward the military are a combination of fear, envy, and admiration. This last attitude stems from the government's successful use of long-standing Korean nationalism to foster a belief in the eventual reunification of the nation and the expulsion of all foreign elements. This has long been a Korean sentiment, and it is played up big in the North.

In the South, there was more democracy, and for many years the military was seen as a usurper of democratic power. At the same time, there is an ancient tradition of the military "caste" taking over the government in times of crises. The South Korean generals played this theme as long as they could. This was largely possible because the people did not want a return of the Communists from the North. During the 1950–53 Korean War, South Koreans got a taste of Communist brutality and had no desire to sample it again. So the military was tolerated, and eventually removed as dictators in the late 1980s without a bloody revolution. This was another ancient Korean tradition: the primacy of a civil government run by the educated "caste." The booming South Korean economy makes the military a less attractive career than in the North, where it's the best opportunity for prestige and material comfort.

JAPAN: WORSHIPFUL RESPECT

Japan has for centuries all but worshiped the military. Up until 1945, this seemed a reasonable attitude, as until 1945 Japan's military had pretty much never lost a war. Ignominious defeat in 1945 changed the old attitudes for most Japanese. Yet the military are still treated with respect, though not quite as much as before the war. Although the Japanese have officially renounced war, except for self-defense, their troops are still among the best-trained and most disciplined in the world. The size of Japan's armed forces is growing even faster than its economy. No wonder the rest of Asia gets nervous when Japan gives in to U.S. demands that it raise its defense spending. Within Japan, it's becoming more fashionable to talk of a larger armed forces. These developments bear watching.

CHINA: TOO MUCH OF THIS, TOO LITTLE OF THAT

China has always had a great deal of respect for, and fear of, soldiers. China's history is one of empire: conquest of neighbors, invasions by foreign powers, and civil wars led by contentious warlords. These last two have been the major events in China's experience this century. After World War II, the

Communists defeated the last of the warlords, won the civil war, and, until recently, maintained the largest army in the world. The army was a swell place to be, as you were assured of adequate clothing and food, as well as some prestige. In effect, the army was a society and economy unto itself. It built housing for its cadres and troops, ran farms and factories using troops as workers, and in general looked after itself. When China reformed its economy in the 1980s, the army began to appear less attractive. Its size was cut by over a million troops to provide funds for economic development. Ambitious young men saw greater opportunities in the civilian economy, leaving the army with a lower grade of potential recruits to conscript. The Chinese are still aware of the enemies on their borders, and the need for preventing the return of warlords and civil war. But memories of the warlord period grow dimmer each year. And while the armed forces have been supported by the population, in the wake of Tiananmen Square, it remains to be seen how long this relationship can endure as they are used as an instrument of political repression.

SOME ILLUSIONS OF MILITARY POWER

Military power in peacetime is rarely what it appears to be. There are plentiful historical examples.

THE BLITZKRIEG AND THE SITTING DUCKS

Blitzkrieg is a pseudo-German term (invented by an American journalist) meaning, literally, "lightning war." It implies tanks and armored troop carriers dashing into action across the battlefield and deep into the enemy rear. The concept, which was developed in several countries, was theorized as the key to battlefield victory during the 1930s. When it was eventually used in combat during World War II, the reality proved a little different. The blitzkrieg only worked some of the time, and generally with less than dazzling results. It rarely worked if both sides were trying to do it. Blitzkrieg was an attempt to reintroduce mobility in warfare after it was lost in the trench fighting of World War I. Yet the most mobile armies in history, to this day, were the medieval Mongol hordes. The Mongols could move rapidly for months at a time, aided by their lack of any heavy equipment to drag around. The Mongol horses ate grass, and the Mongol riders could subsist on horse milk and horse blood. As time went on, armies collected heavier equipment, particularly artillery. They still used horses, but heavy draft breeds to pull the guns. These large horses could not maintain their strength on grass alone. Thus you had to haul horse fodder along with the guns. Railroads helped, but could be damaged, and didn't always go where one's army wished to go. So increasingly large and complex supply lines tended to hamper military operations.

All this proceeded to get worse until World War I, when several innovations—mass armies, machine guns, barbed wire— and the extraordinary weight of munitions and supplies needed to sustain the troops, horses, and guns brought the armies to literal immobility. But the by-then twenty-year-old truck technology offered some relief. And the tank was introduced, which helped too. During the 1920s and 1930s, truck technology advanced. In addition, tanks and other track-laying vehicles, like bulldozers and tractors, became more efficient. Armored vehicles, particularly tanks, became larger, heavier, faster, and more complex. While these engine-powered vehicles could move several times as fast as horses, they were not as rugged or reliable. This did not discourage armies from wholesale adoption of wheeled and tracked vehicles for large formations, particularly divisions. Horses would still be used in most nations well into the 1950s, but going into World War II there were enough motor vehicles to completely equip 10–50 percent of most major armies, and all of the Anglo-American ones. The result was a "dash" capability, where the mechanized forces, and their heavier weapons, sped on ahead, crashing through enemy defenses, while the slower horse-drawn infantry divisions struggled along behind.

This was the reality of the famed blitzkrieg. It wasn't all that speedy, usually averaging less than ten kilometers a day. The problem was not speed, but mass and firepower. The units involved were large, and their numerous vehicles had huge appetites for fuel, lubricants, spare parts, mechanics, and road space. In many parts of the world, there were not sufficient roads to support all this traffic, and most of the vehicles could only travel on roads. Although tanks and other track-laying vehicles were designed for cross-country travel, these maneuvers were not without risk. Various obstacles like rocks, ditches,

and tree stumps could seriously damage the track-laying mechanism. There was also the danger of antitank land mines, developed shortly before World War II just for the purpose of
stopping tanks. Mines were extremely effective, accounting for
over a third of tank losses in World War II and over two thirds
of all vehicle losses in the Vietnam War. And armies needed
lots of wheeled vehicles to carry food, ammunition, and fuel,
which moved cross-country only with great difficulty and even
more risk of damage. In effect, vehicles were lost at a much
faster rate than troops. In combat, your vehicle-loss rate runs
about five times higher than that for troops: If 2 percent of your
troops are killed or injured in a day of combat, about 10 percent
of your vehicles will be put out of action. Vehicles can be brought
back into action more quickly than injured troops, which accounts for the stop-and-go nature of the blitzkrieg. When too
many vehicles are out of action, the entire unit must halt so
that repairs can be made.

Some nations were a bit more perceptive than others about
how all this 1920s and 1930s blitzkrieg theory would turn out.
All future practitioners of blitzkrieg, including Germany, made
serious errors in working out the details of conducting mechanized warfare. What made the Germans so successful in 1939–
41 was that their opponents were so much worse, not that
German *Panzertruppen* were that much better. Of course, the
Germans were fortunate in that their first use of the technique
was in two "dry runs" against Austria and Czechoslovakia, followed by several live-fire essays against considerably weaker
opponents, which enabled them to gain valuable experience
without taking crippling losses: Operations against the Poles in
1939 and the French in 1940 involved relatively light German
losses against ill-prepared foes. Starting in 1941, the operations
against Russia, which were initially enormously successful,
tended to kill off the German troops faster than they could use
their hard-earned experience in additional battles. This also
highlighted the fact that another source of German success was
their development of efficient infantry tactics. Able tank units
are severely hampered if they lack well-trained infantry. One
of the lesser-known keys of German military success in World
War II was the superb German infantry, who did over 80 percent of the fighting and dying. To this day, the Germans still

consider well-trained and well-equipped infantry as the key to success in battle.

Since World War II, the only nation that has had a chance to practice blitzkrieg successfully more than once has been Israel. The key to its success has been careful preparation, good infantry, and thorough training, areas in which its enemies have proven consistently inferior. The Israelis believe that weapons and technology are not all that important and that they would have been just as successful even if they had exchanged weapons and equipment with their opponents. There is some truth to this, as Israel regularly reconditions captured weapons and successfully incorporates them into its armed forces, using them with equal effectiveness.

The blitzkrieg has had occasional success at high-speed movement in combat with mechanized forces. It's not easy to pull off, as the historical record shows. Be particularly wary of those who say it will happen in the opening stages of any war. Blitzkrieg ability, like fine wine, requires time to come of age.

IF IT LOOKS GOOD, IT AIN'T GOOD

Uniforms were originally introduced into armies so one could tell the good guys from the bad, and both from the civilians. They also had the beneficial effect of making your troops look neat and tidy, and even impressive to the enemy, which was good for your morale and bad for theirs. Uniforms also helped make it easier to keep everyone clean and healthy, as even the ancients noticed that ragged troops died off more quickly than neatly turned-out ones. This originally quite utilitarian expedient quickly became an object of fashion. Fancy uniforms appear to be inseparable from the general image of military power; troops who look good must be good. Yet historically this has not been the case. Impressive uniforms are generally characteristic of armies whose principal interests lie elsewhere than on the battlefield. It's cheaper to look like a real soldier than to be one. Besides, in peacetime what other means do armies have of showing off? Governments that want to impress their neighbors with their military power—or keep politically inclined armies happy—frequently introduce new uniforms. This is much easier than attempting to effect significant changes in tradition, training, technique, and technology. Twenty years of Fascist rule in Italy saw more uniform changes than did either the previous sixty years under a liberal monarchy or the subsequent forty-five years of parliamentary democracy, a sartorial display that was not of much help during World War II. Consider other examples from recent history: The losers in both World Wars, in the Arab-Israeli wars, in Vietnam, in the Falklands, in Uganda, in Chad, and now in Afghanistan would all have won a military fashion show against their opponents, who still managed to outfight them. This sort of thing has been going on for a long time, probably predating the defeat of the magnificently outfitted Hellenistic armies by the simply attired Romans. Among military historians, this phenomenon is jokingly termed the "Sukhomlinov Effect," after Vladimir Sukhomlinov, Russian minister of war on the eve of World War I, one of the most splendidly uniformed soldiers in history. But though he looked, and sounded, like a fine soldier, Sukhomlinov was an incompetent admininstrator and an inept commander, largely to blame for the disasters that overtook Russian arms in the opening weeks of World War I, disasters from which czarist Russia never recovered.

Troops who are successful in combat habitually partake of what might be termed the "Mexican Bandit" look. This image derives from the ill-equipped, unkempt Mexican irregular troops, some of whom *were* bandits (at least some of the time), who outfought the splendidly attired French in the 1860s and the neatly uniformed *Federales* in the Revolution Wars that began in 1911, and outmaneuvered the comparatively well-turned-out gringos under John J. Pershing in 1916. During the Vietnam War, most U.S. troops sported starched and pressed fatigue uniforms. The people at the numerous headquarters were particularly resplendent, with even their combat boots—for office wear!—sporting a shine you could see your face in. Generals flitted about in helicopters featuring Simonize jobs any corporate limo would be proud of. In contrast, the Viet Cong and North Vietnamese Army (NVA) wore dingy black pajamas. U.S. troops actually in the field, particularly those who were better-led soon adopted attire less elegant than that of their commanders. The best American forces, those actually able to go out there and beat the Viet Cong at their own game, on their home ground, regularly partook of the "Mexican Bandit" look, and some extremely successful commando units even preferred the black pajamas.

To a greater or lesser degree, in peacetime all armies try to look good, and one way to do this is by dressing—and drilling—"like soldiers" to the exclusion of many more important concerns. When war comes, it's the army that has been least corrupted by such peacetime pathologies that wins.

THE VALUE OF AN UNWORTHY OPPONENT

The seemingly "unworthy opponents" are the major causes of wars and the most common reason why aggressors lose. The unworthy opponent is rarely unworthy enough to guarantee a quick and painless victory. Most of the wars in this century started because the aggressor underestimated the staying power of his intended victim. In hindsight, war is rarely, if ever, the solution to a nation's problems. We are talking about the nation that does the attacking. The defender has no choice but to resist. Many wars are avoided because some nations correctly estimate the relative strength of their own and neighboring nation's armed forces. This is what has been keeping the relative peace in the Middle East for over fifteen years now. After several failed attempts at war, Israel's Arab neighbors have concluded that Israel's military strength is too much for them to overcome, while Israel realizes that she is not as unbeatable as was once believed. The result is peace, or at least a semblance of peace, although the grievances that ignited the previous wars still remain. What has not been abandoned is terrorism and guerrilla warfare. This is the traditional warfare of an aggrieved party that knows itself to be weaker but is not willing to abandon the struggle for what it wants. Unworthy opponents are usually created out of political expediency; thus Arabs still fight Arabs. Domestic political problems appear solvable if some successful foreign adventure can be concocted. In recent decades, one can point to Idi Amin's invasion of Tanzania in 1978, Iraq's invasion of Iran in 1980, Argentina's invasion of the Falklands in 1982, Burkina Faso's invasion of Mali in 1985, and Iraq's taking of Kuwait in 1990, most of which resulted in disastrous reverses. Some people never learn.

THE AIR-POWER MYTH

Air power became a myth shortly after it appeared on the scene during World War I. The initial function of air power, and still the only one that is consistently useful and cost-effective, is reconnaissance. But the pilots sought more work, and something more exciting than playing chauffeur for a photographer. The first task they pounced upon was preventing the enemy reconnaissance aircraft from doing their job. This made sense, and, naturally, one's own reconnaissance aircraft had to be protected too. And so on.

The next role was attacking ground forces. This is where things began to come apart. Most World War I aircraft carried only one or two machine guns with at most a few hundred rounds of ammunition. While enemy aircraft had no place to hide, their infantry did. And the ground forces fired back regularly and with effect. Once the ground troops realized what poor effect the aircraft had, they took the occasional attacks in stride. Undismayed, the pilots then sought to take larger aircraft and airships on attacks into the enemy rear and even against their cities. But the bomb load was minuscule, and accuracy worse. After World War I, the aviators saw that technology would continue to move forward. Air-power advocates postulated that masses of heavy bombers would dominate future warfare, reducing enemy cities and factories to rubble and winning wars virtually single-handedly. America and Britain believed it, and built thousands of heavy bombers. These devastated German and Japanese cities. But after the dust had settled and survey teams had sorted out the damage and its effects, it was discovered that all that "strategic" bombing had only a modest direct effect on the outcome of the war. In contrast, the results of ground attack by aircraft were highly useful. Undismayed, the "strategic" bomber fans, at least in the United States, continued to push their favorite weapon system. So successful was the heavy bomber crowd that two thirds of the U.S. Air Force's spending on strategic weapons went to bombers even after ICBMs came into service. This despite the fact that it costs several hundred million dollars per nuclear weapon delivered by manned bombers. That's for the newer B-1s and B-2s. The older B-52 can cost over a billion dollars per warhead delivered. In contrast, sea-launched ballistic missiles cost under a hundred million dollars per warhead delivered on target. Land-based ballistic-missile warheads cost about twice as much as aircraft-delivered warheads if you assume that your enemy will attack the missile silos and knock out a fair percentage of them. But cost is not very relevant when the air force controls the bombers and land-based missiles and the navy owns the sea-launched ones.

To make matters worse, the air force consistently dragged its feet when it came to upgrading its ground-attack aircraft for the support of army troops, a role in which it had demonstrated considerable effectiveness. Even the original air-force mission, reconnaissance, is gradually being taken over by satellites. This is fine by the air force, as it increasingly distances itself from anything resembling direct support of the ground forces. What the air force prefers is fighters going after enemy aircraft and bombers taking out enemy airfields. Both of these tasks could be accomplished by missiles. But there are no pilots in missiles, and therein lies the reason for all problems with the myths of air power.

THE MAN ON HORSEBACK AND OTHER MISCONCEPTIONS

Military heroes have, in one instance, been described as "cowards that got cornered." This is not to take anything away from those who serve in the military and suffer, often to the point of injury or death. But the real heroes are those who endure combat day after day without trying to avoid the unpleasant tasks that come their way. Some are recognized, most are not. These are the good heroes. There are also bad heroes. These are mostly the senior commanders who get credit for things they haven't done and then proceed to believe all the flattering lies others shower on them.

Now there are peacetime heroes and wartime heroes. The wartime variety are more authentic. But armed forces spend most of their time at peace. Many reputations are made, and very few unmade, without a shot being fired. Your peacetime heroes are the most dangerous. For in peace, those who look and sound like generals and have attractive wives and a pleasing manner get promoted more rapidly than anyone else: A short, fat, homely officer who is divorced, a poor bureaucrat, and a lousy golfer but happens to be Napoleon reincarnate would have only a slim chance of gaining rank in peacetime. Napoleon himself fit the profile of an officer with poor peacetime prospects, as did Ulysses S. Grant and many other authentic wartime heroes. Historically, the seemingly impeccable generals who command your combat units at the start of a war are rarely still in charge by its end. The senior commanders frequently survive, as someone has to give out the pink slips. There is usually a lot of outplacement to do once the fighting starts. During the American Civil War, George B. McClellan was seen as an obvious choice for high rank, until he had ineptly commanded the Union Army in battle. During Vietnam, William Westmoreland was another shining product of the peacetime military who some would argue put in a less than sterling battlefield performance. Every war has similar examples.

The difference between a peacetime hero and a wartime hero may perhaps best be illustrated by some incidents from the Louisiana maneuvers, held shortly before Pearl Harbor in September of 1941, with World War II already two years old in Europe. These are the largest maneuvers in the history of the U.S. Army, involving over 350,000 men. A lot was learned. For example, over the objections of his chief of staff, the commander of the Third Army in the operation permitted his signal officers to arrange construction of a $200,000 telephone poleline system in the maneuver area before the scheduled start of the exercises. The director of the maneuvers objected, commenting, "Ask your staff . . . how the German Army made such preparations for the campaign in Poland." George S. Patton, who commanded an armored division during the war games, provides an interesting contrast. Patton decided to "steal a march" and attack twenty-four hours earlier than the official schedule. His opponent protested. The umpires concluded that Patton had not acted improperly, since, after all, surprise attacks are not unknown in war. These two incidents had some serious implications for the Allied cause. The losing general in Louisiana was later proposed to command U.S. forces in the 1942 invasion of North Africa. But having been disgraced by Patton, the job went to his erstwhile chief of staff a much more junior, and abler, officer, Dwight D. Eisenhower.

This development was no accident, as the U.S. Army was one of those rare military organizations that actually dismissed a large number of shaky generals and colonels in anticipation of a war, as, for example, in 1916–17 and again in 1940–41. Nor did this inclination to fire generals end there: In both World Wars, the senior U.S. commanders encouraged quick dismissal of ineffective generals. This policy remained a part of the American military tradition, although it is not much talked about and did not always reach the highest levels of command. The policy was also not implemented in Korea, largely because there was no warning when that war broke out. Vietnam was also an exception, probably because it was an undeclared war, not a threat to national existence, and thus not worth the cost of several senior officer careers.

PROPAGANDA AT WAR AND PEACE

Most nations have a deliberate program of putting forward an official version of what their armed forces are capable of. Now this has little to do with reality and everything to do with the current foreign and domestic political situation. This sort of thing can be very effective. Consider the effect of Hollywood's war on a recent president's memories of World War II. Ronald Reagan saw no action in World War II, nor did he serve overseas. But he had seen a lot of movies about the war, and helped make a few, so it's not surprising that his memories were colored more by the celluloid version of events than by their reality. In this regard, he was not alone, as for most Americans—unlike most Britons, Germans, French, Russians, or Chinese—the war consisted largely of cinematic experiences. The average American's exposure to the realities of World War II is today shared virtually worldwide by the average person's understanding of military power in a more or less peacetime environment: They believe what their political and military leaders tell them about war.

Governments get away with this because few people, and certainly very few ordinary citizens, have any realistic idea about what their armed forces actually are capable of. Naturally, there is great disappointment among the citizenry when they discover that things are other than what they were told. Propaganda is a tricky business. Which is another reason for not going to war and finding out just what the military is made of.

PEACETIME DRIFT

Successful combat forces are extremely perishable. A few years of peace will typically reduce a force's combat capability by half, or more. After a decade or two, once most of the combat-experienced troops have died, retired, or otherwise gone to seed, you have lost it all. The loss that is most noticed is the sense of urgency and the no-nonsense attitude of people who have risked their lives in combat and don't want to take any more risks than they have to. These attitudes are hard on the nerves. A few months, or at most a few years, of combat will burn out the most stalwart individual.

Once the fighting stops, few combat-experienced troops are able to maintain this mental edge. Fewer troops who have not been in combat can generate a proper state of readiness. As the years of peace roll on, the sharp edge of combat readiness further erodes. It's inexorable and normal, and fatal the next time there is a battle. Some armed forces maintain more of their combat edge than others. This is where the much maligned military tradition comes in. The drill sergeant who appears as a sadistic party pooper to peacetime recruits will be seen as a lifesaving mentor to those same recruits when faced with combat. A few nations are able to maintain the illusion that all this nasty training has some future purpose. These are the nations that do better the next time there is a war. But even those nations with the most effective military traditions also suffer from peacetime drift. Keep in mind the counsel of combat veterans: "It's not a matter of who's better, it's a matter of who's worse."

THE BEST AND THE WORST

What follows is a listing of the ten nations that have the most capable armed forces, as well as the ten that may be considered to have the least capable ones. There's a lot more competition at the bottom.

HOW TO READ THE CHARTS

Rnk—Rank, "1" is leader in that category, either best of the ten best or worst of the ten worst.

Nation—Name of country

Pop—Population, in millions. This, more than land area, is an indicator of a nation's size. A third crucial indicator is economic power, usually indicated by Gross National Product (GNP). Long-term military power is linked closely to GNP, while short-term military power (what nations have available right now) is more a function of how much the nation wants to spend on weapons and defense.

CPWR—Total combat power, land and naval combined.

Land—Land combat power, calculated by combining manpower, weapons (especially armored fighting vehicles and combat aircraft), equipment, and quality. This is not all it appears to be. Nations with large populations are likely to have long borders that must be guarded. This prevents military power from being concentrated for offensive operations. Normally, a nation cannot concentrate more than a third or half of its land combat power for offensive operations. At that, it must have a two- or three-to-one superiority over the defender to insure success. Note that a defender is probably able to concentrate up to two thirds of its land combat power to defense, assuming that it has warning of an attack.

Naval—Naval combat power, calculated by combining manpower, ships, ship tonnage, naval aircraft, weapons, equipment, and quality. While naval power can contribute to land operations, its primary function is to maintain use of the seas by merchant and military shipping, and to deny such to the enemy.

Qual—Overall quality of leadership, training, military tradition, infrastructure, weapons, and equipment. This is a major modifier of raw combat power. Normally, all we see are raw representations of combat power, frequently expressed by head counts and lists of weapons and equipment. This is very misleading. For more detail on the methodology used to determine each nation's quality factor, see James F. Dunnigan's *How to Make War* (Morrow: New York, 1988).

Troops—Armed forces personnel, active-duty troops plus organized, trained reserves, in thousands.

AFV—All armored fighting vehicles, in thousands.

CAC—Combat aircraft, including combat helicopters, in thousands.

WTON—Warship tonnage, in thousands of tons. Instead of

giving the number of ships, which can vary enormously in size, we give the total weight of the fleet. The fleets listed below have ships ranging from under 100 tons to over 60,000. The U.S. and Russian fleets, for example, have about the same number of ships, but you'll note that the total weight of U.S. ships is nearly 50 percent larger.

THE TEN BEST

RNK	NATION	POP	CPWR	LAND	NAVAL	QUAL	TROOPS	AFV	CAC	WTON
1.	U.S.	240	4,900	1,400	3,500	48	2,100	42,000	9,200	3,887
2.	Russia	280	4,700	3,200	1,500	40	3,800	132,000	11,500	2,661
3.	China	1,100	1,830	1,700	130	38	2,800	17,400	5,200	725
4.	S. Korea	44	1,010	970	40	46	600	2,400	460	147
5.	Vietnam	65	842	840	2	40	1,100	4,500	355	46
6.	Germany	61	790	730	60	75	485	17,000	530	247
7.	India	802	680	630	50	44	1,250	4,500	780	200
8.	Taiwan	22	630	570	60	48	424	2,600	560	297
9.	Israel	5	445	430	15	55	149	11,600	680	21
10.	Iran	54	425	420	5	46	940	2,300	60	90

Picking the ten best is largely a matter of picking the ten most powerful. These are not the ten largest armed forces in the world, but the ten with the most real conventional combat capability, omitting nuclear weapons. Actually, after you get past the two Superpowers, the next level contains about twenty nations. Most of the ones not shown on this chart are in Europe, where, aside from the NATO and East European blocs, many of the neutrals have quite respectable armed forces. Curiously, Britain and France don't make the top ten (but just miss) because the nations shown have much larger, and reasonably competent, armed forces. British and French troops are as good as ever; it's just that there are a lot fewer of them immediately available compared to these other powers.

Most of the top ten are also the major powers in their region, but have only modest ability to send forces outside their region. Three members of the "Second 10" (Britain, France, and Japan) *do* possess world-class long-range intervention capability. Britain demonstrated this in the Falklands, France frequently does so in Africa. Japan could do so in the Pacific, which makes her neighbors nervous. Each nation on this chart has an interesting story as to how it got the military power it possesses.

The United States has the world's most powerful combat forces largely because of its navy, which is by far the world's greatest. Yet this designation is deceiving, as comparing ground and naval forces is comparing two very different things. As the world's largest maritime trading nation, the United States has an urgent need to keep the sea lanes open in the event of a war. Also, the Americas are isolated from the rest of the world by vast oceans. You cannot invade the United States unless you can safely cross one of those oceans, and the U.S. fleet exists primarily to deny that safe passage. Large American peacetime ground forces are a recent phenomenon, a result of the Cold War. U.S. ground forces are not organized to defend the homeland—the navy sees to that. The U.S. Army and Marines are largely overseas forces, with several "light" division types that can rapidly be transported to far-off battlefields. In effect, America reverses the usual relationship and has the army supporting the navy.

Russia, as the largest nation in the world, needs a large army to defend itself. Russia also has the misfortune of possessing vast borders lacking natural obstacles. Without mountains, swamps, major rivers, or oceans to dissuade an aggressor, Russia finds itself invaded regularly. It's not just paranoia that causes the Russians to maintain the world's most powerful land forces. Another reason for large ground forces is the enormous number of non-Russians within Russia. These conquered people are restive. The ground forces are largely cadre-strength mobilization divisions. In wartime, the armed forces would grow to 10 million troops in over three hundred divisions. The Russian Navy is a new development. A large navy is very much a luxury in which Russia attempts to indulge from time to time, usually until economic reality intervenes, and it is likely to be one of the first victims of the military budget cutting its current economic program will bring about. In the late 1980s, it began to scale back its naval operations drastically. Next you will see serious cutbacks in shipbuilding.

China, like Russia, is a large nation with vast borders, but has the advantage of natural barriers in many frontier areas. The Indian border is guarded by high mountains, the Vietnamese, Laotian, and Burmese frontiers are rugged jungle, and Japan must cross the sea to invade. Only the frontiers with Russia and Korea are somewhat open. Three traditional opponents have been Russia, Japan, and Vietnam; Korea has historically been a friendly client state. The primary strength of the Chinese military comprises a large, nonmotorized infantry force. Most equipment is 1960s technology. Unlike Russia, China has a homogeneous population and up to 50 percent volunteers in the military. Forces have been cut back through the 1980s along with economic growth and modernization of weapons and equipment. Her largest military asset is the size of the country and population plus a historical willingness to resist invaders with any means at hand for as long as it takes.

South Korea is a major military force because of the continuing state of war with North Korea. The troops are well trained and equipped with modern weapons. Its naval and air forces are particularly good, and include a marine corps patterned after the U.S. model. A robust and growing economy permits military strength to be maintained and expanded.

Vietnam maintains large ground forces to cope with hostilities with China and occupation duties in neighboring countries. Equipment is largely 1970s vintage. Economic problems are forcing cuts in military spending and in the number of troops under arms. The need to solve economic problems will cause military power to decline, particularly as combat veterans age and leave the service. During the 1990s, Vietnam will drop out of the top ten.

Germany has traditionally been a high-quality military power. Currently, the recently reunited Germany possesses the most numerous and efficient forces in Europe. Although most of the troops are conscripts, the levels of training, equipment, and enthusiasm are all first-rate.

India, like China, has an ancient military tradition. Its armed forces are not as large, but are more modern and better led than those of China. Another similarity to China is the desirability among its populace for obtaining a position in the army. Both nations are fairly poor, and a military career means steady employment and pay. India successfully adapted Western (British) military techniques and traditions to its own ancient customs. Wide use of Russian weapons reflects the lower educational and skill levels of the troops and is more in line with the capabilities of potential opponents.

Taiwan, like South Korea and Israel, is driven largely by fear to maintain large and effective armed forces. The Taiwan Chinese were the losers of the Chinese Civil War, and from the late 1940s to the present they have held the island of Taiwan against several mainland Chinese reconquest attempts. The troops are well trained, well led, and well equipped. Although without combat experience for over four decades, they would probably give good account of themselves for an army so long away from the battlefield.

Israel is the most obvious case of military strength generated by the constant threat of annihilation. Surrounded by larger nations sworn to destroy her, Israel had to develop superior military forces or perish. Israel has a mobilization army, one of the few such forces in the world. The full strength of these forces is available in less than seventy-two hours. These forces have the most modern equipment, superb leadership, and thorough training. Israel faces one significant limitation, however: the nation's economy is largely shut down by this mobilization. Israel cannot fight a long war; she must win within a few months or lose everything.

Iran (formerly Persia) has always been a major military power in its region. Strong enough to keep Russia at bay and dominate neighboring Arabs, she has an impressive military tradition going back thousands of years. The recent revolution and war with Iraq have not seriously diminished her military power, although its composition has changed. There is far more combat experience now, and a lot fewer high-tech weapons. Despite peace with Iraq, Iran continues to upgrade and reequip its armed forces, but troop quality will probably slip as combat-experienced personnel age, and religious priorities once more take precedence over military ability.

THE TEN WORST MILITARY POWERS

RNK	NATION	POP	CPWR	LAND	NAVAL	QUAL	TROOPS	AFV	CAC	WTON
1.	Zaire	36	6	6	0	11	50	230	20	1
2.	Bangladesh	108	28	27	1	24	91	56	30	9
3.	Mexico	87	33	29	4	18	260	250	88	87
4.	Colombia	32	35	34	1	21	66	290	76	32
5.	Philippines	59	39	31	8	24	115	350	88	162
6.	Burma	41	41	40	1	21	186	110	22	8
7.	Argentina	33	42	23	19	34	75	1,100	160	183
8.	Thailand	55	74	68	6	22	400	1,200	180	55
9.	Ethiopia	46	84	83	1	23	228	1,750	160	8
10.	Indonesia	175	90	84	6	29	281	840	84	168

There's a lot of competition for the Ten Worst. So many smaller nations have such militarily insignificant armed forces that we came up with different criteria for the Ten Worst. The first criterion is size: A nation had to have at least 30 million people. This recognizes the ancient historical fact that small nations mostly survive by the good graces of their neighbors, not military power. It's not unreasonable for a small nation to abandon any serious attempts at maintaining armed forces of the same quantity and quality as much larger neighbors. But the larger nations do raise large armed forces, if only because they have the resources to do so. Some nations do much worse than others in creating armed forces, and the above lists shows those who have made the biggest mess of it. What we are really saying here is that given their size, these nations could easily have much larger, or at least more efficient, armed forces. In some cases, what they have is good, but there's just not enough of it to provide real security. Yet real, or sufficient, security is a slippery concept. Although Zaire holds down the number-one—the bottom—spot on the "Worst List," this wretchedly governed nation really has no imminent fear of foreign invasion. The principal function of the armed forces is to suppress internal rebellion and keep other military units loyal. Thus, as a police force, Zaire's military is adequate. As an effective national armed force, these same troops are an abject failure. Each country has a different reason for this failure, and the most common factor is relative freedom from potential aggressors.

Zaire is a large nation in Central Africa that has more to fear from internal unrest than from external aggression. The government and economy are very inefficient, and this carries over to the armed forces, which are nonetheless sufficient to keep things more or less orderly. Unfortunately, when tested by occasional insurgencies and foreign incursions, the Zairese armed forces have been found wanting.

Bangladesh, which was part of Pakistan until India aided it in breaking away in 1971, is one of the poorest nations in the world. Basically a client state of India, it thus has no reason to create armed forces commensurate with its size. What it has is sufficient to handle occasional internal-security problems.

Mexico has not bothered to build up its armed forces, since the United States defends North America from foreign invasion and is much too powerful for Mexico to challenge militarily. This seems to satisfy everyone, but has led to some problems when an internal-security issue arises.

Colombia, like most Latin American nations, exists under the U.S. defense umbrella. The only reason for armed forces is to discourage unfriendly neighbors. In this case, the last time Colombia had such territorial disputes were in 1903, when the United States supported the secession of the province of Panama with warships, in order to build the Panama Canal, and in 1940, when she clashed with Peru over some real estate on the Upper Amazon. Thereafter, Colombia's major security problem has been internal unrest, and the nation's armed forces have not demonstrated much ability in that area. The vast amounts of illegal funds from the drug trade have apparently had an impact on military efficiency.

The Philippines, as an island nation, has no neighbors who can just walk in. The nearest significant military power is China, and China has refrained from bothering the Philippines for several thousand years. Except for World War II, the major military problem has always been, and continues to be, internal unrest and rebellion.

Burma has a long military tradition, having fought successful wars with India, China, and smaller neighbors over the centuries. After World War II, Burma adopted a more pacifistic and very isolationist attitude, and this is demonstrated by the decline of its armed forces. Several warlords operate in isolated portions of the country, further focusing the armed forces on police matters.

Argentina is one of the most industrialized Latin American nations, but this has not resulted in noticeably efficient armed forces. For much of the country's history, these have existed primarily for internal security and prestige reasons. The 1982 Falklands War with Britain demonstrated Argentine military shortcomings for even the slow learners. As with the rest of Latin America, the hemispheric security provided by the United States has one drawback. Nations rarely get a chance to use their armed forces. There have not been many wars between Latin American nations, so there is not much opportunity to see just how unprepared the armed forces have become.

Thailand is one of the few non-European nations that has not been conquered at one time or another by a European one. This was a result more of diplomacy than military force. Like its neighbor Burma, Thailand takes advantage of the military

backwater it occupies and doesn't spend overly much energy
on military affairs. What there is, is good, but there's not much
of it.

Ethiopia is an ancient nation that has maintained independence largely because it's isolated in an inaccessible part of
Africa. In modern times, Ethiopia has had to make do with
outdated technology and methods. In the 1970s came revolution and a new social order. Revolution turned to civil war, and
the one result was an awareness of how inept the armed forces
were. Although Russian and Cuban aid kept the government
troops ahead of their opponents into the early eighties, this aid
was cut drastically in the late eighties and the armed forces
have resumed their collapse.

Indonesia is, like the Philippines, an island nation with no
nearby major military powers. For centuries, India and China
had only mild interest in it, but never enough to invade. Ironically, both Indonesia and the Philippines were eventually conquered and colonized by far-off European nations. When the
Europeans departed, little modern military technology was left
behind. Indonesia's armed forces have been put together in a
very haphazard fashion, and this has come through in their performance.

"I Read It in . . .": Where Do We Get Our Military Information?

·3·

What role do the media play in military matters? How effectively do the media cover military affairs? What impressions of the military and military power do the media give leaders, citizens, and the troops themselves?

While we think of ourselves as a literate society, surveys of how people spend their time show that for every hour spent reading, seven hours are spent in front of a television. Not only that, but most people get their news not from reading but from television. News is a highly perishable product, and even newspapers cannot match the immediacy of television. Most people have at least a passing interest in military affairs, yet TV is the least capable medium for explaining what is going on in military situations. TV lives on headlines, and military affairs are so outside the understanding of most people that headlines are likely to mislead more than inform most of the time.

SOURCES OF THE NEWS

Few people get their news from one source. There are a number of media in the news business.

TELEVISION

Television news reaches about 80 percent of the population, and nearly all adults are capable of comprehending it. The average American watches TV about ninety minutes a day. TV is the most widely used medium, and 98 percent of U.S. households have at least one set. Most television viewing is for entertainment, but 50 percent of the population view TV news largely to the exclusion of other media. You would think the usage would be higher, but radio and newspapers continue to hold their own despite substantial declines since the 1940s.

RADIO

Although many thought TV would greatly reduce radio usage, this has not been the case. There are approximately as many radios in the United States as there are people, and more people are exposed to radio broadcasts daily than to TV. Over 90 percent of radio listening is a secondary activity, something you do while actively engaged in doing something else, such as driving. Despite this, radio news, which is as headline-driven as television news, reaches 90 percent of the population. This is greater than TV, although more time is spent with TV news.

NEWSPAPERS

Another predicted victim of TV, newspapers have taken a beating, but still hold their own as a major news source. In 1950, when only 9 percent of American households had TV, there were 354 newspapers sold each day per 1,000 population. In 1990, with a television in practically every home, there are only 260 newspapers sold per 1,000 population. About 60 percent of the population are regular newspaper readers, with about 10 percent more taking a paper on Sunday. College graduates are about 10 percent more likely to read newspapers than the national average. Readers spend about half an hour with a paper, and a third of the population gets nearly all its news from papers rather than TV.

MAGAZINES

Some 75 percent of the population reads magazines. Less than half of those readers get any amount of news from magazines. But magazines are the most common source of in-depth treatment of newsworthy stories. Magazines that handle this sort of thing reach less than 10 percent of the population. But these people are the decision makers and opinion leaders, so magazine impact is higher than readership numbers would indicate.

BOOKS

About half the population reads books, but most of the 2 billion books distributed each year are paperback novels. Nonfiction treatments of current events and related subjects in book form, such as the one you are holding, have about as much circulation as the news magazines. Again, while this does not mean much on an overall population basis, many of the movers and shakers are likely to be influenced.

CLASSIFIED REPORTS

While the news media scurry around trying to find out exactly what's going on in military affairs, there are a few thousand people who have access to the real thing: the secret reports from the massive U.S. intelligence effort. While over 4 million Americans have security clearances, most of them have access only to narrow technical data concerning their job. The big-picture data is available to only a very few; senior officials, mostly and, more significantly, members of their staffs. The staffs are the really important ones here, for it is these relatively low-ranking military and civilian personnel who actually have the time to do anything with their access. Senior officials simply get briefed periodically, by their staffs. While these briefings go into more detail than even the most verbose TV news program, and the "audience" can ask questions, it's still a fairly passive process.

As a rule, the more narrowly based the medium, the more detailed and accurate the information conveyed is likely to be. Television and radio have to reach out to an enormous audience if they are to justify their sponsors' fees, and thus provide the least detail. Since people can be selective about the newspaper and magazine articles they read, the coverage can be more intensive. Selectivity is still higher among those reading books, who express their willingness to accept detail by paying for it, so coverage is even more extensive. Classified data are the most detailed, most expensive, and least used. This pattern not only affects the treatment accorded news in each medium, but also the way in which each medium obtains and processes the news.

SOURCES OF THE SOURCES

Because much data on contemporary military operations are classified, it is difficult to get accurate information quickly. This has led to a large body of military information that is part fact and part speculation. Such data have to be handled with special care if they are to be useful and not misleading. Different media effect this with varying degrees of success.

TELEVISION

The TV news organizations have developed their own style of collecting news. Because they are the most immediate media, they must move fast. Television news viewers expect the latest developments, even if covered only in a cursory manner. There is neither time nor resources to allow reporters days, or even hours, to work up a fast-breaking story. The TV news hounds rely heavily on outside sources and experts who can not only provide the background on a military item, but can also give on-air interviews on a moment's notice. Naturally, not all the time on a typical thirty-minute newscast (which includes seven to ten minutes of commercials and promotions) is for immediate items. Many pieces are continuing stories that can be done with fewer time constraints. But then the reporter runs into the problem of severe restrictions on how much can be said. One advantage of TV news is that because of its immediacy, anyone eager to get an item out fast makes a phone call to the station. This means that a television news report can be mostly hearsay, as there is little time for the reporter to dig: Newspapers are also moderately subject to this problem, but make liberal use of qualifiers such as "Ms. Jones said" or "Mr. Smith alleged." TV does this too, by putting Ms. Jones or Mr. Smith on the air, which is supposed to let you know that what they are saying may be opinion. But their image on the screen is itself a most authoritative statement, particularly if they are making "eye contact" with the camera.

TV's biggest limitation is the amount of information it can handle. The actual number of words in a typical half-hour newscast is about two thousand. This is several hundred less than the average front page of *The New York Times* or other major newspapers, which also have headlines and pictures, and with all the stories continued inside. Books average about 500 words to the page, while magazines fall somewhere in between, both again with treatments spread over several pages. So with television we're talking about a very concise presentation, usually about a hundred words per minute. The people who read the news on the air can actually deliver more than a hundred words a minute, but TV is a visual medium and a lot of airtime is taken up with visuals at the expense of words. While pictures may have exceptional impact, newspapers and magazines use them too. But you still need a few of those words, and on TV you don't have many and these even are often squandered as well. Moreover, TV programmers have found that too many words of news will put off or confuse viewers. So there are frequent breaks in the news reading while the anchors and reporters simply chat with one another.

As a result of word restrictions and the emphasis on presentation, there is a tendency toward form over content in TV news. This is not generally a problem, because most of the topics covered are "soft" items. There's no difficulty if you get the facts mixed up when dealing with some celebrity's sex life or a natural disaster. But military affairs are more complex and replete with commonplace myths and misunderstandings. It's one thing to perpetuate Hollywood myths; pushing the military myths is another matter. Because even the most in-depth television news shows cannot go very deep, military affairs are invariably ill-served, as is the audience that uses that medium as its primary source of information. Of course, most people tend to be aware of the limitations of television. When a really important story breaks, newspaper sales usually rise. But news about the military does not often break with the force of a presidential resignation or major natural disaster. The problem with regard to military coverage lies in the day-to-day treatment of commonplace events and developments.

NEWSPAPERS

Newspapers have a tradition of aggressive research and reporting of the news, and they really shine when it comes to military affairs. Reporters, some of whom are former military personnel or have academic backgrounds in such fields as military history, are allowed to specialize in military affairs. They will spend years, even decades, as a military correspondent. This enables them to develop a fairly comprehensive understanding of the military, of military problems, and of military practice, while building up networks of contacts within the military and the civilian organizations that support the military. The stories that these reporters work up are so extensive that the authors can fatten them up still more and turn them into books.

THE WIRE SERVICES

Collecting the news is no trivial task. One way both newspapers and television networks supplement their own news-gathering efforts is to rely on the wire services. The wire services, so-called because a century ago they distributed their reports over the telegraph wires, are actually the principal collecting organizations. The largest is the Associated Press (AP), which has 3,000 employees, most of them in the United States. Nearly all large and medium-size newspapers subscribe to the AP electronic news feed, and some 96 percent of American newspaper readers are exposed each day to AP news. About 5,000 different stories and reports (current events, financial, sports, and so on) are prepared daily by the AP. The other notable wire services, such as United Press International and Reuters, not to mention those in the non-English-speaking world, provide similar, though less extensive coverage. Wire-service treatment is essentially newspaper-oriented. TV and radio stations can use them, but have to rewrite the material to condense it, while most newspapers print it as it comes in, with occasional editing to shorten a piece.

MAGAZINES

Magazine reporting on military affairs differs from newspaper reporting in three main respects. First, the magazine stories are customarily longer. Second, the magazine lead times are longer, so a magazine article cannot handle a fast-breaking situation. Third, magazine articles tend to contain more opinion than newspaper items.

There are numerous magazines that specialize in military affairs, and they ordinarily do an excellent job of it. In fact, one of the primary sources of information on Russian military affairs is the numerous Soviet military journals. These magazines are published by the Russian military for two purposes. The principal goal is simply to keep the troops (especially the 20 percent who are officers) informed about developments. The other objective is to provide a forum for officers to debate changes in how the military operates. This is a common function of the military press in all nations, but is particularly prevalent in Russia. Despite their closed and secretive society, the Russians realize that there has to be a free exchange of ideas if there is to be any progress. They are also avid students of military history, strongly dedicated to studying the past and getting all they can out of the experiences of earlier times.

The Russian military-oriented magazines are the best source of what is going on in their armed forces because the articles are written by officers and troops on active service. This is important, as all military organizations, not just the Russian, are somewhat restrictive in what they allow their troops to say to superiors. For over a century, the best way for a novel idea to overcome the usual institutional inertia that prevails in most military organizations has been for the originator to write an article. In these magazine pieces, the author can say in print things that might get him in trouble if said out loud.

In the West, writers for civilian news magazines, political journals, and general-interest magazines seek out military authors and use them as sources of material. The military authors

may have ideas too radical or upsetting for the military journals. After all, the editors of the military journals are usually
officers themselves and well aware that publishing an article
gives the ideas contained therein some degree of legitimacy.
Senior officers are then under pressure to answer the article.
Military writers with unpopular ideas can thus get the ball rolling by discussing their findings with civilian writers and reporters. This can occasionally backfire, as the military author's ideas
may really be off the wall, but the result can lead to a useful
airing of views. The military journals in the West rarely hesitate
to publish strange ideas, and all military authors have to worry
about from their own organizations is accidental leaking of classified material. Preventing this is the purpose of the editorial
review by the military for all articles written by military personnel.

The West also has a great many academic, commercial,
popular, and hobbyist-oriented military magazines, devoted to
history, technology, collecting, and other aspects of military affairs. These publications are commonly of high quality, with
active and retired military personnel making regular contribu-
tions, supplementing the efforts of experienced scholars and
knowledgeable hobbyists, and they too may be used to air unpopular criticisms or float highly innovative ideas about the military. Some of this is done through newspapers as well.

BOOKS

Books have traditionally used the most reliable sources.
But this is the case only some of the time. So-called "scholarly
books" do indeed go as far back to the origins of a situation as
it is possible to get. But many academic works are so arcane
that they are not very useful for any practical purposes. A lot
of serious works on military affairs are published as "scholarly
books." This means that few are sold, or read. It's difficult to
determine which are breakthrough works and which are just
more academic droning. However, relatively few of the books
published on military affairs are scholarly works, and most of
those that are cannot use the best (classified) sources. The military books that consistently sell the most copies are those featuring pictures of uniforms and equipment, or action novels.
The books that have more impact, for better or worse, are the

"trade books" (like the one you are holding), which are distributed to the bookstores (the "trade") and are widely available.

Military-affairs researchers must contend with classified information that is usually, but not always, unavailable. This was not always so. Up until World War I, it was common to see most technical details of military equipment in widely available publications. This is still very much the case in the West, although most of the fine detail may be classified. In the West, there are many manufacturers of armaments and many customers. There are many trade journals, and the manufacturers release a lot of information in their marketing efforts. This has produced a vast amount of semisecret information. Types of material that are top secret in Russia are openly published in the West. Oddly enough, many Russians have a hard time believing that all these readily available data are real, thinking instead that they are disinformation released to mislead them. Established ways of thinking die hard.

Another valuable source for people writing in this field are the numerous official government publications related to military matters. These range from field manuals issued by the services to the transcripts of hearings before congressional committees to reports of investigative bodies such as the General Services Administration or the Congressional Budget Office. While their output in this regard is less voluminous, there's some similar Russian stuff too. An extraordinary amount of useful information may be found in these, though their sheer size, and generally turgid prose, may be off-putting to some. Most government-created material is very honest, the bureaucrats being quite eager to make accurate claims about their accomplishments.

Diligent researchers can, and have, produced data that are functionally identical to the classified stuff. Good researchers have something else going for them when predicting the performance of new weapons: the incremental development of military technology. While there is much talk about scientific breakthroughs, these are overstated. Breakthroughs are infrequent. Mostly there are gradual increments, step-by-step additions developed from existing technology. In the peacetime military, this effect is made even more useful by the exceptionally long time it takes to develop military technology. The average military system takes five to ten years to get into the field, two or three times longer than equivalent civilian systems. Using these trend-line techniques, diligent researchers can work up a convincing case without official access to state secrets.

CLASSIFIED REPORTS

Military information rests on a bedrock of classified reports, secret documents that the military prepares for itself. Thousands of these documents are churned out each year, and range in size from a few pages to several book-length volumes. *The Pentagon Papers* was just such a report, prepared as a multivolume collection of data, reports, and analyses on what actually happened during the Vietnam War. *The Pentagon Papers* was classified and never meant for public distribution but, like so many other secret reports, was leaked in 1971, leading to considerable public furor. But after the dust had settled, it transpired that most of what was in *The Pentagon Papers* had already been published in bits and pieces over the previous few years. So much for secrecy.

There are some serious problems with classified reports, even if you get your hands on them. They are not noted for their veracity or accessibility. The veracity problem is not due so much to outright lying as to uncertain data, institutional bias, and wishful thinking.

Uncertain data is the result of a number of problems. First, when working with classified information, there are restrictions on how you can go about it. Any classified data outside your immediate area can only be obtained, if at all, via complex and daunting procedures. It's common for people working on classified projects to rely on unclassified data out of desperation. A more insidious problem with classified research is the difficulty, if not impossibility, of getting many people to review your work. Thus the errors that normally creep into any research find it easier to remain undiscovered and uncorrected in classified projects. Not all classified reports suffer from these problems, but it is difficult to detect which do. You can't just grab a classified report and run down to the library to double-check the facts. At least not unless you want to get arrested.

Institutional bias is another major problem with classified reports. Each agency preparing these research reports does so to support the organization's work and goals. While this is true of research done for any institution, studies done for purely scholarly purposes make a point of being neutral. Organization-sponsored research cannot afford such neutrality, so the researchers know from the beginning that there are certain goals their work must support. Some of the goals are legitimate, such as an air-force study on the performance of certain types of aircraft. However, suppose the study was to determine what type of ground-support aircraft the air force should build to assist the army. Further suppose the air force would prefer to use a modification of an existing fighter rather than a totally new purposely designed and built aircraft. One can imagine how great a temptation there may be to do the study a certain way.

Wishful thinking has much to do with the inclinations of whoever happens to be preparing the report. Aside from partaking of institutional bias to a greater or lesser degree, the preparer of the report is influenced by the problem of uncertain data. As his, or increasingly, her, career may be partially dependent on the perceived quality and value of the report, padding or otherwise cooking the data to make the end product more impressive is a constant temptation, particularly given that few knowledgeable people are likely to review the results.

Classified reports must be taken with a grain of salt. Many of them are eventually declassified, and if this happens after many years, the errors and biases are more obvious. For freshly minted reports, the pedigree is less certain. Do not be overly impressed when someone beats you over the head with a classified report to prove a point. Especially when your tormentor will not disclose exactly what's in the report because "it's secret."

USES AND ABUSES OF THE PRESS

Despite its acknowledged problems, television news is still a primary source of information on current events. Many people, even those who try to read the paper regularly, find themselves at the end of a hectic day with only enough energy left to stare at the TV version of the news. It's better than nothing, but that's not the major problem. TV news is pervasive, more people watch it than read print accounts. This means that TV news creates an image of how events are, or were, for a majority of the population. The television version gains substance simply through repetition. TV is a visual and thus easily re-membered medium. Most people will remember the television version of the explosion on the USS Iowa in April of 1989, warts and all, but few will recall the more thorough newspaper accounts. Multiply this by the scores of military-affairs pieces run each year and you have a large, significantly large, portion of the population receiving a fuzzy and distorted impression about armed forces and wars and the people who serve in them. These distortions will become more dangerous as the practice of filming "simulations" of news events using actors spreads. This is nothing new: It was done in Vietnam, and even the fa-mous World War II picture of the marines raising the flag on Mount Suribachi was a reenactment for the photographer. But the practice is becoming more commonplace. A picture may be worth a thousand words, but today the words are carefully ed-ited before you see them.

Many of the normal distortions are not really the fault of the TV news and the techniques used in video journalism. The major problem is that the most common news reported on tele-vision is of events close to people's lives. It's not for nothing that human-interest stories have taken over the medium in the last twenty years. In the last decade, the "happy talk" format has also come into wide use, a technique whereby the on-air talent carry on a friendly banter while they toss off the news nuggets. In this way, even political and financial matters can be brought down to a human level. Many of us vote, and most of us have to deal with money, so the connection is easily made. Crime and disasters in general also have an angle most people can identify with.

But when TV news gets into the areas of technology and military affairs, most people's eyes glaze over. It's no big deal if people don't really understand the TV news version of tech-nological developments. Although panic-sparking reportage on medical developments or nuclear power often causes problems, the physicians, engineers, and scientists usually manage to eventually clarify everything one way or another, and people mostly accept the fact that they don't really understand what all those nerds and mad scientists are up to anyway. Military affairs are different. Even the appointed (or self-appointed) ex-perts have a hard time making sense of military affairs. Sensibilities are sharpened during wartime, but drift into fantasy and hypothesis in peacetime. The TV tendency to seek out the sensational and fanciful in news matter means that military affairs are regularly treated as contemporary science fiction with a dollop of burlesque thrown in. One can make a case for not showing military operations too realistically. When this was done during Vietnam, television audiences became quite appalled. But that was after a war began: The major impact of TV reporting on military affairs in peacetime is to get the audience to understand what to expect. To date the public has not been prepared for any reality that someone with combat service has experienced. The print media does a better job of this, but reach a much smaller audience. And many of the print users still have all those striking video images burned into their consciousness.

A good notion of the differences in the way in which the print and the video media treat a military story may be gained by looking at one that broke while this volume was in preparation. There were several such. The U.S. occupation of Panama might seem to have been an obvious choice. However, this was a "war," and as such received far more intensive treatment than the norm for military-related stories. Moreover, much of the coverage was essentially political in content. The Iraq-Kuwait War deserves a book of its own. A more typical incident was the turret explosion aboard the battleship *USS Iowa* on April 19, 1989. The table at the end of this chapter contains a summary of the treatment accorded the *Iowa* incident by *The New York Times* and several television networks. Print coverage was considerably more extensive than that on TV, and continued long after the incident had passed from the screen. In addition to reporting the facts, print coverage also dealt with a broader variety of issues and provided greater analysis than did television.

Several broadcasts spent a few hundred words, a significant effort for TV, discussing the issue of battleship obsolescence. *Iowa* and her three sister ships were laid down fifty years ago. For most of the intervening period, they have been in mothballs, and so they have had active lives of less than fifteen years each, only about half their operational life-expectancy. Although updated in many aspects, they *are* still big, expensive to operate ships based largely on half-century-old technology. Nevertheless, several characteristics of these ships make them suitable for modern warfare. First, they are far less vulnerable to modern naval weapons than any other ships afloat. Their armor was designed to defeat one-ton armor-piercing shells, which no other ship currently fires. Although current antiship missiles can do great damage to modern ships, they would bounce off these fifty-year-old "relics." The second advantage of these ships is that their very size provides ample room for lots of high-tech modern equipment. *Iowa*-class battleships have been outfitted with modern electronics and cruise missiles. In any fight with an enemy task force, an *Iowa* would give better than it got and be the last ship afloat. This is the ultimate definition of control of the seas. Even against submarines, the battleships have an advantage, as their hulls were designed to take several torpedo hits before even slowing up. On the downside, these battleships are hideously expensive to run. Three or four modern cruisers could be operated for the $50 million annual cost of keeping one *Iowa* going. But in a slug-out with half a dozen missile cruisers, the latter would be sunk or dead in the water while the battleship would still be moving and fighting. The only reason navies don't start building battleships again is because they are so expensive. Building one today would cost several billion dollars. Actually, Russia *is* building a class of battle cruisers, a form of "lite" battleship popular before World War II, but may be forced to cut back on this program in favor of their aircraft-carrier program as their defense budget continues to shrink. The United States has these four battleships only because they were put into storage ("mothballs") after World War II, instead of being scrapped. They were brought out again for service in Korea, and one served in Vietnam. In those wars, their primary service was artillery support for ground troops, using their highly accurate sixteen-inch guns, a function they can still perform better than any other ship afloat. Several newspaper articles dealt with many of these points, which were largely ignored on TV.

While the $250–350 million spent to reactivate each vessel refurbished much of the ship's equipment, there were some questions about the thirty-year-old ammunition. This was a subject the TV news could only cover in passing. In theory, the ammunition, particularly the propellant for the shells, can be kept usable over decades if it was stored in a climate-controlled space and tested periodically. The problem was not instability, as with dynamite, which can explode spontaneously if left too many years. The crucial thing with artillery propellant is reliability and predictability. Heavy artillery is accurate only if you use propellant of a known strength. For this reason, much care is taken in its manufacture, and when samples are test-fired, small variations that occur from batch to batch are noted and passed on to the end user. If the propellant is not stored under stable conditions, extremes of heat or cold will change the chemistry of the propellant and with that its power.

When the newly recommissioned battleship *New Jersey* was deployed off the coast of Lebanon in 1983, it was found that her sixteen-inch guns were not as accurate as expected. Although the newly formed crews were part of the problem, old ammunition long in storage was also a contributing factor. Both deficiencies were quickly attended to, but not before the press jumped on the navy for foisting this obsolete and ineffective warship on U.S. servicemen. The press was braying after a familiar target, the often shabby weapons and equipment the troops find themselves stuck with. The press, and sometimes the troops, have a hard time figuring out which weapon is a turkey and which is a lifesaver. The *Iowa* incident was an example of this confusion. Before, and after, the *Iowa* explosion, the navy had an abundance of volunteers for service on the battleships. These sailors are being practical, since no ship will be safer in combat than an *Iowa*-class vessel. Yet the turret explosion was not totally unexpected. Anytime you work with explosives, there is always some chance of a catastrophic accident. While the cause of the *Iowa* accident may never be known, two highly possible ones are a ripped "powder" bag (the explosive propellant "chips" are stored in silk bags) plus a spark from an electrical failure or a sailor intent on suicide.

Accidental explosions of munitions have been a not-uncommon cause of battleship accidents. The loss of the battleship (actually an uprated heavy cruiser) *Maine* in Spanish-controlled Havana Harbor in 1898 was just such an accident. The press jumped to the conclusion that the Spaniards had done the deed with a mine. Later investigation showed that it was caused by the ship's poorly maintained ammunition exploding. Several countries have lost battleships in this fashion over the years. Nor have turret explosions been unknown: The U.S. Navy suffered three in this century. What cannot be anticipated is that someone might deliberately create such an accident. If the "suicide" theory is correct—and this can never be proven "beyond a reasonable doubt"—then a great deal of the controversy over the "safety" of these ships is based on unsound concerns.

Military affairs are complex and are perhaps made more so because we are rarely exposed to the details of military operations. What we see of military affairs on television news is invariably more misleading than informative. The print media today are much better than at the time of the *Maine* explosion, but fewer people read these longer reports. Information is power, and lack of information is a problem waiting to happen.

NATIONAL AND LOCAL STYLES

The accompanying analysis of reportage on the *Iowa* incident shows only one of the two major styles of newspaper reporting, the "national press." The major metropolitan dailies (*The New York Times, The Washington Post,* the *Los Angeles Times,* and so forth) all maintain their own staffs of specialized reporters instead of relying entirely on the wire services, and give more extensive coverage than many other dailies. In contrast, TV coverage is much the same nationwide because of the use of network news. For this reason, high-level political and military decision-makers insure that the major papers are available whenever they are in some out-of-the-way area. Local papers outside the major metropolitan areas do not give military affairs as much play, unless it has something to do with a local military base, defense plant, or member of the armed forces.

Naturally, your average senior political or military official will not rely solely on TV. These people have access to intelligence reports as well as official accounts of events. Moreover, the military compiles reports from many different newspapers and periodicals for distribution to key people. These cut-and-paste jobs don't arrive as speedily as the newspapers, but do give their readers a broader choice of reporting to choose from. This is important, as the various major papers don't speak with one voice. For example, *The Washington Post* treatment of the *Iowa* incident contained more technical detail and, naturally, profiled a local resident who died in the explosion. The major dailies, and the network news departments, are always out to outdo each other. Since television news has the edge on timeliness, the papers concentrate on ferreting out important, or simply interesting, or sensational, information about an event. Many senior officials have assistants monitor all major news networks for information. Likewise, the major papers and periodicals are watched for military and political information. Reporters can go where spies can't. Moreover, there are more reporters snooping around than spies, and the government doesn't have to pay the reporters, or take the heat when some news hound gets caught where he shouldn't be.

THE TABLOIDS

Tabloids are the print version of television. Tabloid newspapers essentially aim for the broadest possible readership, and, commensurate with the basic rule that the larger the audience, the less informative the medium, they provide relatively poor coverage, habitually sensationalistic and shallow, with no systematic follow-up. And like television, the tabloids rarely admit to mistakes. At that, at least they provide more words to a story than does television. Frequently, the words are just "borrowed" from some other print medium, or simply invented. The tabloids have given new meaning to the term "inventive journalism." Unfortunately, the tabloids are read by millions and believed by many of them.

NEWSMAKERS

Another reason for watching how the media handle an event is that the journalists not only report the news but may help to shape it. And once in a while they may help make it. This is not new. The American Revolution was fueled and sometimes directed by the colonial press. The course of the Civil War was also heavily influenced by the press. The Spanish-American War was triggered by press coverage of the *Maine* explosion after years of lurid reporting about the revolution in Spanish-controlled Cuba. Many readers will also remember the influence the press had on the course and outcome of the Vietnam War and the Iran Hostage Crisis. Even totalitarian nations can no longer control their press sufficiently to eliminate the occasionally inflammatory influence on their population. Moreover, worldwide radio broadcasts by the BBC and Voice of America get through with the truth—or a reasonable facsimile thereof—even if the local state-controlled press is spouting the current party line. These broadcasts, in conjunction with the thousands of foreign correspondents from major Western media, provide many nations with a valuable adjunct to their own intelligence organizations. Moreover, the information released through these open channels eliminates one problem that bedevils users of normal intelligence: "Do the other fellows know what I know? Well, of course they do, unless they're deaf." The intelligence collected openly by journalists is frequently questionable. But because it is gathered and released quickly, errors are readily spotted and new angles pursued. In more than one recent crisis or conflict, one of the best sources of information has been the media reports. An excellent example of this phenomenon at work occurred in the immediate aftermath of the California earthquake of October 17, 1989, when for some time the White House essentially repeated what was being said by the various television news organizations. Although the earthquake was a domestic natural disaster, the pattern was very similar to that which sometimes occurs in fast-breaking diplomatic or military situations abroad. In essence, the media were fueling government decision-making. This is not always the case, as on occasion a government can control what the media are passing on to the public, as did the British government during the Falklands War and the United States during the Grenada, Panama, and Iraq campaigns: In these cases, the media were, at least in the opening stages, more or less dependent upon official sources for information.

There are dangers in this system. Leaders, under pressure to make decisions quickly, and faced with incomplete or contradictory information from their own intelligence sources, are tempted to use the more plausible reports from the open media, whether or not those reports have any substance. The news organizations are in the habit of sounding authoritative no matter how shaky their sources. This causes all parties involved to make risky decisions without even knowing it.

PRESS RELATIONS

For many decades, the totalitarian Communist countries took advantage of the freewheeling foibles of the Western press, and the strictly controlled Communist media, to "work the press." Russian intelligence officers, skilled in the art of disinformation (carefully planted lies and deceptions) spread false, but tantalizing, information to the scoop-happy Western and Third World press. These deceits were reinforced by the controlled Communist press pushing the same line, often by quoting the more believable Western or "nonaligned" press, where the disinformation had been planted in the first place. Where they could, Communist agents infiltrated, bribed, or subsidized Western and Third World media. This put Western intelligence agencies on the defensive, as they had to clear away the disinformation before presenting a more accurate analysis of what was really going on to their leaders and fellow citizens. Among the many myths perpetuated by this process was the stability of the political order in Communist countries, the viability of Communist economies, and the prowess of Communist military forces. Communist-supported revolutions in Third World and Western nations also got a public-relations and image boost from these activities. All this came apart in the 1980s, as the disintegration of Communist economic and social systems was reacted to in the form of rebellious behavior by their peoples. You can lie to all of the people all of the time, but eventually the deceit comes back to haunt you.

To a lesser extent, the same game of disinformation and media manipulation is used in the West, where special-interest groups attempt to play the press for their own agendas. It's not for nothing that the public-relations (PR) business in the West has an unsavory reputation. Much of what the Western PR firms do is not nearly as wicked as the practices of their Communist and totalitarian counterparts. The Western press is pretty independent-minded and not fond of being manipulated by the PR crowd. Also, many PR techniques are fairly benign. The press release is the most widely used technique, although the more insidious mat release is less well known, or liked. The mat release takes its name from the practice of sending already typeset news stories on "mats," which can then be placed right on the printing press with other material from the newspapers' own reporters and published as if the mat release were just another news story instead of a message from a special interest. Mat releases are still commonly used in weekly real estate sections of newspapers. You can usually tell a mat release because its typeface is a little different from the one the paper normally employs. In these days of electronic journalism, with even print reporters relying heavily on computers, there are even electronic versions of the mat release. The ready availability of video equipment has created a television version of the mat release, in the form of well-edited, carefully slanted video "press releases," which are distributed by lobbyists, corporations, and even members of Congress to local TV stations lacking extensive news-gathering resources. These can be spotted by paying attention to the "reporter" presenting the story or to the tape's attribution. If they are unfamiliar, be alert.

Reporters are always eager for a bit of inside information. Government and industry officials are willing to comply if the resulting story will serve their ends. The most common form of this is the news leak. Military affairs are rife with this sort of thing, which has serious implications for how military power is used. The leaks by government (including military) officials are designed to further some favored program or to defend a project under attack in the press. Defense-industry leaks follow the same pattern, although they are mostly used for the purpose of defending some weapons project.

The military maintains hundreds of uniformed PR specialists, who play the game for their employers. Not all journalists are equally adept at sorting out the PR that is information and that which is self-serving propaganda. As a result, much of what makes it into the media is not what is, but the image some special interest wishes to promote. For some military organizations, this process is a matter of life and death. The U.S. Marine Corps (USMC) is a prime example of this. The USMC is officially a part of the navy, yet it is commonly considered a fourth service, even to the point of having its commandant (who is nonetheless a subordinate to the chief of Naval Operations) as a member of the U.S. Joint Chiefs of Staff. This curious arrangement is a direct result of very successful USMC lobbying and PR efforts over the years. No other marine-infantry organization in history has ever established itself in such a powerful and independent status. In effect, the USMC has freed itself of interference from the army, whose functions it duplicates, and the navy, for whom it works. Moreover, the USMC have even obtained its own air units, with marine pilots flying fixed-wing and helicopter aircraft. All this is largely due to the shrewd use of public relations, the press, and the lobbying efforts of the USMC. Much of the favorable treatment the marines get is no accident, but the result of systematically working the press for decades. The other services envy the success of the Leathernecks, but have not been able to match it.

However, the other services are not fighting for survival, as the marines are; only for a larger piece of the defense budget. Unlike most nations, America does not have a unified military command. This is partially to curtail any chance of military interference in the civilian government, and partially out of habit. The net result is that the four services (army, air force, navy, and USMC) constantly maneuver to grab a larger piece of the budget, mostly at the expense of another service. This has made the media a battlefield for the services and their defense-industry suppliers. We're talking hundreds of billions of dollars in play each year.

Washington, D.C., is one of the more intense battlegrounds for these struggles to control what the media report on military affairs. In D.C., 15,000 news media personnel struggle with the thousands of PR professionals, consultants, lobbyists, politicians (supported by over 20,000 personal staff), and tens of thousands of military staff. All of these people are looking for a story, or a way to influence one, and have an effect on what ordinary citizens get for news and what military and political decisions are made. Senior decision makers are influenced by this torrent of print and video information because it is so immediate and persistent. Another crucial factor is the need for these decision makers to respond to the impressions their constituents get. Most people do not have access to classified intelligence reports, but are inundated by media reporting. Thus the press becomes a major player in the decision-making process. And media reporting is not all you think it is. There is always an extra "spin" on the reporting.

THE "SPIN FACTOR"

All the players in the media game attempt to put their own slant, or "spin," on the way news that affects them is presented. The most obvious way this is done is through the press release. Most of these press releases are preventive, or "apple polishing": Attempts to enhance the image of the military in general and to shore up defenses in areas that are likely to become controversial and harmful in the future. Examples abound. One of the more frequently seen are the thousands of releases simply announcing the achievements of military personnel in their hometown newspapers. Others simply spread the word about good deeds by the military: charity drives, heroic acts by military personnel, or the participation of military units in disaster relief. These positive releases far outnumber any information released on failure or scandal within the military. Thus, whenever there is a scandal of some sort, the media audience will have all those good deeds to offset the bad news.

When an embarrassing event gets a lot of media attention, the military PR staffs shift to "damage control" efforts, which is where most of the lying and deception go on. The longest-running and highest-volume deception campaigns are those surrounding defense procurement programs. After over three decades of this nonsense, the press and the public have become a bit cynical about the excuses and inability to solve the problems. Although defense procurement is more efficiently run than other government purchasing programs, this is scant comfort to taxpayers who continually see multibillion-dollar programs go over budget, miss schedules, and then sometimes not work when the shooting starts. From the vantage point of shooting blanks, the most obvious problem is the smoke that gets thrown into everyone's eyes as the press releases trying to paper over the scandals go flying back and forth.

The B-2 Stealth bomber is a classic example of a defense procurement project trying to evade the potentially fatal attention of the press. First, the project was kept "black," or hypersecret, for over five years. When the project finally came out in the open, the only information available was the official press releases. This was nothing new, as there have always been some "black" projects, usually involving intelligence-collecting (satellites, recon aircraft, etc.), which are ordinarily secret throughout their existence. The F-117 Stealth fighter (actually a light bomber) and the B-2 were both kept black and for more reasons than just the stated one of keeping the technology from the Russians. Both aircraft were using technology that was radically new and untried. The technology was very advanced, very difficult to perfect, and very, very expensive. Over $25 billion was spent before the B-2 even flew, and projected costs are over $70 billion for 132 aircraft. Air-force planners knew that the cost of these bombers would run into popular opposition in an era of declining defense budgets. There would also be criticism for building a new bomber when two strategic bomber systems already existed, one of which was totally new, in addition to cruise and ballistic missiles. Instead of being defensive about it, the air-force PR crew went on the attack. First, press releases stressed the ability of the Stealth bomber to negate Russia's extensive air-defense system. This distorted the situation, as most Russian air defenses would still be available against the much larger fleets of non-Stealth aircraft. Moreover, the Stealth bomber is intended for strategic warfare, where ballistic and cruise missiles would have the best opportunity to do all the dirty work of delivering nuclear weapons. This argument also avoided the questionable effectiveness of Russian air defenses, which are regularly penetrated by civilian airliners, not to mention Mathias Rust's tiny single-engine plane, which landed in Moscow's Red Square in 1987. In the face of this, the PR effort then stressed that Russia would have to spend more upgrading its air defenses than the B-2 would cost. This assumed that the Russians would, or could, make such a move when their economy was stalled and they were cutting defense spending. This argument also makes the B-2 an economic, not a military, weapon, which neatly sidesteps the issue of whether the Stealth bomber would work at all. This last question shot down still another PR effort: to imply that the B-2 would be used to go after Russia's mobile missiles. These road and rail mobile missiles would escape attacks by ballistic and cruise missiles. But the B-2 PR team allowed as how the B-2 could cruise around Russia looking for mobile missiles and destroy them. All this would take place after a nuclear exchange. The "mobile missile hunter" argument was soon withdrawn in the face of public skepticism and ridicule. Next came the argument that, with a 10,000-mile range, the B-2 could be used to bomb anyplace in the world from U.S. bases, "economically": Arguably the 1986 raid on Tripoli could have been executed by three or four B-2s using precision munitions and one or two tankers, all flying from the United States. Yet with fourteen large aircraft carriers, this capability seems to be present already. Another constant theme was that, as $25 billion had already been spent, it would be a shame to "waste" it by not building the aircraft.

While the military PR organizations appear to lose many of their battles, they do succeed when they manage to muddy the water, and people's perceptions, of what is really going on. For example, military doctrine of how wars are to be fought is revised periodically in response to changing political requirements. In the 1960s, doctrine stressed "counterinsurgency" (antiguerrilla warfare), although the military regularly ignored this political directive and spent only modest sums on "Special Forces." During the 1970s, doctrine again emphasized mechanized warfare, and in the 1980s it shifted back to "low-intensity warfare" (another form of counterinsurgency). Strenuous PR efforts accompanied each of these shifts as the troops, and the public, were reassured about the wisdom of these doctrinal shifts. These new doctrines were created for a number of reasons, not all of them military and not all of them capable of surviving close scrutiny.

In addition to these major shifts in policy, there were the usual smaller PR campaigns in support of questionable weapons systems. Some weapons have been killed despite these efforts, such as the Sergeant York antiaircraft system plus one attack helicopter and several new tanks. Nevertheless, the U.S. Air Force has demonstrated a remarkable ability to recover from PR and legislative setbacks. The B-1 bomber program was shut down in the 1970s, only to be revived in the 1980s. Military and industry PR played a large part in this, as well as the similar revival of the MX ICBM. This is not a purely American phenomenon. In Europe, even among the neutral nations, there are many of the same struggles over defense budgets, with the same pattern of wins and losses, and masses of citizens wondering which way is up.

HOW THEY GOT IT WRONG

The media have a pervasive influence on how we perceive past military events. Those perceptions are the basis of how we cope with current and future military events. It's important to remember that much of what we consider as "common knowledge" about military affairs are simply myths that were enshrined as fact via repetition in the popular press. Even so hallowed a belief as the "embattled farmers" of the American Revolution who defeated the Redcoats by hiding behind trees is largely erroneous, fostered by two centuries of media repetition of patriotic rhetoric: The principal battles of the Revolution were all fought in formal stand-up European style. Below are some examples of how some more recent myths contrasted with reality.

CHINESE HORDES IN KOREA

The first year of the Korean War (1950–51) was very much a back-and-forth affair. First the North Koreans swept all before them, including some U.S. units thrown hastily in the way. Then United Nations (largely American and South Korean) forces pushed the North Koreans back almost to the Chinese border on the Yalu River. At this point, the Chinese entered the war and sent UN forces scurrying back into South Korea. Finally, UN forces recovered and pushed the Chinese back to approximately where the border is today. Then everyone settled down to two years of trench warfare and peace negotiations. One well-developed fallacy came out of the war, the myth of the Red Chinese hordes, who were most often described as masses of Chinese infantry surging out of the darkness. Accompanied by the sound of bugles, whistles, yells, and other noises, these hordes would fall upon American troops with savage ferocity and overwhelm them by sheer numbers, with total disregard for casualties. The impression being conveyed was one of inhuman disinterest in the survival of the common Chinese soldiers on the part of their callous commanders. The reality was quite different.

Chinese Communist infantry tactics had been developed over several decades of increasingly successful combat against Japanese and Chinese Nationalist troops. The Chinese had plenty of manpower, but not much in the way of weapons and equipment. So they adapted, and those who survived years of fighting became quite skillful. A key ingredient of Chinese infantry operations was mobility. The troops traveled light and could outmarch just about any other army in the world. They preferred fluid situations, where this mobility, plus the discipline and diligence of the troops, would give them many advantages.

Before they unleashed a large number of very vulnerable infantry against an enemy position, they carefully scouted that position. Chinese attacks were usually meticulously planned, and every assault group, which consisted of half a dozen or so troops, had a specific task. The assault groups habitually rehearsed their attacks under the direction of seasoned and industrious leaders. The assault generally took place at night, to further protect the troops. Specially trained engineers would sometimes go in first to clear mines, cut wire, and remove other defensive obstacles. Along with the engineers, small groups of especially skilled scouts would move up to kill any defending troops in outposts. At the same time, the assault groups were silently moving to their jumping-off positions just in front of the enemy lines. Depending on the situation, this might be less than a hundred meters from the enemy, occasionally at a few hundred. Normally, the Chinese wanted to have their troops as close as possible to the enemy position before launching the assault. One reason for the careful preparation was the Chinese lack of radios. They had very few of them, although they laid wire for field telephones whenever possible. In general, once the operation began, everyone had to carry out his prescribed role no matter what because of the lack of communication during the battle. Communications were limited to flares, shouting, and noisemakers like whistles and bugles. In the immediate battle area, the bugles and whistles were more efficient than anything the United States had. Moreover, all that noise was good for Chinese morale. Only when a Chinese soldier couldn't hear any more whistles or bugles did he know his side was beaten. Silence indicated that most of the leaders were out of action and it was time to pull back and reorganize or stand and die, depending upon orders.

The hordes that American troops saw right in front of them were the assault groups. Several of these groups were led by a senior leader. If everything worked, the assault groups achieved surprise and were on top of the defenders before many Chinese got hit. Early in the Korean War, the Chinese tactics worked quite well. Terrified American survivors of such attacks told eager journalists about the overwhelming Chinese hordes. Soon, the troops began telling jokes about the subject: "How many hordes are there in a Chinese platoon?" This illusion of "hordes" of Oriental infantry reminded Americans of World War II Japanese "banzai" attacks, which actually *were* often ill-organized mass charges against American positions. But the Chinese attacks were much smoother articles.

For a while, the Chinese seemed unbeatable. By 1951, most U.S. infantry units had worked out ways to defeat these Chinese tactics. The solution was not difficult: more outposts, more mines, more wire, and more alertness. While the Chinese infantry tactics could be devastating if they achieved surprise, they had catastrophic consequences if anything went wrong. This was largely due to the numerous and efficient U.S. artillery. If an outpost detected the early stages of an attack, heavy artillery barrages came down on likely Chinese assembly and jumping-off positions. Several hundred artillery shells could easily cripple the attacking forces before they got anywhere near U.S. or Allied lines. Indeed, in the face of better-trained and more alert U.S. infantry and artillery, there were not a lot of successful Chinese attacks in 1951. The Chinese were also stymied by the static "trench" nature of the war after 1951. Robbed of the advantages of a fluid battlefield, the Chinese lost several key elements of their doctrine (surprise, mobility, encirclement of the enemy, etc.).

For the rest of the war, few U.S. troops saw a Chinese horde. But the GIs read the papers, and that's how many found out about the Chinese hordes. The folks back home learned of the hordes the same way, helped along by a few motion pictures that depicted them in all their hordish fervor. Outside of intelligence personnel or the more inquisitive frontline commanders, few knew what was really behind the apparent "hordes" of Chinese.

U.S. GROUND FORCES IN VIETNAM

A recent myth is that our ground forces won most of their battles against Viet Cong and North Vietnamese infantry. Such was not the case, and this time it wasn't the press that was most at fault but the senior commanders of U.S. forces, both in Vietnam and at the Pentagon, plus an intensive PR campaign.

Vietnam was an odd war in many respects. One important characteristic was the concentration of the people exposed to enemy fire in an unusually small number of combat battalions. At its peak, there were only eighty-one U.S. Army infantry battalions in Vietnam, plus about twenty-four battalions of marines. There were also a dozen army tank and armored recon battalions, plus six of marines. So the "frontline" strength of American forces in Vietnam was only about 123 battalions. And it was the infantry that took most of the punishment. The 105 infantry battalions contained fewer than 90,000 troops, out of a peak U.S. strength—all services—in Vietnam of 536,000 in 1968, of whom about 330,000 were army and a further 75,000 marines. This was a ratio of one combat soldier for every five support troops within the combat zone. If you include the support troops for Vietnam forces back in the United States, the ratio climbs to well over ten to one.

The army endured 238,000 combat casualties, including 30,000, dead; the marines about 100,000, including some 13,000 dead. The marine figures are the key here, for proportionally far more marines are infantrymen. On average, an infantryman had a better than 50 percent chance of being wounded or killed in combat during his one-year tour. Add in the figures for non-combat disease and injury and the chances of getting hurt were over 60 percent.

But these numbers don't tell the whole story. Most American casualties were from booby traps and mines. U.S. commanders claimed victories by launching large "search and destroy" operations. Using superior mobility with helicopters and massive firepower from aircraft and artillery, attempts were made to pin down Viet Cong (VC) forces so they could be blasted. The VC quickly learned how to cope with these operations, and constantly lured U.S. forces into ambushes. When American troops got around to calling in their artillery and aircraft, the VC would withdraw, or get so close to U.S. troops ("grab the enemy's belt") that the superior American firepower would hammer both sides.

U.S. commanders turned these embarrassing operations into victories by developing the "body count" approach to determining victory, partially because the press was demanding some "objective" criteria to back up the army's claims. So the troops would count the VC bodies on the battlefield. The body counts were invariably higher than U.S. casualties, and thus victory could be proclaimed. It soon became apparent that either the average VC had nine lives or there were a lot more of them out there than anyone thought. Actually, not as many VC were being killed as claimed. Because so much emphasis was placed on the body count as a means of keeping score, the count was not scrupulously done. Several subterfuges were employed. The easiest was to simply multiply the number of bodies found by some number to account for the enemy dead "carried off" during the battle. This "carrying off the dead" routine did sometimes occur, but not so frequently as the inflated body count indicated. The second trick was to count all non-U.S. bodies. There were generally a lot of civilians in the battle area, and their dead bodies would be counted as VC dead. The infantry knew this fraud was going on, but their primary objective was to get out of Vietnam alive, not audit the books. One thing that tipped some people off was the low number of weapons recovered, frequently only one for every ten bodies. The official story was that retreating VC would recover weapons from fallen comrades. The VC did try to do this, but it did not occur frequently enough to explain the consistently disproportionate body count to weapons captured ratio. In fact, the number of VC killed was never accurately known. Aside from battlefield deaths, many were killed by artillery fire or air strikes when there were no U.S. infantry around to count the bodies. Indeed, some American troops held as prisoners of war are known to have been killed by B-52 raids or artillery barrages, though still officially—and politically—listed as "missing in action."

What did happen on the ground was an endless cycle of green U.S. infantry units getting chewed up by experienced VC and North Vietnamese units. The reasons for this were clear enough. First, the U.S. troops were nearly all recruits who had been hastily trained and ineptly prepared for combat. They spent a year in Vietnam and then went home and got out of the service. Worse, the troops in a unit were never all in Vietnam as a group for that year. Men were rotated into units as "replacements" whenever they were needed, and rotated out precisely on the day that their year "in country" expired. This did not encourage unit cohesion, which invariably remained poor but could have been overcome had there been adequate NCOs and officers. But effective battlefield leadership was grossly lacking. Many of the senior NCOs had World War II and Korean experience, yet these men needed only one tour in Vietnam to realize that the system wasn't working. The army underwent a massive loss of such experienced NCOs as the war progressed. Many of those who weren't killed retired or simply refused to reenlist. Many senior NCOs who did not have twenty years in the ranks left the service anyway, forfeiting their pensions. In response, the army selected recruits with "leadership potential," ran them through a special NCO course, and sent these fresh "shake and bake" NCOs directly into leadership positions. The green troops and instant NCOs were then led by equally inexperienced officers. Indeed, if anything, the officers were less prepared than the troops they led.

WHY ALL THAT POOR LEADERSHIP?

On the theory that it would be good for their education, the army adopted a policy of giving as many officers as possible some "troop experience." As a result, most officers spent six months or less with combat units. These officers were as inadequately trained as their NCOs and troops. Moreover, since they stayed in the field only half as long as the troops, they rarely attained the expertise in combat of their more senior NCOs and men. An example of the army's attitude could be seen in their response to inquiries about the short duty tours of combat-unit officers. The army pointed out that the average platoon, company, and battalion commander in World War II served less time with their units than did the Vietnam officers. The implication was that the Vietnam era officers actually had more combat experience than had their fathers in World War II. What the army failed to point out—possibly failed to realize—was that while a World War II combat unit did indeed run through officers at a rapid rate, this was due either to combat injuries or getting the boot for gross incompetence. After all, in World War II, units experienced intense combat not just for days on end, as was the case in Vietnam, but for months and even years. The big difference in World War II was that the 15–20 percent of officers who proved capable, and lucky, stayed in action, got even better, and were promoted. By the end of that war, some of the best battalion commanders were in their late twenties, and many of the best company commanders were barely out of their teens. There was none of this in Vietnam. Worse, it was more difficult to smoke out the incompetent. Toward the end of the war, entire battalions would "pretend" they were out beating the bush for VC, while, in fact, they were staying as far away from the VC as they could. In this they were merely imitating a favorite practice of the South Vietnamese Army—"You don't shoot at me, and I won't shoot at you."

In addition to fudging the body count, the official reports on most battles were doctored as well. These were made to sound as though U.S. forces operated with disciplined professionalism. Talking to the troops and looking at the casualty figures presented a quite different story. Most often, U.S. units were lured into ambushes by VC units that constantly patrolled the battle area and had better intelligence. Although VC troops—who were in for "the duration"—lacked many radios, much artillery, or any aircraft, they were more experienced and better trained than their American opponents. They were also better motivated. It was their country, and the Americans were seen as foreign invaders and the South Vietnamese as corrupt collaborators. After the first encounters with massive American firepower, the VC found that the best tactic was to get as close to U.S. units as possible, so that the GIs would be reluctant to use their firepower lest they take casualties from friendly fire. In fact, for a good deal of the war as much as 20 percent of U.S. losses were due to so-called "friendly fire": This was ten times the comparable official rate for World War II.

True to their guerrilla origins, the VC did not stand and slug it out. They inflicted as many losses as possible with their ambushes and then withdrew. Whatever the respective losses, the fact that the enemy had left them in command of the field—a traditional measure of military success—created the impression that the U.S. troops had won. But it was difficult for the Americans to know how much damage they had done. What was known was that there were always VC combat units out there. No matter how much they were hammered by B-52 bombs or artillery, there was always a VC ambush waiting for U.S. infantry.

Some infantry units did perform admirably. There were the rare units that were able to latch on to combat-experienced officers and NCOs. And the U.S. Marines had much better success against the VC than the army. These successful units, both army and marine, played the game the VC way, operating light, moving fast, and hitting hard. But these successful tactics were not widely imitated. So the VC survived, and ultimately they prevailed. The U.S. forces did not succeed on the ground.

There are many examples. On August 18, 1965, two com-

panies of U.S. Marines tangled with a North Vietnamese Army
(NVA) battalion and suffered twenty-nine dead and seventy-
three wounded, about 25 percent of strength. This effectively
wrecked the companies for some time. NVA losses were estimated at over two hundred dead, about 50 percent of strength,
not counting wounded, but the NVA typically recovered from
these losses much more quickly than the Americans or South
Vietnamese. More important, since the NVA often carried off
their dead, estimates of their losses were problematic. The only
times enemy losses were confirmed were on those rare occasions when enemy documents were captured. But American
losses were broadcast around the world, and the U.S. Marines
were involved in some extremely bloody actions, as at Hills
861/881 during April and May of 1967. The marines took over
nine hundred casualties while tangling with the NVA 18th and
95th Regiments. The marines took longer to rebuild their shat-
tered units than did the NVA, who essentially held the ground
when the fighting was over. On November 17, 1965, the U.S.
Army's 2nd Battalion/7th Cavalry Regiment lost 155 dead and
121 wounded at Landing Zone [LZ] Albany. The NVA 66th
Regiment lost an estimated 400 dead but was back in action
much sooner. In January 1967 these two units had a rematch at
LZ 4 with about the same results. On November 11, 1967, the
66th Regiment tangled with the U.S. 1st Battalion/503rd Airborne ("Task Force Black") and inflicted over 170 casualties.
Eventually, the NVA 66th Regiment had the area all to itself.

The media were extremely ineffective in communicating
American tactical and operational failures in Vietnam to the
public. The media were also remiss in not clearly pointing out
that there were two quite different enemy armies in Vietnam.
The Viet Cong (VC) were a classic guerrilla force that went out
of its way to avoid encounters with U.S. combat units. The
North Vietnamese (NVA) were a regular army patterned on the
Russian model, although heavily modified in accordance with
local conditions and their guerrilla origins. The NVA were more
willing to take on U.S. units, while the VC specialized in setting booby traps and ambushing noncombat elements.

In general, adverse coverage of the war effort in South
Vietnam revolved around corruption, allegations of atrocities,
and morale problems, rather than substantive questions about
battlefield performance. Overall, the troops were depicted as

uniformly capable, brave, and well led. For most of the war, the majority of journalists accepted the official version of events, even after many of them had become disillusioned with the war. The U.S. Army told a different tale, indirectly, after the war. From the mid 1970s through the 1980s, there were massive changes in the way the army trained, organized, and prepared to fight a war. Somebody was paying attention.

WHO WON THE TET CAMPAIGN?

While U.S. ground forces took a beating when trying to fight the Viet Cong and North Vietnamese in the bush, it was a different situation when the enemy came out of the jungle. Such was the case during the Tet Offensive of 1968.

Prior to Tet, America's political and military leaders had been promoting the impression that the war was being won, that we were beginning to see "the light at the end of the tunnel." The massive VC offensive during Tet in 1968 proved an enormous blow to the confidence of the armed forces, and seriously undermined domestic support for the war. Press coverage stressed the completeness of the surprise, and lingered over the devastation and the casualties that friendly forces incurred. This led to serious questions about William Westmoreland's judgment and the effectiveness—and honesty—of U.S. intelligence, which had seriously underestimated VC strength. Criticism grew when Westmoreland declared that we had decisively defeated the VC and then immediately called for more troops. Journalists, who had heretofore more or less endorsed the official perspective on the war, began to take a more jaundiced view of events. One result of this was that stories of poor U.S. morale increased significantly after Tet, as did stories that focused on U.S. casualties: Even today, the average American believes that most of the troops who went to Vietnam became casualties and that more U.S. lives were lost in that war than in World War II, neither of which is incorrect. But who had actually won?

Defining victory is rarely simple. The general consensus at the time was that Tet had been a VC victory and that the war was going badly for the United States and South Vietnam. A lot of misconceptions were involved in this popular conclusion. To be sure, American estimates of VC strength and intentions had been in error, though by no means as seriously as it seemed at the time, nor deliberately, as was claimed by some. Tactically, despite the advantage that surprise gave to the VC, U.S. and South Vietnamese forces had reacted rapidly to the offensive, and the VC made no permanent gains. Moreover, as a result of Tet, the VC were virtually eliminated as a combat force. This went largely unnoticed in the press because there were no correspondents with the VC, and because North Vietnam greatly increased its troop strength in the South. This was why Westmoreland had called for additional ground forces, to be used in conventional operations against conventionally organized and equipped foes. So, although the United States and South Vietnamese forces had achieved a significant tactical victory, and the VC had suffered a disastrous defeat, the North Vietnamese—though not the VC—won a major political victory.

THE U.S. MARINES IN LEBANON

"The Marines have landed and the situation is well in hand" went the initial reports when the marines occupied Beirut Airport in 1982. A year later, there had been no radical improvement in the political, or military, situation because of the marines' presence. This generated a lot of stories casting aspersions on the marines' military prowess. After local terrorists sent a truckload of explosives into the marine barracks in October of 1983, the marines became fair game in the media. The print media presented a pretty balanced story of what was going on, but only for those who were willing to plow through the thousands of words of military and political reporting from Beirut Airport and marine headquarters in Washington. The video news left one with a series of snapshots, and snap answers for what had happened and why. The truth of the matter was that the marines had been doing this sort of thing for over a century, but rarely with so much political and media attention paid to their every move. Overexposure in the media and over control from Washington essentially left the marines with no opportunity to do what they were proven experts at. The marines were sent in to pacify the area, but the leadership in Washington kept changing the rules. When the marines became aggressive in defending their positions, the media jumped all over them for a story, and Washington usually recoiled from the attention.

After all, the marines were on a diplomatic mission, so what was all that marine combat we were seeing on the evening news? In the past, there would still have been all that violence, and probably a good bit more, but the folks in Washington would have read about it days or weeks later after the marines had pacified the area, and there was no opportunity to second-guess what they were about. Even such a minor incident as a marine stopping an Israeli tank became a major media, and later diplomatic, event. The marines in Lebanon, or at least their last battalion commander, also caught the diplomatic fever. After the dust had settled on the marine deaths, the battalion commander admitted that he had taken it upon himself to interpret his mission as largely a diplomatic one. For this reason, he felt it counterproductive to take any strong defensive measures like building fortifications, dispersing the troops, or giving the sentries live ammunition.

The entire Beirut entanglement was doomed to failure because the marines were not allowed to be marines and were instead used as chessmen in a game instead of acting as players. The real issue was micromanagement from afar and trying to run a military operation in a media spotlight. The real problem is a military organization being able to readjust itself quickly to cope with a wide range of missions it can be called upon to perform short of full-scale war.

RUSSIAN WEAPONS CAPABILITIES

In general the more technical a subject is, the more likely journalists are to make mistakes. This is particularly true when it comes to weaponry. One cannot understand the capabilities of a particular weapon without having used it and comparable weapons in a variety of circumstances. Few journalists have this experience. One author who deals with military hardware was for a time the butt of jokes about never having fired anything except a 105-mm gun. Weapons look impressive, even ones that don't work. And, real turkeys aside, you can never really tell whether or not they'll work in combat. The press apprises us of problems with our own weapons, much less so of problems with Russian equipment. This is natural, inasmuch as we live in an open society that airs its dirty linen in public, while Russia is a closed society that keeps this sort of thing close to its vest. This can lead to some extraordinarily inaccurate reportage. It happened again with Iraq in 1990.

Repeatedly, the media accord Russian equipment pretty favorable treatment. Part of this is because they're parroting what they hear from the professionals. Going to the military leaders, who presumably ought to know more about the capabilities of Russian equipment, is not always helpful, since they may actually know very little, but will pretend that they do. Moreover, U.S. generals and admirals are not normally inclined to bad-mouth Russian stuff, perhaps out of professional courtesy, or perhaps because next year's budget is never far from their thoughts. The intelligence crew also play a part, making sure that our senior officials don't say anything that would let the Russians know just how much we *do* know. As a result, when a new piece of Russian equipment turns up, strange things can happen in the media. Take the T-80 tank.

When the existence of the T-80 was first reported, the U.S. Army issued statements describing its "probable" capabilities along with sketches of its "probable" appearance. Several sectors of the media merely picked up on these press releases and repeated them, creating the impression that the Russians had introduced a decisively innovative tank. A few reporters and military analysts kept their heads and inquired a bit deeper. Their conclusions were that the T-80 was essentially an incremental improvement on the T-64 system, which had been in service for a decade. Although a good tank, the T-80 had several flaws. The army's statements as to its "probable" characteristics were based on what the army thought a new Russian tank would have, which in turn were based on what the army would have liked to see in its own newest tank. In the case of the T-80, the media were more or less misled by the army, which was misleading itself. This has not always been the case, and the media sometimes err in their treatment of hardware without any outside help, as in the case of "reactive armor."

Reactive armor really isn't armor at all, in a traditional sense. Actually, it's blocks of explosive placed over a tank's regular armor. When struck by an antitank projectile, the explosive reacts quickly and detonates outward, sending fragments of material from the reactive armor container toward the incoming round. Depending upon the type of round, this reduces penetrating power by 25–70 percent. First deployed by Israel, some reactive armor was captured by Syrians from a wrecked Israeli tank in Lebanon in 1982 and passed on to the Russians, who were already working on something of the sort themselves. By 1987, Russian tanks in Germany began to be equipped with it. Press reports began suggesting that NATO's hundreds of thousands of antitank projectiles were obsolete. Clearly, the Russians and Israelis had hit upon something significant, and questions were raised in the media as to why the United States didn't have it, on the theory that if "they" were spending money on the stuff, it must be good. A degree of panic slipped into some of the coverage: "The introduction of reactive armor to the Group of Soviet Forces in Germany means that there has been a decisive shift in the military balance on the Central Front."

Although the media expressed considerable concern, reactive armor was in fact not very effective, and certainly not decisive. It had a number of drawbacks. It was very expensive, heavy, dangerous to friendly infantry, and could damage a tank's communications and fire-control electronics. Most important, it didn't always work as intended, and tank crews were not keen about carrying several hundred pounds of explosives on their hulls. The military professionals were only mildly concerned about reactive armor because they were aware of its drawbacks, and realized that it could be defeated by relatively simple modifications to existing antitank projectiles. Israel had adopted it for some of her older, less well protected tanks, as a stopgap. Russia needed it as a "quick fix" because she was having problems with her version of British-developed composite armor, and was intimidated by all those NATO antitank weapons. By 1990, it became apparent that many early users of reactive armor were moving away from it and back toward the more stable, and predictable, composite armor.

The result was that reactive armor had virtually no effect on the military balance. In fact, Russia has been attempting to improve the armor protection of its tanks throughout the 1970s and eighties. This first consisted of adding 0.8-inch plates of additional armor to the front of their T-72s, plus varying arrangements of extra armor to the turret. Every four or five years, the Russians discarded one protection scheme and tried another. They were clearly worried about the vulnerability of their tanks, and seemed unable to come up with a satisfactory solution. The Western press rarely paid attention to these continuous developments, even though they were regularly reported in the military press, with photographs.

The media have made several similar errors in reporting on the capabilities and numbers of other Russian military equipment. Some of this is due to Russian secrecy, plus a general lack of understanding of military hardware. After all, most of us have no idea what a tank is supposed to be capable of. One result of this is that outside of the technical press, the flaws in Russian equipment are rarely mentioned, such as the autoloading cannon that doesn't work very well and has been known to injure crew members, or the highly vulnerable fuel-storage system on the more recent Russian tanks. Similar problems have arisen in terms of coverage of Russia's naval expansion. While their accident-prone ships and submarines have gained considerable attention, there has been much less coverage of the fact that, on average, Russian warships are rarely at sea for extended periods of time, or even that some classes of ships, such as their new "battle-cruiser" design, do not seem to have a specific role.

AFGHANISTAN

Combat operations in Afghanistan were a lot more casual than most press accounts let on. Understanding a guerrilla war is never easy, and the U.S. press has never been very good at it. To put things in perspective, the Russians had about 130,000 troops in Afghanistan. This number was determined by the limited road network, which could not support a larger force. Most of these troops guarded several dozen urban areas and military bases. The bulk of the fighting was done by 10,000 airborne and airmobile troops, who generally didn't make contact when they went looking for action. The sharpest actions were between *Spetsnaz* commandos on their sweeps and ambush missions along rebel supply routes. The Afghan rebels rarely had more than a few thousand fighters in position to attack at any given moment. And because these fighters were "organized" along tribal lines and had a warrior, not a soldier, mentality, there were very few coordinated operations. Groups of twenty to fifty Afghans would walk in from Pakistan, wander around for a month or two, try to find something they could attack without too much risk, and eventually head back to Pakistan, with whatever weapons and equipment they looted from dead Russian or Afghan soldiers, for a few months' rest. These raiding parties were also prone to stay in areas where the fighters had lived before being driven into Pakistan. Western journalists would often accompany these raiding parties, or more frequently the more numerous supply columns. The Russian policy of bombing villages and encouraging the people to flee into the cities or across the border was a deliberate attempt to deprive the rebel raiding parties of support, thus the need for supply via pack animals from Pakistan. So the rebels simply brought their food and ammunition with them, establishing many small bases (camps, really). Many camps were in areas that were highly inaccessible and so could easily resist Russian attack, or even detection, and became bases where rebel raiding parties could pick up food and munitions and get their wounded treated. To the Afghan fighters, this was a reasonable situation. This sort of marauding was the preferred outdoor sport for many Afghan tribesmen at any time, and the Russians made good pickings because they had lots of new equipment. While rebel casualties were quite high, particularly before they received effective antiaircraft missiles, they were already accustomed to one of the world's shortest life-expectancies. With their families safely established in Pakistani or Iranian refugee camps, the rebels could get on with avenging their kinsmen who did not make it safely into exile.

The Russians tried to mount carefully planned and organized attacks on rebel-held areas, but the Afghans would regularly get word of the attack and slip away into the hills. Unlike the Russians, the Afghans traveled light. They frequently operated in areas they grew up in, and knew the trails and hiding places. If the Russians sent out small raiding patrols, they would frequently be ambushed and invariably come up empty.

Once the Russians left, the press was again caught short when the Afghans took to their traditional activity, fighting each other. There was a lot of talk about Kabul falling as soon as the Russians left, which ignored local realities. Hundreds of thousands of Afghans supported the Communists and could be expected to put up stiff resistance. After all, many would die when the rebels triumphed, so the supporters of the government had to hold on even more desperately than before: Similarly, Saigon managed to hold out for three years after U.S. ground forces pulled out of Vietnam. Finally, most Afghans were, typically in wars like this, neither pro- nor anti-government. They just wanted to stay out of the way and survive.

It was not a very newsworthy war, unless you portrayed it as something it wasn't. And most of the time, that's what the media did.

THE ARAB-ISRAELI WARS

Throughout the long and continuing Arab-Israeli confrontation, Israel has benefited from an excellent press. Many cultural, social, political, historical, and religious factors have contributed to this situation. Press treatment has been influenced by the fact that Israel is a modern industrial democratic society, with a brave and beleaguered people having important religious ties to the West, and a strong psychological claim on Western support in the wake of serious questions about Western inactivity during the Holocaust. Then there is the strong Israel lobby in the United States, which keeps a watchful eye out for what it considers "unbalanced" coverage, as well as the sizable pro-Israel voting blocs in many politically vital places. Of no small importance is the fact that lots of Israelis speak English, which makes it easier for American reporters, who, like most Americans, are likely to speak nothing but English. After a while, another element helped strengthen the favorable press that Israel enjoyed: the fact that Israel won, and this in an era—the forties through the seventies—when the West seemed to be losing a lot. The Israelis themselves also proved to be excellent press agents, "working" the press to their ends. In contrast, aside from some romantic notions about desert sheikhs, the Arabs do not have much of a constituency in the West. No Arab state is remotely democratic, none is technologically or socially very progressive, and all are tainted with the hint of religious fanaticism. Worse, none has a free press, which means Western reporters are less likely to bother trying to cover the story from the Arab side of the issue.

The overall result of this has been that the Western press, and particularly the U.S. press, has accepted the Israeli version of events and promoted the prowess of the Israel Defense Forces (IDF). For example, coverage of the 1948–49 War for Independence revolved heavily around the theme of ill-armed, embattled Israeli farmers and shopkeepers contending with six well-equipped Arab armies. In fact, the total number of Arab troops who invaded the Israeli portion of Palestine was roughly equal to the number of defenders. The Arab armies had some 25,000–28,000 men who were poorly equipped, mostly with World War II hardware, very badly trained, save for Jordan's Arab Legion, and ill led. All of the Arab armies had spent World War II doing police work for their erstwhile British or French colonial masters, and so lacked any combat experience. These forces were supported by an approximately equal number of irregulars. Most of the Arab troops were illiterate peasants dragooned into the service for a cause that they barely understood, let alone had a commitment to. In contrast, the Israelis numbered 20,000–25,000 troops, plus about as many irregulars and home guards. They had numerous World War II veterans in their ranks, were fairly well equipped as a light infantry force, albeit also with World War II surplus, were well led, and were very highly motivated. The Arab irregulars and the Jordanians offered the most severe resistance to the Israelis, the other Arab forces being extremely inept. The war was hardly a "David against Goliath" situation, as was widely reported at the time, and since. The Israeli victory in 1949 was the beginning of what may be called the "Invincible Israeli" myth.

Arab-Israeli clashes over the next two decades were all largely reported from the Israeli perspective. The emphasis remained on the outnumbered Israelis with improvised armed forces beating the pants off the militaristic Arabs, with their enormous stocks of Soviet weapons. Regularly, the accounts stressed the Israeli success against "overwhelming" odds, while ignoring the problems that the Arabs faced, not least of which was their military backwardness and their Soviet military advisers. On a number of occasions, the press ignored or glossed over unpleasant realities, such as the French pilots who flew for Israel in 1956, the USS *Liberty* incident of 1967, or Israel's long-standing military links with South Africa. So willing has the press been to support the Israeli perspective that in the wake of the 1967 Israeli victory over Egypt, one American national magazine ran a picture showing an Arab prisoner of war who was pretty obviously being subjected to water torture with a caption stating that it showed Israeli troops giving aid to a captured foe. Of course, the hysterical rhetoric, and vicious behavior, of many of the Arabs did not hurt the Israelis very much. Meanwhile the myth of the "Invincible Israeli" grew.

The Arab-Israeli War of 1973 came as quite a surprise to anyone nurtured on press coverage of the Middle Eastern military situation. Suddenly, the Arabs, or at least the Egyptians, were no longer so inept. And the Israelis made a few blunders of their own. The Israelis demonstrated their basic superiority by going on to win the war, but their early reverses not only had a salutary effect on their overconfidence, but actually helped promote peace, because one Arab leader, Anwar Sadat, soon began to enjoy a favorable press in the West. In addition, some of the press, though not the electronic press, attempted to deal with the organizational and structural changes in the Egyptian armed forces that led to their unexpected success, and to the flaws that had developed in the Israel Defense Forces (IDF) that contributed to its initial failures. This war also brought into the open political strains within Israel concerning the character of the state, the future of occupied territories, and relations with various Arab states, strains of which were reflected in the Israel lobby in the United States, and had to be covered in the press. In more recent years, and particularly after the Lebanese operation of 1982, the image of the IDF in the press has probably not adequately reflected its actual capabilities, due to the character of its activities. Lebanon turned into a quagmire that frittered away the principal assets of the IDF, its flexibility and mobility. In addition, the civil disorder—the *intifada*—which erupted in the West Bank territories in late 1987, involved the IDF in repressive police work, which was bad for its image. These occupation duties, which have very unpalatable aspects, such as demolishing people's houses on suspicion of harboring terrorists, do not play well in the press, particularly given the vocal resistance to such duty by some Israeli reservists, open dissension in the ranks of many of Israel's foreign supporters, and the corrosive effects repressive activities have on morale: About three dozen Israeli soldiers commit suicide each year while on active duty, a rate statistically about three times higher than for the U.S. armed forces, and about twice that of the pre-reunification West German armed forces. So the image of the IDF has suffered. Yet the reality is that it probably remains one of the finest armed forces in the world, and certainly in the Middle East.

WHAT IMPRESSIONS WERE LEFT OVER

We rarely get our military information from those who have been there. Very few people experience combat, even in wartime. Fewer still have ever been in the sort of sustained, grinding combat that is better known as battle, a phenomenon that produces some strange attitudes. This is largely unavoidable, as there are never enough wars, or survivors of combat, to provide all the military journalists the press requires. It is important to understand the types of misinformation that can arise from this situation.

Naturally, many journalists write about subjects in which they have not participated. Most sports journalists have not been athletes, nor have many business journalists been executives. But with most other areas, journalists can talk to people who actually participate in these activities. Yet the majority of soldiers today have not been in combat. The troops only practice for what they may have to do eventually. No one has a great deal of certainty about how things will actually turn out. It's the blind leading the blind, and we have to read the resulting articles and make some sense from them. Actually, that's a bit of an exaggeration, at least most of the time. Many military journalists prepare as best they can, reading a lot about past warfare and talking with others who have done the same. So we have a situation where writers must deal with organized violence when they're not sure what it's all about.

A good case in point is the differences between the current crop of military experts and the older generation. Many of the current military experts, including journalists, academics, and not a few government officials, were hiding out in graduate schools when they were called to arms during the 1950s and 1960s, while the older—World War II through the Vietnam era—crew frequently had a tour in the ranks before entering journalism. The militarily experienced generation, as a group, tended to be a lot less sanguine about military affairs than the newer crew, and thus were less likely to become disillusioned. Those who have been in the military are somewhat more dubious about the predictability and efficiency of military organizations. This attitude cannot help but color one's writing.

A good example of this is "the runaround." Many novice journalists and researchers have complained that when they attempted to get certain information from the armed forces, they were subject to "the runaround." That is, when they phoned, for example, the U.S. Navy Public Information Office in Washington for some information, the folks there referred them to some other agency of the navy, which in turn referred them to yet another, and so forth, in a seemingly endless series of buck-passing. Often their conclusion is that a "cover-up" is in the works, that the service doesn't want the information made available. But while this occasionally happens, the reality is more often less sinister. Experienced researchers and journalists, not to mention military personnel, take this sort of thing in stride, recognizing it as but one manifestation of the extraordinary bureaucratic complexities to be found in the armed forces. For example, in the course of the research for this volume, one of the authors had occasion to make precisely this call in pursuit of a seemingly innocuous fact, the number of admirals in the Naval Reserve. A total of thirteen telephone calls or transfers were required before the answer could be found, sixty-five. No one was trying to conceal the number, which is hardly of enormous military consequence. The shuffle resulted because none of the people in the chain knew the answer, or knew how to find it, it not being the sort of thing regularly asked of them. In contrast, one call to the Office of Marine Corps History was sufficient to establish the number of marine generals on active duty at the end of World War II. This was a question that they were immediately prepared to answer.

Military experience is not the critical factor in making an effective writer on military affairs. It does help, as military culture is quite different than anything found in civilian life, with its own vocabulary, customs, and priorities. This is particularly true when a war is going on. In such cases, most military experience does not apply, as most people who serve never do so during wartime or, if they do serve in a war are usually nowhere near the combat zone.

Military journalists are chosen first for their journalistic skills. They acquire their military expertise in a variety of ways.

Formal military training, or a tour in the ranks, is of some value. Reading military history is commonly given as the most useful preparation for military journalists and, obviously, for writers of books on military affairs. Unfortunately, this can become an incestuous relationship, as most of the books on military affairs are those on contemporary events, and these are increasingly written by people with no exposure to military culture; and thus tend to produce an outlook that is increasingly out of sync with what is really going on within the military.

Hanging around with professional soldiers is also of some help in acquiring a familiarity with military affairs, as soldiers are a fairly affable lot, and quite talkative. This provides a good insight into some aspects of military subculture, though one perhaps overly oriented toward the middle and lower levels. The armed forces do try to make journalists welcome, giving them special briefings, guided tours, and the like. These are designed to present the official point of view, which is unlikely to stir up much dirt that could grab headlines. Yet not a few journalists go along with this program and become quite dependent on official handouts of information.

Throughout this century, military journalists have started out simply being good journalists. If they have prior military experience, that is considered helpful. But first and foremost, they must be able to write clearly and concisely. They are journalists first, military experts second, sometimes a distant second. But military journalists are not reluctant to market their expertise to some of the very organizations they report on. Defense contractors and related businesses have been known to seek out journalists for their insights and to pay them handsomely, a practice that is not widely known. The journalists involved keep it quiet for a number of reasons. They feel that some may question their objectivity if their links to the people about whom they report were known. Others feel their employers would use the outside income against them in salary negotiations. There is also the propensity of journalists to jump on others for accepting fees from organizations they are supposed to be regulating or otherwise watching over. Yet even the authors of this book have done this: performing research for or serving as consultants to military organizations and lecturing to military audiences. Nearly every noted author on military affairs has taken compensation in this way. Some have even entered government service in the civilian bureaucracy of the Defense Department.

The best sources of useful information both within and outside the military are existing written materials and the access the military allows journalists and others to troops, weapons, and equipment. This can be tricky, as the journalists must still dig, otherwise they leave themselves open to manipulation by some very competent military public-affairs officers (PAOs). The military has its own agenda on what it wants shown and how its viewpoint is to appear before the public. Most of this attitude is simply one of getting the official military perspective across, and accepted. At times there is an attempt to cover up, or minimize the damage from, embarrassing incidents. The military makes it very easy for journalists just to accept the material given out and not to probe any further. Only the largest papers and periodicals develop good investigative reporters and provide them with sufficient resources to dig in after an important story. There can be many obstacles, as the military can refuse cooperation without actually saying so. This can become quite a conflict in itself, and the reporter must come well equipped with investigative skills and clout from a major news organization.

Writers in general, and journalists in particular, are very self-confident people. Their ability to express themselves is rewarded by their being considered experts on what they write about. To themselves, their own experience in the military, or lack of it, has little impact on their ability to effectively report on military affairs.

There is no formal training for those who report on and write about the military, save for the courses many military establishments give to those who perform journalistic functions within the armed forces. Few journalism schools offer no special courses in military studies, and the armed forces no longer have "familiarization" programs for journalists, as they did during World War II. As a result, unless a journalist has military experience, or has read widely in military history, practice, and custom, he is likely to be unfamiliar with military organization, equipment, terminology, jargon, and usage. This can lead to some unpleasantness. During the Vietnam War, for example, large numbers of journalists were sent off to cover the war more or less unprepared. As a result, while there was much to criticize in terms of U.S. policy in that conflict, they came away with the impression that everyone in uniform was lying most of the time, the classic example being the oft-repeated line " 'air support' is a euphemism for 'bombing' ": In fact, while the weapons employed may be the same, "air support" is a tricky business that involves putting firepower on targets very close to friendly troops, without harming them, and is thus considerably different from "bombing," which is far less discriminating. Currently, the U.S. military has a number of PAOs who spend most of their time trying to keep journalists from making mutually embarrassing mistakes, while also trying to circulate the official view of things. The army alone has 427 officers and 946 enlisted personnel classified in public-affairs occupations, not all of whom are serving as such at any given moment. This may seem like a lot, but only amounts to less than .02 percent of army personnel, whose activities are supplemented by about a thousand civilian employees. This is one reason why the phones are likely to be busy at the Public Affairs Office. In addition to preparing press releases and fielding questions from the public, the PAOs can also arrange familiarization tours for anyone who asks for them. But that's the catch—there is no standard package or course for journalists. A week of classroom work and field trips to teach journalists the basics would eliminate a lot of the misinformation that gets into print. Even a small handbook would be of value. But this is not done.

Military journalists serve a wide variety of readers. And each writer on military affairs is aware that his tenure lasts only as long as he pleases his audience. Not every publication serves the same type of audience, so the slant given military reporting differs. *The New York Times* serves a nationwide upper- and middle-class audience. Most of these readers are well educated, and many work in scientific or technical professions. The large New York City portion of this paper's readership also reaches most of the financial community and a large number of people with an international outlook. *The Washington Post* has a much larger government and military audience. *The Wall Street Journal,* a truly national paper despite the parochial-sounding name, reaches out to most of the senior and middle managers in the United States, as well as to the many similar people overseas.

While each of these papers takes a different editorial slant overall, and this is reflected in its military articles, the reporting is
habitually thorough and evenhanded. But there are differences.
The Wall Street Journal addresses a largely business audience,
and most of its military reporting reflects this. The *Post* caters
to a highly political audience, and follows a liberal and muck-
raking tradition. Given the nature of peacetime military operations, the *Post*'s military reporters have plenty of material with
which to work. The high concentration of Defense Department
employees in Washington gives *Post* reporters a steady stream
of leads. The *Times* takes a broader approach to issues than the
Post or the *Journal*. This extends to military affairs, where the
Times has a long tradition of accurate and thorough reporting,
something it keeps up, painful as that may be to some who
object to "the Old Gray Lady's" editorial views.

There are several broad problems that all three papers must
confront in their military reporting. First, there is access to information. Much of it comes from the military. The reporters
earn their spurs by learning how to separate the self-serving
hype from the reliable data coexisting in the same Department
of Defense press handout. Next, there is the ability to interpret
correctly what is going on. Here, the reporters are in the same
boat as military-intelligence analysts. Distressingly, reporters
have several million readers keeping score on their accuracy,
while the work of the intelligence analysts is seen by only a
handful of ordinarily understanding and sympathetic users. For
this reason, reporters are much more circumspect than intelligence analysts. Interestingly, many people with access to intelligence reports will still pay close attention to press reports. It
is the press that influences public opinion, and in a democracy
public opinion cannot be easily brushed aside.

The electronic-news people have a unique set of problems.
They do not have much time available for collecting or presenting information in comparison to the print media. In effect,
the electronic media are reduced to not much more than reading headlines. The video half of the electronic media is also
under pressure to show pictures of great visual impact. This
may awe the audience and keep the ratings up, but it does not
help educate anyone about the facts. Because of these conditions, the video journalists tend to be less well prepared than

their print colleagues. The greater reach, and immediacy, of TV gives the video journalists better access to information sources. The video information gatherers have clout, and they know how to use it. The people gathering the information, incidentally, are rarely the ones you see reading it on the screen. An unheralded collection of producers, writers, and reporters do most of the digging, aided by a large number of free-lancers. Moreover, while most television stations have special "editors" or "correspondents" to deal with health and science, business and finance, sports and entertainment, and frequently even food, education, and style, few have a "military editor" to lend coherence and experience to the treatment of a military story. So anyone can report on a military story.

This brings up another problem with journalistic coverage of the military. By and large, the peacetime military journalists are a fairly experienced lot. However, in wartime their numbers grow, as everyone seeks to go where the action is. Indeed, the number of journalists covering wars has been increasing geometrically, at least for Western military operations, as a glance at the accompanying table will demonstrate:

MILITARY JOURNALISTS WITH THE TROOPS

CONFLICT	COMMAND	TROOPS (MILLIONS)	JOURNALISTS TOTAL	TROOPS PER JOURNALIST
Spanish-American (1898)	US V Corps	.025	89	281
World War I (Nov. 1918)	AEF	2.040	38	53,684
World War II (June 1944)	SHAEF	2.600	300	8,667
Korea (Jan. 1951)	UN	.800	300	2,667
Vietnam (Jan. 1969)	Allied	1.400	500	2,800
Falklands (1982)	British	.020	29	690
Grenada (1983)	US	.007	180	39
Panama (1989)	US	.024	350	69
Persian Gulf (Jan. 1991)	Allied	1.750	1,300	577

This table is based on the number of journalists assigned to cover these wars at the time indicated. In the case of the Spanish-American War, this means U.S. troops and journalists in Cuba. For World War I, it is the number assigned to the American Expeditionary Forces (AEF) at the time of the Armistice. For World War II, figures include all Allied forces assigned to the support of the Normandy landings (Supreme Headquarters Allied Expeditionary Forces) plus accredited journalists. For Korea and Vietnam, they include all UN and

Allied forces engaged in or directly supporting operations in the field, and the accompanying press. For the Falklands, the figures include only forces directly involved in the operations in and around the islands, and the journalists who went along with them. For Grenada, the figures for the journalists are limited to those who actually were eventually permitted to accompany the expedition. All the examples exclude personnel engaged in operations in other areas: For the Spanish-American War, for example, this means the 18,000 troops and several dozen reporters who went to Puerto Rico, as well as the 13,000 or so who fought the Spanish in the Philippines, and the more than 25,000 who fought in the subsequent "Philippine Insurrection," not to mention the nearly 300,000 troops who never left the United States. In the case of Grenada, while about 7,000 troops actually landed on the island, they were directly supported by some hundreds of pilots and several thousand sailors. Note that technology has something to do with the increase in the number of journalists. Long gone are the days when Richard Harding Davis or H. R. Knickerbocker could cover a war single-handedly, with pad and pencil. Now they would need a camcorder operator and sound technician. But even allowing for this, the increase has been considerable, even in the Persian Gulf in late 1990–early 1991, where press access was restricted by the Saudi government.

In peacetime, only a few thousand journalists really specialize in military affairs. Since many of the journalists thus sent off to a war are not very familiar with military reporting, these are the journalists who will probably make the most egregious errors, often out of a desire to sound authoritative. While on occasion a newspaper puts an ill-prepared journalist on a military story—one major paper assigned someone who could not distinguish between a "warship" and a "battleship" to cover the December 1989 Bush-Gorbachev summit at sea—this sort of error is particularly common among television journalists. One reason for this is that many TV journalists are "stars" in their own right. As a result, it is not unusual for a noted video journalist adept at covering street crime or political corruption to be assigned to cover a war. The violence may be similar, but the nomenclature is quite different. The several Arab-Israeli wars have been particularly prone to such malcoverage. During the 1982 Israeli invasion of Lebanon, certain aircraft were described by one major network reporter as "Israeli-built Mirage jets," when they were actually made in France, while another cooed over the fact that the Israeli Merkava tank included a special mirror so that the fluid levels in the battery could be easily checked. This sort of thing frequently happens in military reporting: In June of 1989, a BBC correspondent referred to the troops who perpetrated the massacre of the Chinese students in Beijing as "battle hardened," when in fact the soldiers in question had never been in combat until they were called out to slaughter their unarmed countrymen. One of the most common errors in video reporting on military affairs is a penchant for calling any military vehicle with a tread a "tank." Another failing is to equate "casualties" with "dead," when in fact the term includes injured personnel as well. All this comes from the lack of experience common to many electronic journalists. Even with the best intentions, many of these people will make errors. After all, journalists of all types make errors when reporting on matters of similar complexity, as in stories on developments in science or the arts, and even in commonplace matters: Not long ago, *The New York Times* identified a picture of Venice's St. Mark's Square as being "in Rome." But those errors are not as likely to influence public opinion, and possibly political decisions as well.

Military journalists are aware of their influence on decision makers. And so are the decision makers. There are a number of military journalists who have gone on to high positions in the government. The obvious route is as a media director, to get the most out of the press relations. Several have gone on to elected office or other high positions. It's not for nothing that the press is called "the Other Government."

THE RAMBO EFFECT

There is yet another medium which is of great importance in shaping popular—and sometimes official—impressions of the military and military power, one that might not come to mind when thinking about media influence: film. In the World War II and post-World War II eras, the movies shaped an entire generation's perception of war and military life: Again, one only has to recall Ronald Reagan's celluloid-tainted comments about the war to realize this. Film can have an enormously distorting effect on the public's perception of war. For example, as anyone who has seen a war picture can testify, Hitler's *Wehrmacht* was a technologically sophisticated, highly mechanized force. In fact, in World War II about 75 percent of the German Army's ground units used horse-drawn transport. But showing a lot of Nazi troops slogging along with horse-drawn artillery would not be good box office. This is not a petty point. Men entering the army between 1946 and the mid-1960s were admonished by their combat-seasoned officers and NCOs to avoid pulling any "John Wayne" stunts in combat. These young men had been raised on a diet of World War II movies, which continued to run on television until the Vietnam era. John Wayne, a perennial star in such films, was a sort of predecessor of the more recent Rambo character, the Supersoldier who—usually—could not be killed. The battlewise infantry instructors were warning the recruits that sudden death or mutilation was everyone's companion on the battlefield. Combat was not the movies; the blood was real.

In both Korea and Vietnam, inappropriate battlefield heroics, and subsequent losses by inexperienced troops, were noted by combat veterans. Some of these veterans figured out that these foolish and mostly fatal actions were a direct result of the false representations of combat in the media. Movies were the biggest offender, as movies made a more vivid impression with their theater presentation.

The influence of war pictures on public perceptions of the military was enormous in the period roughly between World War II and Vietnam, when virtually instantaneous television reporting came along to promote a rougher, more realistic image. A survey conducted by the navy in the early 1960s concluded that the prevalence of World War II films, whether wartime oldies rerun on television or newer ones run in the theaters, was creating the impression that the navy was an obsolete service. It seems that all those films of guys going after the Imperial Japanese Navy in their Wildcats, Corsairs, and Avengers, or in diesel submarines, was bad for the jet-age, nuclear-navy image that the brass were trying to promote. The army suffered less from this problem because the newer technologies were not too dissimilar from the old, while the air force, which likewise had a lot of old films in reruns, also had B-52s and ICBMs, which had caught the public's attention. Lest we think that the post–Vietnam era public is less susceptible to the influence of film, we might note the popularity of such pictures as *Top Gun, The Hunt for Red October,* or *The Flight of the Intruder,* made with considerable military cooperation, the *Rambo* series of films, or the Rambo-inspired fad for camouflage uniforms and "action figure" dolls for boys. Although condemned by some right-wing elements, the recent spate of films on Vietnam fits this role as well, perhaps to a grittier, more realistic degree than previous war pictures, but sufficiently so as to prompt some leftists to claim that they are glorifying war and the American war machine: *Platoon* was denied first prize at a film festival for precisely this reason.

THE LOST CONGRESSMAN

During 1989, there occurred a tragedy that illustrates one of our basic themes, that fundamentally we don't understand the capabilities and limitations of military power. In August of 1989, Representative Mickey Leland, one of the most effective members of Congress, was reported missing on a routine flight across Ethiopia in the company of several members of his staff and a number of relief officials, while on a tour of refugee camps. At the request of the Ethiopian government, U.S. military personnel and equipment were dispatched to assist in the search for the missing aircraft. As the days dragged on without results, some of Representative Leland's friends and associates charged that the armed forces were dragging their feet and not doing all that they possibly could to find the missing congressman. These critics overlooked the fact that some 600 troops and many airplanes and helicopters had been moved thousands of miles on short notice, to a country with which the United States had no military ties, that these forces had quickly established a practical working relationship with their Ethiopian counterparts, and that they had immediately commenced operations. Moreover, the critics also failed to note that the search area amounted to some 100,000 square miles—as great as Italy or Britain—of extremely rugged, very undeveloped, and sparsely populated terrain. Stung by such criticism, the air force provided the representative's staff with a detailed briefing that turned their criticism into praise. The wreckage of Representative Leland's airplane was found several days later, and there were unfortunately no survivors. There is a lesson to be learned from this incident. The critics of the progress of the search were misled by their own assumptions as to the capabilities of the armed forces. The troops went into action, and they did not perform as expected. The criticism was sparked by erroneous assumptions about the capabilities of the troops. Curiously, Representative Leland had no high regard for the military, voting "in favor" of defense only about 3 percent of the time, a matter in which presumably his friends and staff concurred, yet their expectations of the abilities of the armed forces were still unrealistically high. Or perhaps these antimilitary views went hand in hand with an unwillingness to keep up on what the military was doing, how they went about it, and what the troops were actually capable of.

The armed forces are partially to blame for such misunderstandings, as they try to promote an image of enormous skill, efficiency, and flexibility. But much of this image is created by the media, political leaders, and public figures who comment upon the activities of the armed forces. And not all of this boosting of the defense establishment's prowess comes from its friends: Inveterate foes of the military contribute as well, by their often imaginative fantasies about military machinations, cover-ups, and power. As a result, there is a general misunderstanding of the abilities and the limitations of the armed forces throughout society. This lack of perspective as to the capabilities of the armed forces can be dangerous. Recent calls from a number of persons of widely divergent political views to commit American ground troops to assist in the struggle against Latin American drug cartels are a case in point: The troops are neither trained nor equipped to function as policemen, and would have at best limited utility. Worse still, sending them into countries such as Colombia, Peru, and Bolivia could involve them in clashes with endemic revolutionary groups that are known to have ties to the drug trade, which could lead to an escalation from police functions to counterinsurgency in countries with differing cultural, political, social, and economic systems. The last time that happened was in Vietnam, and a Colombian operation would produce far more GI drug addicts, plus plentiful opportunities for U.S. troops to be bribed and otherwise subverted.

* * *

The influence of the media on military perceptions and policy has probably never been higher than at present. In some ways, this is a healthy trend, since it has stimulated considerable debate with useful results. But it has also had a deleterious effect, in that the debate is frequently focused on nonessential aspects of military policy, such as the politics of base closing or the intricacies of budget cutting. The aging of the real veteran population, those who served under fire, coupled with the abolition of the draft, is leading to a society in which the number of Americans having some familiarity with the realities and complexities of military life will be quite small. Rather than living through the military experience, more citizens will know only the more dramatic theatrical version, which was probably also written, directed, and acted by nonveterans (such as Sylvester Stallone). Only a few films like *Platoon* are an exception. The influence of the media on military policy is likely to increase, as they will increasingly provide the principal source of information on military affairs not only to the pubic, but also to the political and military leadership. This raises serious questions as to society's ability to create and maintain military forces able to meet the contingencies likely to develop in the next generation. The United States is stuck with its Superpower status, and the military obligations that entails. Yet Americans remain essentially isolationistic, pacifistic, and antimilitary for a great power: Most Americans cannot read a soldier's rank insignia, something taught in elementary school in most European countries. Moreover, most Americans are not even aware of the differences in attitudes toward the military between themselves and Europeans, and non-Americans in general, who are far more realistic about having armies and navies. These views lead to emotional reactions toward military power. This is an attitude that causes more death and destruction when America does go to war. It's a national vice, but also a national virtue.

WORDS VERSUS PICTURES: COVERING THE NEWS IN PRINT AND VIDEO THE CASE OF THE USS IOWA TURRET EXPLOSION

There are numerous sources of news, some easy to absorb, others requiring more effort. The two ends of this spectrum can best be seen in how TV and newspapers cover the same event.

To demonstrate this, we selected an event that took place during the writing of this book and compared the degree of coverage given the event by TV and newspapers.

At about 10:00 A.M. on Wednesday, April 19, 1989, there was an explosion in the Number 2 sixteen-inch gun of "B" turret on the battleship *Iowa* as she was engaged in training exercises some 330 miles north of Puerto Rico. Although an official navy investigation tentatively concluded that the disaster was probably sabotage, specifically an elaborate and successful suicide attempt by one of the members of the gun crew, it can never be known for certain what the cause of the explosion was. With forty-seven sailors dead, one of the navy's most lethal peacetime training accidents ever, the incident raised questions about the fleet's four battleships, as well as navy personnel selection and training. The incident was handled differently by the video and print news media, as the following material demonstrates.

SUMMARY OF TYPICAL TV NEWS COVERAGE: NEW YORK CITY AREA USS IOWA TURRET EXPLOSION, APRIL 19, 1989

CBS News, April 19. During the afternoon, there were several headline teasers broadcast that had the same effect as short news bulletins. Although conveying little information, these promotional items let people know that something had happened and that CBS was on the case. Then, on the local CBS *Six O'clock News,* the *Iowa* incident was the lead item. It was treated thus:

Brief announcement
File film and tape of the ship
Interview with Norman Friedman, naval analyst, about 25–35 words
Reaction of President Bush, about 10 words
Family hotline number given

Total presentation was about 105 seconds, perhaps 100 words of information were delivered. Note that on the same broadcast, news of new video releases got about the same amount of time. Sports coverage was about 220–240 seconds.

* * *

On the six-thirty *CBS News* with Dan Rather, the *Iowa* incident was also the lead item.

Introduced with the phrase "Aging relic of World War II"
Fresh tape of the ship showing damage to "B" turret
File tape of the ship in action
Comment by USN spokesman, about 20 words
Comment by President Bush, about 20 words
Short historical piece on the ship
Comment by retired Rear Admiral Gene LaRoque, of the Center for Defense Information, critical of the recommissioning of *Iowa,* about 35–45 words
Graphic showing the structure of the turret

Presentation was about 3.5 minutes (under 400 words). By comparison, commercials and promotions ran about 6–7 minutes. Twelve other items were covered, including a report on a vacation scam and a follow-up report on the *Exxon Valdez* oil spill of March 24, 1989, which each received about 3 minutes.

On the *MacNeil/Lehrer NewsHour* on April 19, the *Iowa* incident was the lead item.

File tape of the ship
Graphic of the turret structure
Reaction of President Bush, about 25–30 words
Historical note on battleships and their recommissioning

Presentation ran about 3 minutes (300 words).

CBS News, April 20
Afternoon: Headline teasers broadcast regularly.
CBS Local News at five-thirty, *Iowa* incident was the lead item.

New tape showing damage to the ship
Coverage of memorial service
Notice of two local sailors who died in the accident

Presentation ran about 1–1.5 minutes (under 150 words).

* * *

CBS News at six o'clock. *Iowa* incident was again the lead item.

New tape of the damage
Landing of the dead at Dover AFB
Recap of the events
Comment of commanding officer, Second Fleet, about 30 words
Graphic of turret and probable nature of accident
Comments of President Bush, about 8 words
Announcement of the Appointment of a Board of Inquiry
Interviews with families of two of the dead from the New York City area
Short piece on the debate over home-porting *Iowa* in New York

Presentation ran about 2–2.5 minutes (about 200 words).

CBS News at six-thirty with Dan Rather, *Iowa* incident was the lead item.

Landing of the dead at Dover AFB
Memorial service at Dover AFB
Comments of President Bush on the obsolescence question, 20 words
New and file tape
Animation showing probable nature of accident
Comments on the incident by: A defense analyst, about 20 words; A member of Congress, about 6 words; A navy spokesman, about 15 words
Coverage of the families and recap of the arrival of the remains
Remarks of commanding officer, Second Fleet, about 40 words
Tape of the secretary of the navy at Dover AFB
Chaplain discussing impact on the families, about 25–30 words

Presentation ran about 7 minutes (over 600 words) with a strong slant toward the alleged obsolescence of the ship.

* * *

MacNeil/Lehrer, April 20: the *Iowa* incident was the lead item in the News Summary

Arrival of bodies at Dover AFB
Comments of the commanding officer, Second Fleet, about 50–60 words
Recapitulation of the events

Presentation ran about 2 minutes (200 words).

NBC Nightly News, April 20, at six o'clock, *Iowa* incident was the lead item.

Recapitulation of the events
Arrival of the remains at Dover AFB
Memorial service at *Iowa*'s adopted elementary school
Chaplain's statement on problems of the families, about 20 words
Mention of the work of the Navy Family Service
Interview with relatives of the dead

Presentation ran about 6 minutes (nearly 600 words).

Fox News, April 20, at six o'clock, *Iowa* incident was the lead item. Coverage was similar to that by NBC.

TYPICAL MAJOR NEWSPAPER COVERAGE

DATE/ITEM	WORDAGE	ILLUSTRATIONS
Apr 20		
General Summary (p. 1, right)	880	5
Families	320	
Home-porting Controversy	240	
Recommissioning Controversy	360	
Information Hotline	40	
Total	1840	
Apr 21		
General Summary (p. 1, center)	1200	2
Return of Dead	360	
List of Casualties	360	
Total	1920	

DATE/ITEM	WORDAGE	ILLUSTRATIONS
Apr 22		
Reaction in Norfolk	700	2
List of Casualties	400	
Home-porting Controversy	800	
Total	1900	
Apr 23		
Inquiry to Be Held	1120	2
Apr 24		
Return of *Iowa* to Port	520	
Apr 25		
Memorial Service	960	3
Possible Problems over Repair	740	
Total	1700	
Apr 29		
Home-porting Debate and Repair	820	
Apr 30		
Report of Misfires	200	
May 3		
Report on Repair	520	
May 5		
Cost of Repair	280	
May 6		
Status of Repair and Inquiry	440	
May 25		
Foul Play Suggested	660	
May 26		
Foul Play Follow-up	720	2
May 27		
Foul Play Follow-up	640	1
May 30		
Rebuttal on Foul Play	320	1
June 3		
Inquiry to Focus on Suicide	720	
July 19		
Tentative Conclusion of Suicide	800	1
July 20		
Controversy over Conclusions	1220	
September 5		
Report Cited as "Inconclusive"	400	
September 7		
Report Will Say "Probably Intentional"	600	
September 8		
Navy Issues Report on Inquiry	800	1
Excerpts from Report	1280	
Total	2080	1
September 13		
Congress Asked to Review Inquiry	400	
September 19		
Gun Testing Not Involved in Blast	680	
September 21		
Senate to Investigate Incident	120	

DATE/ITEM	WORDAGE	ILLUSTRATIONS
October 5		
Reprimands Issued Certain Officers	80	
October 12		
Navy Denies Maligning Sailors	400	
November 5		
Criticisms of Navy Findings	1320	1
Survey of Recent Navy Accidents	580	
Total	1820	1
November 7		
Insurer Pays Claim on Seaman	160	
November 11		
Charges Dead Were Looted	200	
November 18		
House Panel to Investigate	600	1
December 12		
Iowa Captain Disputes Part of Report	540	1
December 13		
House Subcommittee Critical of Report	340	
December 14		
Survivors Deny Shipmate's Involvement	440	1
May 25, 1990		
Navy Reopens Inquiry	800	
May 26		
Navy Tests Challenged	1450	2
June 11		
Navy Investigators Again Criticized	880	1
Grand Total	c. 35500	27

SUMMARY OF TYPICAL MAJOR NEWSPAPER COVERAGE: THE NEW YORK TIMES USS IOWA TURRET EXPLOSION, APRIL 19, 1989

Word count excludes pictures, captions, and headlines. Illustrations include pictures, maps, and diagrams. Articles are listed with an abbreviated summary of contents.

SUMMARY: THE VIDEO IOWA VERSUS THE PRINT IOWA

More people get their news from TV than from newspapers. Moreover, TV newscasts are usually seen in their entirety, while most printed news is read only partially, if at all. Knowing this, print journalists structure their stories like a pyramid, with the headline, followed by one or more smaller but wordier subheads, and then the essence of the story in the first paragraph, followed by the body of the story.

The detailed accounts of what happened on *Iowa* were not seen on TV, and the incident was largely referred to in only a few words.

The disparities between television and newspaper coverage of this incident were substantial, over six to one in word count. Yet both forms of media covered the incident in their normal fashion, and both served their audiences in a manner these audiences had come to expect. It's no accident coverage on TV is so brief. Decades of experimentation, competition, and studying the audience have caused broadcasters to use this concise format. The average item on TV takes up all of ninety seconds (100–200 words). Newspaper readers want more detailed coverage, but they also want the ability to pick and choose what they read and when they read it.

Within weeks and months, even more detailed and lengthy magazine pieces were produced. Finally, books on the incident will almost certainly be written, including a level of detail even naval architects and weapons experts could appreciate.

While detailed *Iowa* coverage was maintained in the print media, by April 21, *Iowa* had been upstaged on the TV news by the Central Park jogger rape, with occasional remaining network coverage being focused on the families of the *Iowa* dead and the return of the ship to port. On April 26, the death of Lucille Ball occupied at least six minutes on each of the network prime-time news broadcasts, and at least one station ran a special half-hour program about her. By then nothing was seen on TV news about the *Iowa* affair. Its moment had come and gone.

In mid-May, lurid stories began to circulate about a possible murder or suicide stemming from a "special" relationship between two of the ship's crew. This received regular TV coverage over a period of several weeks, mostly of thirty to sixty seconds. On June 2, there was a seven-minute treatment of this question on *A Current Affair,* which at least had the saving grace of trying to explain how the whole story got started. Meanwhile, more detailed print reports put this story in a more accurate perspective. On TV, all you got was, "Someone said someone did this," while a day or so later an equally brief report said, "It's probably not true." You had to get a printed account to really see what was going on, so at least the terse TV reports were selling a few newspapers to the curious. Finally, on July 18, *NBC News* obtained a copy of the preliminary findings of the navy's board of inquiry, which did conclude that the explosion was a case of sabotage, possibly due to a suicide. Newspaper coverage over the next two days stressed the inconclusive and controversial character of the report by the board of inquiry, since no direct evidence was found that could support any mechanical or electrical reason for the blast, or, indeed, the suicide theory either. The video medium did not have the airtime to mention the controversial nature of the report, or to explain that it was possible to reconstruct the state of the turret before the explosion, just as crashed aircraft are put back together to discover what went wrong. Given the available evidence, and the armed forces' nearly ninety years of experience with battleship turrets, it seemed sabotage was the most likely cause of the explosion, although, as is often the case in these situations, the real reason will probably never be known with any certainty.

The final navy report was issued in early September. It was given extensive coverage in the press, including editorial and op-ed pieces (which have not been listed above), but none of the network news programs devoted more than a minute to it. The report revealed that chemical remains of a detonator were found in one of the gun barrels. The chief suspect, a gunner's mate who stood right next to the breech, would have been able to slip a detonating device between one of the bags of propellant. The navy investigators theorized that the force of the propellant bags being rammed into the gun breech activated the detonator, causing the propellant to explode back into the turret. The shell was only propelled a short distance up into the barrel. The force of the exploding propellant wrecked the inside of the turret and killed the crew members. The report was cautious in its wording, noting the inconclusiveness of the findings, and went on to recommend disciplinary action for several officers involved in training and supervising the turret crew. A week later, however, a Virginia newspaper reported that the navy had been conducting secret unofficial propellant tests in the turret. This was picked up and given somewhat sensational play in some of the electronic media, which suggested that the experiments had contributed to the explosion and that the inquiry had ignored this fact. Their version of the story turned out to be inaccurate: The navy had been conducting propellant tests, but these involved *reducing* the charge from six to five bags of powder to see how this would effect range and accuracy. More-over, the board of inquiry had looked into these experiments, with the conclusion that they could not have caused the fatal accident, as the charges used were, as one petty officer's testi-mony put it, "way inside the safety realm with the gun." The print media followed up the story more carefully, and included citations from the investigation report concerning the experi-ments. But the apparent flaws in the official inquiry prompted calls for a further inquiry, with the result that in late September the Senate Armed Services Committee announced that it would conduct its own investigation into the explosion, partially at the urging of the family of the sailor identified as the probable cul-prit in the blast, who are seeking to clear his name. By late October, the FBI had issued its own report on the matter, which was at variance with the navy's. Meanwhile, an insurance com-pany paid off on a policy covering the sailor in question, the captain of *Iowa* announced that he disagreed with the "suicide" hypothesis, and the House, itself skeptical about the official re-port, convened its own investigation. The case continues. A "definitive" explanation for the disaster will probably prove definitively elusive.

The media will continue to search for an angle or lead that will "solve" the mystery of what went wrong in the *Iowa* tur-ret. This is good. But if this search is not tempered with some knowledge of how things work on a warship, it will only create more confusion. This is bad.

Aside from the sparse nature of the TV news about *Iowa*, there was a tendency to avoidable errors. About half of the video journalists—including several of the "anchorpeople"—could not pronounce the word *turret (tuh-rut)*, referring instead to the *"tour-ette."* One of the anchors referred to "black pow-der" in an explanation of how the guns were loaded: Black powder went out of use in the last century, along with muzzle-loading cannon fired from sailing ships. Of course, print jour-nalists also made some grievous errors—one, in an extreme example of silliness, referring to battleships as a technology "out of Nelson's day"—but the audience is smaller, and the piece in question was clearly indicated as signed opinion, whereas a TV journalist's error in this regard reaches a wide audience. These errors represent exactly the same type of carelessness that per-vades television news treatment of many technical fields, such as science. The number of errors in reporting military affairs is greater, so great that most military people simply take for granted that the video medium will, on average, get it *approximately* right only some of the time.

A SAMPLER OF MILITARY "EXPERTS"

Not everyone who appears in print or on TV as a "military expert" has much experience and knowledge to back up that title. One of the authors of this book regularly appears on one TV news show or another as a "military expert." Once a TV anchor who had not previously worked with him asked how he came to be a "military expert," to which he replied, "Because you [TV people] say I am."

Some experts are more expert than others, but it's difficult to tell who is really on the ball, or at least on target. One measure of expertise is actual service in the military. As explained elsewhere in this book, this is not a crucial factor. But it helps, and it was interesting to see who among the commonly accepted "military experts" actually experienced a bit of what they are expert about.

A SAMPLER OF MILITARY "EXPERTS"

NAME	MEDIUM	BORN	SERVICE
Government Officials			
Aspin, Les	House Armed Services Committee	1938	USA
Atwood, Donald J., Jr.	Deputy Secretary of Defense	1924	None
Ball, William L., III	Secretary of the Navy	1948	USN
Bush, George	President	1924	USNR
Cheney, Richard	Secretary of Defense	1938	None
Nunn, Sam	Senate Armed Services Committee	1941	None
Quayle, Dan	Vice President	1947	ANG
Rice, Donald B.	Secretary of the Air Force	1939	USA
Stone, Richard P. W.	Secretary of the Army	1925	RN
Webster, William H.	CIA Director	1924	USNR
Scholars and Journalists			
Adde, Nick	Times Publishing	1953	None
Black, Norman	Associated Press	1953	None
Bode, Ken	NBC	1939	None
Brokaw, Tom	NBC	1940	None
Budahn, P. J.	Times Publishing	1947	USA
Carrington, Tim	*Wall Street Journal*	1951	None
Cushman, John H.	*New York Times*	1954	None
Dionne, E. J.	*New York Times*	1952	None

NAME	MEDIUM	BORN	SERVICE
Donnelly, Tom	Times Publishing	1953	None
Dunnigan, James F.	Books	1943	USA
Dupuy, Trevor N.	Books	1914	USA
Ewing, Lee	Times Publishing	1944	USA
Fialka, John	*Wall Street Journal*	1938	None
Fineman, Howard	*Newsweek*	1949	None
Francis, Fred	NBC	1945	USAF
Gordon, Michael R.	*New York Times*	1951	None
Graham, Donald	*Washington Post*	1945	USA
Greenfield, Jeff	ABC	1944	None
Hadley, Arthur	Books	1924	USA
Halloran, Richard	*New York Times*	1930	USA
Hennings, Peter	ABC	1938	None
Isby, David C.	Books	1953	None
Kinsley, Michael	*New Republic*	1951	None
Kondracke, Morton	*New Republic*	1939	USA
Koppel, Ted	ABC	1940	None
Kramer, Michael	*US News*	1946	USAR
LaRoque, Gene	Center for Defense Information	1918	USN
Lehrer, James	PBS	1933	USMC
Luttwak, Edward	Books	1942	None
MacNeil, Robert	PBS	1931	None
Martin, David	CBS	1943	USN
Meyer, Larry	*Washington Post*	1941	USMC
Mohr, Charles	*New York Times*	1929	USNR*
Moore, Mollie	*Washington Post*	1956	None
Moskos, Charles	Books (Northwestern U)	1934	USA
Nofi, Albert A.	Books	1944	None
Pasztor, Andy	*Wall Street Journal*	1949	None
Perle, Richard	*US News*	1941	None
Philpott, Tom	Times Publishing	1952	USN
Prados, John	Books	1951	None
Rather, Dan	CBS	1932	None
Rasor, Dina	Media	1956	None
Reed, Fred	Columnist	1946	USMC
Robinson, Barry	Times Publishing	1948	USN
Rochelle, Carl	CNN	1938	USNR
Rogers, David	*Wall Street Journal*	1946	USA
Shapiro, Walter	*Time*	1947	None
Smith, R. Jeffrey	*Washington Post*	1954	None
Summers, Harry G.	*US News*	1932	USA
"Suvarov, Victor"	Books (real name Vladimir Rezun)	194?	USSR**
Taylor, Paul	*Washington Post*	1949	None
Trainor, Bernard	Harvard	1928	USMC
van Creveld, Martin	Books	1946	IDF
Van Vorst, Bruce	*Time*	1932	None
Wallace, Chris	NBC	1947	None
Wilson, George	*Washington Post*	1927	USN

*Died June 17, 1989
**A Russian military intelligence officer who defected*

This table does not attempt to list every government official associated with the military, or every journalist and scholar who regularly reports on military topics. Nevertheless, the people listed here are likely to be regarded as having some expertise in the military.

"Medium" refers to the "pulpit" that the person occupies. For government personnel, this is their official post. For the journalists, this is the newspaper, magazine, network, features syndicate, or other body. "Books" indicates that the person is either an academic scholar or free-lance commentator specializing in defense affairs. Times Publishing may not be familiar to most readers. This company publishes several weekly newspapers for military personnel and their families (*Army Times, Navy Times,* etc.) that share a core of common material plus special items specific to each service. The Times Publishing papers are highly regarded in the military, partially because they are independent of the military and partially because they do a good job of journalism. The Center for Defense Information and Media are defense watchdog organizations.

"Born" provides a convenient guide to when each person attained eligibility for military service, usually between the ages of eighteen and twenty-six. As the nation was at war in 1942–45, 1950–53, and 1965–72, this datum also provides a convenient guide as to the circumstances under which service was rendered. For example, World War II era vets were mostly born between about 1910 and 1925, Korean vets, 1917 and 1934, Vietnam vets, 1937 and 1954. This is a rough guide, as some people enlisted while underage, and professional soldiers can serve during wartime when in their fifties and sixties. The above date ranges are for those eligible for conscription.

"Service" indicates the branch in which the person spent his military career: ANG, Army National Guard; IDF, Israel Defense Forces; RN, Britain's Royal Navy; USA, Army; USAF, Air Force; USAR, Army Reserve; USMC, Marine Corps; USN, Navy; USNR, Naval Reserve; USSR, Russian armed forces. The people indicated served in all ranks, from private on up to a lieutenant general of marines, Bernard Trainor. Some had unusual careers, such as Army Secretary Richard P. Stone, who went to Canada to enlist in the Royal Navy at age seventeen, eventually rising to flying officer. Some saw action, such as President Bush, who was the youngest USN combat pilot in the Pacific during World War II, and others did not. It should be noted that the people who did not serve were not necessarily neglectful of their obligations as citizens: Several were 4-F, physically or otherwise disqualified from serving. This status could change depending on how desperate the need for manpower was. During World War II, many 4-Fs of 1941 became eligible for service by 1944 because of heavy combat losses and the realization that even a slightly handicapped person can perform many of the noncombat jobs. In peacetime draft periods, 1948–50, 1953–64, many of those classified 1-A (fit for service) were never called, and some of those so classified during wartime were not called because peace came. One of those on the list washed out of ROTC due to poor eyesight. It *is* true that many highly skilled and successful people of today were prime draft bait during the 1960s. And many of these current leaders and opinion makers basically avoided (or "dodged") the draft. In other times, this would have been considered a disgrace. But the Vietnam War was different. The government never had the nerve to actually call it a war and officially mobilize the nation for it. The feeling then was that many people would oppose such a mobilization. Thus the war was largely fought by those who either believed in it, were very patriotic about military service, or were simply resigned to their fate. Many of those who avoided the war did so out of conviction. But many more did so out of convenience. The old line "Did you serve?" acquired a host of new meanings during and after the Vietnam War. Ask Dan Quayle.

By some accounts, one person listed as having no military service actually had a very unusual experience. Born in one of those countries that never lets you off the hook for conscription, he migrated to the United States some years later. As an adult, he acquired some reputation as a writer on military affairs and was invited to speak at an official conference in his native land. When he landed at the airport, he found his hosts, who included some high-ranking defense officials, there to greet him, as well as a detachment of military police, who arrested him for desertion. The matter is alleged to have been resolved by a ministerial decision to swear him into service and then immediately discharge him.

The War of the Analysts: Intelligence

·4·

*H*ow does intelligence work influence governments in the use of military force? Who collects intelligence, and how do they do it? What problems affect intelligence work? How successful have the intelligence specialists been?

A major cause of shooting blanks is poor, or misinterpreted, information about the other side. This problem has got a lot more attention, and money, in the last fifty years than ever before. The United States alone spends over $20 billion a year on intelligence collection and analysis, about 20 percent of world intelligence expenditures (which for many foreign intelligence agencies includes a lot of domestic snooping). Unfortunately, all this attention to the problem, and money spent on it, has not entirely turned the situation around.

INSIDE STUFF

While government and military officials depend on the press for much of their information on military affairs, there are also a variety of journalists within the government. These are the military-intelligence analysts, who create the numerous reports designed to keep senior decision makers informed. Some analysts are regular military personnel, but most are civilians who work for the armed forces or various civilian intelligence agencies such as the CIA. These investigators not only piece together information from numerous sources, but also attempt to organize and present these largely classified data as clearly as possible. This effort involves editors and graphic designers who spiff everything up for delivery as a document or a slide-show presentation. In effect, the government intelligence agencies are publishers, as well as authors. Their output takes many forms, including newspapers, magazines, books, films, computer data bases, and plain old reports. Most of this is never seen by the general public, although there are enough intentional leaks to give most citizens an inkling of its extent.

Intelligence analysts are really not much different from the journalists and academics who are also trying to explain what's going on. Indeed, some of the civilian analysts are recruited from among journalists and academics, although many more are recent college graduates, and there is a sprinkling of former military personnel among them as well. One result of this is that a lot of the professional analysts have no more military experience than do the "amateur" ones. In the United States, this situation is made worse because CIA analysts, who increasingly have no military experience, look down on the uniformed ones, who have such experience, mainly because CIA people belong to a very independent organization. The uniformed analysts are more likely to belong to one of the military intelligence organizations and thus less able to "go anywhere and say anything" with their analysis and opinions. This is a simple example of the problems that can crop up with intelligence analysis.

Intelligence analysts must answer the same questions about foreign nations and armed forces as the open media. The main difference is the amount of detail and secrecy associated with the analysts' work. Some of the analysts' work does reach the public. When you see "the CIA reports," or some such, take a closer look.

Worldwide, over a hundred billion dollars a year goes into intelligence gathering and analysis. National leaders turn to their analysts' reports in times of crisis. What these leaders find in these documents decides the fates of nations.

IMPRESSIONS

The intelligence people know that finding the answers is only part of their job. If they cannot put their conclusions across to their clients, they have failed. The point of the exercise is to find out what is transpiring in the dark corners of other nations and make your superiors aware of what these developments are and what they mean.

The concept of using the latest publishing techniques to put intelligence information across was developed to a high degree during World War II. The practice was initiated by a German intelligence officer, Reinhard Gehlen. He had to deal with Adolf Hitler, who was reluctant to accept unfavorable intelligence. Gehlen decided that adding some zip to the presentations would make them more convincing. Bringing in editors and graphic artists, Gehlen had striking presentations prepared. Hitler was still unhappy with the information, but was impressed by the presentation and thus accepted the conclusions. This enabled the Germans to make more rational decisions and fight more effectively. This also made World War II last longer. You could blame it on those editors and graphic artists.

The concept has been carried forward, especially in the United States, to sometimes ridiculous lengths. Nightly, thousands of U.S. intelligence specialists labor through till dawn so that senior officials can get their multimedia intelligence briefing shortly after breakfast. The presentations are capable of getting across large quantities of information in a short period of time. But it is the quality of the data, and the analysis that produced them, that make all the difference. Like fighter pilots, a small percentage of analysts score most of the kills, but the audience at these briefings rarely knows if an ace or a dud produced the material for today's show. Worse yet, the summaries take the edge off crucial information. Blandness is the usual result, so as not to offend or overly excite. There is a bureaucratic urge to present the situation as under control, even when it isn't.

ERROR OUT OF CHAOS

Different analysts come up with divergent perceptions of the same events. You would expect differences between analysts from different nations. But in the United States you get differences within the intelligence establishment and even within the same agency. All of this serves largely to confuse the users and cloud the situation in general. Such chaos makes it more likely that the "official" analysis of a situation will be the wrong one. Eventually, the more accurate, but unpopular, analysis surfaces after the smoke clears. Then people wonder why the more accurate analysis was not the official one used in the first place. When there are a number of differing analyses to choose from, decision makers usually make their selection on the basis of that which most closely conforms to their preconceived notions. Most intelligence failures are not entirely the fault of the analysts. They are a group effort.

WHAT INFORMATION?

The ultimate purpose of intel [intelligence] analysis is to determine another nation's capabilities and intentions. In most nations, all this information is summarized in one report. In the United States, this is called the National Intelligence Estimate (NIE). The NIE summarizes all the intelligence work done and, more important, makes estimates on what future moves other nations, and the United States, are capable of. Since the NIE must be made concise so that rushed senior officials can absorb it, there are ample opportunities for misunderstanding or misinterpretation.

The NIE is the ultimate goal of all intel information, but along the way much of this data is used for such things as early warning (alerts when someone is getting ready to attack us), crisis support (readiness to increase the speed and quantity of analysis when a major crisis develops), targeting (updating lists of targets for strategic nuclear weapons, and conventional warfare as well), counterintelligence (keeping an eye out for spies), covert action (looking out for opportunities for "dirty tricks" operations and readiness to support them), operations (the day-to-day functioning of senior headquarters requires a constant flow of fresh intelligence), and gaming support (political and military games require accurate, or at least realistic, details for their exercises).

The data for the National Intelligence Estimates come from a number of other intelligence activities, each having its own separate purpose. Most of the material comes from basic intelligence work. Basic intelligence is the bedrock upon which all other intelligence analysis is done. It consists of several separate areas, each with its own specialists, customs, and analytical tools. For example:

Order of Battle Intelligence ("O/B" or "OB")

Referred to in the trade as "bean counting," this consists of tallying all of another nation's military units, with an analysis of each unit's composition in order to give a rough idea of the relative balance of forces between the two nations. Among those powers able to afford them, reconnaissance satellites have made this sort of work a lot easier, as it is difficult (but not impossible) to hide an armored division, warship, or air base.

Weapons and Equipment (or Scientific and Technical) Intelligence

This has always been a difficult area. Learning the operational characteristics of weapons and equipment can't be done very thoroughly unless you actually get your hands on the stuff, which is not always possible in peacetime. Although large quantities of gear tend to get captured in various minor wars, such secondhand stuff rarely includes the latest models, as the Superpowers are content to peddle old or derated equipment to foreign nations. This is not as crucial as it sounds, for it takes a while for new weapons and equipment to be built in large quantities. Russian equipment found on Third World battlefields is similar to most of the gear the Russians themselves hold. There is a more serious problem in determining the operational characteristics of weapons. The Russians, for example, avoid pushing their equipment to its limits in peacetime.

One advantage of the Afghanistan War was the opportunity to let the troops give their weapons and equipment a real workout. The results of this experience soon appeared in the form of new designs and modifications to existing apparatus. While the Russians benefited from this, foreign intelligence organizations also enjoyed a windfall of captured Russian equipment as well as the user reports. This was particularly valuable, as all previous opportunities to obtain Russian equipment came from nations Russia had sold the stuff to. These people would not always use the stuff as the Russians would. Moreover, it's also a Russian custom to hold back some equipment unless there is a really desperate wartime situation. Afghanistan brought out some of the "desperate wartime situation" stuff. Yes, the analysts' task is never simple. In peacetime, much of the information comes from satellite photos and the collection of electronic and other (infrared, sonic, etc.) "signatures" given off by the equipment.

Doctrine and Training Intelligence

This consists of figuring out what the other fellows plan to do in a war (doctrine) and how they go about preparing their troops to do it (training). The source of doctrine can be found in unclassified publications since it's difficult to get the word out to the troops if you make a lot of the doctrine secret. Russia has got away with some deception in the doctrine department because of the oppressive secrecy it has imposed throughout its civilian society. But there are so many resources applied to ferreting out Russian secrets that it's difficult to keep diligent analysts in the dark for long.

Training is a question of quality more than anything else, and this fact remains a mystery to many. For example, articles in the Russian military press complain bitterly about the low quality of Russian training. *Glasnost* has brought forth a flood of such complaints, some from Afghanistan veterans recounting the tragic results of their poor training once they reached the battlefield. Apparently, even Russian senior commanders aren't sure just how good their training effort is. How can foreigners be expected to do any better? Until the recent outpourings in the Russian press, many Western analysts were reluctant to give the Russians significantly low marks in the training department.

Even so, this crucial area of intelligence is not given a lot of respect or credibility by many senior intelligence consumers anyway. It's a very soft and murky area. Other nations have doctrine and tactics quite alien to American ways of thinking, which makes it difficult to get senior officials to comprehend the differences.

Morale and Leadership Intelligence

If doctrine and training are difficult to sort out and analyze, morale and leadership are even more slippery. Historically, these two items have proven to be the crucial elements in the battlefield effectiveness of an armed force. Yet these two items are the ones the intelligence crowd have the most difficulty with. The study of morale and leadership quality is slighted, or even ignored. The Russians pay more attention to it, but are hobbled by ideological blinders. *Glasnost* has revealed grave morale and leadership problems in the Russian military. This appears to be producing a risk of underestimating the stability of Russian forces. In 1991, Iraqi morale was certainly crucial.

Net Assessment

This is the most important aspect of the National Intelligence Estimate. You take all of the above items, plus data on economic, social, and political conditions, and compare them to the same standards for your own troops. Doing so should give you an idea of how well you shape up against a likely opponent. In a way, this is just what military historians do when they examine the interplay of forces that produced a particular result on a battlefield or in a war. Military historians have the advantage of doing their analyses and evaluations after the fact, with lots of original documents and memoirs and such to help. The intelligence analysts, some of whom are themselves trained in military history, must do it before the fact, often with minimal documentation, which greatly complicates their task. It makes such analysis a particularly tricky business and the subject of intense debate. Net assessment conclusions are used to determine which new programs are to be funded, and which existing ones are to be cut back. Under the circumstances, every senior commander becomes an intelligence expert when the accepted net assessment goes against his institutional interests. With all the vested interests in the military, the net-assessment crew must tread very lightly lest they be set upon by all the people disappointed by a dispassionate evaluation of military power. In other words, net assessment is honored more as a concept than a practical tool.

Economic Analysis

Combat capability is a murky thing to pin down because you so infrequently put it to the test. The situation is quite different with economic capability. In a long war, economic potential counts for more than initial combat power. As the Germans demonstrated in two world wars, in the long run superior combat capability eventually falls before an opponent's superior economic power. Keeping track of the economic capabilities of various nations and their likely impact on military power is an oft-ignored aspect of intelligence analysis. Note that Russia pays keen attention to this element, and a major reason for its recent pleas for disarmament is the Russians' realization that they are slipping further behind in strategic economic strength. As China saw earlier, without a strong economy, powerful conventional military forces become more difficult to support, and use.

POLITICAL ANALYSIS

Beyond military factors, there are the political ones that could cause a war in the first place. These political situations, are rather more slippery than the military ones. Military affairs do not exist in a vacuum, but within the context of political and diplomatic affairs. If the intelligence analysis of political events is sufficiently astute, you won't have to use the armed forces for anything more than a threat. It's when political analysis fails that military analysis suddenly becomes crucial. The diplomats are the first line of defense, the soldiers are the last. Unfortunately, political analysis is ticklish because a diplomat's usual initial reaction to something is to "await developments" while a soldier's is to "show them who's boss," which generally sells better with the politicians, not to mention the public.

Assessing intentions is much harder than determining capabilities. For one thing, intentions are more important than capabilities. A lot of generals and not a few politicians have been surprised as a result of assuming that an enemy's capabilities defined his intentions. What a power has may not be so important as how it intends to use it. Sweden certainly has the capability of invading its immediate neighbors, but clearly lacks any such intentions. On the other hand, although Syria lacks the capability of conducting a successful war against Israel, it has certainly attempted to do so on several occasions. Russia spends a lot more effort on these political issues. The Russians place much more emphasis on political control domestically and, until recently, among their allies. Russia also sees lack of similar control as a weakness that it can exploit in wartime.

To clarify the issue a bit, we can divide intentions into two classes: political and military.

First we'll look at political intentions. Each country has national interests defined by many items. Among these are:

• *Physical Security:* A nation's first goal on becoming a functioning entity is the establishment of law and order. Without internal physical security, nothing else can be accomplished. Lebanon through the 1970s and 1980s is a classic example of how debilitating prolonged disorder can be. Iran in the late 1970s lapsed into civil disorder, but immediately snapped back once Iraq invaded. Any nation in the throes of a prolonged civil war or revolution will eventually achieve peace on the terms of whichever party wears out first. This form of endurance contest changes a nation's attitude toward warfare for several generations. A population that has been through any type of war does not want to repeat the experience anytime soon. But threats of physical dismemberment can also be important, and no population wants to see its national patrimony lost to some foreign scum. In trying to determine a nation's political intentions, a major factor is how much value the population places on maintaining physical security. Also, it's not surprising that a nation at war is capable of mobilizing considerably more resources than when it is at peace. Threats to life and limb produce a nationwide rush of adrenaline. In contrast, a period of prolonged civil disorder will sap a nation's strength and will.

• *Economic Security:* Nations that feel physically secure will place greater emphasis on economic security. They are willing to go to war over economic issues when they feel that another country is somehow harming their economic prospects. Sometimes the threat to economic security is real, sometimes not. Iraq invading Kuwait in 1990 is a prime example.

• *Aspirations:* A nation that is physically and economically secure may still have aspirations that can bring it into conflict with another nation, or itself. The two world wars in this century began over national aspirations that had little to do with physical or economic security. This can be manifested by sheer public opinion (occasionally inflamed by the media) or by the machinations of wayward leaders.

Keeping tabs on political intentions requires one accurately to gauge constantly shifting public opinion, regularly volatile economic conditions, and the extremes of which national leaders are capable. It's not an easy task. The analyst must be able to track all these indicators and give reasonable warning before any particular situation gets out of hand. The difficulty of doing this successfully can be seen in the number of times were are surprised by unexpected wars and disorders. Even in hindsight, it is difficult to see how one could have predicted Russia's 1979 move into Afghanistan, Argentina's 1982 invasion of the Falklands, Uganda's 1978 invasion of Tanzania, Iraq's 1980 advance into Iran, Lebanon's descent into chaos during the 1970s and 1980s, or the Chinese use of force against dissidents in 1989. On the other hand, the U.S. occupation of Grenada in 1983 and the Iraqi invasion of Kuwait in 1990 were accurately called by several observers shortly before they took place. Military intentions are somewhat easier to measure, although it doesn't always do you much good, as a senior official can change his mind quickly. Military intentions can to some extent be defined by military capabilities. A nation that does not possess nuclear weapons can be safely assumed to have no intention of starting a nuclear war. Taking the examples mentioned above, we can see the problems inherent in making accurate estimates as to the intentions of the powers involved.

Russia certainly had the ability to invade Afghanistan, and had done so in the past. But the constraining factor was always, "Why bother?" The Afghans had never been subdued before and were quite content to remain fairly neutral regarding Superpower affairs. The country had long existed in a state of barely controlled chaos that precluded any sustained political or military action beyond its own borders. In retrospect, the Russians now attribute the decision to invade as a rash move on the part of a senile leadership. This is not the first, or last, time a war started for that reason.

Argentina had the ability to send a few battalions of marines into the lightly defended Falklands. They had long disputed British ownership of the islands. But after more than a century of leisurely diplomatic dueling, no one really expected a war over the matter. Indeed, Argentine relations with neighboring Chile were far more strained, due to similar territorial disputes. In hindsight, the invasion was a desperate move by a military dictator attempting to keep the peace at home with some patriotic military adventurism abroad, on the assumption that Britain was too weak or too disinterested to react. The 1978 Ugandan invasion of Tanzania was a very similar venture, though in this case the territorial question at issue was even less important, and a war even less predictable. These were not the first, or last, times that this sort of thing has happened. The difficult task for the analyst is determining when a dictator will recklessly force the issue.

Iraq's 1980 invasion of Iran was similar to the Falklands and Uganda situations. A dictator sought to achieve a national aspiration by attacking a more powerful neighbor. The principal difference was that this neighbor was in the midst of a revolution and civil war, which suggested it might be an easy mark. One thing an analyst learns from these situations is that dictators don't hesitate to gamble national survival on the chance of some questionable gain. In such situations, the analyst should be a good student of history, and acknowledge the strong role chance and whimsy play in human affairs.

Lebanon's civil war was something that could have been predicted, based on historical experience in the area. But the degree to which the country would splinter was unprecedented. This war demonstrates how complex these situations can be. Syria, Israel, Iran, the Palestinians, and the numer-

ous Lebanese factions are all responsible for this protracted
agony. Analysts have a hard time just keeping all the groups
sorted out.

China in 1989 was a different story. Westerners often ignore how different Chinese culture is. It's not just the language
and form of writing, but the fundamental attitudes of the people. China, for example, has never had a body of codified law
that was scrupulously obeyed by rulers and ruled alike. China
developed a workable system of custom and tradition that func-
tioned in the place of a written legal system. While Chinese
science had earlier developed many interesting new technologies, the culture did not encourage exploitation of these technologies. In the West, exploitation was encouraged, along with
laws rewarding the exploiters with patents and copyrights. China
is different, and intelligence analysts must gauge the difference
and communicate this to their customers.

In contrast, consider the Grenada affair. The United States
was openly opposed to the "New Jewel Movement," with its
revolutionary rhetoric, flirtatious relationship with Cuba, and
support for extremists in other eastern Caribbean states. The
increasing radicalization of the regime, culminating in a bloody
coup that brought to power an even more extreme faction, spread
a pall of fear over the small English-speaking states of the region. These developments, plus an increasing Cuban presence
and the large number of American students on the island, coupled with Ronald Reagan's recollection of what the Iranian
Hostage Crisis had done to Jimmy Carter's presidency and his
desire not to "lose" a country to communism, led several observers to predict an American invasion about a fortnight before it actually occurred. Still, only a few observers came to
this conclusion.

Even fewer people predicted the Iraqi invasion of Kuwait
in mid-1990, but the signs were clear to a number of observers
of the region. Iraq did have a long-standing, if long-dormant,
claim on Kuwait, some legitimate complaints about Kuwaiti exploitation of certain mutually held oil reserves, and serious concerns about the enormous sums that it owed to the emirate.
The rhetoric emanating from Baghdad certainly pointed to a
military adventure, as did extensive troop movements in the
weeks and days before the invasion. But only a few professionals, including the CIA, saw these as presaging war. There were

several reasons for this, not least of which was perhaps an American inclination to look upon Saddam Hussein as a more or less "friendly" factor in the convoluted politics of the Middle East. The prediction business is not always predictable.

Some understanding of the complexities of the prediction business may be gained from taking a look at the CIA, not the one of film and fiction, but the real one.

THE "REAL" CIA

The world's largest intelligence organizations are Russia's KGB and the United States' CIA. Less is known about the KGB. The CIA, existing in an open society, is another matter. Most of the people in the CIA, or any other modern intelligence organization, are not spies, known in the trade as "spooks." The majority—well over 95 percent—are "buffs" (researchers), "nerds" (technicians), or "flakcatchers" (managers).

Buffs are people obsessed with knowledge about some obscure corner of the world or an equally arcane topic, such as the mathematics of cryptanalysis, chemical engineering, African politics, or Siberian tribal customs. These people research everything that has any possible relation to their peculiar interest and compile the data thus accumulated in elegant and unusual ways. Helping them do their thing keeps a lot of translators and computer technicians busy. Sometimes the results may not seem to have much use. But you never can tell.

Nerds are the technicians who operate the expensive and quite capable equipment used to photograph and eavesdrop on much of what's going on in the world. The nerds are whizzes at computers, and the enhancement of photographs, radio signals, telephone conversations, and other such electronic magic. Nerds are too productive for the analysts, delivering far more data than can be sorted out efficiently.

The flakcatchers are the managers, who direct the buffs and nerds while trying to figure out what their own superiors want in the way of information. Some of these people are themselves former buffs and nerds, generally unhappy with having become administrators. Others are political appointees or civil servants, who may or may not have experience in or an aptitude for intelligence. The flakcatchers also have the unenviable task of defending their analysts' work against incredulous or disappointed customers. Senior officials regard the nerds and buffs as, well, nerds and buffs. The flakcatchers spend a lot of time overcoming these prejudices. Their job is not made any easier by the unexpected or unwanted results the nerds and buffs come up with.

There are still some "spooks" around, since neither the nerds nor the buffs can figure out everything, nor can they look inside people's heads or have access to the Kremlin's paperwork. But James Bond notwithstanding, most spooks lead dull, boring lives, mostly as low-level or mid-level functionaries. They spend a lot of time building up spy networks. The foot soldiers in these networks are usually "recruited" through blackmail, or volunteer their services out of ideological conviction or, especially in the West, out of greed. The great value in these networks is that their dull routine eventually provides access to plans, codes, secret technology, and the like, and to other persons who may also be recruited as spies. The people who recruit and control these spies, or "run their agents," are specialists and comprise less than 2 percent of the CIA's personnel. This includes those who run the more spectacular operations that set up, and support, guerrilla movements in foreign nations. Most "covert operations" consist of no more than delivering cash or other favors to people willing to support U.S. positions.

The foreign intelligence apparatus of the KGB is structured essentially like the CIA. The technologically poorer KGB relies less on gadgets and more on spies. But even the relatively low-tech Russian intelligence system collects enormous amounts of data.

This arrangement presents many paths to success, or to failure, in the intelligence business. The most dangerous area is the relationship between the people who use intelligence analysis and those who direct the buffs and nerds collecting it. The users don't know exactly what they want or, worse, have already made up their minds and basically want the intelligence crowd to confirm their positions. This is very common, and shows how persuasive other media can be. The people presenting the news on TV and radio have considerable influence with senior government decision makers, especially in a murky or fast-breaking situation. This is true even in Russia, where secrecy is so tight that many people who could use certain information cannot get it. Russian government officials are keen users of Western media, to a greater extent than their own, to find out what's happening in their own country. But access to information is not the primary problem, only one of a complex of difficulties.

The most common problem of intelligence organizations is getting the questions right. It is a classic problem when two dissimilar organizations, the intelligence ones and their government clients, have to work together. Each has different methods and goals. To understand this problem, let us refer to a similar but more widely understood problem: computer software. Getting software written is much like getting a useful analysis out of an intelligence organization. The primary problem in both fields is making the people who build the beast understand what it is you, the user, need. In the software business, you are always at risk of being misunderstood by the programmers. This is largely human nature at work. Management has one idea about what the software should do, and the programmers, because of their different mind-set, may develop quite a different conception of the project. Once computers came into widespread use several decades ago, this clash of perceptions has been one of the major obstacles in the way of effective software development. The problem is usually overcome, but at great cost, as the software is rewritten time and again until it does what the users want and not what the programmers think the users want, or what the programmers feel the users *should* want. Of course, sometimes the programmers are right, though the users may be reluctant to admit it. The big difference between software development and intelligence work is that you can run the software and everyone can see if it works, and what it does. With intelligence analyses, you never really know what unintended results your analysis will have. You may not even be getting what you think you're getting. Indeed, you may not be sure that your analysis is doing more harm than good.

How does one evaluate the veracity and accuracy of an analysis? It's largely a matter of perception and opinion. An intelligence report on the state of the Russian Army could be dead-on accurate, and there would still be numerous opportunities for different interpretation of the intelligence findings, as the reports are called. A good example is the role and mission of the Russian Navy. When the Russians began to build up their navy from a coast defense force to a high-seas fleet in the 1960s, there was a lot of uncertainty over how they intended to use this much larger fleet. At first the assumption was that the Russians were emulating traditional Western navies. In other words, seeking control of the merchant-ship routes. After all, the Russians were putting a lot of effort into expanding and improving their submarine forces. Two decades of examining Russian military literature and observing Russian naval exercises, however, had led to another view. This interpretation holds that the Russian fleet was expanded to deploy and protect strategic ballistic missile submarines, with a secondary mission to keep U.S. carrier forces, and their nuclear-armed aircraft, away from Russia. The Russians have consistently held that U.S. carrier aircraft equipped with nuclear weapons can hit many targets inside Russia and are thus really strategic weapons. Things are not always what they first appear to be until you look at the situation from the other side.

Analysts, and their managers, are well aware of the problems of interpretation, and strive to make their reports as acceptable (to their superiors) as possible. But some situations are more receptive to unbiased analysis than others. There is always going to be some political flak.

Unbiased intelligence findings are at most risk when they are at the direct request of a senior government official. This occurs mostly in support of a defense-budget item or particular diplomatic initiative. There's a lot of politics in these situations, and intelligence agencies are not immune to the notion that "the customer is always right," especially when the customer controls budgets and promotions. Intelligence is the dog that gets wagged by the policy-making tail. If this sounds like putting intelligence before politics, it is. Political decisions ought to be based on information, not justified by it.

Fortunately, much of an intelligence agency's output is generated for other reasons. Most information gathering and analysis are done simply to keep up-to-date. From this comes frequent dry runs, as the agency tests its capabilities by asking itself the kind of questions it expects from its consumers. However, one never can be sure what the customers will need. Often the customer doesn't even know.

Finally, we have unpredictable world events. If some dramatic and unexpected political, military, or diplomatic event occurs, the intelligence crew must drop everything to serve the nervous requests rushing in from their customers. When something surprising happens, like the Russian invasion of, or withdrawal from, Afghanistan, lots of midnight oil is burned to collect all available information and get a coherent analysis on the table as quickly as possible. Meanwhile the customers fume about the apparent inability of their intelligence agencies to supply them with information before the event.

THE RIGHT TOOL FOR THE RIGHT JOB

To meet these demands, the organization of the CIA and most other intelligence agencies follows a common pattern. There are large numbers of information gatherers. All those nerds and buffs, not to mention the spooks, collect far more information than can be analyzed. This has always been the case. Even the introduction of computers has not eliminated this bottleneck. The smaller number of analysts, some of whom are also nerds or buffs, are still locked in an unequal struggle with the mountains of data the information gatherers scoop up. It's no wonder that old-fashioned spies have fallen from favor; their contribution to these avalanches of data is really quite minuscule. What keeps any spies employed at all is management's need to find missing links between all those bits of data. While electronic surveillance, satellite reconnaissance, and textual analysis of documents can yield a lot of information, they are still not capable of looking inside people's heads. Listening in on phone conversations and reading messages helps to some extent, but there are still surprises if you can get to talk with someone from the other side. Logic and dispassionate analysis of the facts are not always the final arbiters of political and military decisions.

THE UNBEARABLE UNPREDICTABILITY OF SPYING

Spies are much more labor-intensive and considerably less reliable than nerds, buffs, and analysts. At least the latter three groups can be kept in one place and under some control. Spies, and field agents in general, will on occasion wander all over the landscape. They have a well-deserved reputation for getting into unexpected mischief. The goodies the spies obtain are open to more debate than the carefully documented analysts' reports. These data are generally highly valuable, but equally risky because you never know if it's real: Spies can be fooled or even "turned" into working for the other side.

Where the spooks cause the most commotion is when they attempt to shape events rather than just report on them. Some agents try to influence, or even otherthrow, foreign governments. Being on the spot, recruiting local help, and buying what loyalties and information they can, American agents have long realized that they have the wherewithal to mold events. While this can be a useful extension of the diplomatic process, it is not without danger. These activities mostly don't work as they should and leave a bad taste behind. Once in a while they really blow up and make matters worse, tainting the entire intelligence community. The Iran-Contra scandal is a recent example. The excessive attention the spies and dirty-tricks types attract causes most people to lose sight of the much larger contribution of the nerds, buffs, and analysts.

GOLD-PLATED GOSSIP

People in the intelligence business make a lively trade in what is essentially gold-plated gossip: Their data are little more than talk, and just as frequently are gathered at such great expense as to merit association with precious metals. This is part of an ancient tradition involving attempts to make sense of whatever mysterious and unpredictable maneuvers foreigners may be up to. In the old days, much of the information came from merchants, travelers, and diplomats. Occasionally, professional spies would be used, but this was not always necessary. The diplomats, tourists, and businessmen were quite observant. The major problem was, and is, interpreting the information.

WHOSE REALITY?

Diplomatic and military history are rife with instances where two nations seriously misinterpreted each other's intentions. War itself is a result of diplomatic misunderstanding reaching the point where only violence seems capable of resolving the differences. How often do the combatants realize, after the war is over, that their disagreements were not so great after all? Compounding this problem is the one of disagreements within a nation as to what should be done in response to another nation's real or perceived actions. In the United States, you have several different attitudes toward Russia, Third World insurgencies, and any number of other foreign-relations issues. America also has disagreements with her European and Asian allies on these matters. Whose reality is the real one? Arguably, there is only one reality in these situations, that of the other party. But do the Russians actually have a clear idea of what they want to do? Do Third World revolutionary movements have a fixed agenda of goals and methods? Does a petty dictator in Latin America, Asia, or Africa? Beyond keeping himself in power, the answer is likely to be no.

Even when Stalin ruled Russia with an iron hand, up to 1953, there was no certainty that Russian policy would not quickly change, simply because when Stalin changed his mind, there was no debate about how fast the new direction would be followed. Some assert that Russia became more predictable after 1953, when it began using a collective leadership that would haggle over new policy. Perhaps, but most of even that leadership's deliberations and decisions were kept secret from most people, including Russians. It has since come out that Brezhnev rammed through the decision to invade Afghanistan in 1979, despite the opposition of many military and civilian leaders. But this was not known at the time, and there was much fear in the West that the Afghan adventure presaged an ominous new direction for Russian foreign policy.

Third World governments and rebel movements follow the same patterns of initially inexplicable behavior. Some of these are led by dictators, others by collective leaderships. All are prone to secrecy and indecision. So why bother with prodigious intelligence gathering and analysis efforts at all? A good question. Ultimately, we do it because it does give us an edge. By studying potential opponents and possible allies, we can gain a sense of what they might do and what they are most likely to do. The key point here is that intelligence analysis, by its very nature, is an approximate solution. But it is hard for intelligence professionals to sell this approach. Their customers want clear guidance after they've paid billions to support massive intelligence organizations. Many users are aware of the necessarily imprecise nature of intelligence analysis. But many others are unaware of the problem, or choose to ignore it. Domestic politics cause policy debates that degenerate into the defense of very simplistic positions. For example, a common position in Soviet policy debates has been that America is intent on surrounding Russia with hostile neighbors as a means of preparing to conquer it, or at the very least smashing the Communist party. American political debates portray Russian foreign policy as dedicated to conquering the world. The reality, in both nations, is a lot more versatile and imprecise. Some Russian leaders still believe in world hegemony, but most are intent on simply holding on to what Russia already has. In America, the advocates of "rolling back" communism and "liberating" Russia are usually shouldered aside by those concerned with more pressing domestic issues. All of this complicates the intelligence analyst's job immensely. It's not enough to know what has to be said, you must say it to each listener in a different way in order to be understood.

THE EXPERTS FIGHT BACK

Intelligence work takes on the appearance of a struggle between the analysts and the users of their analyses, but this only happens some of the time. Ordinarily, users are quite content to take whatever analysis they are given, especially if it is presented in a spiffy fashion. Unhappy users are placated by being given what they want or, more commonly, raw data. The users can then perform their own analysis. This is a tricky game to play, as there are several degrees of raw data. Users aren't going to listen to tapes of Russian fighter pilots' chatter. The average American user doesn't even speak Russian, and most Russian users are no better off with English. The analysts use the "raw data" ploy to get irate users off their backs and to escape blame when it is discovered that the raw data left the user worse off than if he'd taken analyzed stuff. Analysts are often regarded as overeducated drudges. Too many users feel that anyone can sort things out from all this information, and proceed to concoct their own explanations. This generally results in their home-brewed analysis exploding in their faces. Surprisingly, this doesn't always result in increased regard for the abilities of the professional analysts.

The intelligence business deals with several large bureaucracies. The user organizations comprise the senior military, legislative, and executive leaders. The key personnel involved comprise no more than a few hundred people in a large nation, and perhaps several score even in a mid-size nation. In addition to the officials who make decisions based on intelligence analysis, there are even more aides, assistants, and other staff workers with access to the analysis. In the West, the press is also a user of sorts.

The analysis community consists of hundreds of thousands of people, only a few of whom are senior people who "deliver" the analysis to the users. In some nations, this senior person is a career civil servant; in others, a short-term political appointee is the norm. The deliverers make a big difference. Thus, for a number of organizational reasons, there are wide differences in how well analysts and users get along. Consider the principal national variations.

THE UNITED STATES: INTELLIGENCE GIANTS VERSUS THE USER HORDE

The United States has a complex and unstable system. Oliver North's free-lance intelligence operations were nothing new in American history, and certainly not new in the history of intelligence. This is complicated by the presence of several official intelligence agencies, although the CIA is technically coordinating all of them. In practice, this is a sometime thing, as some of these other agencies are themselves huge operations. The DIA (Defense Intelligence Agency) and the NSA (National Security Agency) are each large bureaucracies. DIA is a combined agency for coordinating all military intelligence, but there are still separate intelligence organizations, for the army, navy, and air force. In effect you have four organizations here, each pulling in a different direction. While the three services have their own specific needs for intelligence and analysis, the DIA looks at overall military intelligence needs and is more influenced by the civilian management of the Defense Department. The NSA is primarily a technical agency, in charge of breaking codes and using billions of dollars' worth of satellites, computers, and other gadgets to collect information. The CIA is the NSA's largest customer, as the CIA's principal responsibility is gathering together and analyzing data from all sorts of sources. But the DIA, which does a lot of specific military analysis, and the NSA, which does hardly any end-user (government official) analysis at all, disagree with what the CIA does to their data. The most common symptoms of these disagreements are contradictory assessments of the same situation by the military (DIA) and the CIA. There were a lot of these disagreements during the Vietnam War, and the squabbles continue to the present. People are a mite quieter about it, but the differing opinions as to what is reality continue.

The user situation is most complex in the United States. Technically, the CIA has but one user: the president of the United States. But in practice the hundreds of advisers, appointees, and staffers who support the president are the users who matter. In effect, all these people consume the CIA analyses and literally perform yet another analysis. Even when the CIA briefs the president directly, the others will still be consulted for opinions. Members of Congress also get to play, as they are responsible for appropriating funds for the CIA and have gradually assumed more of an oversight role to insure that the intelligence people play it straight. Because the intelligence community all, in theory, work for the president, it is not unknown for the CIA to filter its analysis in order to push the boss's favorite ideas. When the legislators find they have been misled, they become upset. This has led to regular battles between the Congress and the intelligence people. To avoid these ugly incidents as much as possible, the CIA has made the legislators users. This has made the CIA's job much more difficult, as its primary boss, the president, frequently pushes a policy different from that preferred by the Congress. The legislators themselves represent a wide spectrum of views. So while a particular analysis may please the president, it can be guaranteed to upset at least some of the Congress. Because of this adversary relationship with the legislature, the press gets dragged in. The journalists are always looking for a good story angle, and what better material than a few juicy CIA items leaked by an irate legislator, a manipulative president, or the CIA itself?

In reality, however, leaks are big trouble for analysts. A leak is either just a carefully selected portion of an analysis, or information specifically put together to influence someone. In other words, leaks are usually not objective, but slanted to support a particular position. In the United States, leaks have become something of an institution. People are still prosecuted from time to time for releasing classified information. Prosecutions occur only when someone within an intelligence organization leaks material, although most leaks are from users who have legitimate access to analyses. This is an important distinction to the intelligence people. Insiders have access to "raw" data, whose exposure could give other nations an idea of how the United States collects data. The analysis reports are opinions based on many sources of raw data, so there is less likelihood of damage when only the analysis is leaked. Customarily, the leakers get away with their actions, with the thanks of their peers or superiors.

There is also a lot of official and aboveboard leaking. The United States is an open society, and its citizens expect a lot of information from the government. After all, America is the only nation with a Freedom of Information Act. As a result, the United States is the world's primary, and regular, source of detailed information on military affairs. Much of the authoritative and copious data on armed forces, weapons, and equipment that appears in the press was released by the U.S. intelligence agencies. They don't always release it voluntarily, but the custom is to do so, and the CIA and other agencies have regularly complied for many years now. This open attitude also manifests itself in the defense industries. Trade publications regularly discuss in great detail weapons and equipment under development, as well as doctrine and tactics for their use. All of this makes the intelligence analysts work much harder.

With all this other information floating around, it's difficult for the analysts to make themselves heard above all the amateurs. The intelligence agencies do retain a vital edge: They have the raw data. They have all the satellite photos and huge amounts of electronic data. But as they frequently discover, the best is drowned out by someone who is louder, or simply more eloquent. And if an item makes the network news, all most people will remember is what the anchor said, not what the CIA meant.

RUSSIA: ONE BIG GUY, ONE LITTLE GUY, AND NOT MANY USERS

Russia has two major intelligence organizations. The larger is the KGB, sort of a combined CIA/NSA/FBI and Praetorian Guard for the national leadership. The FBI is included because the KGB also takes care of internal security and counterintelligence. The smaller organization is the GRU, or military intelligence. This is the equivalent of the DIA, but it is not, technically, subordinate to the KGB, as the DIA is to the CIA.

Secrecy is a historic obsession with the Russians. As a result, they are remarkably good at it. In the face of superior American satellites and electronic data-gathering capabilities, they have set up a nationwide deception organization. This outfit is also considered part of the intelligence apparatus, as secrecy and information are considered two edges of the same sword. This is especially true if you are able to make the enemy believe what you want him to believe. To the Russians, the ability to manipulate the enemy's knowledge of you is more valuable than information about the other side, and this attitude goes well with Russian capabilities. The Russians do not have satellites with the capacities of their American counterparts. Nor does Russia have all the computers and other electronic gadgets found in the West. What the Russians do have is several hundred thousand people who are carefully selected, well trained, and very well cared for. Surveys of Russian citizens indicate that KGB officers are considered to be at the top of the social pecking order. This is not to say that the Russians like the KGB; they simply respect it and recognize that anyone belonging has access to the best amenities Russia has to offer.

Aside from material goods, mostly from the West, KGB staff are a law unto themselves. A KGB officer can only be arrested by another KGB officer. This is another way of demonstrating that the KGB is the guardian of those things the Russian state holds most dear, namely, information and security within its own borders. While the police take care of routine security, the KGB concentrates on treason in its many forms, plus the intrigues of foreign powers. As events in Romania in December of 1989 demonstrated, the Romanian version of KGB internal-security forces, the Securitatae, were murderously loyal to their deposed overlords. This is what the Securitatae were trained to do, in imitation of their KGB mentors. Don't expect it to be any different in the other hard-line Communist nations, such as Albania, North Korea, and Russia itself.

It's also important to keep in mind that the current KGB grew out of the prerevolutionary secret police, the Okhrana. During the Revolution, many Okhrana operatives saw the handwriting on the wall and joined the new revolutionary secret police, the Cheka. This new agency has seen many changes of name—OGPU, NKVD, KVD—but even today a common nickname for KGB personnel is "Chekist." The KGB, like the Cheka before it, comprises the professional paranoids in Russia. It seemed only natural that the secret police should be in charge of spying on foreigners as well as on Russians. The KGB is relied upon more than the Foreign Ministry for analyzing the motives of potential enemies of the state.

Analysis is different in Russia. The Russians are great believers in quantification. Their Communist doctrine places great emphasis on the inexorable logic of calculation. As a consequence, KGB analysis can be more straightforward. There is not as much emphasis on trying to figure out what other nations are thinking and what they are apt to do. It is taken for granted that all foreign nations are basically hostile. Some are seen as less hostile than others, but eventually all of them will take a jab at Mother Russia if given half a chance. The KGB's job is to see that none of these predatory foreigners get a chance to do any permanent damage. Data are compiled and put into calculations that show the probability of various actions by internal and external enemies.

KGB analysts have no real competition within Russia. The GRU is competition of a sort, but the GRU is supposed to stick with strictly military matters. While this includes military technology, most of the really techie stuff is supposed to be done by the better-equipped KGB. The GRU goes after the information on the organization and equipment of foreign armed forces as well as their military capabilities. There is some overlap and competition in the field, but when it comes to a shoving match, the KGB usually comes out on top. Note that the KGB is also responsible for monitoring the loyalty of the troops, and taking action if any officer or soldier gets out of line. This automatically puts any combative GRU operative at a disadvantage because the KGB also keeps an eye on the loyalty of GRU personnel. However, because the KGB is so much larger than the GRU, the GRU military intelligence types feel a certain superiority. The GRU must get by with a lot less, and yet they regularly outperform their KGB equivalents.

Another difference from the CIA is the KGB's emphasis on industrial espionage. Because Russian industry is technologically inferior to that of the West, the KGB is the primary agent for stealing technology that cannot be bought legally. The KGB takes great pride in its accomplishments in this area and devotes considerable resources and many of its best people to it. At least the results in this area are easier to quantify.

There are a lot fewer users of intelligence analysis in Russia. Part of this is because of the mania for secrecy. But another major reason is the structure of the government. Russia is not a democracy. There is no functional legislature, not yet anyway. The journalists are all state employees and do what the boss wants, which does not include digging around for state secrets to publish. There are only a few dozen officials who have access to most of the KGB's analysis output, and these are all career officials who have been around for quite a while. Everybody knows everyone else. There's a lot less game playing with analysis because of this.

Russians have a unique perspective on analysis. They have a more rigid attitude toward running things. They develop, and follow, five- and ten-year plans for defense and industrial projects. Their analysis is more of a routine function, a side activity to the crisis management all governments must be prepared for. Russian intelligence analysts have a military background and spend a lot of time preparing contingency plans just as they would for the military General Staff.

Much of what Americans call intelligence analysis the Russians call academic research. At any time, thousands of senior military and KGB officers are in postgraduate study programs. They perform studies that resemble the intelligence analyses regularly prepared by CIA analysts. One thing these officers and many CIA analysts have in common is their training in history. Few people have seen many samples of both nations' studies, but those who have say they are quite similar in their academic rigor.

EUROPE: BOUTIQUES, DEPENDENTS, AND PROFESSIONAL USERS

Russia and America together employ over a million people in collecting and analyzing intelligence. This probably comprises over half the people so employed worldwide. The other hundred or so nations with intelligence staffs share fewer than a million personnel. With such smaller resources to work with, different methods have to be adopted.

The model for most intelligence operations is found in Europe, particularly the three larger nations: Britain, Germany, and France. Each of these nations has made a contribution to the European model of intelligence operations. Although the Russian and American organizations are quite different, both have borrowed heavily from these models; the Russians from the Germans, the Americans from the British. Both nations are also in debt to the French work of the past three centuries.

The European model is derived from centuries of using diplomacy as a mask for espionage. This technique can be traced back into antiquity. The first diplomats were, in effect, legal spies who played by a mutually agreeable set of rules. The first of these were probably "heralds," who performed the invaluable function of providing some means for warring groups to communicate. During battles, each side's heralds would stand together off to the side to take—and compare—notes. To this day, when one agrees to "exchange ambassadors," one is also agreeing to allow a number of highly skilled foreign intelligence professionals into your midst. But much has changed since the days when a monarch would dispatch some clever favorite to a foreign court. In those days, data collection and analysis were done by the same person. Users of intelligence were those who later sat down with the diplomats and discussed the situation. The notion of an "intelligence service," in effect the invention of modern methods of intelligence collection and analysis, is the product of the last few centuries. Although similar agencies existed in antiquity, for our purposes they began with the emergence of the nation-state in Europe during the Renaissance and the Reformation, accelerating with the Industrial Revolution and the consequent growth of government control. As economies, and armed forces, became more complex, so also did the need for effective intelligence data and analysis. A second major development was the emergence of counterintelligence. This only became possible as countries evolved into nations and created national bureaucracies and police forces. These are all relatively recent developments, largely of the last three or four centuries.

As armed forces became much larger, they also developed a more systematic approach to intelligence. A hundred years ago, the major European nations all had both diplomatic and military intelligence organizations. Unfortunately, these two branches of government operated largely independently. There was nothing like the KGB or CIA to act as an umbrella organization to combine intelligence from all sources, analyze it, and then present a unified assessment of what was going on out there. The two world wars forced European nations to make their diplomats and soldiers cooperate.

After World War II, most European nations found themselves with well-developed diplomatic and military intelligence organizations, as well as umbrella organizations for combining intelligence. As with Russia, considerable resources were devoted to counterintelligence. Overall, in most countries internal security still employs far more people than external intelligence. More important, the separate intelligence agencies of the army, navy, and air force are frequently (collectively) larger than the central intelligence organizations. The European nations have adopted the attitude that they cannot compete with the Superpowers, so they don't bother trying. They put most of their efforts into supplying specific intelligence for their diplomats and the individual branches of their military. Each of the European powers—whether NATO, Warsaw Pact, or Neutral—has certain strengths and weaknesses in its intelligence community, which is due partially to the historical evolution of their intelligence services, and partially to the differing specific needs of the nation in question. As a result, some of them can be quite good in areas where other powers have no direct interest.

Fourteen of these countries belong to NATO, along with the United States and Canada. As an organization, NATO has few intelligence capabilities. But it does serve as a framework for exchanging and analyzing intelligence information that is of use to the organization as a whole. Being a military alliance, NATO requires plans for potential wartime situations. To support this, NATO members contribute substantial amounts of their own analysis to further the development of war plans. They also cooperate in several intelligence-gathering ventures, for example, jointly owning and operating a number of AWACS early-warning aircraft.

The NATO nations have arrangements with the United

States to exchange information. Basically, it's a barter arrangement. When the French, British, or German intelligence services pick up a juicy morsel, they regularly (but not always) pass it on to the CIA. The Americans reciprocate by regularly passing on items from their worldwide network of electronic sensors.

Secrets don't stay secret forever. Nowhere is this more true than in NATO, and the West in general, where a number of nations share the same secrets and each has a different security situation. The net result is that once a nation's secret information becomes "NATO information," you can expect it to become known to the Russians before too long. As a practical matter, NATO members assume that different levels of secrets will have a half-life: a period in which there is a 50 percent chance that the Russians will get their hands on it. This half-life varies from a month for low-level stuff to a year or more for the most valuable secrets. This is caused by the multiplicity of nations holding these secrets and their differing security arrangements. West Germany was particularly porous because East German agents could so easily blend in and penetrate local security. After all, even a German couldn't always tell the difference between an East German and a West German. Europe also has a lot of people sympathetic to the Russian bloc, or who simply succumb to greed, as many American traitors do.

The situation among the NATO powers is quite different from that among the Warsaw Pact nations. While in NATO the members are fully sovereign, in the Pact the relationship was essentially one between "Big Brother" Russia and its six "Little Brothers." The East European intelligence organizations were very much under the control of the KGB and simply acted as its junior branches. Russia placed great emphasis on control of its allies' intelligence and secret-police organizations. East Europeans politicians might speak, and even act, independently of Russia, but they all knew that their local versions of the KGB had very close ties to their Big Brother in Moscow. This was one reason why Russia allowed East European nations flexibility in their domestic and foreign policies. There were always numerous pro-Russian individuals within the internal-security forces of these East European nations. Until recently, however, no leader in these nations could proceed too far from the

Russian line without risking unpleasant reactions from his own Russian-trained and Russian-influenced secret police. And despite *glasnost,* the power of the secret police remains enormous.

ISRAEL: THE MOSSAD

Israel is something of a special case. To begin with, Israel lives on a more or less permanent war footing. This lends a great deal of immediacy to the need for reliable information. While the Israelis have very good electronic means for procuring information, they rely heavily on their excellent personnel resources. Israel has numerous non-Jewish as well as Jewish sympathizers in other countries, not merely in the West, but also in the Soviet bloc and even in the Arab world. In addition to these informal sources of information from foreign parts, many Israeli citizens are former residents of the very nations that pose the most serious threats to Israel's survival, providing them with a valuable pool of reliable people to serve as agents and analysts. Moreover, Israeli analysts are quite good, perhaps as a result of a tradition of centuries of venerating scholarship. Because Israel has such good sources of information, and such an excellent capacity for analysis, the Mossad is called upon to cooperate with the intelligence services of other powers on matters of mutual concern. That there is such cooperation with the United States and several other Western powers, as well as South Africa, is well established. There are also hints that from time to time the Mossad has worked closely with Russian and even Arab intelligence agencies: One or two coups that would have replaced mildly hostile Arab leaders with more rabid ones seem to have been frustrated by a timely word from the Mossad.

The degree of success achieved by the Mossad has been impressive: For some years, it had an agent, Eli Cohen, who was so well regarded by the highest people in the Syrian government that they almost made him defense minister. This expertise has given the Israeli political leadership an enormous advantage. To be sure, there have been a few serious blunders. The most glaring was the failure to predict the 1973 Arab offensive, largely as a result of effective deception measures undertaken by Egyptian intelligence. That failure had to be paid for on the battlefield. Others—such as the still unexplained attack on USS *Liberty,* or the Pollard affair, in which an Israeli espionage ring was uncovered in the United States, or the erroneous assassination of an Arab waiter in Norway—have usually been covered up rather effectively. In general, Israeli intelligence delivers the goods to the political leadership as needed.

THIRD WORLD: KEEPING THE "SUPREME GUIDE" IN POWER

While the Superpowers and their allies know—or think they know—everything about everybody, Third World nations generally know little about anyone. Bad intelligence work is more of a factor in shooting blanks by Third World powers than in the blunders of the more developed nations. Third World countries have no impressive intelligence gathering and analysis bureaucracies to keep them informed. The president will just turn to a crony and ask for opinions. Sometimes this works, but mostly it doesn't. Moreover, in many cases, the "Maximum Leader" may not even do that, relying entirely on his own judgment. That works even less frequently than consulting one's accomplices. And in the Third World, failure is the first step toward civil disorder, revolution, and worse. In these nations, the best sources of information are open ones, which are mostly not all that bad. Most Third World nations need detailed intelligence on armed opponents much closer to home. While U.S. intelligence analysts worry over how many nuclear missiles and tanks Russia has, the average Third World intelligence officer is in a dither over how many people want the current president dead and what means they have to do it. While for the big boys intelligence work concentrates on technical stuff, the average Third World operative is more concerned with politics, especially domestic politics. In many Third World nations, opposition politics takes the form of tribal wars, army mutinies, assassinations, massacres, coups, civil disorders, and perhaps a drug lord or two with an "investment" to protect. So internal developments have to be studied carefully if the regime is to maintain itself in power, certainly more carefully than what's going on in the neighboring Third World country, beset by many of the same problems.

Surprisingly, the Superpowers have an edge on many of the Third World nations even in terms of intelligence concerning their internal political situation. Funds and personnel are expended lavishly to obtain the best information money can buy on who is up to what in various Third World nations. This results in piles of exotic information that is rarely used, such as the names of infantry company commanders' girlfriends. It's usually not prudent to pass a lot of this stuff on to the leader of the Third World nation in question, lest your contacts be compromised. The Superpower intelligence operatives in these countries run around with a suitcase full of greenbacks, collecting information from anyone who seems likely to have some worth buying. A Third World intelligence officer could do this too, if he had the money, but normally they are broke. There are exceptions. Through the 1980s, Iran has been sending over $50 million a year into Lebanon to support Shiite extremists. This money buys a lot of things, including information. But the Iranian efforts are a rarity among Third World nations.

So Russian and Yankee hotshots collect all these lovely data, analyze the hell out of them, and usually lock them up where they will do no one any good. Well, at least the sources will be able to enjoy their gratuities without fear of having to explain their talkative behavior.

A CRITIQUE OF PURE REASON

Intelligence gathering and analysis are but the first step in supplying the answers to questions like, "Are our armed forces sufficient?" While many senior decision makers only look at the intelligence reports, many others look to electronic games and models. These devices, largely computer programs, play out future wars and battles. Based on the results, decisions may be made to build new weapons, to organize new units or reorganize old ones, to develop new plans, and so on. While all this gaming and modeling might seem the reasonable thing to do, it doesn't work out that way in practice. Although commercial firms also use games and models with great success, the military has been less fortunate. The primary problem in the uniformed services is that there is rarely any reality against which to check game and model results. A commercial firm can model a new marketing campaign or manufacturing process and then proceed to the real thing. Mistakes will still be made: No model or game is perfect. But the constant exposure to reality teaches civilian model builders and gamers a lot of interesting tricks and techniques. With few combat experiences to sharpen their insights, military modelers and gamers not only have to rely more on guesswork and estimation, but also have to be wary of senior officers insisting that they know how to get these things right. This combination of ignorance and hubris has turned military modeling and gaming into a fantasy land where you can believe or disbelieve whatever you want and it will make no difference.

The reason for this bizarre situation can be traced back to the success of Operations Research (OR) and systems analysis in World War II. Put simply, OR attempted to look at how things work, and so a systems analyst might have been termed a sort of "efficiency expert." OR analysts worked out optimal techniques for air warfare, antisubmarine operations, and hundreds of other tasks, and thousands of lives were saved because of them. After World War II, it appeared that war-gaming and combat modeling would be a natural for OR. The then-current mode of war-gaming was based on German techniques developed in the early 1800s, although subsequent German war-game developers were actually using a number of OR techniques, many of which were cloaked in historical detail and interpretation. Thus one vital aspect of German war-game methods was ignored as American OR people took over war-gaming after 1945. The Germans used a very historical approach as the basis for their gaming of future battles. This was not unreasonable, as weapons and equipment during the 1800s were not evolving as quickly as they would a century later. Moreover, American historians did not get as deeply involved in military modeling as did their German and other European counterparts, and there were fewer American than European senior officers with advanced historical degrees. The development of the nuclear bomb, jet aircraft, and electronic equipment seemed to eliminate the usefulness of historical data. When the post-1945 OR crowd saw the future as a chaos of change and innovation in weapons and equipment, there were few military officers willing to caution them. OR teams would re-create combat from the ground up. When computers became widely available in the 1950s, it seemed that military gaming would never be the same.

In some respects, the OR people were correct. Combat

models, static re-creations of isolated tasks, seemed to work well with OR techniques: Analyzing the functions of a gun crew or individual pilot was manageable with OR tools. To this day, OR techniques make weapons and related equipment easier to use and more efficient. But even in this area, real combat exposes flaws in the logic of the OR approach. This is because troops will handle weapons and equipment in a logical and reasonable fashion during peacetime exercises. When there are real bullets flying about, though, the attitude changes. The difference between life and death is using weapons and equipment in ways that were never before considered. This effect is always discovered during periods of sustained combat, and forgotten shortly thereafter. In wartime, the OR workers can make the minor adjustments dictated by experience to perfect their techniques. In peacetime, there is a certain drift from battlefield reality.

What applied to models was even more apparent in war games. The Germans used war-gaming techniques extensively throughout World War II. They may have lost the war, but they won many a battle and inflicted more casualties than they suffered, partially because of their skill in the use of war games. By abandoning the lessons of history, OR war-gamers let themselves in for over three decades of blind alleys, embarrassing failures, and a general distrust of war games by all concerned. The basic problem was that when the OR approach attempted to re-create something as complex as entire battles, its results regularly diverged from historical outcomes for similar actions. This was explained away as an irrelevancy, since the modeling being done was of battles not yet fought. The future would be different, or so the line went. When history caught up with these models, there weren't enough excuses left to deal with the doubts.

Two notable disasters resulted from the OR approach, the Bay of Pigs and Vietnam. Neither operation was properly gamed in the traditional fashion. Indeed, the Bay of Pigs does not seem to have been gamed at all, even using OR techniques. While Vietnam was subject to extensive gaming, this was mostly in the form of number crunching, with no attention paid to the history of Vietnamese resistance to foreigners or to potential political developments. The ultimate downfall of any OR-based war game was in the unpredictability of the human element, and in fact the OR approach had generally ignored or "normalized" the human component. Yet wars will always involve people, who will continue to do unpredictable things.

Of most concern is the continued invocation of war-game results to back up one policy or another. Needless to say, many times war-game results are what the decision maker wants to see. Those who create and run the war games have few illusions about what is expected of them. While some good work is done, when important issues are at stake, war-game results are not allowed to drift into any area that would threaten decisions already made. When the Japanese Navy war-gamed their proposed 1942 Midway operation, the umpire disallowed the loss of several aircraft carriers. This game was an important factor in determining their final plans for the actual operation, which ended with the disastrous loss of four carriers, totally changing the balance of sea power in the Pacific. Lest one feel smug about how foolish the Japanese were, the U.S. Navy has been known to assume carriers are immune to attack when it conducts war games in preparation for World War III.

POLITICAL INPUT

Analysts are not perfect, nor can you expect them to be on the mark every time. One major problem analysts have is the frequent possibility that a foreign leader will indulge in some apparently random act. This happens more than one might think, for any number of unpredictable reasons. Although we like to think human beings do things for rational reasons, not all political, military, and economic decisions are made after careful, dispassionate, logical, and calculated consideration. Most analysts are familiar with this problem and are also aware that their own usually unpredictable political leaders can throw them curves. While large institutions can have the general trend of their policies predicted with some accuracy, whenever there is a strong-willed political leader, there is traditionally a good chance for unexpected new directions to appear suddenly. Many of the more famous "surprises" and "failures" in the intelligence business can be traced to these wild-card situations. Staying close to the thinking of a powerful and unpredictable leader is no easy task. What with all the dictatorships in the world, it's a wonder there are as many accurate intelligence analyses as there are. Most of the major failures were largely caused by unpredictable leaders. The Israeli intelligence failure in 1973 and the similar American problems in anticipating the 1979 Russian march into Afghanistan or Iraq's 1990 invasion of Kuwait were the result of "illogical" decisions. The decisions may not have seemed illogical to the decision makers involved, Anwar Sadat, Leonid Brezhnev, and Saddam Hussein. And such failures do not necessarily imply treachery or malfeasance on the part of the intelligence community.

HOW IT WORKS

The best way to understand how intelligence works is to take a look at some examples. Each of our cases deals with a separate type of intelligence situation, to better illustrate the different problems involved in disparate areas of interest.

THE MISSILE GAP

In late 1962, Russia and the United States came as close as any two nations have to firing nuclear weapons at each other. One component of this near-nuclear war was the belief, by the United States, that Russia had parity in strategic nuclear weapons and that the emplacement of additional Russian missiles in Cuba would tip the balance in Russia's favor. The truth, as later revealed, was quite different. The United States had nearly a hundred operational ICBMs, plus several hundred long-range bombers. Russia had a dozen operational ICBMs and less than a hundred long-range bombers. The U.S. misconception had begun in 1957, in the aftermath of *Sputnik,* when Nikita "We Will Bury You" Khrushchev proclaimed that the USSR now had the ability to destroy any country in the world. Given that our failure to loft an artificial satellite before the Russians suggested we had a lot to learn about rocketry, both the CIA and the air force concluded that the Soviets were very much ahead of us in missile technology. While the two agencies disagreed over just how much ahead the Russians were, both predicted that by 1961 they would have an enormous superiority: The CIA said there would be 500 Russian ICBMs; USAF said 1,000. In 1961, a reassessment of the data concluded that the earlier estimates were too high, with the result that they were revised downward to rough parity. This seemed like a major revision, but the reality was that the United States was very much ahead. Khrushchev had been scoring some points with his boasting, and many analysts had swallowed it whole. While in retrospect some critics have claimed the overestimations were deliberate efforts to inflame the situation and inflate defense budgets, it was really the result of Cold War paranoia and the extraordinary difficulties attendant upon penetrating Russian secrecy.

RUSSIAN OIL PRODUCTION

Russia essentially has a coal-based economy. In the 1960s, an effort was made to greatly expand oil production. The Russians attempted to locate and open new oil fields and proceeded to exploit their existing reserves more intensively. As a result, petroleum production grew markedly into the 1970s, with consequent beneficial effects on the Soviet balance of payments, when the Arab oil embargoes of that decade drove the price of oil through the roof. But while certain techniques can be used to pump oil faster, thereby raising annual yield, such aggressive exploitation leads production to decline in the long term: You get more oil now, but less overall. So as Russia expanded its output of oil, it was mortgaging its oil future. This did not go unnoticed in the West. In 1977, the CIA publicly predicted that if current trends continued, Russian oil production would peak within two to three years and then begin to decline markedly. This did not occur as predicted, and there was some comment about the "failure" of the CIA. Yet from about 1984 to 1985 Russian oil production actually did peak and then began to decline, albeit a bit less precipitously than the CIA had predicted. The CIA's 1977 estimate had been wrong not in substance, only in detail. Given the difficulties of securing accurate information on the Russian economy, the original prediction was not too far off. This illustrates a serious problem concerning accuracy in intelligence analysis. Depending upon the type of information desired, the degree of accuracy possible may vary enormously. With regard to political intentions or military capabilities, a high degree of accuracy is a must. But this is not necessarily the case with regard to many other types of information.

COMPETITIVE STRATEGIES

In the late 1980s, there arose the concept that the West could use its resources more effectively against potential military threats from Russia by developing weapons and tactics that took advantage of weaknesses in the Russian system. This might seem somewhat obvious for what was supposed to be a novel idea. The reality was that weapons and tactics development had heretofore been done without any systematic study of how potential opponents planned to fight. The assumption had always been that the other fellow would be like us, only different. But not different enough to bother with. This, it turns out, is to some extent a universal trait; but so is competitive strategies. We always seek ways to exploit an enemy's weaknesses. The unique aspect of the competitive-strategies concept was to not just see enemy weaknesses, but another culture's different way of doing things. Analysis revealed that many of these differences were unavoidable. In other words, nations were stuck with what they were whether they wanted to be that way or not. Thus the Russian tradition of waging war by throwing huge masses of troops and, since 1939, tanks at their opponents was not likely to change. It was also noted that during World War II, those German commanders who were most successful against the Russians were those who took advantage of the predictable Russian fighting habits. The Germans lost that war because too often their units were ordered to operate in a way that did not take advantage of Russian habits. For example, Russian attacks were usually in great strength, but relatively uncontrolled once they got under way. If you stood in front of them, you would be crushed. If you stood aside and stayed out of their way, you could hit them in the rear or flank and destroy them. All of this was easier said than done, but many German commanders managed to pull it off consistently. Note that the Germans used the same tactics successfully during World War I.

When competitive strategies was first proposed in the late 1980s, it was intended largely as a means for overcoming a chronic shortage of money in the U.S. defense budget to pay for all the new weapons being produced. The first "competitive strategy" put forward was the use of superior American technology against the most vulnerable Russian system: armored vehicles. Advances in microelectronics, sensors, and a thirty-year-old armor-piercing technology combined to produce inexpensive antitank (AT) weapons that could be dropped in front of enemy tanks. There, the AT weapons would wait until an armored vehicle approached and then attack it with about a 30–50 percent chance of destroying or crippling it. The Russians could also produce these weapons, but not in large quantities and not as cheaply. Moreover, the Russian ground forces have far more armored vehicles than Western armies and would suffer the most when these new AT weapons were deployed. As a bonus, these AT weapons are also very effective against railroad engines, which the Russians depend on to move additional forces into East Europe and supply them. All this is a classic application of competitive strategies. The Russian strategy is to mobilize an overwhelming number of armored vehicles. The most effective counterstrategy is to develop (as the West can) an inexpensive robotic AT weapon that will attack these swarms of Russian armored vehicles without exposing Western troops to attack. This turned out to be the only easily identified and implemented application of competitive strategies. For the concept to bring about a more intimate relationship between analysis and force development, other situations had to be found.

This has proven more difficult because of the ambiguity in most military matters. Picking out the Russians' massive use of armored vehicles was fairly easy. After all, what else were they going to do with all those tanks and APCs? It was no secret that Russia had a massive number of armored vehicles. Russian use of armored units in World War II was also well known, as well as published writings by Russian commanders about how they would use their ground forces in a future war. While similar writings exist for their other forces, these air, naval, and missile units are organized quite differently from their Western counterparts. When attention turned to aircraft, warships, marines, commandos, and ballistic missiles, the opportunities became murkier.

To give strategists some insight about Russian tactics for these other forces, the intelligence analyst must sort things out. This has caused some problems, as we are dealing with a lot of classified intelligence material and an obviously different Russian approach to military affairs. Still and all, it turned out that Western navies and air forces were already practicing competitive strategies without calling them that.

For example, the Russian Navy has a number of ship types not found in the West (cruise missile subs, battle cruisers) and a much different proportion of some types found in the West (many more diesel subs, corvettes, small missile boats). The same pattern exists in the Russians' air forces and, to a lesser extent, in their ballistic missile forces.

The new (post-1950s) Russian Navy initially presented some very difficult problems for intelligence analysts. For decades, it was assumed that Russia's large submarine fleet was intended for commerce raiding, in a style similar to the German U-boats of the world wars. Gradually, it became apparent that the Russians were more defense-minded, and planned to use their hundreds of subs to keep Western carriers and amphibious forces away from Russia. Most other Russian ships, including their helicopter carriers, were meant to chase Western subs. When this strategy was accepted by many Western analysts in the 1980s, it also became apparent that Western naval forces were *already* practicing competitive strategies. Most Russian subs are much noisier than their Western counterparts and, more important, Western sensors are much more effective than Russian ones. To give you an idea of the problems the Russians face, one of their most widely used antisubmarine weapons is a depth-charge mortar with a reach of five to six kilometers. Most Western subs use wire-guided torpedoes with several times that range. This means that Russian ships would rarely get a chance to use these mortars, as Western subs can detect and attack the ships carrying them without much danger of getting depth-charged.

The Russian air forces posed less obvious problems. Unlike Western nations, Russian and Warsaw Pact air forces make greater use of specialized aircraft. Most Russian aircraft are either ground attack or interceptors. One reason they have so few multipurpose aircraft is that they don't allow their pilots much time in the air to practice because they cannot produce aircraft durable enough to sustain a lot of training flights. Thus the average Russian pilot is trained for one type of mission, and may not even be very good at that. Russian tactics are also quite different. Western pilots are given a lot more freedom once they are in the air. More Western aircraft have powerful radars, or are accompanied by "Wild Weasel" aircraft that carry even more electronics. This enables Western aircraft to sort things out as they go. Russia relies more heavily on "positive ground control." Under this system, which is consistent with the traditional Russian way of running a battle, ground controllers sit in front of radar screens and tell the pilots where to go and when to fight. The Russians are aware of the vulnerability of this system and have gone to great lengths to protect the ground controllers, their radars, and the security of their communications with the pilots. Western air forces have been equally energetic in developing ways to attack the ground-controller system. This is an example of competitive strategies, but the problem is to dig deeper into Russian air-force procedures and tactics to reveal additional opportunities.

Competitive strategies is old wine in new bottles. The concept is as old as warfare itself and has been diligently applied by various U.S. military agencies for quite some time. For example, as early as the American Revolution, patriot inventors developed submarine weapons to take on the much superior British surface fleet. That's competitive strategies. But by placing competitive strategies in the spotlight and making a lot of noise about it, friendly innovators are encouraged to try anything and potential opponents terrified of what might result.

THE RUSSIAN DEFENSE BUDGET

For many years, the CIA asserted that Russia devoted about 6–8 percent of its GNP to defense. Then, in 1976, the CIA abruptly revised its estimate upward to something between 11 and 15 percent. Some folks claimed that this revision was a deliberate attempt to fuel the arms race. Actually, it was a very good example of the problems faced by intelligence analysts. Reliable financial and economic data on Russia are hard to come by. Even senior Soviet officials and economic planners have access to data only on a "need to know" basis and may have to rely on data appearing in Western publications. For example, a Russian economist authorized to develop a computerized model of some aspect of Soviet industry was once actually provided with various Western reference works as his sole source of data. For many years, the official Russian defense budget hovered in the vicinity of 20 billion rubles, or about $32 billion at the highly artificial official exchange rate. Aside from some Russian sympathizers, no one in the West took this figure seriously, given that it was only about the same as the combined total of very real pounds and francs that Britain and France spend for much smaller armed forces. So the CIA had to guess. Estimates of real Russian defense expenditures ran up to some $200–$250 billion, a figure that was based on calculating what Russian equipment would cost if produced in the West. Unfortunately, this estimate was inaccurate. In the West, labor costs more than goods, there's a free market in raw materials, and money has real value, while in Russia goods are more expensive than labor, access to raw materials is controlled, and money is worth whatever the government says it is. So the actual figure was anybody's guess. In fact, the Russians themselves didn't know what their "defense budget" was. The announced figure was apparently mostly for personnel costs. All the hardware costs were included in the budgets of various ministries, such as the Ministry of Medium Machinery, which makes the nuclear weapons, none of which published detailed budgets. To make matters worse, prices that various enterprises must pay for raw materials, semifinished goods, machine tools, and other resources vary according to official schedules: In effect, a factory making military equipment pays less for things than one making civilian goods. The official schedules are subject to negotiation, with politics and not economics playing the major role. So there is really no way of determining what the Soviet Union spends on defense. But the CIA tried. Further complicating matters was the fact that no one knew what Russia's GNP was, so that had to be estimated as well. Comparing its estimate for Russia's defense spending with its estimate for its GNP, the CIA came up with the 6–8 percent of GNP figure. But by the mid-1970s it became increasingly clear that the CIA had seriously overestimated the vigor of the Russian economy. This led to a reduction in the estimated GNP, and a consequent rise in estimated proportion devoted to defense to 11–15 percent. Matters rested there into the late 1980s, when *glasnost* and *perestroika* began to become the catchwords in Russia.

Glasnost in Moscow brought forth comments from Russian economists that the Soviet economy was neither as large nor as efficient as previously thought in the West, running perhaps as low as $1 trillion (less than Germany's) a year, not the assumed $2 trillion (just below Japan's). The effect was to indicate that Russian military spending consumed over 20 percent of the GNP, rather than 11–15 percent. Mikhail Gorbachev further complicated matters when he announced that Russia's "real" defense budget was about 78 billion rubles, plus another 3.9 billion in military-related space outlays. This translates into about $125 billion at the official exchange rate. The problem is, once again, that, aside from some Russian sympathizers, no one in the West takes this figure seriously either: It's only about twice the combined British, French, and West German expenditure. And only a few months after this announcement, the Russians revalued the ruble by about 90 percent, from $1.60 down to where it had always been on the black market. On this basis, the 81.2-billion-ruble defense budget is worth only about $12 billion, an amusing figure. So far no one has come up with a better figure than the CIA's, including the Russians, who openly admire the CIA's economic analysis. The basic problem with calculating the Russian defense budget is that you cannot, at least in the Western sense of free markets and convertible currency. In Russia, the currency is only part of the "medium of exchange." Each ruble has attached to it what it is permitted to purchase. Rubles spent on defense can buy anything. A ruble spent by a coal miner can buy very little, which is why there have been so many strikes among coal miners.

PREDICTIVE PROWESS OF MILITARY AND INTELLIGENCE PROFESSIONALS

The craft of intelligence reverses the old saw that "Victory has many fathers, but defeat is an orphan." In the intelligence business, successes are likely to go unnoticed and unrewarded save within the very narrow confines of officialdom, while failure is likely to taint ever-widening numbers of individuals in the intelligence community. We will never be able to have perfect intelligence. The difficulties of obtaining accurate intelligence are going to be with us forever. The problem is not merely that intelligence-gathering techniques or analytic skills must be refined. Far more important is to get political and military leaders, and the public at large, to understand the strengths, weaknesses, and limitations of our intelligence collection and processing procedures.

As we have seen, though, it's easier to be wrong than right in the intelligence business, and the following list demonstrates just how. Note that successful armies possess intelligence people who are right most of the time. The failures, however, are more instructive.

PREDICTIVE PROWESS OF MILITARY AND INTELLIGENCE PROFESSIONALS

PREDICTION (DATE)	PREDICTOR	ACCURACY	MILITARY RESULTS
"Scott Is Lost" (1847)	Wellington	V Poor	None
A Long and Bloody War (1861)	Scott	V High	Useful
The Zulu Are Mere Savages (1879)	Chelmsford	V Poor	Disaster
Home Before the Leaves Fall (1914)	Everyone	V Poor	Disaster
France Will Fall in Thirty-nine Days (1914)	Schlieffen	Poor	Useful
A Long and Bloody War (1914)	Kitchener	V High	Positive
America Will Not Enter the War (1917)	German Army	V Poor	Disaster
The Bomber Will Triumph (1921)	Douhet, Mitchell	Poor	Useful
China Is Ripe for the Taking (1937)	Jap. military	Poor	Negative
Finland Will Not Fight (1939)	Stavka	V Poor	Disaster
Air Power Will Beat Britain (1940)	Göring	V Poor	Disaster
The Germans Won't Attack (1941)	Stalin	V Poor	Disaster
Japan Must Win in Six Months (1941)	Tamamoto	V High	Disaster
"Japs Can't Fly" (1941)	RAF, USAAF	V Poor	Disaster
Japan Will Strike Southward (1941)	USN	V Poor	Disaster
Russia Is Collapsing (1942)	Hitler	V Poor	Disaster
Bomber Tactics and Targets (1943)	USAAF	Poor	Mixed
The Germans Can't Attack (1944)	Eisenhower	V Poor	Mixed
China Will Not Enter Korea (1950)	MacArthur, CIA	V Poor	Disaster
"The Bomber Gap" (1955)	NSA	V Poor	Useful
"The Missile Gap" (1957)	CIA, USAF	Poor	Useful
Castro Is a Pushover (1961)	CIA	V Poor	Disaster
Israel Will Not Attack (1967)	Nasser	V Poor	Disaster
The VC Are Finished (1968)	CIA, Westmoreland	V Poor	Disaster
The Arabs Won't Attack (1973)	Israel	Poor	Disaster
Iran Can't Resist (1980)	Iraq	Poor	Disaster
Britain Will Not Fight (1982)	Galtieri, etc.	V Poor	Disaster
The PLO Can Be Crushed (1982)	Sharon	Moderate	Mixed
Eastern Europe Won't Fall (1989)	All	Poor	None
Panama Will Fall Within a Few Days (1989)	USA	Poor	Mixed
Warsaw Pact Is a Formidable Opponent (1989)	NATO	Poor	Not Much
Iraq Won't Invade Kuwait (1990)	USA	Poor	Disaster
An Invasion of Kuwait Is Safe (1990)	Iraq	Poor	Disaster

Accuracy: V High (Very High), High, Moderate, Poor, V Poor (Very Poor). Military Results of prediction: Positive, Useful, Negative, Disaster. An inaccurate prediction can sometimes have useful results, by improving one's preparedness or military position in unexpected ways: For instance, although the bombers which were built were never so effective as predictions in the 1920s and 1930s, they did prove useful in wartime. Even a militarily disastrous outcome could prove useful or positive in a political way, as when the Falklands War resulted in democracy in Argentina.

NOTE: While some of these events are also covered in the chart in Chapter 1, Shooting Blanks and Great Wartime Disasters, here the emphasis is on intelligence problems only.

"Scott Is Lost" (1847)

When the United States went to war with Mexico, world opinion assumed Mexico, a "military" nation, would win. Winfield Scott, the senior U.S. military commander, proposed a simple strategy: Land an army on the east coast of Mexico and march on Mexico City, there to dictate a peace. Apprised of this, the Duke of Wellington, no mean soldier himself, remarked, "Scott is lost." But Scott went on to do precisely what he said. Wellington's analysis, which was supported by the bulk of European military opinion, failed to recognize the strengths of the U.S. military and political system, and the weaknesses of Mexico's. The man closer to the action, Scott, had a better understanding of the situation. This is a common circumstance.

A Long and Bloody War (1861)

Winfield Scott is now recognized as one of the most capable military leaders in American history. The commanding general of the Union Army at the beginning of the Civil War, he drew up a plan that assumed massive mobilization of the nation's manpower and economy and several years of heavy fighting. Scott's plan was dismissed by his contemporaries as the fevered musings of a senile mind—he was then about seventy-five—and he was sent off into retirement. Scott proved to be correct, and most of his 1861 "Anaconda" plan was eventually adopted. A classic example of popular feelings crowding out more experienced and well-reasoned analysis.

The Zulus Are Mere Savages (1879)

Lord Chelmsford was thought to be an expert on military and African affairs. His assessment of Zulu military effectiveness proved disastrously off the mark and cost the lives of many

British troops. Chelmsford, naturally, made his estimate more on the basis of conventional wisdom about "naked savages," than from examination and analysis of the facts as they stood.

Home Before the Leaves Fall (1914)

World War I began in a swirl of illusions and errors in judgment. Nearly all the participants believed that the fighting, which began in August, would be over before October. The only thing that happened in October was that everyone ran out of artillery ammunition and thus began digging the trench systems that changed little until 1918.

France Will Fall in Thirty-nine Days (1914)

Alfred von Schlieffen, the general who drew up the German plans for the opening stages of World War I, was certain that German troops would be entering Paris thirty-nine days after the war began. His prediction was close, but not close enough. The plan called for the Germans to perform, in wartime, feats of marching that would have been considered impressive in peace, while assuming that the French would largely ignore their advance. In the end, the exhausted Germans were stopped some forty kilometers from Paris. Note, that it was a still very close-run thing. The French were on the ropes when the Germans (or, more correctly, a handful of General Staff officers) decided that no further advance was possible. This was the second mistake von Schlieffen's General Staff successors made. Their first error was to weaken the forces attacking France so as to strengthen those defending against the Russians. This change was not in itself crucial, but it didn't help. In hindsight, though, the German plans were wrong. For the next four years, both sides more or less sat there and shot each other to pieces. The Germans had not planned for any outcome but the fall of France within six weeks. At best, the "perfect plan" gave Germany the territorial cushion necessary to endure the subsequent carnage on the Western Front with something of an advantage over its foes.

A Long and Bloody War (1914)

Lord Kitchener, a senior British general, was among the few military leaders in 1914 who saw that the conflict would be a hard one. His assessment enabled Britain to prepare for the war a bit more quickly than the other participants. In a bit of bad luck, Kitchener was killed at sea in 1916 (while on his way to evaluate Russia's prospects), thus depriving Britain of his accurate appraisals during some of the most crucial periods of World War I.

America Will Not Enter the War (1917)

Late in 1916, the German General Staff concluded that the only way to win the war was to resume unrestricted submarine warfare. When it was pointed out that Germany had given its word to the United States that this would not occur, the General Staff concluded that (a) the United States would not enter the war, (b) even if it did, the U.S. Army was too small to affect the outcome, and (c) even if the United States was able to improvise a large army quickly, the submarines would prevent it from reaching Europe in time to affect the war. They were wrong on every count, as a consultation with their ambassador in Washington would have told them.

The Bomber Will Triumph (1921)

Misinterpreting the effects of innovative technology is nothing new. During the 1920s, two air-power zealots, the Italian Giulio Douhet and the American William Mitchell, made loud, and widely accepted, predictions about the future of air power in war. They were incorrect, but they caught the public imagination, and their errors were not discovered until it was much too late. But at least there were lots of bombers available for all sorts of missions that were useful. Note that despite this experience, the U.S. Air Force still maintains a major bomber force.

China Is Ripe for the Taking (1937)

Japanese military commanders were feeling pretty cocky after World War I, having defeated China, Russia, and (technically) Germany in recent wars. Throughout the 1920s, Russia and China were engulfed in internal turmoil. Both nations seemed incapable of offering significant resistance. Japan had occupied portions of Russia's Far Eastern territories after World War I, but had been forced out by a combination of growing Red Army strength and American refusal to support the Japanese. The situation in China seemed more promising. Regional warlords were fighting each other, and Japan already occupied portions of Manchuria. By late 1937, the generals controlled the Japanese government and predicted to themselves that a full-scale invasion of China would succeed because they foresaw no effective resistance. They were wrong.

Finland Will Not Fight (1939)

Having cut a deal with Nazi Germany, the Russian military command *(Stavka)* felt a territorial dispute with Finland could be settled by force because the Finns would be unable to resist the much larger Red Army. The Russian generals ignored their own history. Up till 1919, Finland, then a province of Russia, had been the source of some of their toughest combat units. The Finns had not lost their fighting ability, and the subsequent war proved a huge embarrassment for the *Stavka*.

Air Power Will Beat Britain (1940)

Hermann Göring, the head of the German Air Force *(Luftwaffe)*, was also a close friend of Adolf Hitler. But above all, Göring was a strong believer in air power. He convinced Hitler that it was worth risking the *Luftwaffe* in a large-scale air assault on Britain. German intelligence had overlooked the new British radar system and novel air-defense tactics. The Germans knew of the new British Hurricane and Spitfire fighters, but did not have a clear idea of the numbers available or production capability. Deceived by the success of the *Luftwaffe* in Poland and France, the conquest of Britain from the air seemed a possibility. It didn't work, and thereafter Göring began to spend more time with his drugs and stolen art, while Hitler tried to find another way to win the war, by an attack on Russia.

The Germans Won't Attack (1941)

Russia's dictator Josef Stalin signed an alliance with Nazi Germany in 1939. In accordance with the treaty, Russia and Germany proceeded to carve up Eastern Europe. In 1940, Germany gobbled up most of Western Europe. In 1941, German forces went after Greece and the Balkans, and began to appear on the Russian border in great numbers. Russia's intelligence service was not asleep, and made numerous reports of Germany's intentions to invade. Even Britain and the United States tried to warn Stalin. But he refused to believe it, and did not fully do so until the invasion had been under way for several days. Russian forces, which had been massed on the German border for an eventual attack, were not alerted to the impending German advance. The Russians took catastrophic losses because of Stalin's refusal to believe what his intelligence officers knew about the coming German invasion. This is a classic example of the customer ignoring reliable information.

Japan Must Win in Six Months (1941)

Admiral Isoruku Yamamoto had lived and studied in the United States and knew better than the more provincial generals who ran Japan the awesome economic and military power of America. He warned that if the war came, Japan would have to win a decisive military victory in six months if it was to have any chance of surviving a counterstrike by the Americans. Yamamoto was right, but few of his fellow flag officers paid much attention to his prediction until it was too late.

"Japs Can't Fly" (1941)

Until 1942, no one in the West knew quite what to make of the Japanese. A xenophobic, closed, medieval, and economically nondescript nation until the late 1800s, Japan had quickly adopted Western ways. After defeating Russia in 1905, Japan had brought in Germans to help build a modern army and British advisers to help create a modern fleet. When aircraft became more common and effective as weapons of warfare in the 1920s, Japan designed and built its own. Observers from the British and American air forces watched this activity with some alarm, but ultimately decided that the flimsy Japanese aircraft and intense Japanese pilots were simply no match for Western machines and men. It turned out that the Japanese planes were flimsy because they preferred more nimble and maneuverable aircraft. The Japanese pilots were intense because they were the product of an extremely selective training program. These pilots also considered themselves heirs to a medieval warrior tradition that had contempt for death, and any opponents. British and U.S. pilots soon found this to be a formidable and lethal combination.

Japan Will Strike Southward (1941)

As the United States and Japan drifted toward war in the summer and fall of 1941, U.S., British, and Dutch intelligence all concluded that the Japanese offensive would be directed toward the south, to the Philippines, Malaya, and Indonesia. Allied intelligence became fixated with this idea. And they were correct, but the Japanese were also intending to hit Pearl Harbor hard and fast at the very start of the war, and hints to this effect were simply overlooked. So the Allies—and particularly the United States—suffered a major reverse. Later, in 1942, Allied intelligence became equally obsessed with the notion that the Japanese would eventually head for Australia. After the war, it was learned that the Japanese had no intention of stretching their lines that far. The Japanese strategy, logically enough, was to build as compact a defense perimeter as they could while incorporating populations they felt would be amenable to Japanese leadership. The Japanese were wrong on that score, but that's another story.

Russia Is Collapsing (1942)

The German invasion of Russia in 1941 was a near success, for, although Russia did not immediately crumble, as Adolf Hitler expected, it seemed that such enormous losses had been inflicted that Russia would inevitably fall. Hitler's generals, and their intelligence experts, knew better. The German offensive of 1941 came to a halt from exhaustion and unexpected Russian reserves, just short of two major objectives, Moscow and Leningrad. These cities were heavily fortified through the winter of 1941–42. When the warm, dry campaigning weather came in the spring of 1942, Hitler decided to head south, to seize Russia's primary oil supplies on the Caspian Sea. To do this, the major city of Stalingrad had to be taken or isolated and bypassed. When the Germans hit Stalingrad, they encountered stiff resistance. Some German forces were sent on toward the oil fields further south. Instead of putting a screening force around Stalingrad and concentrating on grabbing the more vital Russian oil, Hitler ordered that Stalingrad be taken in the belief that this would break Russian resistance and allow an advance to the north into the rear of the Moscow defenses. All of this assumed that the Russians were hanging on by their fingernails, which was true only in those areas the Russians did not consider vital. This tactic allowed Russia to gather a huge reserve of infantry and mechanized forces. German intelligence was not ignorant of this reserve, but Hitler would have none of it. He ordered the battle of Stalingrad to proceed. Then, on November 19, 1942, the Russians unleashed their counterattack: Stalingrad and the German Sixth Army were surrounded, and the tide had turned in the Russian-German war. Good intelligence is not worth much if you don't pay attention to it.

Bomber Tactics and Targets (1943)

When the Japanese attacked in the Pacific in December 1941, the U.S. Army Air Force had already deployed the B-17 four-engine heavy bomber, which soon went into mass production, along with the similar B-24. Such weapons had never been used in combat before, so it was not surprising that the doctrine developed for them in peacetime proved somewhat wanting when the shooting started. The heavy, long-range bomber was designed to fly in large formations, each bomber using its half-dozen or more machine guns to throw up a wall of fire against enemy interceptors. Each bomber was equipped with a Norden bombsight, an electromechanical marvel that could, during peacetime tests, drop bombs on a factory four miles below. In combat, things were different. The Germans, for example, created efficient early-warning systems, including radar, which allowed them to concentrate their fighters against the bomber formations. Enemy antiaircraft guns disrupted the huge bomber formations. The Germans developed long-range cannon for their interceptors, as well as air-to-air rockets that, while unguided, usually hit something when fired into the dense bomber formations. Air-force intelligence failed to anticipate any of these enemy innovations, but the bomber crews coped. More machine guns were mounted, more armor was added to vital parts of the aircraft, and "flak jackets" were invented for the crew. Formations were modified for more efficiency, and long-range fighters were developed to escort the bombers all the way and keep enemy interceptors at bay. The escorts were also used for "flak busting," attacks on the German antiaircraft defenses, and electronic countermeasures were invented to deceive German radars. This left one problem that was never fully addressed: which targets should be hit. There were a limited number of bombers and a massive number of targets. Should the bombers go after power supplies, fuel sources, munitions plants, aircraft or tank plants, transportation, or what? The air-force target intelligence people were not able to agree what the key targets were, so they kept switching from one target system to another. These switches were in response to political and military leaders. Thus the bombers were called to support other operations, such as the Normandy invasion or trying to stop the V-1 and V-2 missile attacks. Eventually, by early 1945, attacks on transportation and fuel systems began to have an effect. After the war, it was found that the most vulnerable system was the electric power plants: There were not many of them, and they were easy to damage and difficult to repair or replace. The target intelligence people had believed that the electrical power system was too flexible and too dispersed to be vulnerable to bombers. They were wrong. If they had figured out the electrical power system's vulnerability in 1943 or 1944, the war could have been shortened by six months or more.

This is a good example of the problems caused by the introduction of a new weapons system: First you have to get the thing to work, then you have to figure out how to use it to best advantage.

The air-force generals of World War II can be forgiven for

assuming that their bombers were having a devastating effect on the enemy economy and will to resist, since there was no direct way of assessing the damage. But once the war was over and the research teams of the Strategic Bombing Survey turned in their reports, there could be no arguing with the failure of their wartime policy. Rather than face facts, the fly-boys ignored them and continued to insist on the success of their methods, with consequent warping of U.S. military efforts in both Korea and Vietnam.

The Germans Can't Attack (1944)

By December 1944, it was thought that the German armies were on their last legs and incapable of a large-scale attack. The Allies had been reading Germany's coded communications for years, and these messages gave no indication of any planned offensives. But most German forces were now fighting from inside Germany, where it was possible to use very secure cable-based communications instead of radio. The Allies did not have a lot of taps on the German telephone system, so the planning messages for the German December attacks against Allied armies were not detected. Opposite the Ardennes area of Belgium, some intelligence analysts did note several armored divisions assembling, but no one got excited enough to risk the lives of agents by sending them into enemy territory to get a closer look, believing instead that those units were to be a counterattack reserve for the battle north of the Ardennes, where Allied forces threatened to overrun the vital Ruhr industrial region. The prevailing wisdom was that the Germans would not attack in the difficult Ardennes. The prevailing (or at least the majority) wisdom was wrong, leading to the Battle of the Bulge. It was ironic that four years earlier French and Belgian intelligence experts reached the same conclusion, that the Germans would not move large forces through the Ardennes. Lightning does strike twice, especially in intelligence work. But this time the Germans failed, due to overwhelming Allied matériel superiority and five years of experience dealing with the blitzkrieg.

China Will Not Enter Korea (1950)

After three months of hard fighting, U.S.-led UN forces began to chase North Korean invaders out of South Korea. The

American commander, Douglas MacArthur, felt that China would not come to the aid of its ally, Communist North Korea. The CIA and other Western intelligence agencies did little to change MacArthur's mind. Yet despite signs to the contrary, including captured Chinese soldiers and open radio announcements from the Chinese government, the UN (largely U.S.) intelligence people were reluctant to admit what they saw unfolding before them until it was too late. Chinese armies proceeded to chase UN forces right back into South Korea at great cost to all concerned.

"The Bomber Gap" (1955)

Before the "missile gap," there was the "bomber gap." The U.S. intelligence and air force folks got it into their heads that the Russians were turning out hundreds of long-range bombers and that soon the Western democracies would be in grave peril from this air armada. Some say it all began in the mid-1950s at a Russian military parade. The Russians had their dozen or so heavy bombers fly over Red Square, and then fly out of sight and come around again, and again. Neither satellites nor U-2 high-altitude recon aircraft were available at that time, so there was no way of checking just how many bombers the Russians had. U.S. intelligence experts, or at least the people they worked for, erred on the side of paranoia, and this led to a huge bomber-building program. When the dust settled a decade later, it was realized that the Russians never had many heavy bombers and never intended to build many either. This error greatly fueled world tensions, but at least it prompted the United States to improve its early-warning and bomber forces. Actually, the reaction to this imaginary problem is still with us. More is currently spent on U.S. strategic bombers than on the more effective and efficient ballistic missiles.

"The Missile Gap" (1957)

Right on the heels of the bomber gap came the missile gap. Long-range ballistic missiles carrying nuclear warheads became practical in the late 1950s, and the United States assumed the Russians were going all out to build these beasts. The Russians were going all out, but had little to show for it. When the Cuban Missile Crisis came along in 1962, the United States had many more ICBMs than Russia. At that point, most Russian ballistic missiles were shorter-range IRBMs that couldn't reach the United States except from Cuba. As usual, the truth of this situation was not sorted out for another decade. Meanwhile, the United States and Russia waded into a costly missile-building contest. By the late 1970s, Russia had closed the real missile gap that had always existed by virtue of the advantage the United States had from the early 1960s.

Castro Is a Pushover (1961)

The Cuban Revolution of the late 1950s was not unexpected; that its leader would proclaim himself a Communist was. As often happens in the intelligence business, one error begets another. The CIA concluded that the Cuban population, or at least a significant portion of it, wanted nothing to do with godless communism and would rise up in revolt if a force of Cuban Freedom Fighters could be put ashore. Well, the force was, the people didn't, and Cuba is still under Communist rule. It turned out that most of the people willing to lead a rising had already departed for Miami by the time the Bay of Pigs invasion was launched in 1961.

Israel Will Not Attack (1967)

Following their humiliating defeat in 1956, the Egyptians built up their armed forces so that they could, with Syrian, Jordanian, and Iraqi assistance, eliminate Israel once and for all. The Egyptian leader, Gamal Abdel Nasser, convinced himself that if he moved his forces through the UN Peacekeeping Force to the Israeli border, he would be able to advance directly into Israel. Although Israel stated plainly that this action, and several others the Arabs took, would cause Israel to attack, Nasser refused to believe it. A more serious Arab intelligence lapse was the refusal to accept the superiority of Israeli troops. The Arabs had, on paper, a better than two-to-one advantage in all major weapons systems. But in the previous two wars with Israel, Arab forces had been beaten despite even more favorable odds. Israel did what it said it would do, and in six days defeated all the Arab forces arrayed against it. Those who ignore history are inclined to repeat it.

The VC Are Finished (1968)

After three years of heavy combat, President Johnson and his advisers were eager to proclaim the Vietnam War won. The American generals in Vietnam were eager to proclaim a victory, but were having a difficult time keeping score. The South Vietnamese Communist guerrillas (Viet Cong, or VC) were taking a hammering, but collecting information on the ground was difficult. Unlike conventional wars, there were few recognizable enemy units. The VC were largely organized as a secret society, comprising thousands of tiny groups, each generally of only a handful of people. Most of the VC were part-time fighters, going out at night a few times a month to make war on the South Vietnamese government or U.S. forces. The rest of the time these VC were farmers, urban workers, or even South Vietnamese government employees. It was difficult to find out how many VC there were and almost as difficult to determine how many were killed in combat. The VC tried to take their dead and wounded with them because if a dead VC was identified, his comrades might be found out. A lot of innocent bystanders were also killed, and U.S. commanders, pressed to get a high "body count," soon counted every dead body in sight. This muddied the water for U.S. intelligence even more. South Vietnamese intelligence was not the most efficient, and American analysts could not agree among themselves how best to interpret the muddled information that was available. As a result, at no time did the United States have an accurate picture of the military situation in Vietnam. This was not understood at the time, and the U.S. command remained consistently optimistic when it might better have been more cautious about the imminence of victory. This is what made Tet so devastating to political support for the war.

The Arabs Won't Attack (1973)

After defeating three Arab nations in six days during the 1967 war, Israel made three mistakes. First, the Israelis lost track of the relative combat power of their armed forces and that of their Arab enemies. Second, they believed that their intelligence services were very unlikely to miss the signs of a pending Arab attack. And third, they had no idea that they were making mistakes one and two. The Israeli problem was not one of collecting data, but of improperly acting on them, which is a common problem with intelligence disasters. As is typical, the causes of faulty interpretation were partially political and largely due to attitude. The Israeli government was warned of an impending attack in late 1973, but decided that it was a false alarm similar to one they had earlier in the year. The Israelis thought they were on top of things. They weren't.

Iran Can't Resist (1980)

Iraqi intelligence capabilities were never that great. British Broadcasting Corporation (BBC) short-wave newscasts served as a principal source of fast-breaking events across the border in Iran. What firsthand reports Iraq did get back from Iran spoke of chaos and sectarian strife. The shah's carefully stage-managed regime had appeared very strong. Now the religious fundamentalist revolutionaries made Iran look like a country coming apart at the seams. The Iranian armed forces, a pillar of the shah's power, were being purged while young, untrained, and poorly armed revolutionary guards were rampaging about the country, searching out Islam's enemies. While this was largely true, even if one learned of it only from the BBC, what Iraq's leadership missed was the religious and patriotic fervor that the revolution had unleashed. Iraq's population had for many decades been suppressed. Enthusiasms similar to Iran's could be fatal to an Iraqi. In a common pattern, Iraqi leadership tended to see Iran in Iraqi terms. The Iranian chaos must be bad for Iran. The Iranian military was being taken apart, and there was nothing but wild-eyed revolutionary guards to take its place. With this interpretation of intelligence on Iran, it seemed a reasonable decision to invade and settle a long-standing border dispute, which crucially ignored the significance of the fervor gripping Iran, and Iran's much larger population, which would prove more than a match for the invading Iraqi soldiers.

Britain Will Not Fight (1982)

The military dictatorship of Argentina was facing dangerous domestic unrest in 1982. President/General Leopoldo Galtieri, the senior officer, approved a plan to invade the British Falkland Islands, off the coast of Argentina. These islands, inhabited by 1,500 people, had been claimed by Argentina for over a century. The dispute was a fairly cordial one, as Argentina was an Anglophile nation. The middle and upper classes sent their children to local versions of the classic British "public" schools; English, the British version, was favored as a second language; and there were a number of British-style social clubs. The British, in turn, spoke fondly of traveling to "the Argentine" for a holiday or to visit kin who had migrated. British arms industries supplied many weapons to the Argentine armed forces, and there was a long-established trading relationship between the two nations. Galtieri thought he understood the British. The thinking was that if the Falklands were seized quickly, and with minimal bloodshed, the polite British would adopt their stereotypical stiff upper lip and agree to talk over the new arrangements. But Galtieri, and his intelligence advisers, apparently knew British manners better than British history. The United Kingdom was quick to fight over seemingly trivial matters. It was another case of wishful thinking overcoming available intelligence.

The PLO Can Be Crushed (1982)

Israel is, in many ways, sitting on an impossible situation with its Palestinian population and the PLO (Palestinian Liberation Organization). A large portion of the Palestinian population lives outside of Israel, and most of it supports the PLO. Many Arab states also support the PLO, providing money, weapons, and bases. Lebanon was such an Arab state, but when civil war broke out there in 1975, partially over the presence of so many heavily armed PLO fighters, the PLO strength actually grew amid the chaos. As more PLO fighters settled into Lebanese bases, raids across the border into Israel increased. Finally, in 1982, the Israeli defense minister, Ariel Sharon, convinced the Israeli leadership that an attack into Lebanon would clear out the PLO. Israeli intelligence was operating on thin ice here, as the situation inside Lebanon was armed anarchy. Sharon's use of intelligence estimates was a mask for a desire to do something, anything, to stop the PLO raids on northern Israel. In the short term, the Israeli operation was a success, as the PLO was forced to leave Lebanon. But the large Palestinian refugee camps in Lebanon remained. Arab nations were willing to take a few thousand PLO fighters, but not several hundred thousand Palestinian civilians. The Israelis soon pulled out of Lebanon, rather than become embroiled in the civil war, or a conflict with Syria. Within a year, PLO members began to trickle back into Lebanon, and within a few years, the PLO had armed units operating there once more. This episode shows that intelligence is a murky business. There are no sure things, particularly when a civil war is going on in a nation noted for past civil conflicts that spanned decades.

Eastern Europe Won't Fall (1989)

In the space of about six months, the unthinkable happened. Nearly every Communist government in Eastern Europe fell from power, and Russia did nothing save recognizing the new non-Communist regimes and political parties. The conventional wisdom since the 1950s was that Russia would never give up control of Eastern Europe without a fight. With rebellion stirring in Russia, Eastern Europe liberated itself, often in surprising ways. Meanwhile the Cold War had become so much a way of life that some Cold Warriors speculated that it was all an elaborate trick.

Panama Will Fall Within a Few Days (1989)

Since 1903, the United States has been intimately involved in Panamanian affairs. The former province of Colombia gained its independence by agreeing to let the United States build and run the Panama Canal. By the 1960s, this relationship caused unrest in Panama, and in the 1970s the United States agreed to turn the canal over to Panama by the end of the century, while retaining certain military rights. Meanwhile economic distortions created by the canal caused similar political aberrations. The canal threw a lot of money into the local economy (ac-

counting for about 10 percent of the GNP), creating "two Pan-
amas." Half the people were quite well off by Latin American
standards, while the other half were sunk in the more typical
Central American rural poverty. Out of this situation came the
military coup of 1968, led by officers of humble origins. The
officers' gimmick was to extort money from the wealthier half
of the population while passing some of it around to the less
wealthy half. Meanwhile Panama was made a wide-open nation
to all manner of illegal schemes. As long as the generals got a
cut, anything was possible. When the United States finally decided to invade and return to power a recently elected government (kept from power by the generals), it was thought that the
generals' minions would quickly fold. Such was not the case.
Thousands of men owed their prosperity to the generals, and
as they were armed, many of them put up a sustained fight.

Warsaw Pact Is a Formidable Opponent (1950–1989)

A very expensive intelligence failure, driven by over forty
years of Cold War rhetoric. When the Communist governments
of Russia and Eastern Europe crumbled in 1989, it became obvious that the armed forces of those nations were equally inept.
This was contrary to four decades of expert and official opinion
in the West. There were always intelligence analysts in the West
who insisted that the Warsaw Pact was not nearly as formidable as it appeared to be. But the political and emotional clout
behind the "Mighty Monolithic Soviet Empire" image was such
that any defects of the Warsaw Pact were played down. The
result was an arms race that brought Russia to its knees and
did great damage to the economies of the Western nations that
also participated. This development was not so much a failure
of intelligence as it was a prime example of what happens when
existing policy dictates how intelligence information is to be
interpreted.

Iraq Won't Invade Kuwait (1990)

As with most intelligence disasters, this one required the
efforts of many people to bring it off. Although Kuwait (and
Saudi Arabia) had been quite generous with Iraq during Iraq's

1980–88 war with Iran, there was no way they could be generous enough. Iraqis were dying; the Bedouins in Kuwait and Saudi Arabia were only spending a fraction of their excessive (in Iraqi eyes) oil wealth to help (from the Iraqi perspective) defend all Arabs from the Persian menace. Iraq piled up over one hundred billion dollars in debts fighting Iran to a standstill. When the cease-fire with Iran came in 1988, Iraq's credit was exhausted. Lenders and suppliers pressed for repayment and cut off supplies, war-weary Iraqis cried for reconstruction. Iraq's dictator, Saddam Hussein, demanded a $30 billion "gift" from Kuwait and Saudi Arabia plus forgiveness of debts. The prospective donors asked to negotiate and Saddam saw a way out by seizing Kuwait. The Kuwaitis assumed Iraq would keep its distance because Kuwait and Saudi Arabia were cozy with the United States. But Iraq had been developing better relations with the United States, and even stomached the indignity of a female ambassador from America. Iraq, like most Arab nations, did not look favorably on women in high government positions. But the ambassador in question made the mistake of not telling the Iraqis that the United States would strongly oppose any tampering with Kuwait's borders. Greed, need, and a convenient misunderstanding got Kuwait dismembered and Iraq into a fatal situation.

An Invasion of Kuwait Is Safe (1990)

Once the Iraqis were in Kuwait, they had to deal with a situation gone terribly wrong. While the Kuwaitis made some horrendous diplomatic mistakes to bring on the invasion, Iraq found itself equally in danger from a world united against it. The UN bestirred itself in one of those rare shows of unanimity and passed resolution after resolution condemning Iraq and, worse yet, authorizing an embargo and the use of armed force to restore Kuwait. As with many intelligence failures, this one was the result of Iraqi domestic policy shoving aside dispassionate analysis of the situation. In hindsight, the Iraqis could see that there was little likelihood that the United States would abandon one of its Persian Gulf allies to a rapacious neighbor. But hindsight is never an adequate replacement for foresight.

AND NOW THE GOOD NEWS

In the intelligence business, failure gets more attention than success. There are several reasons for this. Failures are more noticeable and generate a lot of anger and demands for "someone" to "do something." Success is best kept secret, lest the other fellow figure out how you do it and change things so you can no longer do so. For example, recon satellites cannot see everything. Some of these birds are more effective at seeing through clouds or camouflage than others. If your subject finds out your satellites' weak spots, he can exploit these to make it more difficult for you to see anything. The same problems apply to electronic intelligence and the use of spies. In the latter case, secrecy is literally a matter of life and death.

There are several different types of successes. The more mundane ones have to do with simply keeping track of a potential opponent's armed forces. When the subject is a vast and secretive nation like Russia, this is no trivial undertaking. Success is relative, as the recent INF treaty revealed that Western intelligence services had apparently made substantial errors in determining how many SS-20 ballistic missiles the Russians deployed. Or had they? These may not have been errors. The U.S. intelligence agencies may have released inaccurate figures to conceal their true detection capabilities. You never know. Similar gaffes, real or imagined, have been revealed in the past. These problems may have a lot to do with the success of Russia's "deception" forces, which consist of a nationwide bureaucracy led by a senior army general.

Yet the overall size and composition of the Russian armed forces has been tracked with good accuracy since the 1960s. Where most intelligence systems fall down is in the analysis of senior leadership decision making. Counting tanks and ships is one thing, determining what generals, admirals, and politicians are going to do is much less predictable. It's not an "intelligence failure" if the other side's leaders do something bizarre and illogical; this is considered a normal aberration. Good intelligence can determine what the opposition is capable of and is most likely to do. But this covers a wide range of possible moves. For this reason, the "failure" to predict the Russian moves against their East European satellites in 1956 (Hungary) and 1968 (Czechoslovakia) were not failures in the same sense as those discussed above. It was widely assumed within intelligence circles that the Russians would not let any of their satellites leave Russian control. There was some static about not knowing of the details of the 1956 operation, but there were no recon satellites then, and so the Russians had an easier time pulling off a surprise operation. In 1968, there were satellites, although quite crude by current standards. More was known about Russian moves during that operation, but U.S. intelligence agencies were reluctant to reveal how much they knew for fear that the Russians would respond by making surveillance more difficult. The Russians almost invaded Poland in 1980, and the satellite technology was much better. Information about Russian troop concentrations on the Polish frontier were leaked to the press, but not to the extent that the Russians could determine anything new about Western intelligence capabilities.

Some 95 percent of the CIA budget, and 97 percent of its personnel, are devoted to intelligence collecting and analysis (the remainder are devoted to "special operations"). The investment has regularly paid off. One troublesome aspect of this success is that no one outside the intelligence agencies can keep score. Major breakdowns in the information gathering and analysis system can have catastrophic consequences. For example, as more nations obtain ballistic missiles and nuclear weapons, there is greater probability that these systems will be used. Western and, in this age of *glasnost,* Russian intelligence agencies are the first, and perhaps only, line of defense in preventing a nuclear war. Even a minor nuclear war, with one nuclear missile fired by one Middle Eastern nation into another, could be a catastrophe. It certainly would a horror for the people getting hit, but there is always the possibility of triggering other use of nuclear weapons. It's up to the intelligence community to sniff out these nuclear wars in advance so that diplomatic, or even military, action can be taken to stop them. Reform in Russia (and other former Communist states) is placing even more demands on the intelligence community. Intelligence success is easy to take for granted; intelligence failure is often disastrous, and too late to do anything about.

The "9 to 5" Soldiers: The Profession of Arms

⚔️

·5·

What do the troops do? How do soldiers prepare for war? Are we sure our training methods are adequate? How does the workaday routine of the troops influence their perceived combat ability as opposed to their real combat ability?

Your average soldier is little more than a civil servant with heavy weapons. In fact, the vast majority of uniformed personnel don't even operate weapons or otherwise participate directly in combat. Soldiers are often considered the least effective government employees. This has a lot to do with the inability to test the troops' capabilities short of actual combat. When such a test does appear, the troops rarely cover themselves with glory. Armed forces historically attempt not to be better than a potential opponent, but merely less inept.

PAPER BULLETS

Peacetime soldiering is not risk-free. Career soldiers have much to fear from the usual dangers of working in a large bureaucracy. It is not real bullets that peacetime soldiers fear, but the dreaded "paper bullets." These missiles are fired in the bureaucratic skirmishes that, for the professional soldier, are far more dangerous than real battles. Real bullets can lead to injury or death in combat. Paper bullets can have worse consequences, as in a ruined career. A soldier has much more to fear from paper bullets than from real ones. After all, he spends most of his time fighting uniformed bureaucrats, not armed enemies. There's no honor, glory, or heroic memories for those gunned down in bureaucratic conflict during peacetime squabbles, to watch helplessly in disgrace as their careers fall to pieces.

This situation creates a major image problem for the military. The average citizen thinks of the troops as being constantly prepared for combat, a battle-ready band of hard chargers chaffing at the bit. Actually, most soldiers have more in common with people working for large corporations; the uniforms and insignia simply make it easier to determine who outranks whom. About one in five of the troops is regularly reminded of the possibility of combat because he is in a combat unit, but even here the troops are overtaken by the demands of organizational gamesmanship. As one infantry battalion commander put it, after decades of peacetime soldiering, "I know a lot about running a motor pool and mess halls." In peacetime, a successful battalion commander must see to it that all his vehicles are kept in top shape and that the troops are fed well. Combat readiness comes later, after all the paperwork is sorted out.

In most armed forces, you are constantly followed through your career by a voluminous personal file. The most important documents in this file are the periodic evaluations by superiors. These are the most deadly of all paper bullets. Just one negative fitness report can destroy a soldier's career. And as the good reviews all tend to be very good, even a merely satisfactory one can have dire consequences. Naturally, even the most well-intentioned officer will think twice before doing anything that would possibly offend a superior. Without combat conditions to prove a maverick officer right, most will play it safe. While civilian organizations also rate their "officers," there are things like profit-and-loss reports to show who is really doing a superior job. The situation in the military breeds a complacency and uniformity that has more to do with not rocking the boat than it does with adjusting to the constantly changing needs of modern warfare.

This situation is nothing new. Ever since professional armies were first established several thousand years ago, there have been serious problems with the troops getting out of shape in peacetime. Actually, the situation is not too bad in the United States or Europe or even Russia. It's much worse in most other countries. A glance at any newspaper will reveal that many nations have problems with their armed forces, such as when they take over the government, massacre their own countrymen, or go into the drug business. Given such developments, then, one of the greatest innovations of modern times might be the invention of "paper bullets" (military bureaucracy), for very often they keep the troops in line in peacetime. European nations in the late 1600s were the very first to turn their troops into bureaucrats, keeping them busy with administrative struggles when there wasn't a war going on. The famous Jean Martinet, who rose to become a major general in the service of Louis XIV before succumbing to "friendly fire" while storming a fortress, flourished during this period; his name is now the common term for fastidious attention to detail and rigid discipline.

The bureaucratic approach was also necessary as warfare became more expensive. Standing armies are costly enough without the enormous additional expense of actually having them wage war. Paper bullets may be debilitating to the combat readiness of the troops, but are less of a bother than restless soldiers looking for something to do.

THE GENTILITY FACTOR

Until this century, armies wore their fancy uniforms into the field and, while the troops may have become somewhat ragged marching around looking for the enemy, everyone would spruce up before the battle. This was not because of vanity or the generals' desire to simply look good. The primary reason was to gain a psychological edge. If your troops were well turned out, they felt more confident, and if they looked better than the opposition, the enemy would in turn suffer a drop in morale.

But by the mid-late 1800s, longer-range infantry weapons made these "stand up and march in formation" battles obsolete. Victory went to the side that could approach the other fellow without getting shot to pieces. It took armies more than two generations, and millions of casualties, to fully appreciate these new techniques. Fancy uniforms were out, green and brown and khaki battle dress were in. But the fancy uniforms did not disappear; they were saved for peacetime parades and any occasion where the troops might benefit from dressing up. This created something of a morale problem for the senior officers, who never quite got over the thrill of leading masses of splendidly attired troops in combat. A perverse trend set in whereby during periods of peace, battle dress gains bits of color and refinement at odds with combat requirements. But this is a symptom of deeper problems. In peace, many of the rough-and-ready practices of wartime are replaced by more genteel methods. For example, when in a defensive situation during a war, troops tear up trees, buildings, and whatever else is necessary to build fortifications. In peacetime, this would cause a lot of damage. Besides, there are not a lot of bombed-out towns available for peacetime training in wartime construction of fortifications. There are not enough forests available for trashing either. Holes in the ground must be filled in after exercises, if only to leave the next bunch of trainees someplace to dig. The net result is the practice of being "neat" in peacetime. This neatness became such a habit that wartime construction techniques had to be learned under fire, usually with substantial friendly losses.

Similar problems were encountered with maneuvers. Peacetime maneuvers are done without benefit of enemy fire. Real combat is slow and unpredictable because the troops become understandably cautious and deliberate in the face of imminent death or mutilation. So peacetime commanders strive to speed things up in training exercises. When these officers and their troops encounter real opposition, it's quite a shock and very bloody.

FUTURE SHOCK

Gentrification is an old problem; technological change is a relatively new one. New technology gets caught up with the gentrification problem to produce overoptimism about the effectiveness of new weapons. Part of this overoptimism comes from the process accompanying the introduction of the new weapons. The people pushing the new stuff are understandably enthusiastic, and their enthusiasm understandably clouds their judgment. They're not going to get these weapons funded and accepted if they simply say the new gadgets *might* be better. No, they have to preach nothing short of a "revolution in warfare" after the introduction of this splendid new piece of hardware.

New technology will continue to be a problem, partially solved by occasional small wars that enable the new stuff to be used and the effects examined. This is not always a perfect solution, as peacetime prejudices carry more weight than a few combat experiences. Earlier in this century, it took considerable experience with the machine gun before most officers accepted the fact that infantry tactics would have to be drastically changed. Tanks and aircraft had similar difficulties getting properly integrated into ground combat, and aircraft carriers and submarines caused a lot of problems for naval tacticians. Today, missiles, electronics, and nuclear weapons cause anxiety among those who must figure out how to fight the next war.

THE ORDER OF PRIORITIES

While every government declares that the purpose of having armed forces is to provide a sufficient defense against foreign enemies, this declared goal is rather low on the actual list of priorities. Keeping in mind that the armed forces are the most heavily armed and, probably, the most disciplined group in the country, many governments have a more pragmatic list of priorities for the troops.

PRIORITY 1: KEEPING THE TROOPS HAPPY

Happy troops are not likely to be angry troops. When the soldiers get angry, they do what troops are trained and equipped to do: Go to war against the object of their anger. This is often the government they are supposed to be protecting.

If there's no foreign enemy to fight, and nothing to keep the soldiers occupied, the troops will find something else to do. For example, in addition to making war on their own government, the wayward soldiers indulge in unauthorized massacres of the local citizens, go into business for themselves, or get into some other mischief, such as starting an unauthorized war with a neighboring country. This is a common pattern in Third World nations. But this phenomenon is not unknown in the history of any nation. For example, the United States was created when its citizens, whose legally authorized militia constituted a considerable army, became unhappy with the British colonial government. The result was the American Revolution and a defeat for the colonial government. Moreover, the substantial portion of the U.S. population that had actively sided with the British suffered serious harm and many sought refuge in Canada and other parts after the war ended. In a sense, the American Revolution began as a military coup by the colonies' armed forces (the militia), which outnumbered the regular army troops from Britain.

The American Civil War was another occasion where unhappy troops, again in the form of militia, brought on a lot of local bloodshed. In this case, the militias of the seceding states (and regular officers from those areas) organized into armies that brought forth the bloodiest war in American history. One might regard this as another attempted coup, which did not succeed. Seen in this light, Americans should think twice before they look askance on nations that suffer from one coup after another. European nations have long suffered the same pattern of unhappy armies and resulting strife. Britain suffered its own civil war in the 1600s. France has experienced several bouts of civil war, saw much of her army mutiny in 1917, and had a brush with rebellious troops as recently as the early 1960s when paratroopers protested Algerian independence. Germany had several private armies marauding through its territory in the wake of World War I. And during the last 150 years, Russia and China each endured one of the bloodiest civil wars of all time. All of these sad events were brought about by unhappy soldiers.

It's no wonder that most nations take strenuous measures to keep the troops from getting too restive. There are several ways to do this. We can boil the most effective techniques down to the following short list.

1. Pay Them Off

This is what makes mercenaries effective. Pay troops, any troops, enough to keep them content, and you have a reliable army. However, mercenaries usually can be hired and fired at will, while the national armed forces are around permanently. Well-paid troops are also, well, expensive. You probably can't afford too many of them. Worse still, the troops quickly become accustomed to their high pay levels and eventually expect more. Generous pay alone will not solve all your problems. The usual compromise is to pay the officers, and perhaps the NCOs, or most of them, well, and then fill out the ranks with short-term conscripts. The draftees are very young, are paid very little, and are let go before they become too discontented. Another solution, seen in many Third World nations, is to turn the armed forces into a criminal enterprise with each unit a different "gang" led by its commander in the role of a local crime boss. The commander shares the loot with his troops, as well as making payments to his own superior for "protection." The troops themselves can be given license to shake down the local civilians for whatever they can get. Panama and Haiti, to name but two examples, are burdened with this soldier-gangster syndrome. Even the well-paid volunteer forces in Western nations do not have smooth sailing. If pay scales do not keep up with what's available in the civilian sector, the most able troops will not stay in uniform.

2. Terrify Them

This was one of the major developments of the "Age of Reason" during the 1700s. Armies of that period used troops trained intensively to move about in precise formations. Their muzzle-loading muskets were not very accurate, unless forty or so troops fired all at once in the same direction. This technique required disciplined movements by large bodies of soldiers. It was found more efficient to terrorize the troops into compliance than it was to reach them with reason. Prior to this, the best troops were highly trained fighters who were led by competent commanders. The terror system developed in the 1700s worked quite well, and even after the weapons became more complex and tightly organized units had to spread out, the terror approach retained its appeal with many armed forces. Russia is the only major military power that still uses a large dollop of terror to keep its masses of conscript troops in line. In combat, Russian officers are still authorized to summarily execute any reluctant or insubordinate soldier. Many other nations allow this practice, officially or otherwise. Moreover, most armed forces use some form of terror to condition their combat troops to the very real terrors of combat. This is what you hear about when veterans describe their initial training ("basic" or "boot camp"). Part of the terror is the separate set of laws under which the military may operate. In effect, the troops are no longer protected by whatever legal system they enjoyed as civilians. Military law contains more rules that the wayward trooper can run afoul of. The punishments are more severe, and prosecution is more expeditious. Company or battalion commanders have authority to act as judge and jury for minor infractions and impose penalties on the spot. These traditionally consist of days or weeks of confinement to barracks after duty, fines, or reduction in rank. Officers get gentle treatment, although Russia does not hesitate to throw officers into jail for a few weeks and then restore them to service. Most nations expect better from their officers, and will dismiss any found guilty of offenses that would simply imprison a soldier for a short period. This goes back to the ancient tradition of "an officer and a gentlemen." Yet everyone in uniform is expected to fear the more draconian laws that set troops apart from civilians.

The complexity of modern warfare works against the terror approach, but it can still be made to work for short periods or in special circumstances. Those few remaining jobs that bring troops face to face with the horrors of combat still require the same iron discipline of the eighteenth-century musketeer. Indeed, this sort of discipline is even more needed today, as the eighteenth-century soldier was almost always fighting while in a tight formation, shoulder to shoulder with his fellows. Warfare today constantly finds the combat soldier out of sight of his fellows and depending on not much more than his training and discipline to do what needs to be done while a lot of unseen strangers are trying to kill him. The majority of troops, however, are working in a less frightening environment. And while we know that terror does not work very well in modern factories or offices, it is equally ineffective against soldiers performing similar jobs. Terrorized troops in nonterrorizing situations can find any number of ways to get back at their tormentors without risk. Two quite different styles of leadership and training are required for the combat and noncombat troops. Too often, the more easygoing styles find their way into the combat units. In peacetime, this is not very noticeable. In wartime, it is fatal.

3. Let Them Run Things

If you want to eliminate the possibility of your armed forces taking over your government, why not roll over and let them run the show? Usually, the troops notice that things are not going well, seize the initiative themselves, and simply take over. It's a common pattern in over a third of the world's nations, and is particularly true in small, poor nations where the military is one of the few well-organized and disciplined institutions. A similar pattern develops when the wealthier people in the nation simply put the troops on the payroll, which is common in several Latin American nations. Since these wealthy families are basically plundering the nation anyway, putting money into the pockets of officers and troops is a sound investment. Haiti is an extreme example of this. The result is, you find some members of these families looking after business affairs while others serve as officers in the military. Keeping it all in the family, so to speak. This technique rarely does much for military capability. The troops become little more than heavily armed enforcers for their paymasters. The bright side is that such nations rarely go picking fights with their neighbors. There is occasionally a revolutionary movement or two keeping the troops busy anyway. One of the many dark sides of this approach is that feuds among the soldiers, or their civilian paymasters, lead to bloody changes in government.

PRIORITY 2: KEEPING THE TROOPS BUSY

Better-organized nations keep the troops out of mischief by giving them something to do, anything except fighting. War is the last thing you want, as it is expensive and unpredictable, so more productive tasks are found. It's a common practice in many less wealthy nations for military units to run their own farms in order to provide some of their own food. China does this, and Russia assigns large numbers of soldiers each year to help out with the harvest. Many other countries use their troops for various civic-action programs, such as building roads, schools, hospitals, and clinics in impoverished areas. Turkey, for example, drafts more college graduates than it can use in its officer corps. Many of these university students would not make good officers, but it seems such a waste to use them as privates. So the college grads are given commissions and sent off to teach school in the impoverished provinces for a year or two, as a sort of uniformed, domestic Peace Corps. Nations with conscription regularly use variations on the Turkish approach. Even the United States had a program for conscripts possessing postgraduate science degrees, before the draft was eliminated in 1973. These talented young troops would not be given commissions, but were shipped off to research centers where they could put their technical training to use for two years, an approach that solved the problem of having a sizable number of young people not being called up, which created resentment and low morale among those who were conscripted. And in most nations, military personnel are also on call to lend a hand in the event of natural disasters.

Training for war is one way to keep the troops busy. One would think that this would be a primary activity in all armies, but actually, in many, if not most, nations it isn't. First of all, most troops are not in combat-related jobs, but in support positions. The support personnel move supplies, repair equipment, and push paper. Depending upon the nation in question, for every "fighting" soldier there are from three to six "supporting" soldiers. The case of the United States is one of the more extreme. In the U.S. armed forces the combat specialists are outnumbered by about 6.5 to 1 by the support troops. There are about 2,000 military occupational specialties for enlisted personnel in the U.S. army; and of these, 51 are legally closed to women because persons holding such assignments "will routinely engage in direct combat."

OCCUPATIONAL SPECIALTIES OF
U.S. ENLISTED PERSONNEL

Transportation & Materials Handlers	425,500 (23%)
Administrative Workers	296,000 (16%)
Combat Specialists	277,500 (15%)
Vehicle & Machine Repairers	220,000 (12%)
Electronic & Electrical Repairers	185,000 (10%)
Service Workers	148,000 (8%)
Engineering, Scientific, & Technical Workers	111,000 (6%)
Health Specialists	74,000 (4%)
Machinists & Precision Workers	55,500 (3%)
Construction Workers	18,500 (1%)
Media & Public-Relations Workers	18,500 (1%)
Human-Services Workers	9,250 (.5%)

Source: *Defense '88*, September/October 1988.

The combat specialists would be unable to perform their duties unless supported by the noncombat specialists. After all, the armed forces need drill instructors (each category supplies its own, consuming up to 5–10 percent of personnel), aviation mechanics ("Vehicle & Machine Repairers"), medics ("Health Specialists"), signal troops ("Electronic and Electrical Repairers"), and computer operators ("Administrative Workers") just as much as they need riflemen ("Combat Specialists"). The U.S. also has an exceptional number of "Transportation and Materials Handlers" because American troops must travel long distances to fight.

But keep in mind that the ultimate expression of combat power is the infantry platoon. Until your infantry occupy enemy territory, the war isn't over. There are only about 3,000 infantry platoons in the U.S. armed forces, and each infantry platoon is supported by, among other professionals, half a dozen media and public-relations specialists, many of whom are working for other branches than the infantry. Altogether, only about a seventh of the approximately 1,850,000 enlisted personnel in the U.S. armed forces are combat troops. However, more than half of all enlisted personnel, about 1,060,000 men and women (57.3 percent), are in the tactical and mobility forces. In wartime, these people would either be directly involved in inflicting harm upon an enemy or working directly in support of the other troops who do so, and will frequently find themselves serving under fire, and in a pinch sometimes as infantry as well: A medic is a "health specialist" not a "combat specialist," but serves in combat nonetheless. And in the event of mobilization, the number of "combat specialists" will initially grow a bit more rapidly than that of some of the other categories. However, because the U.S. armed forces have to "commute" to a war, as recently demonstrated in the Persian Gulf, the number of support personnel will always appear disproportionate to the number of combatants.

The supporting troops are theoretically present in sufficient numbers to sustain the fighting troops in a real war. In practice, wartime needs are usually underestimated and, as a bonus, the military budget can be kept down in peacetime by deliberately ignoring these support requirements. The expensive major weapons systems are considered more important. In any event, the support needs of peacetime operations are much less than wartime requirements. So there is not enough useful work for the support troops in peacetime, and too much for them in wartime. Like government workers everywhere, the peacetime support troops either invent tasks or simply find something else to do. It's not unusual for peacetime support troops to hold other jobs, which consume far more energy than their military tasks. The combat troops are in an even more ticklish situation. For the fighters to practice means large expenditures for fuel, spare parts, and ammunition. Such noisy activity also upsets local civilians, already concerned about the cost of all the matériel consumed in training. So the fighters spend a lot of time on guard duty, doing combat or marching drills on the parade ground, or doing not much of anything, but looking good while doing it. Largely idle, and most likely bored, combat troops are a common sight in less disciplined nations. The larger, and wealthier, nations can keep their combat troops employed in realistic training. But this is a luxury most nations forego. The only combat many peacetime troops see is against their own fellow citizens. Idle soldiers have, for centuries, been a ready means to keep unhappy citizens in line, or at least terrorized.

PRIORITY 3: KEEPING THE TROOPS EQUIPPED

Armed forces are more than just a lot of well-disciplined civil servants. At least to outsiders, the substance of a nation's armed forces is usually calculated according to equipment holdings. Tanks, aircraft, and warships can be seen and counted. All this hardware also encourages the troops, impresses the civilians, and heartens the politicians. The bad-news aspect of this is that much of the stuff may not be maintained very well and is thus not very reliable. The equipment is also expensive to operate, so a common method of reducing the military budget is simply to use equipment less, often a lot less. The troops don't mind so much, because it's a lot of work to keep the stuff operational, not to mention using it on a regular basis. The local politicians are not too upset about low readiness, as it makes effective interference by the troops less likely. But not much less likely, as your average coup only requires a few hundred infantry and some armored vehicles.

Should a hostile neighbor become restive, there is another problem in getting the ill-maintained gear up to snuff. This is very difficult, if not impossible. The spare parts for complex weapons are as difficult to obtain quickly as the weapons themselves, which is a nasty little deceit nearly every nation's soldiers play on themselves and the country they are preparing to defend.

In most Third World nations, there is a severe lack of technically trained personnel. Despite special low-tech weapons from Western manufacturers and simpler Russian equipment, there is still a lot of skill needed to keep tanks and jet aircraft operational. Ammunition is also a problem. Although shells are built to take a lot of battlefield abuse before firing, they can be dangerous if handled too haphazardly. A common practice is to keep the munitions safely locked up much of the time. Indeed, most munitions sent to many Third World nations are never used, but are lost due to accidents or merely degrades to uselessness. An example was seen during the Falklands War, when many Argentine aircraft bombs failed to explode. Most of them were decades old, and their explosive components had literally died of old age. A more extreme example is Libya, which has piled up billions of dollars' worth of weapons. The Libyans have few qualified troops who can use, much less maintain, all this stuff, and much of it is slowly decomposing in the desert. Libyan soldiers, like most of their peers worldwide, follow a highly structured daily routine. But, like soldiers everywhere, they are likely to be skilled at avoiding the more irksome tasks. It's not for nothing that one meaning of the word *soldiering* is as a synonym for avoiding work.

PRIORITY 4: KEEPING THE TROOPS PREPARED

This is the least likely use of troops. After keeping the soldiers happy, busy, and equipped, there may be no money or energy left for something as intangible as combat readiness. You would think that nations would put great emphasis on doing whatever is necessary to get their forces ready for combat, but there are several good reasons against it.

1. Most nations do not get their troops ready for combat, so why should you? Despite the official word on the importance of combat readiness, it's no secret that this is rarely achieved. If no one else does it, why should we? Nations take a close look at their neighbors and act accordingly. Few leaders are foolish enough to admit this, but one must be practical to survive.
2. It's very expensive to get troops fit for combat. It's particularly difficult when you're never really sure that you've done it right until there's a war. So why waste all that money in peacetime, just so long as your armed forces are doing better, or looking better, than those of your neighbors. While no nation spends more on uniforms than on weapons, some come closer than others. Parades are no idle exercise, as rulers have known for centuries: Get the troops looking sharp a few times a year and then march them past admiring (or frightened) citizens and foreign dignitaries. Make sure your obedient press presents these events in the best possible light. This is a case of the pen being mightier than the sword. And its a lot less expensive.
3. It's too tempting having troops who are combat ready in peacetime. This might lead to military adventurism. While invading a neighbor's country may succeed, it would definitely be costly. Thus unready troops are a double bargain: Less money need be spent to train them, and there will be less likelihood that they will get into some expensive altercation with a neighbor. Combat-ready troops are usually eager for combat, especially if they have never been in

combat. Their commanders are keen to see their lads kick some ass in action, although officers who have been shot at are much less eager to fight anyone. In small countries, a few of these hotshots, or the leader's confidants, mouthing off to the press are enough to get a war fever going. Even in larger nations, there is a feeling that if one does not use this combat capability from time to time, the troops will lose their edge. As many an American officer remarked during Vietnam and the Gulf War, "It's the only war we've got." Ambitious Russian officers were equally eager to get to Afghanistan to strut their stuff.

NATIONAL LIFESTYLES

The armed forces that a nation has are, to a great extent, the ones it deserves. Armies, navies, and air forces necessarily reflect the character of the societies that create them. As a result, the strengths and weaknesses of a military are very much the same as its society.

UNITED STATES

U.S. officers are almost all college graduates, most of whom have received their commissions through ROTC (Reserve Officers Training Corps, taken by students concurrently with their college studies). The rest are from the military academies and OCS (Officers Candidate School, for prior enlisted troops), plus a number of direct commissions for medical officers and other specialized personnel. In wartime, the majority will come from OCS (including non-ROTC college grads) plus a small number of battlefield commissions for exceptional enlisted personnel. In peacetime, most of the ROTC officers spend only a few years on active service before joining the reserves or National Guard (state militia). In wartime, these officers are called up with their units. The reserves and National Guard play a large role in U.S. military power, and there is something of a caste system between RA (Regular Army) and reserve commissions. Only military academy graduates and a few very distinguished ROTC officers receive RA commissions; the rest are technically reserve officers. Army Reserve officers may serve twenty or more years on active service, but will always be at a disadvantage to

RA officers in terms of promotions and choice assignments. The marines put reserve officers into reserve units if they don't qualify for a regular commission after three years of active service. So, while all officers are equal, regular officers are just more equal than the others.

Applying for a regular commission can be a difficult process if you have ever had any trouble, like offending a superior or getting a less than outstanding performance review. This system came about early in American history, when the state militias (National Guard) contained the bulk of the nation's combat power and provided most of the troops in wartime, either directly or by organizing volunteers, who were raised by individual states and communities: The smaller number of full-time troops answerable to the federal government wanted to distinguish themselves from the often ragtag militia units that answered to state governors in peacetime. With the enormous growth in peacetime forces after 1945, the system has got a bit muddled, and the designation RA has lost much of its former significance. Today, the state militias are much more integrated with the federal forces. In prior times, the militia had their own distinct uniforms, varying from state to state and even unit to unit. In fact, the old militia system was a descendant of an old British (and European) system whereby wealthy notables could raise a unit and appoint themselves its commander. This system operated during the Revolution and Civil War, but declined after 1865 as the states, and later the federal government, took more control. It's important to keep in mind that in peacetime the National Guard units are under the control of state governors, and the states get very touchy if the federal authorities interfere too much with their local armed forces. There is also a lot of local political influence in National Guard affairs, which varies greatly from state to state and even within states. This is a somewhat extraordinary situation, as few industrialized nations allow local politicians to control such large military forces.

The quality of U.S. military personnel is quite high, compared to the civilian labor pool for comparable personnel—that is, managers (officers) and workers (enlisted). Most enlisted troops—over 90 percent—are high school graduates. Indeed, enlisted-personnel standards are relatively higher than those for officers. That is, your average enlisted soldier is of much higher quality than the average civilian worker compared to the qualitative edge military officers have over civilian managers. One major difference between military and civilian organizations is that the average age of all troops is lower. After twenty years, military personnel are eligible for half-pay pensions. At that age, in your late thirties or early forties, you are still young enough for a second career. Most of the turnover in personnel occurs with the first-term enlistees, of whom only about half reenlist. After that, an increasing percentage reenlist every four or six years because they are getting closer to that twenty-year mark that makes them eligible for a pension.

The U.S. military has gone through several major changes in the past few generations. In the 1920s, it consisted of long-term volunteers. This was a small force, in the American tradition. The quality of the troops was low, another American tradition. Things started improving during the Great Depression in the 1930s, as many talented but unemployed men sought refuge in the military. At a time when strength was being reduced still further, higher recruiting standards could be enforced. This meant that the privates were pretty good. Conversely, most of the NCOs, originally recruited during the twenties, were of decidedly lower caliber compared with their subordinates, despite a number of World War I veterans: Most of the more able World War I vets had got out right after that war, when civilian economic prospects looked much better. World War II brought in some 12 million new people. While most of these were let go by 1946, a lot of those who remained were combat veterans. Then the Cold War came along in the late 1940s; conscription was restored and put a lot more people in uniform, just in time for Korea. The Korean vets provided the backbone of the armed forces right into Vietnam, which in turn produced another generation of combat veterans. Many of the Korean combat vets got out during or shortly after Vietnam, if they weren't killed off first. The Vietnam War was poorly run at the grunt level, and it was particularly hard on experienced NCOs. Nevertheless, from the late 1940s into the 1970s, the armed forces continued to have a large number of combat veterans, and a lot of conscripts.

When the draft was eliminated in 1973, two things began to happen. First, the combat veterans began to become scarce, either retiring or not reenlisting. Second, technology became more pervasive. Even the combat arms became infused with massive amounts of high-tech weapons and equipment. This had been going on for several decades, but now reached the point where tank crews, artillerymen, and infantry were spending a lot of time working with computers and other instruments built into their equipment. Fortunately, after a rocky start, the volunteer army allowed for an unprecedented upgrading in personnel quality. The Vietnam experience had soured many people on a military career, so the military was forced to retain a lot of low-quality people in order to maintain force levels. Through the late seventies, inept troops and officers were let go as higher-quality personnel became available to take their place. Unfortunately, a lot of good people voluntarily left in disgust at the same time, giving rise to the phrase "the Hollow Army."

The marines began their transformation in 1976 by raising recruit standards. By 1978, the improvements were very obvious. Through the 1980s, the military achieved personnel quality levels never before attained, whether in peace or war. Troop quality is higher than at any time in history, which is just as well because the weapons and equipment are more complex than any time previously. One result of this resurgence of the military as a career is that the United States now has a lot more officers and enlisted personnel who are serious about their profession, which may mark the beginning of a peacetime military tradition that the United States has lacked in the past.

The United States is one of those nations that does not hesitate to spend a lot of money on actually using all this expensive gear in peacetime. America also leads the world in the development of realistic simulators. This not only makes training less expensive, but allows the troops to do things with their "simulated" equipment that could get them killed or injured if they tried it in combat.

Unlike most other nations, the United States has also eliminated a lot of nonmilitary tasks from the troops' schedules. There is little KP (Kitchen Police, helping out with the cooking), and many housekeeping tasks, like cutting grass and painting buildings, are contracted out to civilians. More so than most nations, U.S. troops spend an enormous portion of their time actually preparing for combat. In addition, unlike the troops of some other powers, such as Russia, U.S. troops don't help with the harvest or grow vegetables. And where the average foreign conscript is in the service for two years or less, the average American soldier now serves for at least three times that. This improves the American training-to-duty ratio. A typical two-year conscript would spend a quarter or more of his service time learning the necessary skills. A U.S. soldier, in for over six years, can be trained to a higher degree and be on the job for nearly 90 percent of his service time. While most personnel in noncombat jobs go to work like any other civil-service worker, the combat troops spend most of their time training with their expensive, complex, and usually effective weapons and equipment.

The quality and quantity of training in U.S. combat units has increased significantly since the 1950s. The Vietnam experience gave American forces an undeserved reputation for ineptitude, but many troops in the bush did quite well overall, considering their flawed training and poor leadership. Indeed, going into the 1990s, U.S. forces are among the best-trained and best-equipped in the world, a formidable combination on the battlefield. There are still problems, the primary ones being some crucial weapons that don't work too well and leadership quality that is still uneven. While General Westmoreland took a lot of heat for his performance in Vietnam, officers stamped out of the same mold continue to proliferate throughout the armed forces. Nonetheless, the performance of U.S. forces in the Persian Gulf showed vast improvement over previous efforts. But then, you must remember the old military adage about victory going not to the best, but to the least inept.

RUSSIA

Russian officers are nearly all college graduates (some may have also attended special military high schools), and all but a few specialists come out of the large number of military colleges, similar to the four U.S. military academies. The remainder are college grads who receive their commissions through military training while in college. These are technical specialists of one sort or another, including doctors. Increasingly, officers come from families with several generations of service as officers: Currently about 55 percent of them are the sons of officers. This is another old Russian tradition that has survived the transition from czar to commissar. Officers are keenly aware that they are a separate caste with higher living standards than most other college-educated Russians.

The troops are a cross-section of Russian society, being largely conscripts. Nearly all nineteen-year-olds are called, except for the top few percent who are in college and the bottom 10–20 percent who are physically or mentally incapable of military service. About 8 percent of all potential conscripts are turned down for having been in trouble with the police (mostly juvenile delinquency, but some "political" crimes). College students, until recently, were taken, comprising about 5 percent of conscripts, and most of them went into NCO or technical jobs. In 1989, the new Russian legislature forced the military to release the college students from service. The military complained, reasonably enough, that the loss of these bright young lads would have a bad effect on combat readiness.

Most Russian recruits have had some "pre-military" training in secondary schools, so they are rather better prepared for military life than Western recruits, at least on paper. Recent reports in the Russian press indicate that this preparation can be woefully deficient, particularly among Asiatic recruits. This means that the regular units that receive these ill-prepared recruits must assign NCOs and officers to basic-training duties. Naturally, the quality of this impromptu training varies, and many conscripts never complete the psychological transition from civilian to soldier.

As the troops are in for only two years—three in some specialties—the pre-military training allows them to spend most of their service time learning useful military skills. At least that's the theory. In reality, they spend a lot of their time maintaining equipment. Most Russian divisions are not at full personnel strength, although all have full complements of weapons and equipment; and all this gear must be maintained. Most complex weapons and equipment cannot just be put into cold storage, not if you want to get it up and running in any reasonable length of time when a war is declared. Over a third of Russian divisions contain only 10 percent of their authorized personnel, mostly officers with a few enlisted personnel, and these troops devote a substantial amount of their time to keeping the equipment ready for combat. Throughout the 1980s, articles in the Russian military press severely criticized the low state of military training. What was particularly surprising was the accusation that the units most severely criticized were those that were given the most time and resources for combat training. These were the full-strength Russian divisions in Eastern Europe. It is taken for granted that troops in the understrength units back in the heartland might be ill trained. But the divisions in Eastern Europe are the best equipped in the Russian Army and get the most capable officers and recruits. This may say more about the shortage of capable manpower than anything else. When troops are conscripted, the best 20 percent are taken into the KGB/MVD security forces, the paratroopers, commandos (*Spetsnaz*), and the technical units of all services. The air force, navy, and rocket forces are particularly in need of competent manpower. A third of Russian combat divisions are at or near full strength, and these receive the best of the remaining troops, which means that the second-line divisions have a very high proportion of less able troops. Most of the conscripts from non-Russian parts of the country go into these units. One might conclude that running a second-line division is something of a nightmare for the officers unlucky enough to get assigned there. Not only are their troops less capable to begin with, but many of them don't even speak Russian.

No matter what the quality of the manpower, all Russian military units are driven by the officers' desire to achieve their "norms." "Norms" are a peculiarly Russian notion. The "norms" are standards of performance upon which a unit, and its officers, are measured. As the Russian officer corps is very much a career force, attention to norms supersedes everything else. To some extent, all armies have "norms" against which the performance of the troops is measured. But in the Russian Army this idea has a number of interesting side effects. Often the norms in force were developed decades in the past (largely during World War II) and have not been updated to account for subsequent developments in weapons, equipment, and tactics. The only constant has been that failure to achieve norms can still cripple an officer's career. The inspectors who monitor compliance are equally insistent on strict adherence to the norms, whatever they may be. Exceeding one's norms can also have pernicious effects, but that's another issue. The sociology of the Russian armed forces is such that officers have no real interest in the feelings or well-being of their troops. After all, the conscripts are gone in two years, and life has always been hard in the Russian Army. So the troops are driven relentlessly when things have to be done. As with the rest of Russian society, much time is spent in doing little. When the deadline for some important norm approaches, there is a flurry of activity. The Russians call this "Storming the Norm," and this haste to achieve the requirement results in the shoddy goods that Russian industry is noted for. This is one reason most Russian weapons and equipment are simple and robust by Western standards. Mindful of their own habits, Russians build their military gear to mesh with the attitudes and practices of their troops.

Although Russian peacetime routines are designed to get the most out of the lowest common denominator of troops, weapons, and equipment, the Russians do have exceptional units. This is no accident. They have several hundred thousand well-trained ground-combat troops, primarily in the airborne and commando forces. Although still mostly conscripts, these troops are largely volunteers for this type of duty. The officers are picked from the most able available, and all concerned are given additional material and laudatory benefits to encourage them. With less equipment to maintain and a strong sense of mission, these troops spend much of their time out in the field practicing for war. Unlike many of their peers, no harvest or permanent guard duty for these guys; they are groomed to fight and fight well. This was demonstrated in Afghanistan, where regular combat units were fairly useless compared to the airborne and commando units.

For the bulk of the troops in the armed forces, duty consists of dreary living conditions, made worse by the out-of-the-way location of military bases. Officers and career NCOs will usually spend their entire twenty or so years' service with the same unit in the same location. Most conscripts are sent off to their units within days of induction. They will stay with these units for their entire period of service. Although 10 to 20 percent will go to a technical course first, most training takes place at the unit level. While the official training schedule is extensive enough to take care of every waking hour, in practice many of the troops find ways to make free time for themselves. If the officers are inattentive enough, and many are, the troops get into mischief, such as stealing military equipment and bartering it to the locals for booze and better food. Parents who can afford it send their conscript sons money, to be spent on better food, and vodka. Some military equipment uses alcohol and this drinkable stuff has a tendency to disappear if not carefully monitored. Unlike the West, where "industrial" alcohol is made unfit for human consumption, the Russians know better and leave their stuff drinkable. The poor medical care in the military causes enough losses without more from denatured alcohol. Actually, the medical care is not much worse than in civil life, but the crowded, unsanitary conditions for most of the troops make for more disease. Note also that dental work consists largely of extractions, without painkillers.

The Red Army is a rough outfit to belong to, and the Russians rightly depend on this to make it a tough organization in wartime. The increasing number of non-Russian troops in the armed forces is taking some of the edge off the traditional durability of the army. The security forces take few non-Russians, and the several air forces—Tactical, Air Defense, and Strategic—and the navy not many more, leaving most of the Asiatics and other minority groups to the ground forces. This makes the daily routine in the army even more uncomfortable. Most of the officers—94 percent—are Russian, Ukrainian, or Byelorussian, and have little to do, or in common with, their non-Russian troops, who in turn are taught a basic vocabulary of Russian military commands, but otherwise keep to themselves in small groups that speak the same language. This unpleasant lifestyle for the troops causes the officers to distance themselves as much as possible from them. Indeed, continuing a long Russian tradition, the troops are usually treated as very inferior beings by their officers. Morale suffers, and perhaps military performance as well. Nor, despite Afghanistan, have the Russians had many combat veterans around since the late 1940s to help keep things honest.

Following World War II, a unique lifestyle in Russian military history has developed. Until 1945, Russia had never experienced an extended period of peace and short-term conscription. Until the late 1800s, only a fraction of those eligible were conscripted, and they were taken in for over twenty years. Between World Wars I and II, there was short-term conscription, but the social conditions were hardly peaceful. After 1945, there was peace, and three things changed. First, the conscripts were better educated than at any other time in Russian history. Literacy came late to Russia, with universal literacy not being achieved until well after World War I. Second, the NCO corps declined to insignificance in the decades after 1945. In Western armies, NCOs (Noncommissioned Officers) are the foremen and supervisors. Western nations have learned over the centuries that good NCOs are needed to train the troops and keep order and discipline in the ranks. Officers are managers and leaders, a caste apart. During the pre-World War I period of twenty-year Russian conscripts, it was easy to promote the most able troops to NCO rank because they were stuck for the duration and NCOs had better pay and living conditions. During the period of war and revolution from 1914 to 1945, it was also easy to identify and select able NCOs because living conditions were better in the military. But after 1945, the harsh conditions of military service discouraged enlisted troops from voluntarily staying in uniform to build a veteran NCO corps. In theory, Russian units have as many NCOs as Western ones. But the Russian NCOs are conscripts selected upon induction for a few months' NCO training. After that, they are sent to units where they are caught between their conscript peers and their officers, who consider the young sergeants no more than glorified privates.

While a considerable number of troops, in excess of a half-million, passed through Afghanistan, most immediately went back into civilian life when their tour of duty was over. The few who remained in the service, mostly officers, were insufficient to influence a force that numbers nearly 5 million.

CHINA

The military in China have a complex history. There were no modern armed forces, in the Western sense, until after World War II. China's old feudal system of government, and equally feudal military, came apart in revolution and civil disorder early in this century. The 1920s were filled with civil war, and the 1930s saw more of the same plus resistance to the encroaching Japanese. The Chinese forces involved were basically private armies led by a number of warlords. German, Russian, Italian, and American advisers were brought in by various factions to upgrade the troops, but these efforts met with limited success until the Communists finally defeated all the other factions in 1949 and gained control of the entire nation. At that point, the millions of Communist troops were still part guerrillas and part regulars. The Korean War (1950–53) was the first time the Chinese came up against Western forces in a major war. The Chinese did not do so well, except initially, and eventually suffered over a million casualties in the process. They did fight the better-equipped UN forces to a standstill and demonstrated a willingness to substitute troop casualties for material shortcomings.

After Korea, strenuous efforts were made to rebuild the Chinese forces on the Russian model, with the help of Russian advisers and equipment. But in the early 1960s, there was a diplomatic break with Russia, and all Russian aid was withdrawn. Then came the Cultural Revolution of the late sixties, and early seventies, which paralleled an attempt to recast the armed forces into a gigantic guerrilla force, with dire consequences for those who raised objections. If you had been a Chinese soldier in those years, this would have been somewhat confusing. When things finally settled down in the late 1970s, the Chinese realized that they had the largest army in the world, but one armed mostly with 1950s technology and trained to fight the warlords who had disappeared three decades earlier. Meanwhile the tensions with Russia from the late 1950s through the Cultural Revolution and into the late seventies had resulted in the appearance of nearly fifty lavishly equipped Russian divisions on China's northern borders. Firefights between Russian and Chinese border troops brought the tensions to a fever pitch in 1969. The Chinese knew that they were outclassed by the Russians, who had all sorts of modern technology. Still, it was a bit traumatic to discover that their troops could not cope with much less well equipped, but veteran, Vietnamese troops during a number of border battles in the late seventies.

By 1980, China found itself surrounded by enemies and its ill-equipped armed forces possibly not up to the task of defending the nation. Among its other problems, the armed forces were fairly isolated from society, which in an earlier day had been deliberate, in order to prevent the troops from being contaminated by confusing them and compromising their loyalty. The troops were mostly volunteers, plus conscripts, and until the economic surge of the 1980s, those accepted for service were among the best people available. Life in the military was secure and involved a lot more than weapons and maneuvers. The armed forces, particularly the army, ran their own farms and factories that employed the troops part time. Despite several reorganizations, the forces were under the control of commanders who presided over their own private empires. The government allowed this, and prevented military cooperation with local government and Communist party officials in order to maintain a system of checks and balances. The navy and air force spent more time on military matters, if only because their more complex equipment required more attention. During the 1980s, attempts were made to professionalize the forces. Strength was cut by nearly 50 percent, and many of the nonmilitary operations were shut down. Even with these cuts, it was difficult to attract high-quality volunteers, for the economy began to boom. Better economic opportunities not only siphoned off better people, they also cut the military budget. The dramatic results with economic reform made investment in the civil sector a much more attractive prospect. Although new equipment was built locally or bought overseas, the arms budget was cut continually through the 1980s. Entering the 1990s, the Chinese armed forces are smaller, more professional, better equipped, and not certain that they have achieved any gains in military capability. The troops are spending more time on military affairs, but uncertainty among officers and the civilian leadership makes the armed forces a potentially volatile place to be, particularly given apparent strains between the political and military leaderships, and among the military leaders themselves.

BRITAIN

It has been nearly a thousand years since Britons last lost a foreign war on their own island. This achievement is no accident. Historically, nations become nations through the existence of a professional military force and maintain their independence by means of military force. Britain has been quite successful at this, and has done so through a combination of tradition and innovation. Being able to unify these two contradictory elements has been the key factor in its success. For all their apparent stiffness, the British take a very no-nonsense attitude toward warfare and the military, and have been responsible for many innovations. Compared with other major nations, their armed forces have been small, and this has created an intimacy and familiarity that result in a valuable sense of unity. Moreover, the British carefully nurture the local character of their military units. Most army combat units are recruited from particular localities, and this adds to their cohesion and enthusiasm. No one wants to do a bad job in front of the neighbors. They pay close attention to drills, as do most armies, but manage to be more consistent at it. They take good care of their equipment, a habit many other armed forces are apt to avoid. The military is ordinarily well respected and attracts relatively well-qualified officers and troops. In the past two centuries, Britons have been in the forefront of military innovation and have benefited from the wisdom of experience. After suffering embarrassing defeats, as in the American Revolution, the Crimean War, the Zulu War, the Boer War, and World War I, they have not hesitated to borrow good ideas from others. While management/labor relations are commonly quite bad in the civil sector, the military is quite efficient. The combat troops train hard and long, and the service troops deliver a level of support that is the envy of many other nations.

ISRAEL

The armed forces of Israel are unique. Only Switzerland and Sweden have anything similar. The regular armed forces are quite small, and most of the manpower is supplied by reservists who are called up for a month or more each year to provide troops as needed. Most men, and many women, remain in the reserves for decades. It's common to have tank crews that have been together for over a dozen years. This continuity provides combat troops who are the most capable in the world. The only similar forces in size and capability are those in the U.S. National Guard, where troops also remain in the same units for decades. The Israelis have an additional incentive to prepare for combat: They are never very far, in time or space, from a real war. This adds an edge to their training and preparation that is difficult to duplicate in any country not similarly threatened. Because the "regulars" are very much a minority at all levels, and because of the pervasive wartime environment, there are fewer of the bad habits that professional armed forces are prone to develop. The Israeli armed forces are very straightforward and efficient in their day-to-day operations. The biggest casualty of the 1987–91 Arab uprising in Israel has been the training time lost because reservists had to be called out for crowd control. This extra duty has also cost Israel some $500,000 a day, which prevents spending on purely military items. Yet it was this very system that enabled Israel to deploy so many trained (if not in riot control) troops to deal with the civil disorder within its Arab population. While the riot duty caused considerable loss in training time, it did not appreciably lower the readiness and skill level of the nearly half-million Israeli troops. The regulars continue to man most air-force and navy units while keeping the training and equipment-maintenance programs going for the reservist ground troops, who comprise the bulk of Israel's armed forces. The reservists continue to come in for their annual training, and because Israel is so small, many reservists commute from their homes to the training bases. For many Israelis, it's much like a second job, albeit an onerous and dangerous one.

As can be seen, the military patterns of different nations can vary considerably. Most nations have a unique military culture, whether their armed forces are efficient or not. To be sure, some recently independent countries do not have uniqueness in their armed forces. Usually, the armed forces of new nations reflect the model of the former colonial power, though in a few cases a deliberate political decision has been made to adopt a different model. As they evolve, the armed forces of these nations will develop their own "style." As in the case of older nations, this style may be good or bad. any only the test of war can demonstrate the difference.

COMPARABLE OCCUPATIONAL COMPENSATION FOR MILITARY, GOVERNMENT, AND CIVILIAN EMPLOYEES

Most military jobs have equivalents in the civilian sector.

CIVILIAN OCCUPATION	MILITARY SKILL LEVEL	MILITARY BASIC CAREER	GOVT	CIVIL	ADVANTAGE
Academic Professor	Mid/0-3 (Capt)	28.2 35.8	33.0	34.5	3.8%
Air Traffic Controller	Senior/E-6 (SSgt)	18.0 22.9	34.0		−32.7%
Aircraft Mechanic	Mid/E-5 (Sgt)	14.1 17.9	33.3	41.6	−57.0%
Auto Mechanic	Mid/E-4 (Spc)	12.5 15.9	23.7	24.6	−35.5%
Civil Engineer	High/0-5 (LtC)	40.1 50.9	45.0	56.1	−9.2%
Clerk/Typist	Entry/E-3 (PFC)	9.5 12.1	12.2	15.0	−19.6%
Command Sergeant Major	Senior/E-9 (SgtM)	33.4 42.4			
Computer Operator	Mid/E-6 (SSgt)	18.0 22.9	17.2	21.0	8.9%
Electrician	Mid/E-5 (Sgt)	14.1 17.9	24.3	28.0	−36.0%
Infantryman	Entry/E-3 (PFC)	9.5 12.1			
Lawyer	Upper/0-4 (Maj)	32.4 41.1	43.9	59.1	−30.4%
Meatcutter	Mid/E-4 (Spc)	12.5 15.9	21.5	25.0	−36.5%
Nurse (RN)	Mid/0-2 (1Lt)	24.1 30.6	24.6	27.0	13.4%
Paramedic	Mid/E-4 (Spc)	12.5 15.9	18.0		−11.7%
Photographer	Mid/E-5 (Sgt)	14.1 17.9	22.1	26.0	−31.1%
Physician (MD)	Senior/0-5 (LtC)	40.1 50.9	56.0	78.9	−35.5%
Plumber	Senior/E-5 (Sgt)	16.6 21.1	22.8	27.8	−24.2%
Police Officer	Entry/E-3 (PFC)	9.5 12.1	23.1		−47.7%

BASIC CAREER ANNUAL SALARY ($THOUSANDS)

Sources: Bureau of Labor Statistics; Army Regulation 611-201

GETTING PAID

In general, government employees are paid less than persons doing the same job in the civilian sector. Government jobs are still seen as attractive because there is much less chance of losing one, even for poor performance. For military personnel, the pay difference is even greater than that for civilian employees of the government. The data on this table must be understood to be approximate only, as it is difficult to compare differences in the way the military, the government, and the civilian sectors compensate their employees. Although all types of statistics are passed off as authoritative, those dealing with employee compensation are extremely imprecise: They usually omit medical coverage, pension funds, and other "fringe benefits," such as employee discounts and bonuses. In the case of military personnel, for example, room and board, extensive medical coverage, PX privileges, moving allowances, and the like are fringe benefits most civilian workers do not receive. On the downside, military personnel, particularly those in combat units, must make unexpected trips to the wilderness for field training exercises, and must live with the constant threat of real combat. Those who make the military a career—"Lifers"—come off better if you count the pension and retirement benefits that Uncle Sam pays. Rolling all these benefits in, professional military personnel are compensated at levels about 27 percent higher than their announced salaries. Noncombat personnel also do rather well in this regard. As a result, ill-educated minority youths have found the military a good way to get a leg up on life. Contrary to the popular perception, black males are underrepresented in combat units. Most of the black youths who pass the U.S. Army's stringent enlistment standards opt for jobs requiring technical training that will increase their civilian employment opportunities. Moreover, one of the prepublication readers of this volume, an army captain teaching at West Point, noted that the chart demonstrated that in his present assignment he was better off economically than he thought. Unfortunately, when he goes back to being an infantryman, this will change: On the basis of compensation for hours worked, combat personnel are far behind their government or civilian counterparts, even if all fringe benefits are included.

The table is fairly self-explanatory. Figures are in thousands of 1987–88 dollars. Those for military compensation are based on standard pay rates for personnel, including seniority differences in some instances, but excluding special allowances. Government compensation figures are based on Federal employment, except in the cases of Academic Professors, which are based on state university compensation, and Police Officers and Paramedics, which are based on compensation in major cities. Civilian-sector figures are derived from Bureau of Labor Statistics data. Where no figure is shown, there is no comparable occupation in that sector. "Occupation" is the type of job being performed. "Skill Level" is divided into "Entry," "Mid," "Upper," and "Senior," to represent gradations from novice to master, with the military equivalent given on the basis of

"E" for enlisted and "O" for officer grades, followed by the comparable army title in parentheses. "Military" shows standard pay at the indicated grade and prescribed seniority levels: "Basic" refers to compensation without fringe benefits, and "Career" includes the 27 percent "Lifer's bonus." "Govt" and "Civil" show Government and Civilian compensation for the same skill level. "Military Advantage" shows career military compensation in terms of the percentage by which it is greater (+) or less than (−) that for civilians performing the same tasks, except in the case of those trades for which there is no civilian-sector equivalent, and where the government-sector figure is used. There are no occupations in civilian or government employment for Command Sergeant Major or Infantryman. Note also that the "fringe benefits" enjoyed by civilian employees have not been included in these calculations, which would lower the "Military Advantage" in all cases.

As can be seen, while in "blue collar" occupations there is not much to choose from between government and civilian-sector employment, in most "white collar" and professional occupations government compensation tends to fall well behind civilian. Moreover, even including "fringe benefits," military personnel fall considerably below comparable civilian personnel performing the same duties in virtually all categories.

Some notion of the seriousness of the difference between military and civilian compensation may be gained by noting that the average salary of all personnel in the armed forces is only about $20,300, which is just about the same as the $20,850 that is the average wage for persons employed in the United States. The average income for all civilian government employees with a dozen years on the job is about $30,000. Enlisted personnel earn an average of only about $17,100 a year, just about per capita income, while warrant officers make about $30,600, and commissioned officers $36,800. This is one reason why the armed forces offer reenlistment bonuses, of as much as $20,000 a year in the case of certain medical specialists. Even these sums do not do more than bring the income of military personnel a little more closely into line with that of civilians.

Those troops who make the service a career will retire between grades E-6 and E-9 if enlisted and O-5 or above if an officer. This makes the situation a bit more favorable, but only if you are willing to accept lower income (relative to civilian employment) until you reach higher rank. This also explains why so many troops, after their first term of enlistment, leave to get a higher-paying civilian job with their newly acquired skills. This opportunity is used to induce young people to enlist in the first place. And there are also the "occupational hazards" to which military personnel are apt to be subject. Nonetheless, do not underestimate the patriotism, unit pride, and sense of service among military personnel, particularly those in the combat arms.

Officers and
Gentlemen: The
Implied Experts

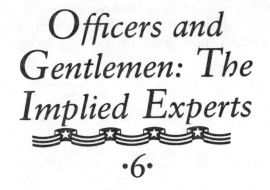

•6•

*H*ow do the officers shape the military? What types of officers are common in armed forces? How can we tell who will be a successful commander in wartime? What methods of selection, training, and management of officers are best?

Also, who are the most competent experts on the capabilities of military power? Some would say it is the soldiers themselves, particularly the officers. But consider the complexity of modern military organizations, and the hundreds of different areas of specialization. Does a competent infantry officer have a real understanding of the overall capabilities of the military forces of his nation? What about the successful commander of an aircraft carrier or nuclear submarine? The leader of a fighter squadron? All of these people may be expert at their specialties, but the sum of military power is a combination of their knowledge, and more. In the military, you start out in one speciality and frequently stay there. Even most of those who rise to high rank do so on the basis of their skills in their one particular area. Those who become the commanding officers of an army, navy, or air force are usually expert in one aspect of their own service's specialties and have considerably less understanding of the other specialties. And they are even less knowledgeable about the abilities and limitations of the other services.

These senior commanders must rely on the advice of others, who are in turn taking advice from still more junior specialists. This is not an unusual situation in any large organization. But the military has a problem peculiar to itself in that most officers have never had a chance to actually *do* what they were trained for, and gain practical experience. Despite the impression you might receive from the media, only a few percent of the world's hundred million troops are involved with combat at any given time. Even Afghanistan did not add a lot of combat experience to the Russian armed forces. Ten years of fighting there involved only a few hundred thousand troops in actual combat. And most of those were conscripts who were all too eager to finish their two years, get out of uniform, and forget the whole thing. The hundred thousand officers and career NCOs who served, whether they saw combat or not, will make good use of their exposure to "the real thing" throughout their careers. But in the Russian armed forces the experts who wield the most clout are those who study the history of combat. Afghanistan is perceived as but a small part of this history, with World War II still seen as the principal source of experience and wisdom. The Arab-Israeli wars and the Gulf War will continue to carry more weight than the experience in Afghanistan fighting "bandits," because those wars were conventional conflicts in the style, if not the scale, of a world war.

The Russian attitude is shared by most other major military powers, with the exception of the United States. In the United States, there has been a vacuum of expertise in military history. This was not always the case. As recently as World War II, historical studies were still the premier source of combat experience, and several of the officers who rose to high rank—George C. Marshall, Dwight D. Eisenhower, George S. Patton—were themselves well versed in military history, as was President Franklin D. Roosevelt. But during and after World

War II, the Operations Research (OR) crowd demonstrated the usefulness of their skills. Since OR proved immensely valuable in solving some problems for which there was little or no historical precedent, such as the proper way to hunt submarines or to select targets for strategic bombardment, OR soon largely displaced historical study as a source of ideas, experience, and inspiration. This was not the case in most other nations that used OR. But in America it was not until the 1980s that historical analysis began to make a comeback. Meanwhile the failure of OR to handle the complexity of warfare as a whole created a serious problem, witness Vietnam. As history provided a basis for peeking at the future of warfare, the renunciation of history left U.S. military planners blind. The analysis of the future provided by the OR community left senior commanders planning in the dark. This state of affairs did not bother most officers. Many were not even aware of the situation.

The reasons for this situation are not unusual. The armed forces are highly regimented and disciplined organizations. Questioning authority, or anything else, is not encouraged. But there is another, more pedestrian reason for this passive attitude. Put simply, by the latter part of the twentieth century, the military has become very much just another civil-service job. In this century, the ratio of noncombat to combat troops has tended to go beyond one to one. In the past, nonfighters in the combat forces were a minority, and often a very small one at that. The accompanying table gives some idea of the extent to which this phenomenon has affected the U.S. Army, which has probably gone furthest down this road.

PROPORTIONS OF COMBAT AND NONCOMBAT TROOPS IN
U.S. FORCES

PERIOD	YEAR	COMBATANTS	NONCOMBATANTS
World War I	1914	87%	13%
	1918	66	34
World War II	1939	88	12
	1945	57	43
Korea	1950	67	33
	1953	60	40
Vietnam	1964	75	25
	1972	53	47
Present	1990	57	43

In this table, "Combat Troops" refers to personnel who normally serve under fire in the performance of their duties. Note that during each of these four wars the proportion of combatants to noncombatants declined markedly. Although the noncombat "troops" are necessary to help the combat troops sustain the fight, as they became the majority, a certain change in attitude has taken place. Few people in or out of the military like to admit it, but the "profession of arms" has become just another job to most of the troops. One result of this has been to reduce the prestige of the combat troops. Indeed, so numerous have the "swivel chair hussars" become that some thirty years ago the U.S. Army introduced a special insignia, "Combat Leadership Tabs," to indicate people who actually were qualified to hold combat command, so one could tell the fighting soldiers from the administrative ones. There has not been sufficient recognition for the fighters, as frequent articles in military journals indicate. In wartime, the situation breeds resentment and hostility by the front-line troops, who must endure the terror, pain, and squalor of combat, toward the rear-area troops who live a comparatively quiet, comfortable life. In an effort to keep the support troops more attuned to the concerns of the combat troops, the ground component of the Canadian armed forces now requires all troops involved in specialty training to spend at least one night alone out in the woods, while the U.S. Marines insist that all noninfantry marines keep up their ground-combat skills. How effective this approach will be can only be determined in wartime, but at least it shows an awareness of the problem.

The vast majority of the senior officers in the world's armed forces have never experienced combat. Many of them have spent their entire careers struggling with problems not much different from those faced by people in civilian management jobs. While combat experience, or at least service in a combat unit, is still considered desirable for senior command, even this attitude is slowly eroding. Successfully negotiating the management perils of peacetime military organizations calls for a particular set of skills. These are not always the same skills that provide competent leadership in combat. History is full of sad tales of civilians attempting to lead combat forces in wartime. And increasingly, the fine-looking fellow in the splendid uniform is not a soldier—he's simply a fine-looking fellow in a splendid uniform.

An additional problem is that not only is an increasing proportion of the officer corps noncombatants, but the overall proportion of the officers in the armed forces is rising. Consider flag officers (generals and admirals) in the U.S. armed forces. On VE-Day, the end of World War II in Europe, the U.S. armed forces had about 11,950,000 people on active duty, of whom about 2,220 were generals or admirals, a ratio of about one flag officer to every 5,380 other persons in the service. In 1991, the combined number of personnel in the U.S. armed forces, including the reserves, the National Guard, and the Coast Guard, was about 5,550,000, of whom about 1,665 were generals or admirals, a ratio of about one flag officer to every 3,333 others. So upon mobilization, the armed forces in 1991 would have had about 46 percent of their strength on VE-Day, but fully 75 percent of the flag officers, which suggests a certain amount of inflation. These figures can be examined in another way, in terms of the change in the proportion of flag officers to the principal combat units that they supervise.

RELATIVE GROWTH IN NUMBERS OF FLAG OFFICERS

	1945	1991
Army: Generals per Division	14	27
Navy: Combat Ships per Admiral	1.8	1.4
Combat Tonnage per Admiral	7,867	11,083
Aircraft/SLBMs per Admiral	53	27
USMC: Generals per Division	13	20
USAF: Aircraft/ICBMs per General	244	17

These figures assume mobilization of all reserve components and the Coast Guard, elements that are almost always omitted in comparisons between the armed forces of 1945 and those of the present. As can be seen, there has been an increase in the proportion of generals and admirals with regard to the forces that they command. Now there really aren't all that many more flag officers actually commanding the troops: A 1991 division had the same number of generals as did a 1945 one. However, the servicewide number of flag officers has increased markedly. There are a number of factors at work here. For example, the central command structure of the armed forces, what is now the Joint Chiefs of Staff, remains essentially what it was in 1945. In addition, the air force was then still part of the army and thus had no administrative tail, while today it provides its own supply, medical, financial, and other administrative services. The increase in technology and the nature of war has also played an important role in raising the numbers of flag officers. There was no space program in 1945, no electronic or satellite reconnaissance, no computerized data processing, and few flag officers served as project managers or military attachés. In addition, today there are proportionally far more aircraft in the armed forces than in 1945: The army, for example, has some 9,000 aircraft, mostly helicopters, whereas in 1945 all flying machines were in the then–army air forces. While the air force and the navy, in addition to aircraft and ballistic missiles, also have hundreds of cruise missiles. One of the key indicators of the technological change is the "Combat Tonnage per Admiral" figure. This suggests the greater size and complexity of modern warships, and their increasing automation: A World War II destroyer ran no more than about 2,500 tons and had 350–400 men in its crew, while its far more capable modern descendant runs 5,000 tons with a complement of about 300. Changes in the way the armed forces are organized and administered also account for some of the increase. A number of flag officers serve in billets that either did not exist in 1945, or required far fewer personnel, such as the CIA, the Department of Energy, the DIA, the National Security Council, the National Defense University, the State Department, various combined staffs, the several historical centers, and so on. Finally, some of the excess is necessary as a contingency in the event of mobilization, though in realistic terms the United States would require a minimum of two years to even begin building armed forces on the scale of those of World War II: The chief stumbling block lies not in securing people for service but in the difficulty of increasing the output of equipment. This pomposity of generals and admirals may seem excessive, but in fact is not nearly as numerous as the numbers maintained by certain other powers, such as Britain, where the ratio of flag officers to others is one to 537. In general, the smaller the armed forces, the higher the proportion of flag officers: At the end of the Civil War, the

Union Army totaled over a million men on paper, with about one general for every 2,500 others, while the Confederate Army had about 400,000 men, with a ratio of 1 to 1,500, and during the Waterloo Campaign of 1815 Napoleon had about 1 general for every 750 of his 123,000 men.

Comparisons to similar developments in civilian management ranks after 1945 are difficult. The government does keep track of the composition of the civilian labor force. In these statistics, there is a category for "Managers and Administrators" (M&As), the civilian equivalent of military officers. The worker to M&A ratio has gone from over ten to one at the end of World War II to about eight to one in 1990. At the moment, U.S. industry is in the midst of an enormous purge of its management ranks, so the ratio may go back up to 1945 levels. The ratio in the U.S. military was about ten to one in 1945 and is nearly seven to one now. In Russia it's five to one, but many Russian units are skeletal, with a disproportionate number of officers.

There is no similar statistic for civilian "generals," as numbers on senior ("General Grade") civilian managers are not compiled. We might note that recent moves to make the management of civilian firms more competitive with foreign, especially Japanese, firms have consisted of sharp reductions in M&A ranks. A similar movement has not been noted in the military, perhaps due to a perceived lack of competition from the Japanese.

Now the reason all these people hold commissions as officers is because they are presumed to be ready to lead in war. But it is commonly accepted, even in the most efficient armies, that some peacetime officers will prove inadequate in combat. The assumption is that only a few officers will be found wanting when the test comes: The reality is far more serious. At times, the failure rate reaches catastrophic proportions, as in the French Army in the opening phases of both world wars and in the U.S. Army in Korea. No one has ever been able to develop peacetime training techniques that can predict with reasonable precision how successful an officer will be in combat. We can't even be certain that our training methods are culling the obvious incompetents from those who may be successful. For example, we traditionally lavish considerable attention on those graduating with honors from the military academies. During the

Civil War, about a third of the generals on each side were graduates of West Point. Yet only about 16 percent (35 of 217) of Union West Point generals and only about 13 percent (18 of 139) of Confederate West Point generals ranked academically among the top five members of their classes, which ran to 33–55 graduates. And of these fifty-three men, only one achieved unquestioned distinction, the Confederacy's Robert E. Lee (second in his class). Among his academic peers, we can count several officers lacking in intestinal fortitude or battlefield skill, such as the Union's George B. McClellan (second) and Henry Halleck (third), and the Confederacy's Braxton Bragg (fifth), while some of the most successful generals in the war were hardly notable for their academic record. Though the Union's William Tecumseh Sherman did rank sixth in his class, George H. Thomas was twelfth, Ulysses S. Grant was twenty-first, and Philip Sheridan thirty-fourth (after doing so poorly he needed five years to graduate), while the Confederacy's Thomas "Stonewall" Jackson was seventeenth and James Longstreet fifty-first, only six from the bottom. Moreover, about a dozen men who had washed out of West Point eventually became generals. Though admittedly none attained great distinction, all were good tactical officers, such as the Confederacy's Lewis Armistead. So academic credentials do not necessarily a general make: In 1819, the director of the Danish military academy remarked "That fellow will never make a soldier," with regard to the unimpressive intellectual and professional development of Cadet Helmuth von Moltke, who led the Prussian Army in the spectacular series of victorious wars in 1864–71 that resulted in the unification of Germany. Currently, the United States and Russian military academies seem to be nurturing more future McClellans, Westmorelands, and Sukhomlinovs, rather than Grants, Stonewall Jacksons, or Georgi Zhukovs, or Moltkes. This is the dark side of military tradition.

Historically, not even military service has been a prerequisite for distinction as a commander. In the Civil War, about a third of the generals on both sides had absolutely no prior military credentials, and yet several of them became quite competent field commanders. The most notable of these men were the Union's James S. Wadsworth and the Confederacy's Nathan Bedford Forrest and Wade Hampton, all of whom were wealthy landowners and businessmen before the war, as was

Oliver Cromwell before the English Civil War. By the early twentieth century, advances in military technology made it less likely that an amateur could become a successful general. Still, Lawrence of Arabia was such a successful amateur, as was Manuel Tagueña, a twenty-three-year-old physicist with no prior military experience who, on the outbreak of the Spanish Civil War in 1936, volunteered for service with the Republic and within two years was turning in a credible performance commanding a corps, later going on to serve with distinction in the Red Army during World War II. Actually, it was quite common for civilians to achieve high rank in World War II, although not usually as generals. The Russians, Americans, and Australians in particular had many successful battalion and regimental commanders who had been civilians when the war started. Technology has made enormous strides since then, but it is a point worth meditating upon.

Successful wartime leaders have personality characteristics that make them less suitable for peacetime leadership. A good wartime military leader is impatient and ruthless, and frequently is a nonconformist as well. A good peacetime military leader is more of a manager and diplomat, and most definitely a team player. In peacetime, the people who don't quite fit in are likely to have very pedestrian careers: Of the seven most successful Civil War generals (Lee, Longstreet, Jackson, Grant, Sherman, Thomas, and Sheridan), three (Grant, Sherman, and Jackson) were civilians when the war broke out, either because opportunities were better or because they couldn't make it in a peacetime army. Peacetime officers don't have an armed opponent threatening their very lives, but they do have political and military superiors who can terminate their careers with a casual remark. The junior officers take their cues from their seniors. Although the lower-ranking officers have a more civil-service attitude, they must prepare themselves for the more political attitudes of the high command. So when war comes, there is a severe case of culture shock: The senior commanders, removed from the actual fighting, cling to their peacetime ways, while the junior officers facing the realities of the battlefield are in a new world. The result is a painful, and costly, learning process. With war, it is not unusual for a significant proportion of a nation's generals to be found wanting: In the major wars of this century, about a third of division commanders have had to be fired for incompetence within ninety days of entering combat, and this is one reason why the generals and admirals who are leading a nation's forces at the end of a war are ordinarily not the same lot who commanded them at the onset. Vietnam was an exception, primarily because no one wanted to admit it was a war or that the United States was losing it. But then, this was the primary reason why so many citizens opposed the entire affair. The voters expressed their displeasure by putting the military on short rations (low budgets) for nearly a decade.

Armed forces are frequently incapable of dealing with the shock of combat for several reasons. Some problems are peculiar to a particular nation while others are universal. These include normally serious problems in selecting and training leaders. Most nations have flawed national memories of what war is all about. A recollection of the harsher realities of warfare is not something that is carefully maintained in the national memory. The "glory" is favored over the less appealing aspects. This is human nature, or good taste, depending on your point of view. Officers and troops join up for more pragmatic reasons than glory or participating in a war. It's a job, generally a pretty good one. It's civil service, so there's a certain amount of security. If it's one of the many nations where the military is a major political force, a uniformed position is about the most secure employment you can get. All you really need is a willingness to terrorize your fellow citizens when the need arises, and the work is customarily neither very difficult, nor very hard, nor very dangerous. Again, this circumstance is more likely in those nations where the people serve the military and not the other way around. Policing the population does not require a lot of skill, training, or effort. Nations that subordinate the military to civilian leadership tend to work the troops harder. But even there, numerous ways exist to take it easy. It's not for nothing that generations of civilians have come to regard "soldiering" as "avoiding work." The result of all this is that ordinarily it is difficult to recruit effective combat soldiers into a peacetime army. Even if you get good candidates, rigorous training schedules are hard to maintain. After all, you go through all that constant training and rarely get to see it pay off in actual combat. This is a paradoxical situation that has existed since the beginning of professional armies. In wartime, many of these problems disappear. But then it's not a matter of which side is better, but which is worse, and the lackadaisical armed forces outnumber the diligent ones. Of over 160 armed forces in the world, only about a third can be said to have any real combat skill.

One of the more subtle problems of selecting effective officers is the aura and symbolism surrounding the rank structure in the military. The officers and troops can be seen as analogous to management and labor. But it goes beyond that. Being an officer is being something very special in many nations. The modern rank structure of the military, unlike similar civilian hierarchies, developed out the feudal system, with its notions of nobility and obligations to a monarch. This gives officers a moderately more glamorous image than their civilian counterparts. Moreover, officers tend to have more power over their subordinates. There is a separate set of laws for the military that establishes more draconian punishments for subordinates than exist in civilian organizations.

While there are a great many national and cultural variations, we can boil most officers down to three types: Younger Sons, Ummpies, and the Armed Hustlers. It is possible for an officer to partake of some of the characteristics of two, or even all three, of the basic types. And a few belong to a number of other types as well. Moreover, a small number of officers will develop into real soldiers regardless of type.

YOUNGER SONS

The Younger Sons are one of the more common types of officer in modern times. Until the last century, the officer ranks of most nations were loaded up with the sons of the nobility. These were usually the younger sons, who would not inherit the family fortune. As nobles were discouraged from going into commercial ventures, they had little choice except the military or the clergy. The snappy uniform and bawdy lifestyle was obviously more attractive than holy orders, so the military did not lack for candidates. Indeed, officer commissions were considered so desirable that you often had to bribe your way into the service or bring considerable influence to bear. This type of officer is still with us, although today they are not idle nobles, merely people looking for a respectable, relatively nondemanding career with good job security. Given the scarcity of wars and preponderance of noncombat jobs, a military career does offer most people a safe, secure, and generally comfortable job. In many nations, these jobs are so sought-after that bribery, or at least some influence, is still required. This is particularly the case in nations with less robust economies. As civilian career prospects go down, an officer's commission appears more attractive. Many Communist and Third World nations suffer from this, but even in Russia there are frequent public outcries about how influence has been used to get someone's son into an officer-training program, and there have even been occasional hints that bribery is not uncommon. Nor is the United States immune to suggestions of untoward goings-on, as witness the 1988 questions about Dan Quayle's National Guard commission.

Some of these opportunistic officer candidates do turn out to be decent officers. But on the whole, this is not the way things work. These fellows may be the most ambitious officers, but the least enthusiastic about the rigors of combat training. History has shown that this type of officer can have an overwhelming influence on the nature of the military, to the extent that military efficiency suffers accordingly. Unfortunately, you don't find this out until there's a war. There are few enough wars to allow the playboys plenty of time to mold the military machine to a less strenuous standard. In many respects, you can't really blame this type of person for the sad state of many military organizations. There are always cultural pressures getting people into the officer corps. Lack of economic and social opportunities are not to be underestimated. And occasionally a Younger Son type turns out to be an outstanding officer, such as Napoleon, Omar Bradley, and many British military heroes, including both Lord Nelson and the Duke of Wellington.

UMMPIES

And then there are the Upwardly Mobile Military Professionals, or Ummpies. Actually, these are the good guys, at least by peacetime standards. The Ummpies want to do it right. Many of them spend more time in school than with the troops. Most rarely deal with troops, as there are many technical specialties that consist largely of highly trained officers, with not many soldiers under command. This is a phenomenon of the twen-

tieth century and has profoundly changed the traditional concept of an officer. The Ummpies are the best example of this
new officer. Under such conditions, it is not surprising that they
become obsessed with developing their career prospects at the
expense of those types who spend a lot of time mucking about
with the troops, and who naturally take a dim view of these
people who rarely command anything but a desk and have only
a passing familiarity with weapons and warfare. Yet all these
people are considered officers, at least to outsiders. Some nations cut through this charade and turn many of the technical
specialties into nonuniformed civil-service jobs. The allure and
prestiege of the uniform and officer rank is strong, and this civ-
ilianization approach has not spread to any great extent. A few
nations have gone a different route, creating a special uniformed "fourth branch" within the armed forces that includes
most administrative and technical personnel whose duties are
not peculiar to the needs of one of the three older branches.
But this hasn't found much popularity, as the uniform betrays
one as something less than a "fighting man."

You would have to be pretty pigheaded, very dedicated, or
somewhat brain-damaged not to get caught up in all this career-
ism. Peer pressure alone causes most Ummpie officers to get
out there and hustle with everyone else or, as many do, leave
the service. So those who stay in will play the game. While
there are variations from one nation to another, the basic drill
is the same. First, the newly minted Ummpie officer has to
choose a goal. Nearly all armed forces have three groups of
officer ranks. The lowest is called company grade in armies and
air forces. These are the lieutenants and captains: Navies call
them ensigns and lieutenants. They are the officers who spend
much of their time with the troops and basically do all the offi-
cer-grade scut work when not commanding troops. Practically
anyone who can function as an officer, and some who cannot,
gets to the top of this grade and becomes a captain, or equivalent, depending on nation or service.

The next level of officers is field grade, majors and colonels in armies and air forces, commanders and captains in navies. This is where the competition begins to heat up. In the
U.S. military, candidates for major have less than a 50 percent
chance of making it unless they have made all the right moves

as a company-grade officer. If they have behaved themselves, and thus have not been "invited" to leave active service, their prospects for success are about 80 percent. The pattern in most other armed forces is similar. The highest grade consists of the flag officers, the generals and admirals, so called because they are authorized special flags to indicate their exalted status. In the United States less than 10 percent of field-grade officers will make it to flag rank. Obviously, competition is fierce for promotion to flag rank. The atmosphere is quite political and, depending upon the country, frequently involves final approval by the national legislature and head of state.

Getting any promotion involves making a number of correct career moves. In the United States, this is known as "getting your ticket punched." In most large nations, the sheer number of officers requires a complex and bureaucratic promotion procedure. The decisions are made centrally, and the successful candidates are those with the right credentials. While the personal element is not completely gone, in the form of senior officers who put in a good word for their favorites, other elements collectively carry much more weight.

The following list summarizes the "right moves." Some nations, and even certain branches of the armed forces of the same nation, may stress one or two of the moves over the others, but by and large these are common to all nations. Note that these "right moves" also apply to other types of officer, such as the Younger Sons. It's just that the Ummpies are more aware of the right moves, and will pursue them in a more systematic fashion.

ACADEMY CREDENTIALS

Although not so important as in the past, to a considerable degree this is still a very big punch for an ambitious officer in the U.S. armed forces. Only about 12–13 percent of newly commissioned officers are academy graduates, but around a third or so of the generals and admirals are. Their impressive credentials—everyone "knows" academy grads are the best—start their careers off with a modest boost. And their fellow alumni in higher ranks have been known to keep a fond eye on them, particularly if they stood high in their class.

COMBAT ARMS

To achieve really high rank, it is usually necessary to start out in the Combat Arms. After all, the ultimate purpose of the armed forces is to fight. In the United States Army, infantry and armor are the ones that really count; Artillery, aviation, and engineers will keep you in the running, with a handicap when compared to the ground pounders. The United States also considers the Special Forces to be a bit too "strange" for those on their way to high rank. (In the Russian Army, being a gunner never hurt anyone's chances, although the Russians apparently also take a dim view of the commando types.) For the navy, it's time at sea as commander or executive officer of a ship that sets you on the way to exalted rank; techies and engine-room types are at a disadvantage. In the air force, you must have served as a combat pilot; driving a cargo aircraft around or keeping the birds flying is not nearly the same thing.

COMMAND

This is the traditional officer's job, and is still recognized as a worthwhile thing to do. But with so many officers and so few troops, it's quite an accomplishment to obtain command of a unit. Many officers in technical jobs can pretty much forget about this one, and concentrate on other matters. In recognition of this, many armies dole out troop command in small portions. This does neither the officers nor the troops much good, as they barely get to know one another before a new Ummpie comes along to get his ticket punched. Surprisingly, most officers do not want to spend a lot of time with the troops. It's grueling work, and you are held responsible when your troops screw up. It's not a case of *if* one of your people will make a mess, but *when,* although if the troops under your command foul up in peacetime, the damage to one's career probably can be minimized. In combat, failure can more easily ruin one's career prospects. Screw-ups in combat can also be fatal to the officer in charge. There is another negative aspect to commanding troops, for if you spend too much time with them, you may not be able to get your ticket punched in other ways.

SCHOOLS

A modern soldier is seen as a well-educated professional. This means schools and degrees. Most nations now require a new officer to have the equivalent of a bachelor's degree, which is largely a post–World War II development. But that's no longer considered enough in many armed forces. Officers sometimes obtain advanced degrees on their own, but the more usual method is to be sent at state expense to a school. There are also a number of advanced or specialist schools within the military that one gets into either because it's required or, more to your credit, by competition. The civilian schools are considered more attractive. They give a more impressive credential, and get you away from the discipline and irritants of military life for a while. One result of this is that there are a surprising number of officers holding doctorates and similar advanced degrees, in addition to having equivalent military school credentials, at least in the U.S. and other Western armed forces. An officer can overdo this: If he spends too much time in school, he may lose his chances at another of the more desirable "punches" to his ticket, such as troop command.

THE "RIGHT REGIMENT"

Serving with a particular unit helps one's promotion prospects. Certain "elite" units are selective in which officers they allow to serve with them. Most elite units are combat units, such as paratroopers or "guards," the head of state's bodyguard, or submarines or fighters, but General Staff Corps credentials are very well regarded in some nations. In the United States, there are no "guards" units or staff corps, but there is the 82nd Airborne Division, the Ranger battalions, and the three Regular Army Cavalry Regiments. All these elite units have a special aura about them, and membership in such denotes that one is a "real" soldier, or an intellectually gifted one. Elite units are likely to be popular with the press, the people, and the politicians, making service with such very desirable. On the downside, these units may be unpopular with the service as a whole, so that being associated with them could be a handicap when serving under "regular" commanders.

AIDE-DE-CAMP

Generals and admirals are permitted to have a number of junior officers on their personal staffs to serve as aides-de-camp, sort of glorified gofers. In addition, all senior staffs have slots for a number of junior officers needed to perform trivial tasks. These selected positions are highly sought-after, as they identify a young officer as a "comer" even if he hasn't done anything to demonstrate particular brilliance. But there is also a danger here. In the United States, for example, extensive service as a White House aide or on the Pentagon staff is not well regarded because these duties smack too much of politics, and few officers having more than the minimum requirement of such duty go on to really high rank. There are exceptions, but the majority of promotions are given out to officers who avoid being tagged as headquarters types.

STAFF WORK

Next to commanding troops in combat, the most tedious task in any military service is staff work. The sections of a staff are very similar to the various departments of a corporation; they take care of the detailed planning and daily administrative grind under the overall supervision and direction of the senior manager, better known as a general or an admiral. This is basically paper shuffling and trying not to get mangled in the inevitable political infighting that characterizes staff relations. One advantage of staff work is that if something does go wrong, it's easier to shift the blame onto someone else. When commanding troops or going to school, you are on your own, and mistakes take on a personal nature. Officers have to have some exposure to staff work, if only so they can better defend themselves against the depredations of the ever more numerous staff organizations. And doing a bang-up job on a staff, particularly as "S-3," or operations officer, is a particularly good "punch" for one's ticket.

FAMILY CONNECTIONS

If your father was an officer, particularly a general, this helps quite a lot. Failing that, some other close relative, such as an uncle, is of some value. This means you grew up in the system and already know a lot of the ins and outs, which gives you a considerable advantage over officers who grew up as civilians. The military is a very social organization, with its own peculiar customs and formalities. Mistakes fatal to your career can easily be made when you are off duty attending some social function with other officers. But if you disport yourself well at these social affairs, one of the few opportunities for your superiors to actually see you, career prospects may brighten. Under these circumstances, you will find it easier to make additional social connections. It's quite common for an officer's career to be made, or unmade, at the Officers' Club. Besides, your high-ranking kin may have served as a "mentor" to someone who is now in a position to return the favor. Both Russia and the United States (and many other nations) have families that produce high-ranking officers generation after generation. The sons of the 1945 generals, for instance, began to turn up wearing stars themselves in the 1960s, and there are more than a few of them out there.

COMBAT EXPERIENCE

This doesn't count as much as one would think, even though the primary purpose of a military organization is to do well in combat. In fact, a certain degree of jealousy and resentment may develop when only a small fraction of officers have combat experience. Grenada was a prime example of this, with many of those who didn't get to go circulating false "horror stories" to smear those who did participate. Moreover, much combat experience is mundane and may consist of events or unpleasant details the officer would prefer not be probed too deeply. This was particularly true for U.S. officers during the Vietnam War. In that conflict, it was common for officers to command a combat unit for only a few months. Often, the most prudent thing for them to do was keep their units out of contact with the enemy, while still allowing their brief sojourns on the battlefield to count as combat experience. Similar situations occurred to Russian officers during the Afghan War. On the other hand, combat experience does impress the politicians who have to approve promotions, particularly in the aftermath of a war. Consider Oliver North's parlaying of his rather commonplace

Vietnam combat experience into an impressive TV performance before a Senate committee: There were hundreds, possibly thousands, of officers with a similar, or more distinguished,
combat record, but he "played" his very successfully to the
media. When the 1990–1991 Gulf crisis broke out, those folks
who saw "combat" in Grenada or Panama had a leg up on
getting a higher command and a little more combat experience.

DECORATIONS

A decoration is the best manifestation of battlefield experience, as you can wear it on your chest. Among other things,
a decoration shows that you were able to rise above the situation, and your peers. Decorations are excellent ammunition when
one turns from fighting the wartime enemy to the "real" battle,
that of peacetime promotional politics. The decorations business sometimes gets out of hand. In Vietnam, the U.S. armed
forces, and especially the army and air force, perverted the system. Awards were given out generously, thus devaluing those
that were obtained for truly valorous actions. After a while, it
became something of a game to gather up as many decorations
as possible. For example, an officer could obtain the Combat
Infantry Badge simply by flying into a frontline outpost on a
supply helicopter a certain number of times. This was quite
common. Some chaplains came away with such "combat" decorations as the Air Medal. Even the Purple Heart, which is
awarded only to those wounded by hostile action, was subject
to abuses, such as when officers with trivial or noncombat-
related injuries received it. The 1983 operation in Grenada
showed that the bad habits acquired in Vietnam lived on, particularly in the elite 82nd Airborne Division. For the Grenada
"campaign," the army gave out more decorations than there
were troops involved: There was no reprise of this routine as a
result of the Panama Operation, nor in the Persian Gulf as many
senior army officers got their knuckles rapped for being too free
with the decorations after Grenada. Still, if you have more battlefield awards than your peers, it's an advantage. Napoleon
made his career partially through the shrewd dispensing of decorations. Hitler made much about the Iron Cross he earned
during World War I service, even though a Jewish lieutenant
was responsible for his receiving the medal. On the positive

side, the United States did demonstrate in a subtle way that some generals had learned from the "decoration abuse" of Vietnam. After the 82nd Airborne's excessive Grenada awards became public, the division commander inexplicably took an early retirement. Normally, command of the elite 82nd leads to greater things, particularly if the unit has seen successful combat. Things *do* change.

MERIT AWARDS

Governments have long awarded exceptional civil servants with medals and honors. The military is no exception. If you can pick up one or more of these awards, it is a signal to future superiors that your former commander thought enough of you to go to the trouble of plowing through the paperwork these awards entail. These awards are ordinarily given to field grade and above, perhaps in recognition that these people have fewer opportunities to get close to the fighting and earn battlefield decorations. Besides, most civilians, and even many members of Congress, don't know what all that "fruit salad" on one's chest stands for and may think you're a heavily decorated combat veteran.

MENTOR

Eventually, an ambitious Ummpie must obtain a mentor in order to achieve high rank. Actually, more than one mentor is advisable, although you have to be careful not to get caught between two feuding mentors. A mentor is a senior officer who takes an interest in the Ummpie's advancement. This is a symbiotic relationship, with the Ummpie expected to demonstrate unwavering loyalty to the mentor. As a result, this can be a tricky undertaking, as the mentor may become entangled in some high-level dispute, end up on the losing side, and take several Ummpie protégés down in disgrace as his career evaporates. While the mentor usually chooses which aspiring Ummpies he will take under his wing, Ummpies must be careful not to get hooked up with a mentor possessing a clouded future. Choosing mentors can be a sticky business. Although one must avoid trying to turn a high-ranking relative into a mentor, a move that is likely to be certain death for one's career, it is in an Ummpie's interest to cultivate every senior official with whom he comes into contact. You never know.

GOOD EVALUATIONS

Most large armed forces have some system whereby senior officers regularly evaluate their subordinates' performance. This is done in writing and is inserted in each officer's file. When promotion time comes around, the records of all eligible candidates are reviewed by a panel of officers. Particularly in the larger nations, most of the reviewing officers will not know the candidates and will therefore have to rely on their records for guidance in choosing the few who will be promoted above the many. As previously noted, the problem with this system is that only one poor, or even average, evaluation can dog an Ummpie for the rest of his career. Ummpies are completely at the mercy of their superiors in this regard. Under these conditions, an ambitious Ummpie is in big trouble if he's serving under a difficult superior. These difficulties can take many forms. The superior can simply be unpleasant. This is the easiest problem to deal with; but what if the superior proves incompetent? Not gross incompetence, but something less that simply causes the organization to perform poorly. Worse, the Ummpie might be working for a superior who asks subordinates to stick their necks out by performing acts that, while not exactly illegal, are unethical or degrade the performance of the unit. In these situations, the Ummpie must choose between career and "the good of the service." Most of the time it's no contest and the damage is done, but not to the Ummpie's career. This is the primary reason that peacetime military units have such a difficult time maintaining efficiency. There will always be people in charge who make mistakes or play games with the rules. In wartime, the results of this are quickly seen. In peacetime, things can be covered up for a long time, at least until there's a war. Commercial organizations have an advantage in that when they screw up, they lose money, which will be noticed in short order. Going bankrupt, or coming close, is the commercial equivalent of losing a battle, and has the same effect of focusing everyone's attention on doing things the right way.

Any such list of the "right moves" includes some that overlap with each other in various ways. The boundaries between the different areas are by no means hard and fast. Just how many of these "ticket punches" are necessary in order to achieve high rank is difficult to say, but the more of them an Ummpie amasses, the better are his chances. The universality of the "Ummpie" officer as a type may be illustrated by noting the Russian experience in this regard.

THE RUSSIAN DILEMMA

The two largest armed forces in the world, the Russian and the American, are very similar in one respect. They both have hordes of Ummpies serving in the officer ranks. Most other armed forces suffer the Ummpie phenomenon to a lesser extent. The primary difference in smaller armed forces is the greater role played by personal relationships. It's hard to get a lot of tickets punched in smaller armed forces, where there is not as much room to move around. As a result, most of the factors that go toward creating the Ummpie phenomenon have to do with larger armed forces and the increasing use of technology. While you can have civilians running complex noncombat systems such as inventory control, you need a military type to run complex systems in ships, in the air, and on the battlefield. Even the infantry has enormous amounts of electronics and computers built into their weapons and equipment. You can't even keep this stuff functional without technically trained officers. The Russians have an additional problem in that most of their troops are young, short-term conscripts: There are very few long-service enlisted personnel compared to Western armies. Thus, besides learning to lead men in battle, Russian officers must also operate and maintain a lot of complex combat gear: Nuclear submarines, for example, regularly have crews of more than 50 percent officers. This is one reason behind the movement within the Russian military to restructure the armed forces from an enlisted force of short-service draftees to one consisting of long-service volunteers or professional troops. Professional troops would mean that the officers could spend more time being officers, leaving all that work normally done by skilled enlisted personnel in Western forces to a new class of professional NCOs. This approach would also mean much smaller Russian armed forces, as the professional troops would demand higher pay and better living conditions than the conscripts currently receive. It would also probably make for much more effective armed forces. Yet given the state of Russia's economy, and the traditional desire for a large army to ward off all the hostile forces on Russia's borders, it is unlikely that we will see this smaller, all-volunteer force anytime soon.

The fact that Russian officers have been publicly calling for a volunteer military force does show, nonetheless, the extent of the discontent with the current system. Implicit in this proposal is a sharp reduction in the number of officers. Many Russian officers feel this would be a good thing. American officers have noted that the U.S. military could stand a little of this medicine too.

Russian officers have presented their case in Russia's many military journals and newspapers. In these publications, which are noted for their relative openness to carefully worded criticism, there have appeared a great many articles concerned more with the standard of living of officers than with their combat readiness or ideological purity. Recently instituted opinion polls among the troops suggest that officer morale is poor.

The current officer system is an aberration even by Russian standards. Before World War I, Russia had a decent NCO corps, and numerous good company officers, many of whom were recruited from the ranks, who could concentrate on being officers. This was one of the innovations of Czar Peter the Great. Being historically minded, one of the useful side effects of "Soviet Military Science," many Russian officers have concluded that this prerevolutionary system had its advantages. These advantages are constantly demonstrated in Western and Eastern European armies that use well-trained officers and NCOs, plus many long-term volunteer troops. Russian officers note that even the East European armies that employ a Western system are more efficient. They also note that the overcentralization that has created an acknowledged disaster in the civilian economy has also wrecked the Russian military. The Russians have just been more forthcoming about the sad state of their economy than that of their military. This is understandable, as the publication of such information falls into the category of giving "aid and comfort to the enemy." But the performance of Russian troops and equipment in the last forty years indicates that there is a problem and that it is getting worse. A steady stream of critical articles in the military press makes it quite clear that many officers are ready for a radical solution to remedy the state of their armed forces. The current economic restructuring in Russia hopes to draw the surplus officers into a rejuvenated civilian industry, where they can be more productive professionals. By creating such opportunities in the civilian economy, the Russians will have removed a major obstacle to implementing an overall reduction in the size of the armed forces—the need for officers to make a living. This solution also addresses several other problems, such as the many ambitious officers who would probably take their chances in a reinvigorated economy.

There could be a danger here. If the economy does prove attractive to ambitious young men, will the armed forces be able to secure sufficient competent new officers? There are many officers who are in uniform simply to make an easy living. These layabouts get away with it because there are never enough officers to attend to the increasing number of technical jobs new, and more complex, equipment creates. The military is already having a hard time getting promising young men into the officer schools. The people, including potential officer candidates, want something different. Already, major cities are not meeting their quotas for officer candidates. There appears to be an interesting social experiment in the offing.

While Russia has traditionally been a closed society, and the military an even more secretive subculture within that society, the Russians have customarily used the military press as a way to expose new ideas to a form of debate. Many ideas are summarily shot down by superior commanders. But if the proposal has some intrinsic merit, it keeps popping up until something is done. The same thing goes on in the West. But there the academic and civilian press provide as much of a forum as does the military press, as there are many independent journals of military history and opinion. Unlike Russia, where the military has its own mass-circulation newspapers plus numerous journals, the West is more open, and civilians also jump into the fray. Much to Russia's chagrin, the "reactionary" Western armed forces are also capable of more rapid change. The United States is a case in point.

THE U.S. EXPERIENCE

Vietnam was a watershed in the evolution of the armed forces in America. The experience in Southeast Asia had a two-fold effect. First, it showed that there were serious shortcomings in the armed forces. To their credit, the armed forces themselves fixed some of these problems during the war, and went to work on many of the others even more energetically after the fighting ended. But the war was also an unpopular one, and Americans soon expressed their traditional distaste for large peacetime military forces by abolishing the draft and sharply cutting defense spending through the 1970s. Worse, the military now had a hard time attracting high-caliber officers and troops. In many ways, the U.S. military hit rock bottom in the mid-seventies. But there were enough dedicated patriots in uniform to initiate effective reform. Policies were changed, higher recruitment standards were enforced, and inept personnel were let go. The big improvement in the U.S. military through the 1980s was not all the additional cash that was spent on equipment, but the remarkable rise in troop quality. The Ummpie phenomenon in the United States has not been an entirely negative thing, as many of the goals being set for advancement were constructive. Russia's big problem is that the armed forces have been one of the few outlets for the ambitious. In America, if you just want to make a lot of money and live the good life, you go into the civilian sector. In Russia, there is no lucrative civilian economy for the ambitious. So its armed forces have filled up with a lot of people who are looking for the good life while trying to avoid the less desirable aspects of a military career as much as possible. In America, you go into the military only if you are interested in a military career or are a member of a minority group with fairly dismal prospects outside of the military. In the latter case, the armed forces benefit from the prejudices of society, since some very able people who may have difficulties in civilian life find the armed forces a relatively discrimination-free environment. The result of this is very good for the service: In the U.S. armed forces, a larger percentage of military personnel are military professionals. In the Russian forces, many officers are simply professionals.

UMMPIES AS GOOD GUYS

As the Russians have discovered, you need to have officers who are more than military professionals in order to make modern armed forces work. Professional career attitudes are a characteristic of all elements of society. Like any other development, there are good aspects and not-so-good aspects to this. One major aspect distinguishing the modern military professionals from their civilian counterparts is the fact that the Ummpie is in uniform voluntarily. The major difference between Russian and Western Ummpies is that the Western officer has a wide choice of careers. By choosing the military, the Western officer concentrates more on the military aspect. This is particularly true with those in combat specialties. A Western infantry officer is there because he wants to be in the infantry. As a result, you see a great deal more enthusiasm and effectiveness. One reason some nations, especially the European ones, have such effective infantry is because their officers stay in the infantry for their entire careers, indeed, often in the very same battalion. In America, there is a tendency for an officer to move about a bit more. By staying in one branch for years, or even decades, a certain expertise is acquired that pays tremendous dividends in combat. Experience is also gained more quickly and profoundly if you want to be there. While there are many eager Russian infantry officers, Russia has a long tradition of putting combat arms officers in truly desolate places and forgetting about them. The Russian forces have another long tradition of discouraging initiative and enterprise. These practices are now creating reluctance among Russia's best and brightest to go for an officer's career, which means standards must be lowered, and doctrine modified to allow for the poorer quality of the officer corps. It's not surprising that most of the combat innovations after World War II have come from the West. Western combat troops have also performed much more effectively during that same period. It does help if your Ummpies are true volunteers.

NCO UMMPIES

Another considerable advantage is if you also have NCOs who take a very professional attitude toward their trade. In most armed forces, NCOs must maintain their effectiveness if they are to be allowed to reenlist. Russia is an exception in that most of its NCOs are simply conscripts selected to supervise their fellow draftees until their own mandatory tour "with the colors" runs out. Unlike Western NCOs, Russian ones rarely serve beyond their required two or three years. In all armies, after their initial term of service, troops are allowed to reenlist only if they are judged capable of doing their job and advancing in it. While most NCOs do not have a college degree, they do undergo many years of training in the military. Some nations even have NCO academies with courses of six months to a year or more. The average Western NCO is usually capable of taking over if the officer in charge is absent. In wartime, many of these professional NCOs are commonly promoted to company-grade officer rank and perform better than newly minted officers straight out of college. Many nations recognize the value of these professional NCOs and provide an intermediate officer rank, known as warrant officers (WOs), who are used largely in skilled positions. Most U.S. Army helicopter pilots are warrant officers, as are many technicians in Special Forces A-Teams. Another common duty for WOs is as senior supervisors in maintenance units or headquarters. Russia has made several attempts to introduce a similar rank. But the difference in living standards between enlisted personnel and civilians is so great that they can't entice troops to volunteer to become warrant officers without giving them benefits on a scale comparable to that for officers. Unfortunately, the officers are not very inclined to accept this former enlisted riffraff into their august company.

FLYING UMMPIES

Air forces have always had a problem with officers as pilots. When aircraft were first introduced to armed forces some eighty years ago, flying was not seen as exclusively an officer's prerogative. Most of the early pilots were NCOs, with the leadership positions filled by officers, who were in many cases not pilots. Today, few air forces still use NCO pilots, although the U.S. Army has a lot of warrant-officer pilots, who do quite well. In a similar vein, some nations have a rank system that calls most pilots officers, but distinguishes between "flying" officers and "real" officers, with the latter earmarked for really high command, while the former can fly, which is all a pilot wants. The primary problem with making all pilots officers is not the additional expense this entails, but the fact that most serious pilots much prefer being fliers to being administrators. As far as a pilot is concerned, he is on the same social level as an officer, but has significantly different goals. Basically, a pilot is a very highly skilled and trained technician. Most important, pilots do not like being forced to give up flying in order to get their tickets punched as they climb through the ranks. Many military pilots leave the service for civil aviation jobs so that they can keep flying, and make more money while they're at it. This phenomenon has had one curious beneficial side effect in the U.S. armed forces, as many of these people also join the reserves or National Guard, where they fly "hot" military aircraft to their heart's content, thereby accumulating ever more experience, to the point where they frequently outperform active-duty pilots. These pilots also cost the military a lot less, as they are only paid for the month or so per year they are in uniform.

GOLD-PLATED UMMPIES

This raises another question, that of differences in officer compensation. Aside from combat specialties, most military officer jobs have civilian equivalents. After all, there are great differences between pay scales of various civil occupations. Doctors and lawyers make more than your average middle manager. But in the military, officers are paid according to rank and longevity. This is not a problem in Russia, where officers make out better than most civilians performing similar specialties. But in the West either you pay bonuses to get doctors, pilots, and similar specialists or you do without. These bonuses cause some unrest among the less well paid officers, and some nations solve the problem by using civilians on many of these specialist jobs. Others pay the bonuses and take the heat. It's also possible to conscript some of these specialists, but you can't keep them for long, so you end up with nothing but young doctors and such. Another approach is to give the specialist a higher entry rank, but this causes ill feeling among those officers who had to earn their rank the hard way. Many officers dismiss the overpaid specialists by remembering that most of them will never reach really high command and, what the hell, they're just a bunch of techies and not *real* officers anyway. Moreover, there's the realization that these people are also at the top of the income pyramid in the civilian world. It's scant comfort, but it's something.

Ummpies constitute a significant proportion of the officers in most modern armies. While they may seem to be a fairly mercenary lot, in fact many very fine commanders were essentially Ummpies, such as Ulysses S. Grant (who proved a lousy peacetime soldier), John J. Pershing, Chester W. Nimitz, and Dwight D. Eisenhower, all of whom originally chose a military career primarily because it offered a free college education.

ARMED HUSTLERS

The third type of officers are basically uniformed thugs with power. They come in several varieties, the most common being revolutionary fighters who came up winners and are now the regular armed forces. These former revolutionaries do not always turn out bad, but they almost always have a hard time adjusting to the tamer ways of peacetime soldiering. Throughout history, trying to domesticate troops who have spent many years soldiering as irregulars has been a difficult task. The old saying "The revolution eats its young" tends to refer to the old revolutionary firebrands getting shot or imprisoned by the new revolutionary government because of an inability to adjust to law and order.

The revolutions producing these people can be either right- or left-wing. Politics does not have very much to do with how these soldiers on the make operate. Sometimes the revolution took place many decades ago, and the hustle has been passed down through the generations. In Latin America, for example, the revolution is mostly the one that occurred over 150 years ago, when the Spanish, Portuguese, and French colonial governments were overthrown. At that time, political power went to a small group of wealthy families. These groups knew that if threatened by popular unrest, the only way to maintain power was through military force. So they recruited officers and NCOs willing to do the dirty work, and conscripted most of the troops from the population. In more recent decades, this phenomenon has manifested itself in many newly independent nations, particularly—and perversely—among those that secured their freedom through peaceful means. Several of these have found it convenient to invent a "Revolution," with the armed forces glorified for victories that never took place save perhaps in the form of a coup, as in Libya and Liberia. In either case, the end result has been a dictatorship maintained in power by force of arms. In a way, it's the ultimate hustle and is quite common. The ranks may include patriots, Ummpies, and general layabouts, but the primary goal is keeping the rulers in power.

Some of these operations, particularly those that have been around a while, are rather sophisticated. If these thugs don't get organized, you end up with little more than a bunch of bandits running things. Bandits are not noted for their managerial skills, otherwise they wouldn't be bandits. So you find the group in power constantly looking for ways to sustain its power. The most popular tools for doing this are the secret police and paramilitary troops. The secret police act as guides for the paramilitary troops in a never-ending effort to stamp out opponents before a new group of revolutionaries replace the current batch in the president's palace. The officers of the secret police think of themselves as military officers and not cops. This is a necessary fiction in order to make the work more palatable. It's a nasty business, and is more easily stomached if you convince yourself that you are doing it for the national good.

THE ARMY BRAT

This is probably an appropriate place to mention a fourth type of officer, the "Army—Navy/Air Force/Marine—Brat," the scion of a family that has sent its sons—and lately its daughters as well—into the officer corps for some time, perhaps even for centuries. All armed forces have some of this type of officer, but they are more common in European services than in the American armed forces. An officer's offspring can also be a Younger Son, or an Ummpie, or an Armed Hustler. For real Army Brats, the choice of a military career was a virtually unconscious one, and they may be considered a separate category unto themselves. As with Ummpies, many fine officers come out of this group, such as Douglas MacArthur, William Halsey, and Matthew Ridgeway.

THE SUPERSOLDIER

There is yet another type of officer, found in limited numbers in most armies, the "Supersoldier." This is the oldest form of officer: the pure warrior. In ancient times, this was the only type of officer. Back then, the leader of the fighting men had to be the biggest, the baddest, the boldest, and the best in battle. As society became more "civilized," this type became less crucial. Larger armed forces equipped with more complex weapons needed more officers who could manage and maintain things. One hundred years ago, it was still common for generals to lead their units into battle. No more. Company commanders might still do that, and more rarely battalion commanders; but the Supersoldier still does, regardless of rank. The Supersoldier is not only at home on the battlefield, but thrives there. He is lucky, in the way of people who make their own luck. While not good insurance risks, Supersoldiers inspire and motivate the troops with them and often change the course of battles. But when the war ends, the military is an inhospitable place for warriors. The peacetime routine does not suit them either. When a warrior isn't fighting, he's a misfit, perhaps a drinker, or a slob, or a womanizer. Periodically, he's in jail for even more unsocial behavior. Some go the other way, being exceedingly religious. This is a touchy subject among professional soldiers, and they react by focusing on the more presentable warrior types like Winfield Scott, Philip Sheridan, James Gavin, Matthew Ridgeway, George Patton, and so on, rather than the more numerous feral types. While the handful of exemplary warriors are nice to admire, you need large numbers of warriors to succeed in wartime. Most warriors are pretty wild people. It's always a struggle to harness their combat qualities while keeping these fighters from self-destructing when out of combat. Distressingly, the initiative and élan that win battles also create chaos in peacetime bureaucratic armies.

There have been several notable Supersoldiers in the U.S. military. Perhaps the most famous in recent years was Lewis B. "Chesty" Puller. Like many "Supersoldiers," Puller started out as an enlisted man. As he rose through the ranks, Puller, who was a protégé of Smedly Butler, another notable marine Supersoldier, was awarded the Navy Cross five times in various "banana wars" and during World War II, and further distinguished himself in Korea, eventually rising to deputy commandant of the Marine Corps. Puller, a talkative, profane man, was an enormous asset in war, but a serious handicap in peace, when he proved politically tactless in talking about the shortcomings of the other services, lambasting the political leadership of the armed forces, or criticizing "softness" in training. Although he had no problems with drinking or chasing women, he was retired as a lieutenant general in 1955: He would never have "worked" as commandant of the Marine Corps, despite being the most decorated marine ever, with over thirty U.S. and seven foreign decorations. Oddly enough, the current Marine Corps commandant is pushing training and personnel programs that Puller would have admired. The current commandant got his job because the then-current secretary of the navy was a former marine infantryman and realized the need for a warrior type at the head of a warrior organization. The more numerous (and more peacetime-oriented) marine generals who lost out in the race for this plum appointment were not amused.

Although fictional, the leading character in Pat Conroy's *The Great Santini* is an exemplary portrait of the problems of a "warrior without a war." Even the manner of his death was typical. It was the way Soviet cosmonaut Yuri Gagarin, the first man into space, met his end, by a thoroughly professional decision to stick with a crippled aircraft rather than to abandon it over a populated area.

Many senior commanders, especially those who have seen a Supersoldier in action, recognize the value of these warriors. Also recognized is the difficulty of maintaining these volatile troops in peacetime. Thus many nations maintain special units that attract the warrior types. Hard training, occasional operations, and a willingness to overlook indiscreet behavior characterize these commando-type organizations. In wartime, such units are not only ready for the most desperate missions, but Supersoldiers who prove to have the real knack for combat can then be promoted and put in charge of regular units. The effect on these units can be electrifying, which is just one more proof of the ancient adage, "There are no bad troops, just bad officers." One Supersoldier in the right place can do wonders.

THE TIES THAT BIND

Military officers possess more firepower than any other official in the government, and they can, and do, abuse that power. Yet all officers share a sense of loyalty toward something, even if it's only their fellow officers. Political beliefs vary all over the lot, but the officer tends to be more conservative than others in the ruling party. The military is more disciplined than any other branch of any government. It is this discipline, and duty to face the horrors of the battlefield, that make the military officer a breed apart.

Officers also represent political as well as military power. The concept of military officers is grounded in the officers' ability to muster sufficient force that will insure the survival of the state. A military officer is basically a uniformed official of the state. One of the major achievements of any nation is creating a corps of combat-effective officers. It's not an easy task and is not always accomplished.

One test of an army's leadership is the number of generals who are sacked in the course of a war. Firing unsuccessful generals is a fairly modern practice. In earlier times, generals were usually members of the royal family or other nobles. As a result, it was rare, although not unheard of, for one to be sacked. At the Battle of Tewkesbury (May 4, 1471), for example, dissatisfied with the unhurried manner in which Lord Wenlock had come up to his support, the Duke of Somerset relieved the tardy nobleman by the simple expedient of dashing out his brains with an ax. While, as one military historian put it, this was "a most effective way to sack a divisional commander," it was an unusual occurrence, perhaps prompted by the fact that Wenlock's leisurely approach had cost Somerset the battle. All this began to change with the rise of the bureaucratic state, and particularly so with the rise of more democratic forms of government. Having lost a battle, in 1757 British Admiral John Byng, the son of a viscount, was tried, convicted, and, as Voltaire put it, shot "to encourage the others."

It was the French Revolution, however, that firmly established the idea that generals should be liable for their failures. During the period from 1792 through 1799, some 680 French generals were ousted. At the outbreak of the Revolution, the

French Royal Army had 1,159 generals, of whom a great many shortly fled the country. Although a large number of new ones were created by the Republic, the actual total number of French generals doesn't seem to have amounted to more than about 3,500 for the entire period. So even without allowing for the Royalist generals who fled the country, about 20 percent were sacked and many more were shifted to less strenuous jobs or retired before they could get into big trouble. Even among those who made general's rank through actual battlefield performance, many would burn out from the stress or reach a level of command they could not handle. While a few of the ousted generals were undoubtedly traitors to the Revolution, and many fell victim to political intrigue or bad luck, a lot of them were incompetent. All these dismissals led to a marked improvement in French generalship: It was better to die gloriously at the head of one's troops than to have to pay for failure by a date with Madame Guillotine. Although during the Second World War Stalin shot some generals—an estimated 200–250—who failed to deliver on the battlefield, among the major powers unsuccessful generals no longer pay so high a price. But when war comes, armies quickly discover their proper priorities and become highly intolerant of anything but victory. As a result, generals lose their jobs at remarkable rates, as a look at the failure rate of division commanders in the principal wars of this century demonstrates. Note that in the chart that follows, many generals who should have lost their jobs, or lost them sooner, avoided this unpleasantness by pulling strings or by simply being good at making excuses. You don't become a peacetime general without developing skills in both these areas. Thus the failure rates shown below can be considered somewhat understated.

Division commanders can be seen as low high-ranking field commanders, or high middle-ranking ones. They command divisions, forces of from about 5,500 to 20,000 men, usually comprising infantry, armor, or cavalry, with healthy doses of artillery and other troops in support. Divisions are the principal tactical organizations responsible for sustained combat in conventional war. In general, the men leading divisions are long-service professional soldiers, with at least twenty years in uniform to their credit. This represents a lot of training and experience, which is what got them their commands in the first place. Nevertheless, as the sample shows, all that "getting ready" was not always enough. Many division commanders in all armies were found wanting in combat. On this table, "Sample" indicates the number of each army's divisions involved in the analysis. In several cases, this number is that with which the power began the war: In World War I, going to war and entering combat were almost simultaneous activities, which was not the case in other wars. "Sacked" is the percentage of the division commanders, or their equivalent, removed from command for reasons that may be considered "less than honorable": that is, they were neither promoted, nor killed, nor captured, nor invalided-out, though the latter three fates might also reflect on their competence. "Note" refers to the lettered comments that follow the table.

FAILURE RATE OF DIVISION COMMANDERS AFTER 90 DAYS OF WAR

CONFLICT	POWER	SAMPLE	SACKED	NOTE
World War I (1914–18)	Austria-Hungary	59	62.7%	A
	Britain	14	0.0	B
	France	100	65.0%	C
	Germany	99	33.3%	D
	Italy	40	52.0%	E
	United States	29	17.2%	F
World War II (1939–40)	Britain	38	36.8%	G
	France	97	20.6%	H
	Germany	122	6.9%	I
	United States	88	17.0%	J
Korea (1950–53)	United States	6	66.7%	K

A. *Austria-Hungary (World War I)*

Figures are based on ninety days from the time Austria-Hungary entered the war in 1914. In this same period, the Imperial-and-Royal Army also sacked 52.3 percent of its seventeen corps commanders. The Austro-Hungarian Empire in general, and its armed forces in particular, were noted for a lackadaisical attitude. No one was surprised at the poor performance of Austro-Hungarian generals. In fact, Russia was depending on it in order to have a chance of quickly knocking Austria-Hungary out of the war. Unfortunately, the Russian Army (and state) had many of the same defects. Note that both nations were burdened with a lot of nobles in the senior military ranks. Russia, however, was not nearly as quick to dismiss battlefield incompetents as were other nations.

B. Britain

Figures are for the ninety days beginning with the first entry of British troops into combat, and so include divisions that did not see ninety days of action. The highly successful British benefited from reforms that had been instituted after the disasters of the Boer War (1899–1902). Their success would change when open warfare began to congeal into trench warfare in the winter of 1914–15. By the end of the war, only about 20 percent of the British generals of 1914 still held equally responsible commands. Although not as exposed to shot and shell, generals tended to be put out of action at a rate nearly as high as the combat troops.

C. France

Figures are based on ninety days from the time France entered the war in 1914. In addition, 33.8 percent of the sixty-five replacement generals were themselves sacked within ninety days, as were 27.3 percent of these twenty-two "third-generation" replacements. During this same period, the French also sacked two of their five army commanders and 51.4 percent of their thirty-seven corps commanders. Only 3.5 percent of the French generals holding divisional or higher command in 1914 still held posts of equal or greater responsibility at the end of the war, in 1918. Despite this horrendous failure rate—Joseph Joffre, the French supreme commander in 1914, holds the record for sacking more generals in a shorter period than anyone in history, about seventy-five in the first month of the war—some of the French division commanders were very successful. Several ended the war as corps, army, and even army group commanders, and at least one was still commanding his division in 1916. The French Army was regarded as a particularly effective military force before the war. This was attributed to the combat experience of many officers in colonial wars and the nationwide desire to build a strong army for a rematch with Germany to avenge the defeat of 1871. But the French had unwisely adopted a flawed tactical system between 1900 and 1914, and those imprudent tactics were the downfall of many French generals who might otherwise have proven able. Also, unlike the Germans, the French military as an institution was not as receptive to more effective ways of doing things. For example, the innovative infantry tactics the Germans used toward the end of the war were first encountered in a captured French document. The Germans proceeded to implement and improve these innovative ideas while the French officer who first developed them never really got the attention he deserved in the French Army.

D. Germany

Figures are based on ninety days from the time Germany entered the war in 1914, and are an estimate based on incomplete data. Firmer figures are available for higher-level commanders, of whom 23.3 percent of the forty-three corps commanders and one of the eight army commanders lost their jobs, as did the chief of the Great General Staff. We should stress that these figures would have been higher had Germany been a republic: Several divisions, corps, and armies were commanded by various counts, dukes, and princes who could not be fired no matter how chuckleheaded they proved to be. As with the French, it should be noted that some of the division commanders continued to perform well for several years, and that a number of them ended the war in high-level posts. Germany was considered to have the most efficient army in the world, and probably did. But four decades of peace had been sufficient to allow a large number of splendid peacetime (but dismal wartime) officers to achieve generals' rank.

E. Italy

Figures are based on ninety days from the time Italy entered the war in 1915. The Italians also sacked 20 percent of their fifteen corps commanders and one of their four army commanders in this period. This was the beginning of the modern attitude of Italians as "better lovers than fighters." It's an undeserved reputation, as most troops and junior officers fought with uncommon courage in the face of inept aristocrats and gentry serving as officers and a weak economy incapable of providing sufficient arms and munitions. Unfortunately, the situation was not improved during World War II, and the misleading reputation continued. Since World War II, Italy has apparently learned from this experience, and has produced several generations of carefully selected and well-trained officers, as well as a world-class arms industry. But military reputations are made in war, not peace.

F. United States

Figures are based on ninety days from the time each division entered combat. The United States also sacked 28 percent of its seven corps commanders. The lower sacking rate for the Americans may be attributed to three factors: 1. U.S. forces entered combat in the fourth year of the war, and so to some extent benefited from the errors of their allies. U.S. divisions were also supplied with experienced British and French advisers. 2. The average U.S. division spent only seventy-seven days in combat, with the maximum being 220 days and the minimum 18. The shortest tenure in command was 2 days, the longest 263. 3. Both the Allies and Germans were worn down by four years of frustrating and bloody trench warfare, while the American troops were fresh and not yet disillusioned. The Germans were shocked by the reckless courage and enthusiasm of the American infantry. Not having seen such élan since 1914, they had largely forgotten what it was like and assumed that most American divisions were specially trained "shock" units.

G. Britain (World War II)

Figures, which include African divisions but not Commonwealth or Indian Army ones, are based on ninety days from the time each division first entered combat. The British generals were not really as bad as the data suggest, but their German and Japanese opponents were much better. Many of the generals the British faced had already gone through their "ninety-day cleanout." So the British were facing a much higher quality opponent.

H. France

Figures, which include commanders of separate brigades but exclude fortress division and sector commanders, are for the campaign of 1940, which lasted thirty-six days. The French also sacked 15 percent of the twenty replacement commanders in the same period. Four of the division commanders (4.1 percent) were killed in action. Lacking a Joffre, the French Army put in a particularly deplorable performance this time around. Had they had tougher leadership, the number of generals canned would have been much higher, probably around 70 percent.

I. Germany

Figures are for the thirty-six-day campaign in France in 1940, and are an estimate based on incomplete data. The Germans were much better prepared for this war than was anyone else, one reason being the superior nature of their tactics, equipment, and training. But perhaps more important was the fact that they had more experience. Prewar maneuvers helped refine their skills and sort out the more obvious incompetents. The unopposed march into Austria in early 1938 was something of a disaster, and steps were taken to avoid a repeat. The occupation of part of Czechoslovakia later that year, and the rest in March of 1939, were also carried out under full wartime readiness, as it was unclear whether there would be resistance, further honing German skills and weeding out less obvious incompetents. The Polish Campaign in September–October of 1939 lasted just thirty-two days and was against a brave but ill-equipped, poorly trained, and ineptly led foe, which further sharpened German skills and led to the removal of any commanders who proved less than excellent. As a result, by the time the campaign in France took place, one would expect that all the German division commanders were top-notch men. And most were. But a few were still found wanting.

J. United States

Figures, which exclude marine and Philippine Army divisions, are based on ninety days from the time each division first entered combat. The comparatively low failure rate of American generals during this war may be attributed to essentially the same reasons as the World War I rate: 1. U.S. forces entered combat late in the game, having learned some from observing the mistakes of the first two years of the war, though not enough—never enough—to avoid making lots of errors anyway. 2. A number of divisions were not in combat for as much as ninety days. This includes amphibious divisions in the Pacific, airborne divisions, and several that went overseas in the last months of the war. 3. In addition, some division commanders had been relieved before their outfits even went overseas, because the extended preparation period allowed the obvious dullards to be identified while they trained their divisions. Large-scale maneuvers before combat revealed that some men were incapable of commanding a division even when the "enemy" wasn't using live ammunition. Moreover, it was common for promising combat-experienced regimental or assistant division commanders to be sent back from North African, Italian, and Pacific battlefields to assume command of new divisions.

K. United States (Korea)

Figures exclude marines, and are based on the first 150 days of the war. Note that several of the divisions in question were not in combat for the full 150 days. In addition, during this period literally dozens of the regimental and battalion commanders in these divisions were sacked, and a decision had also been made to remove the army commander, who was spared this indignity by dying in a jeep accident. The failure rate was particularly disturbing because many relieved commanders had World War II combat experience. The reason for this was that the commanders initially appointed to division and regimental command were not the best available. The occupation forces in Japan, which were the first sent to Korea, were seen as a pre-retirement assignment for a number of older officers, some of whom had spent World War II in staff assignments. Once the bona fide warrior type commanders were brought over from Europe and the United States, the performance of units and commanders improved considerably.

THE SACKING RATE IN OTHER WARS

In American history, the Civil War was something of a watershed for inept generalship. The command problems of the Army of the Potomac are well known: It ran through five commanding generals—one of them twice—before getting one who didn't create disasters, and even he was later eclipsed when U.S. Grant was placed in overall command. There were 583 Union and 425 Confederate generals commissioned during the war. By its end, only 374 Union generals and 299 Confederate ones were still on active duty, though many of the latter lacked commands. Excluding those who died during the war, 67 Union and 96 Confederates—of whom 47 and 77 respectively were killed in action or died of wounds—plus 7 Union and 5 Confederate generals who retired for wounds or other legitimate causes, this represents a failure rate of 26 percent for the Union, and 8.6 percent for the Confederacy. The lower failure rate for the Confederacy may be attributed partially to the fact that the Confederate generals tended to be a mite better than Union ones and partially to the fact that they were fighting an essentially defensive war at a time when technology had given the defense an enormous advantage. A more important factor was that Jefferson Davis's tolerance of failure was greater than the much less generous Abraham Lincoln: It is difficult to believe that a Braxton Bragg (a decent division commander) or a Leonidas Polk (who had some administrative skill) would have long continued at high levels in the Union Army.

For various reasons—secrecy, the nature of the conflict, and so forth—it is not possible to compile data on the failure rates of generals in a number of more recent wars. Even on the basis of partial information, we can at least get some idea of the degree of success that senior commanders obtained in these conflicts.

Vietnam

The character of the Vietnam War insured that no division commander could screw up so obviously that the "old boy network" was unable to cover things up in order to avoid a sacking. A division commander "led" his division for the prescribed year and then returned stateside. There were, however, numerous sackings of lower-level officers. In the year beginning in March of 1966, thirty-one battalion commanders in the 1st Infantry Division were relieved, a rate of about 300 percent, though by some accounts the division commander was himself the problem, as all the new battalion commanders were reportedly six feet or taller. Three years later, during 1969, the able, and demanding, commander of the 4th Battalion, 39th Infantry, relieved fifty-nine lieutenants, eight captains, and two majors, a turnover rate of nearly 300 percent. The battalion's performance improved considerably.

Arab-Israeli Wars

The Israelis have had little trouble with senior commanders screwing up in the early stages of a war. For one thing, aside from the 1948–49 War of Independence, none of their wars lasted so long as three weeks. Another important aspect of these wars is that Israel used brigades (one third of a division) as the major battlefield maneuver unit rather than divisions. In the 1973 war, several of the 32–36 brigade commanders (colonels) reportedly turned in less than sterling performances, though none was relieved on the spot. If we take "several" to mean three to five, then the Israelis had a failure rate of 10–16 percent in a war lasting about eighteen days. The 1967 war saw one of the twenty-five or so brigade commanders relieved outright, a failure rate of only 4 percent in a war lasting six days. During the equally short 1956 war, one of the three division commanders and one of the dozen or so brigade commanders were relieved, failure rates of 33 percent and 8 percent respectively. In addition, after the war many commanders who had performed relatively poorly were also replaced in the course of a general reorganization of the army. This goes to demonstrate that even the best-prepared armies will find some of their peacetime commanders incapable of doing the job in combat.

The Arabs' situation in these wars was different, as they regularly took a beating. In each war, several division commanders were relieved before the fighting was over, but because the wars were so short, many deadheads didn't get the sack until after the fighting stopped. This spotlights another aspect of relieving division commanders, the political one. In all armies, and especially the Arab ones, general officers achieve rank partially through political skill. Removing these officers requires some care, and some of the inept battlefield commanders retained their positions because they did possess superior political skills. The retention of these officers helped assure defeat in subsequent wars, but in the meantime kept the peace on the domestic political front.

Third World Conflicts

Most of these wars are more political than military, so the political skills of the generals counts as much (if not more) as their battlefield expertise. Sometimes the disposal of unsuccessful generals can be brutal. In Ethiopia, which has been engaged in an ongoing series of insurgencies for nearly a generation, government generals who lose big often have a visit from the head of state, Mengistu Haile Mariam, who summarily, and personally, executes them. While this practice is rare—Mengistu had once used it to sack about half his Cabinet—it is not unknown. There is evidence to suggest that unsuccessful Iranian commanders in the Iran-Iraq War paid the supreme penalty as well, and the infighting among Afghan leaders (both Communist and non-Communist) occasionally leads to a firefight.

SUCCESSFUL GENERALS WHO PERHAPS OUGHT TO HAVE BEEN SACKED

This may sound like a bizarre suggestion, but in fact there have been many *successful* generals who ought to have been replaced. Throughout history, there have been commanders such as Hannibal, Napoleon, and Robert E. Lee whose very success has largely obscured the fact that their side lost. These commanders certainly could win battles: They are numbered among the most successful tacticians in history. But they were unable to see that victory in war is more than the sum of victories in battle. When Hannibal refused to march on Rome after his spectacular annihilation of a Roman Army at Cannae (216 B.C.), his subordinate Maharbal remarked, "Hannibal knows how to gain a victory, but not how to use it." Hannibal went on in this fashion for over a dozen years, inflicting so many defeats on the Romans that they decided to ignore his presence in Italy and launched a series of offensives against Carthaginian interests elsewhere. These operations ultimately forced Hannibal to abandon Italy and fight a final battle beneath the walls of his home city of Carthage, a battle that this time he lost.

The German generals in both world wars fall into this category as well. Again we have a number of commanders, such as Paul von Hindenburg and August von Mackensen in World War I, or Erwin Rommel, Heinz Guderian, Walther Model, and Erich von Manstein in World War II, who were wonderful tacticians, but unable to affect the overall strategic picture. While their failure in the Second World War is regularly laid at Hitler's feet, this was not the case in World War I, when the generals had complete control over the country and its military policy. But then, the Germans *did* come closer to strategic victory in World War I. They actually defeated Russia and implemented a treaty ending the war with their Eastern opponent. Many of the divisions in the East were shifted to the Western front, where only the timely arrival of massive U.S. forces prevented Allied defeat in France. During World War II, some of the more successful battlefield generals, like Guderian, Model, and Rommel, did make suggestions for more efficient prosecution of the war. They were ignored, which is just as well. For if Germany had prolonged the war six months, the first two nuclear bombs would have reached their original targets, in Germany, rather than at Hiroshima and Nagasaki. History works in curious ways.

It is worth recalling that one of the most successful generals in American history, Nathanael Greene, never won a victory on the battlefield, yet the series of defeats that he sustained in 1780–81 made possible the liberation of most of the South from British control and helped to set up the American victory at Yorktown that brought the Revolutionary War to a successful conclusion.

Historical experience has shown that it is better to have civilians running wars, as they are more in tune with the political nuances of the situation. But those directing a war must have a grasp of military capabilities. The solution is for civilian leaders to be better informed about military affairs.

Bullets and Ballots:
The Politics of
Shooting Blanks

·7·

What is the proper relationship between politics and the military? How do domestic politics influence the perception and the reality of military force? What effects do military forces have on politics?

Military power is a reflection of social and political reality, the direct result of the social and political conditions in a nation. Military power is very much part of the political process. While in the Western democracies it is taken for granted that the politicians will make the final decision on military matters, such is not the case in most of the world. Western democracies, which essentially tamed their troops generations, even centuries, ago, usually ignore how deeply the armed forces can, and frequently do, get into the political process elsewhere. When military and civilian leadership are mixed together, strange, and often tragic, results usually obtain. Shooting blanks involves real bullets, and real bodies.

Military power ought to be the last resort, to be used only when more peaceful political action fails. The United States military insists that its primary mission is to deter war, not fight it. Unfortunately, what ought to be and what is are very different. Military power is what passes for politics in the many nations ruled or heavily influenced by the military, or by civilians relying excessively on the military. This is particularly common in Third World nations where the largest concentration of discipline, educated, and trained—not to mention armed—people are in the military. In such societies, the soldiers decide to run things because they perceive a lack of discipline, ability, or honesty in the civilian government. Or maybe the soldiers are simply a rapacious bunch of thugs who decide to run the nation for their own benefit. About a third of the nations in the world are presently ruled—mostly misruled—by military regimes.

Nearly every nation, including the more developed ones, has had the military seize power at some point in its history. But as nations become more industrialized and wealthy, economic power overwhelms the brute force of the troops, or at least provides many would-be soldiers with more peaceful opportunities for attaining the good life. This tendency can be seen at work in a number of developing countries right now, including South Korea and several in Latin America. The United States is the only one of the world's major nations that has not, at some time in its history, been ruled by a military dictatorship, although the American Revolution was arguably a rebellion by the legally constituted militia against the royal government. American historians point out that the militia was subject to the political control of the rebellious colonial governments. But those governments were merely local representatives of the crown. Many of those militiamen remained loyal, and some of the bloodiest fighting was between rebel and loyal militia units. This goes some way toward explaining American inability to appreciate how nervous the rest of the planet gets about America's enormous military and political power.

Every nation is at risk for military takeover, as has been demonstrated many times in the last fifty years when military regimes showed up in the most unlikely places, such as Chile and Uruguay, both with long histories of democratic civilian rule, and even Poland, which was the first Communist state to undergo a military coup.

NATIONALISM AND PATRIOTISM

Some call these two ideas noble principles; others call them jingoism. Whatever the labels, nationalism and patriotism heavily influence the use of military power. They are also a large component of domestic politics. It's common for any group to be galvanized by leaders declaring that they are the best, capable of mighty deeds in the cause of the nation, if they just pull together. Sound familiar? The same line is turned up real loud for proposed military adventures.

MILITARY ROLES IN SOCIETY

No nation of any size or significance has ever survived without organized armed forces. Most nations have come into existence largely because their population was armed and willing to fight together as a group. The United States is one of the more notable examples, as were Russia and most of the European nations, drawing in part on the traditions of the ancient Greeks and Romans and partially on those of the European barbarian tribes.

Most other ancient civilizations, such as India, China, Aztec Mexico, Inca, and Japan, recognized the military as a separate caste, with specific rights and duties. The feudal system in medieval Europe was based on such a "warrior" class, and some of the emotional baggage that went along with that distinction survives to this day in the form of military tradition and custom. The military as a branch of the civil service first arose in Europe out of the old feudal military system, as loosely organized kingdoms began to be pulled together into coherent, bureaucratized states.

THE CIVIL-SERVICE DISEASE

Whether the soldiers are a separate class or the populace-in-arms or armed civil servants, there is still a persistent problem with their effectiveness. Populations have long complained of inefficient civil servants, and the military may have been the first state employees to demonstrate this tendency.

There are never enough wars to go around, and keeping

the troops combat ready is a constant, and age-old, problem. Military effectiveness is frequently less important than its appearance, a situation that creates a number of strange developments within the military. The most obvious characteristic, and the one most consistently ignored, is the tendency to put appearance before performance. This makes sense, because military forces historically spend far more time at peace than at war. Survival in peacetime, from a political point of view, depends on looking good, not being good. In peacetime, it doesn't make much difference how combat capable you are because you are not fighting anyone; but, by God, you'd better *look* combat capable. The extent to which capability is sacrificed for appearance varies from nation to nation. For some countries, the trade-off is severe. Third World nations are particularly prone to putting appearance before capability. In some cases, appearance may be all they can afford, if that.

Another problem with administering peacetime military forces is the inevitable interservice politics. This is more than just an army-navy problem. The rivalry between soldiers and sailors for scarce defense budgets goes back thousands of years. Less noticed by the civilians are the disputes among different branches, or "arms," within the army and navy (revolving around tanks, artillery, carriers, submarines, etc.), and within the air force (interceptors, ground attack, ICBMs) as well. Different contingents in each of the major services compete to prove to the government that their particular group is the most valuable to the nation and hence the most deserving of additional funds. Invariably, such interservice rivalries become inextricably interwoven with domestic politics. It is common that many, if not most, civilian politicians have had some service in the military and retain a certain fondness for the experience. While this problem is nowhere more severe than in the United States, it exists, to a lesser extent, in every nation.

UNIFORMED POLITICS

Regardless of country, patriotism and military service always play well in political life. In the case of the United States, for example, of the nation's nine major wars, six (the American Revolution, the War of 1812, the Mexican War, the Civil War, the Spanish-American War, and World War II) produced "hero" presidents: George Washington, Andrew Jackson, Zachary Taylor, Ulysses S. Grant, Theodore Roosevelt, and Dwight D. Eisenhower. The exceptions are World War I, because John J. Pershing refused to run, and Korea and Vietnam, which were both unpopular and unsuccessful wars: Had the latter two turned out differently, it is difficult to believe that Douglas MacArthur or William C. Westmoreland would not have made it to the White House. And as William Henry Harrison's election demonstrates, even a very minor war can propel a "hero" into the White House. The list of "hero" presidents can easily be expanded with Chester Arthur, Rutherford B. Hayes, William McKinley, John F. Kennedy, even George Bush. The difference is, that first group was very clearly elected as a result of a war, while it just helped the political futures of the second. Had Kennedy not run for president few would remember his exploits aboard the unlucky *PT-109* in the South Pacific. George Bush's valiant, and painful, experiences as a World War II carrier pilot were likewise given wide play during his presidential campaign. Compared to Michael Dukakis's tour of duty as a clerk in peacetime Korea, Bush obviously got the better of it. Wearing the uniform during wartime rarely hurts a politician's career.

But there's more. Of the forty men who have held the presidency, twenty-five have been "veterans," a term that originally meant a man who had seen service in combat, but now merely indicates someone who, at one time or another, has seen some sort of military service, whether in war or peace. That service may have been as short as Lincoln's seven weeks of arduous militia duty during the Black Hawk War (1832), or as curious as Reagan's three years of film making during World War II. Excluding the first two elections, in which Washington, a real veteran, ran unopposed, there have been forty-nine presidential elections. A "veteran" ran in twenty-six of these. Excluding five elections in which veterans ran against each other, there have been twenty-one elections in which a veteran ran against a nonveteran. Of these, the veteran lost in only five. In three of those cases, the character of the race was confused by the presence of several serious candidates on the ballot: in 1824, Andrew Jackson lost in a four-way race with John Quincy Adams, Henry Clay, and William H. Crawford; in 1892, Benjamin Harrison, in a three-way race with Grover Cleveland and

James B. Weaver; and in 1912, Theodore Roosevelt, in a three-way race with William Howard Taft and Woodrow Wilson. In the fourth case, in 1836, the veteran, William Henry Harrison, was beaten by Andrew Jackson's favorite, Martin Van Buren, while in the fifth case, in 1856, the veteran, John C. Frémont, was an ardent antislavery candidate from the newly formed Republican party. So nonveterans do not do well. In fact, a nonveteran has not won in the last eleven elections, although there have been five elections in which one has tried.

The situation in Russia is surprisingly similar. Stalin, Khrushchev, and Brezhnev, who collectively ran the USSR for about half a century, all saw extensive military service, albeit largely (but not entirely) in political roles. Clearly, having some military service under one's belt does not hurt one's political chances on either side of the Iron Curtain.

It's unclear to what extent a soldier-turned-politician is influenced by his former military status. Although there is usually an assumption that he will be a warlike leader, this has not always been the case. The United States, for example, did not go to war during the administration of any of the eleven former generals who have occupied the White House. Consider the experience of two former generals who became presidents of their countries, Dwight D. Eisenhower of the United States and Charles de Gaulle of France. Both came to power in the course of unpleasant and unwinnable wars, and both behaved in a remarkably statesmanlike fashion, bringing the wars to a reasonably honorable conclusion. Both proved very effective at dealing with unrest in the ranks, though de Gaulle had the more difficult task here. Yet it is unclear the extent to which either was comfortable out of uniform. Thus, at one particularly acrimonious NATO summit, de Gaulle is said to have pointed to the host of political aides who accompanied them, and remarked to Eisenhower to the effect that "If we could get rid of all these politicians, we old soldiers could solve this problem," to which Eisenhower is said to have nodded in agreement.

Veterans maintain a warm feeling for the branch of the military in which they served. This can have important political results. The U.S. Navy, for example, has done particularly well over the last quarter-century because all but one of the presidents from John F. Kennedy—the first sailor president—on down served with the fleet. Jimmy Carter was very hard on the navy's budget, however, perhaps because he was one of Hyman Rickover's carefully selected "nuclear navy" technocratic officers. One can only speculate what may happen to already huge air-force budgets should a USAF veteran eventually attain the presidency.

Despite bitter battles over cutting military spending, the real struggle is mostly about which faction of the military will get what fraction of the funds. How well a particular military faction does in these budget battles is not always related to the contribution it makes to the nation's defense. Rather, it has everything to do with the skill with which the senior officers of that faction battle for the budget in political infighting.

Budgetary politics consist of some very serious horse-trading between the military, which spends the money, and the legislators, who provide it. With minor variations, this system is found throughout the world. Eisenhower and Khrushchev once exchanged views on the question of how their respective governments allocated funds to the military and found a high degree of similarity. In both countries, the military leaders would say, "The other guys have this excellent new weapon, and in consequence the safety of the nation depends upon our having it too." Despite this measure of similarity, nowhere is the process of developing the military "budget" more complex than in the United States. This is largely due to the fact that a serious regard for military preparedness is a recent development in U.S. history.

Prior to World War II, the United States never had a large military budget to wrangle over except during a few major wars, when everyone was willing to spend like mad. But these wartime spending frenzies left a bad taste behind because of the opportunities created—and regularly indulged in—for corruption. Once a large defense budget became a permanent part of the political landscape, with the onset of the Cold War in the late 1940s, certain rules of behavior appeared. Legislators soon realized that they scored big points with their constituents if their efforts brought military business to their districts. Conversely, this meant that the loss of any military business in their district was also seen as damaging to a politician's career.

The military soon noticed the connection and played this angle for all it was worth. There were two primary ways to spread the money around for the maximum political impact.

One was to choose carefully where new military bases would be located. Bases created a lot of jobs, and if they could be located so that two or even three congressional districts were affected, that would translate into a lot of happy voters. The new jobs involved not just military personnel, but also the civilians who worked for the military, at the rate of one for every two troops, plus all the firms necessary to supply the steady stream of goods needed to keep the bases going. The other angle was procurement, which involved working closely with defense contractors. Building a new weapons system might require only one or two factories to do the final assembly, but there can be hundreds of subcontractors supplying components and services. These smaller outfits are frequently spread out all over the country. Subcontractors are often selected more because of the political clout of their local representative than for the contractor's capability. The ultimate manifestation of this appears to have been the contracting for the B-1 bomber, which was so well spread around that there were subcontractors in forty-eight of the fifty states, and some work was also done in Puerto Rico. Social priorities aside, this is one reason why representatives from inner-city areas are hostile to defense spending, as not much of it gets spent in their districts, which are heavily residential.

Even seasoned antidefense types will become very hawkish in defense of dubious programs if there is a piece of the action in their home districts or states. In 1983, the ballooning deficit resulted in calls for cuts in defense expenditures. John Tower, then chairman of the Senate Armed Services Committee, asked his colleagues to propose program and base cuts affecting their home states. Only three senators responded. Similarly, in 1989, several senators and representatives noted for persistent antidefense voting made a successful bid to save "vital" programs scheduled to be cut, such as the F-14 fighter and the Osprey vertical takeoff transport. These legislators are not being particularly craven; they are simply aware that if they do not support the major defense programs in their districts, they will be held personally responsible for the lost jobs when the projects are terminated. The manufacturer's PR people will see to this, and when a politician occasionally puts principle before politics, the PR crew (and local adversaries) regularly send the officeholder into early retirement at the next election.

For some time, proponents of the military have taken up the idea that a stable percentage of the GNP should be devoted to defense spending on a continuing basis. Unfortunately, since there are no objective criteria on which to base an estimate of the optimal percentage that should be spent, whatever figure is proposed has essentially just been plucked out of the air, or the average for the last few decades is used. Moreover, this notion runs into problems when confronted with the taxpayers' perceived value of the military strength all this money supposedly buys. Many people find it difficult to understand arguments that suggest that cutting $10 billion will so degrade the nation's military as to make it liable to speedy defeat in the event of war, given that the armed forces will still have $290–$295 billion to spend.

DEMOCRATIC COOPERATION

Historically, the normal relationship between civil government and the military has been adversarial. In the past, governments were periodically at the mercy of their soldiery. From time to time, the troops—whether Roman legionnaires, German knights, Chinese bannermen, Egyptian Mamluks, Japanese samurai, Turkish Janissaries, Russian Streltsy, Spanish pikemen, American militiamen (1775 and 1861), or French paratroopers (1958 and 1960)—would mutiny for the purpose of securing some demands. On numerous occasions, in many countries unhappy soldiers—and occasionally unhappy sailors or airmen—were able to install a candidate of their own as ruler, a phenomenon that was even manifested in Cromwellian England in the 1650s. The American Revolution, while instigated by the revolt of a domestic militia raised by the British for defense against the French and Indians, never saw military officers dominating the political scene. This is an important distinction that makes Americans forget that their revolution *was* made possible by a rebellion of organized troops (the militia) and their officers (like Colonel George Washington and many others). The British realized too late that the regular British troops in North America were not able to suppress the larger local militia. The British were much more careful with colonial militia forces after that. For this reason, the 1857 mutiny of Indian troops in Britain's Indian colonies was suppressed by local British forces.

Over the past three centuries, as modern democracies and bureaucratic states began to evolve, techniques for controlling restless troops had to be created. The principal change has been to diminish the "class" difference between troops and civilians. This was easily accomplished by introducing conscription as a means to fill the ranks, a process that was furthered by the fact that the incipient Industrial Revolution made it easier to equip, clothe, and feed such hordes. The introduction of cheap, mass-produced, simple-to-use firearms also eliminated the advantage of the professional warrior, who required years of practice to become a proficient killer.

These mass armies also helped to break up the hereditary officer caste, because there weren't enough blue bloods to command all those troops. This made it easier for growing numbers of ambitious middle-class applicants to become officers. And as governments became more bureaucratized, so too did their armies. These developments helped secure governments from untoward acts on the part of unhappy soldiers.

The use of mass armies was actually an ancient one, going back more than a thousand years, to the Dark Ages and practices common among the tribes from which the nations of modern Europe (and most other nations) descend. These tribes were on a constant war footing. All adult males (and sometimes women, as in the Celtic tribes) were liable for service. Leaders were elected or confirmed by the mobilized warriors. When the tribes settled down amid the ruins of the Roman Empire, a hereditary nobility, leading mercenary troops, gradually replaced the militia. Settled populations were secure populations. It was no longer necessary for every able-bodied male to be armed and trained for combat. More hands were required to produce the larger food supply necessary to feed growing settled populations. With occasional exceptions, such as Switzerland, much of the population was thus reduced to serfdom, and it wasn't until about four centuries ago that something resembling popular government, and citizen-soldiers, began to reemerge, first in the Netherlands, then in England and the United States, later in France, and, by the late-nineteenth century in most of the rest of Europe as well. Note that patterns resembling the older, feudal forms of military organization still persist in many Third World nations.

The newly minted nineteenth-century European "democracies"—not all were genuinely democratic, though all paid lip-service to popular sovereignty—basically turned their troops into armed civil servants, with cadres of career officers and NCOs leading masses of conscripts. The citizens conscripted into the ranks comprised over half the troop strength, and upon discharge provided a trained militia ("reserve") in the event of a large-scale war. This large reserve force proved to be a problem, as it made possible larger armed forces that could be put into combat in a very short time, which made wars bloodier. The reserves were not originally thought to be capable of carrying out large-scale offensive operations at the start of a war, but were considered of some value for their defensive abilities. The reserve troops surprised a lot of observers by being nearly as effective as the regulars. The two world wars of the twentieth century were made possible because of the reserve system, and most industrialized nations still retain this system. One positive aspect of all this is that democracies with large reserve systems are not likely to become dictatorships unless all those reservists go along with the dictator.

The case of Nazi Germany is a good example of how the lack of a broadly based military is dangerous. After World War I, the Treaty of Versailles prohibited the Germans from maintaining a large regular army or a reserve, lest they be used to start a new war. As a result, Hitler's private army of Nazi storm troopers greatly outnumbered the Regular Army. So neither the government nor the army may have had the wherewithal—or the will—to attempt a confrontation with Hitler's storm troopers. The storm troopers themselves were inspired by the post–World War I armed bands (*Freikorps*) that rallied around various warlords in 1919 through the early 1920s to dispute the breakup of the German Reich (Empire). That neither the army nor the government felt inclined to do battle with the storm troopers remains the basis for assuming that all Germans are equally responsible for the rise of Naziism. Yet the government's—and the army's—lack of action may have been based on their assumption that if they chose to use force, they would very likely lose anyway, and get a lot of innocent people killed in the process. We can never be sure, but we do know that the German people were mostly war weary, while those who weren't joined the storm troopers. In other words, the army, though committed to reversing the outcome of the First World War, was inclined to postpone the issue, while the Nazis weren't.

It wasn't just citizen-soldiers who protected the democracies from military takeovers. There was also the question of money. Several democracies no longer have conscript armies, notably the United States, Britain, India, and Japan. These nations don't need all the manpower universal conscription can provide, and preferring to avoid the political price of "selective service," they rely on volunteer personnel. They are also able to pay their lowest-ranking troops the higher wages that only the officer and NCO cadres get in conscript armies. Another important reason why these nations do not need large conscript forces is that they are all geographically protected from ground attack by oceans (or mountains and deserts) or by a lack of significant opponents. Nevertheless, the troops in these nations are still representative of the population. Moreover, there still exist large militia forces (Reserves, National Guards, Territorials) in most of them, just in case. Those who join the professional armed forces of these powers, by and large, do not choose to make the service a life-long career, further preventing the creation of a military caste.

Despite a certain amount of feudal baggage, troops in the democracies are basically thought of as an exotic variety of civil servant. The troops, if married, usually live among civilian families. While much of their socializing is with other military people, they are not out of touch with the general population. Their spouses and children mingle with civilians, and most nations encourage early retirement (after twenty to thirty years), thus forcing the troops to stay in touch with civilian society. These troops retire when in their late thirties or early forties and slip right into civilian life with no real difficulty. As military personnel and their families are also exposed to the same media and cultural influences as civilians, this makes for few readjustment difficulties when they leave the service.

As professional soldiers become less of a threat and are recognized as just another professional group, military service is increasingly seen in a positive light by civilians. Former officers gain an edge in competing for civilian jobs. In some countries—Switzerland is a prime example—service as a reserve officer is considered almost obligatory for any young executive looking to climb the corporate management ladder. Similarly, in the United States, a retired officer customarily finds his former occupation an asset in securing employment. In Russia, retired officers are seen as particularly loyal and reliable employees in a society that prizes these two qualities highly.

Keeping the troops from walling themselves off in their own little caste is only possible if you have a lot of money to spread around. In the advanced democracies, the professional soldier generally has the option to enter the civilian economy, often at a higher wage. Most military jobs have civilian equivalents, and those that are combat-related tend to be filled by people who can manage under difficult conditions. Even an infantry officer is accomplished at many civilian tasks, such as personnel management, maintaining large numbers of motor vehicles and other valuable equipment, and so on. The civilian economy always has a need for such managers.

Less wealthy nations, including Russia, provide fewer alternate opportunities for officers, although they still retire most of them young. The retired officers frequently go into the huge civil service. Russia has had a problem with caste-bound soldiers for centuries, and is one of the few nations to keep its officer class out of trouble under these circumstances. The Russians have done this by paying particular attention to the loyalty of the officers and keeping them out of political affairs. This is accomplished by having a large and efficient secret police, of which the KGB is just the latest incarnation. Russia also has vast, sparsely populated border areas in which to station most of the troops, which further helps to keep them away from potential embarrassments.

Most poor nations are not so well organized as the Russians and thus have constant problems with the military taking over, or threatening to do so. Those nations that have had the benefit of Russian "security advisers" and have adopted Russian methods have had fewer problems with politically ambitious generals and colonels.

THE DICTATOR'S FRIEND

Democratic governments rule only about a third of the planet's population. Most nations are ruled by authoritarian regimes heavily reliant on the police and military or by outright military dictatorships. It may seem surprising that these arrangements do not lead to more international wars. This is largely because the troops are so busy running the country, keeping the population in line, and enjoying their superior status that there isn't much opportunity, inclination, or time left over to prepare for foreign adventures. Yet there is a great amount of actual or potential internal unrest when dictators are in charge. When you count civil wars and revolutions, such governments do lead to more fighting.

In most cases, the generals do not particularly want to run the government. If they can find a politician, or an appropriately inclined general, who is willing to oversee national administration while remembering who his friends are, that's all well and good. Many Latin American nations fall into this category, as do several in Asia and Africa. The military will keep the chief of state in power, and the politicians will see to it that the military is not disturbed or impoverished.

Once left alone, the military have a number of potential tasks and options facing them. In most nations, the soldiers simply want to be soldiers, or something along those lines. Few nations are without one or more hostile, or potentially hostile, neighbors. Many nations also suffer from endemic banditry, secessionism, and insurrection. There is usually plenty of military work to be done. But few officers relish spending twenty years chasing bandits or skirmishing with the neighbors. Every effort is made to keep things quiet and peaceful. Officers in these situations quickly realize that there are more profitable uses for the troops than fighting someone.

LIVING OFF THE REGIMENT

Citizens of Western democracies have largely forgotten the mercenary origins of their armed forces. Armies were not always run by a central bureaucracy that set pay and living standards while carefully disbursing funds. The earliest professional armies were administered by periodically paying the commanders (colonels) of every regiment—500–1,000 men—a lump sum. The colonels then paid the troops and vendors who supplied food and other necessities. Frequently, especially during peacetime, much of the money went into the colonel's pocket and the troops went without pay, uniforms, food, or bullets.

This sort of thing happened for a number of reasons. The colonel may have needed the money for more pressing matters, or it was the custom, or perhaps he was simply a crook who saw the military as a means to enrich himself and nothing else. Nonetheless, this ancient system is still widely found in Third World nations and, with some minor modifications, is occasionally found in more "advanced" nations as well.

Because most Third World forces are spread around the country in permanent bases, it's not difficult for a unit commander to develop local commercial interests, sometimes involving such unsavory things as smuggling, drugs, and extortion, or providing muscle for local "businessmen" who are themselves engaged in that sort of thing. Such activities are nothing new: Similar situations have been recorded for as long as there have been organized military forces. Ancient Greek and Roman generals were never averse to some profitable commercial activity.

IMPACT OF THE MILITARY ON GOVERNMENT

In some countries, the armed forces are more than just a part of the government. At times they *are* the government. At the very least, the military is the most crucial part of the administration. There are three areas where the military has the most impact on government: budgets, administration, and, naturally, defense. The military's impact in each of these areas is not as straightforward as one would think.

BUDGET IMPACT

Armed forces rarely go to war, but they always consume a large chunk of the national budget. Whether the troops are effective or not, they *will* be expensive. The costs rise and fall depending on various political and diplomatic developments. Some of the more interesting of these events to be seen in quite some time are occurring now and will continue to occur throughout the 1990s.

In this century, military budgets have grown faster than the economies that support them. This is partially attributable to the World Wars, which were periods of extraordinary spending on armaments. Since shortly after World War II, the arms race (the Cold War) between the U.S.-led NATO and the Russian-led Warsaw Pact alliances accelerated this trend. The Cold War has been an unequal contest, as the free-market economies of the NATO nations proved far more robust in the long run than the centrally planned Communist economies of the Warsaw Pact nations, but until recently this fact has not deterred the Russians from trying to keep up. Of late, they've been feeling the economic pinch. The United States, with a more vigorous economy, managed this spending contest better, but has also paid an economic price.

The Communist nations have run out of money, and their people out of patience waiting for the good life that a socialist dictatorship was supposed to deliver. U.S. arms spending has contributed to America's having gone from being a creditor to a debtor nation. But other nations still have funds for ever more weapons.

The petroleum-rich Middle East continues to wallow in cash. Through the 1980s, Middle East arms spending directed at the Iran-Iraq War amounted to over a hundred billion dollars of excess military spending. This, in a region that normally spends over 10 percent of its GNP on defense. Here is a typical case of war forcing a government's hand in arms spending. Not only did Iraq vastly increase its defense spending because of the war, but most of Iraq's Arab neighbors reached deep into their oil wealth to support the war against Iran, the traditional enemy of the Arabs. This, unfortunately, led Iraq to invade Kuwait, in order to restore Iraq's finances leading to the Gulf War.

A combination of extensive oil wealth and war potential make the Middle East the region with the largest portion of its GNP devoted to arms. Europe, where military spending takes up 6 percent of much larger and more vigorous economies, is a distant second. In the rest of the world, defense spending consumes between 3 and 4 percent of GNP. Worldwide, money devoted to military affairs is about 5 percent of all wealth created each year (GNP). There are regional differences. For example, on average the nations of sub-Saharan Africa spend 3.5 percent of their GNP on defense; the Americas, 3.3 percent (the United States alone spends 5–6 percent); Europe, 6.2 percent; the Middle East, 12.2 percent; South Asia, 3.6 percent; and East Asia, 3.8 percent. These are hard numbers to pin down, as most nations are not above hiding military spending in other categories. The usual reason for these subterfuges is to lessen the complaints from citizens who would like to see the funds spent on less violent projects. Some nations plead security, while others are simply incompetent at keeping the books straight.

Most nations spend under 4 percent of their GNP on defense, and a few spend over 20 percent. In wartime, the spending can climb to 50 percent, or more. Such high rates cannot be sustained for long, as they mean starving the population and not replacing aging plant and equipment. Those nations that spend 20 percent or more during peacetime have moribund economies to show for it, unless they're floating atop lots of oil.

The most prominent example of excessive defense spending is Russia, which by various calculations spends between 15 and 20 percent of its GNP on defense each year. Despite their recent admission to a "defense budget" equal to about $125 billion a year, apparently even the Russians aren't sure how much is being spent. There are several reasons for this besides the fact that the ruble has no accepted value internationally. To begin with, there is no central accounting system in Russia, or any nongovernmental regulatory mechanisms on the economy. In addition, and more important, is the fact that the Russian armed forces run their own autonomous economy, with mines, factories, farms, and other facilities devoted to producing goods for military use. These installations operate under different rules than do comparable civilian establishments. For example, they have priority access to scarce materials, for which Western defense plants would have to compete on the open market. In the West, this competition drives up costs. In Russia, these additional costs are hidden behind a system of centralized planning. Russia's defense industries also are allocated lots of scarce foreign exchange, with which to procure scarce materials abroad. And workers in defense industries get many special benefits from the government, which thus do not figure in production costs. Some defense installations produce a variety of nominally civilian items (housewares, clothing, motor vehicles, wristwatches, and so forth), primarily for use by military personnel and civilian defense workers. These higher-quality civilian goods are another part of the higher compensation defense workers receive.

The rationale for this separate defense economy is the lack of sufficient production quality in the Russian economy as a whole. While you could get away with selling shoddy clothes and appliances to Russian civilians, the same cannot be done with weapons for Russian soldiers. For one thing, the weapons may have to be used in combat against Western systems. For another, they can be exported for hard (Western) currency and are one of the few types of Russian manufactured goods that must successfully compete on the world market. Historically, the Russian military has had some control over weapons production, and has enforced quality standards. In the face of a lackadaisical work force and no incentives to produce quality goods, the Russian defense chiefs set up their own factories, where quality work was rewarded. Observers have noted that one way you can identify a defense plant is by the number of workers' cars parked in the vicinity; defense workers are several times more likely to own a car than the average Russian. As an added incentive, unsatisfactory defense workers are returned to the nondefense industries, where the living is not nearly so plush. The bottom line, so to speak, is that building any item in the defense industries costs a lot more than the same item built in a nondefense plant. The additional carrots dangled in front of the defense workers do not show up on Russian account books, but they cost the national economy quite a lot. This highlights an important aspect of all Communist economies: Access to goods is more important than the price of goods. There is a shortage of everything in Russia except money. The workers save plenty, but have nothing to spend it on. A government official decides who can buy an automobile or a refrigerator. Naturally, this permission is used as an incentive to extract better performances from the minority of workers deemed able enough to perform the more exacting work required of defense factories.

This Russian system is in sharp contrast to the situation in the West. American defense industries must compete with nondefense manufacturers for workers and other resources. Only in wartime can U.S. defense plants obtain the priorities in funding, workers, and raw materials that Russian defense industries enjoy at all times. In contrast to Russia, Western defense industries have somewhat less capable staff than nondefense companies, a circumstance that arises from the many hassles defense workers must endure. First, there is the need for security clearances and security procedures in general. Next, defense industries are not as competitive as nondefense operations, which discourages many of the more enthusiastic workers. Finally, defense work is smothered by government bureaucrats and regulations. All of this creates the various defense procurement scandals that periodically sweep through Western nations, especially the United States. Communist states have different kinds of scandals, generally much worse, but you rarely hear about them. The current *glasnost* atmosphere in Russia will bring many of these scandals to light.

The United States defense-budget situation is unique, and many are just coming to realize it. At the end of World War II, the United States possessed half the world's production capacity. This was largely because the already enormous U.S. industrial plant was unscathed by the fighting that left most of the remaining major economies in ruins. For twenty years, most of the planet was rebuilding while the U.S. economy reigned supreme in global markets. In addition to filling the economic vacuum with manufactured goods, the United States took up a lot of the slack in defense. A large network of overseas bases was set up, many of which were simply installations established during the Second World War. Half a million troops manned these old and new bases, accompanied by nearly as many more dependents and U.S. civilian workers. Although the Russians put far more troops on foreign soil, the U.S. presence overseas, including dependents, was a historically unprecedented peacetime deployment abroad for any nation. When one considers that the United States had never had very many troops stationed abroad, this was a particularly huge commitment of personnel.

All these American overseas deployments did not come cheaply. The cost of maintaining this web of overseas bases is nearly a hundred billion dollars a year. At the same time, the economies ravaged during World War II are now rebuilt, in most cases with U.S. seed money, so that the U.S. economy now accounts for only about 25 percent of world production. What is out of sync is the contribution many foreign nations with U.S. bases make to their own defense. The U.S. military garrisons have become a bit addictive. The presence of American forces, and the implied assurance that reinforcements will come should there be a war, makes it easy for some nations to slack off on their own defense spending. The most blatant examples of this are Japan and several of the NATO countries. The military in these nations have become accustomed to hearing politicians shoot down their money requests with explicit or implicit remarks that "the Americans will protect us." Though they are less open about the matter, a number of neutrals, particularly in Europe, also implicitly rely on the United States to come to their rescue should they be threatened by Russia.

This situation has led to one of the great defense debates of the 1990s: Should the United States withdraw its forces from overseas bases? It's made more urgent by Russia's moves toward unilateral withdrawal from Eastern Europe. Since 1945, Russia has had more troops in foreign parts than has the United States, about 800,000 to 500,000. But these are overwhelmingly ground forces, and are provided for on a much less lavish standard than American troops. U.S. personnel abroad consist heavily of expensive naval units and combat aircraft, plus lots of costly civilian dependents. Moreover, the expense of maintaining Russian troops in Eastern Europe is a severe burden on the faltering Soviet economy, so pulling them out unilaterally would pay considerable economic, political, and diplomatic dividends. While trade—and loan—prospects with Western Europe will brighten because of the goodwill these gestures create, even bigger gains are likely in Eastern Europe. Nations like East Germany, Czechoslovakia, and Poland supplied many high-tech items for Russia's civilian and military economies. As these nations go through their own political restructuring in the 1990s, it will be important for Russia to see that good relations are not trampled in the process. Removing what are locally regarded as occupation forces will raise Russia's stature throughout Eastern Europe. These withdrawals have already begun.

In America, the budget pressures for troop reductions are coming from several directions. The economists and taxpayers are screaming for reductions in trade and budget deficits. Because defense takes up such a large chunk of the budget, it will be vulnerable. In fact, the U.S. defense budget began to shrink in the late 1980s. But this shrinkage simply gives the military-budget defenders another argument to use in protecting their turf. Even so, the generals and admirals are going to have a tough time because they will be under assault by the Congress and the Department of State, not to mention the Treasury and the voters. The Gulf War will not change this trend.

U.S. diplomats have never been keen about operating in the shadow of the Defense Department. Although the secretary of state, and his senior staff, are the president's men, the career State Department people would like to see State replace Defense as the major player overseas, as was the case before World War II. The large military forces stationed abroad following that war have made the Defense Department into another State Department: witness the advent of officers trained by the military to be "soldier-diplomats." This has not gone down well with the real diplomats at the State Department, and bringing the troops home would take the military out of the diplomacy business.

There will be tremendous pressure to bring the troops back home. The host nations in Europe grasp eagerly at peace offerings from the Russians and would feel more comfortable about bargaining away U.S. troops rather than their own national forces. The U.S. troops they don't control; their own they do. If massive conventional arms cuts are agreed upon, something has to give. Most likely it would be the U.S. forces, which would please American taxpayers, not to mention the Europeans and the Russians. A token force—say a brigade or division—might be left behind to insure U.S. participation in a future war. This is the old hostage routine: The U.S. troops would get hit in any future war, and this would inflame U.S. public opinion and cause reinforcements to be sent. Or so the theory goes. It usually works.

The Europeans, especially the now united Germans, are eager to see U.S. forces go home, if the Russians do so too, because this implies that there is less chance of a war, especially a nuclear one that would lay waste to most of Europe and to Germany in particular. With the Russians and Americans back on their own territory, the risk of major war would be much less.

Those Europeans who see the departure of U.S. troops as a reason for increasing European defense budgets must be careful about what they make of it. There has always been a tacit agreement that all NATO members would preach the gospel of U.S. troops being needed because European nations could not defend themselves alone. American forces can depart now that this is no longer the case. The beliefs that have sustained U.S.

overseas deployments for over forty years can no longer be honored to justify the past.

The departure of U.S. troops puts some pressure on European NATO nations to beef up their forces. These budget adjustments would become part of the maelstrom of negotiation required to deal with Russia's unilateral cuts and proposals for even deeper force reductions. Unlike Russia, and the Eastern European nations, Western Europe is not under as much fiscal pressure to cut back and can afford increases in defense spending. At the very least, the billions spent annually on subsidies for departed American troops could be shifted to national forces.

It is only when radical changes must be made in defense spending that everyone gets really serious about looking closely at just what the armed forces are defending them against. To make a U.S. withdrawal palatable, Russia would have to pull out all its troops in Eastern Europe. The Western Europeans will then be facing Eastern Europeans. After all, U.S. and Russian troops are in Central Europe because of wars that the Europeans themselves started. This is frequently ignored in all the talk about Superpower withdrawal. The outbreak of ethnic strife in Bulgaria, Yugoslavia, Romania, Czechoslovakia, etc., should remind us that there are numerous territorial and other disputes among the various European nations, particularly among the Eastern European nations, which could trigger a war in the future as readily as they did in the past. And then there's the perennial German Question. German nationalism was a major cause of the two world wars, and could rear up and kick off another major European war. Reunification may sound good in Bonn and Berlin, but is much less popular in Paris or Brussels or Warsaw.

The relationships between national budgets and defense policy and expenditures are nowhere more complex than in Europe. In Europe, there are more nations with more money and more troops than anywhere else. There are numerous ancient disputes among many of the nations throughout Europe. The 1990s will see much ferment politically, economically, and militarily because of the lessening antagonism between the Superpowers.

Elsewhere, the military effects on the budget are less dramatic and more predictable. Lacking a believably aggressive neighbor, the military has a difficult time getting much money out of the government. This lack of financial support is one key element in many of the military takeovers around the world. Argentina is a case in point. Up until the disastrous war with Britain over the Falkland Islands in 1982, the military government was able to get over 4 percent of the GNP for the armed forces. Most of this went into the pockets of the soldiers, with over 60 percent being expended in personnel costs. Officers and career NCOs took a disproportionate share of this money, as most of the troops were conscripts getting minimal pay. After the war, a civilian government took over, and defense spending quickly fell to under 2 percent of Argentina's GNP. By the military's reckoning, the combat power of the armed forces was reduced even more, to about one quarter of what it was before 1982. These dire assessments, plus several unsuccessful coups by disgruntled officers, demonstrate the relationship between the budget and a peaceful military.

The military impact on national budgets and economies varies enormously. When defense spending goes above 5 percent a year in peacetime, you can expect eventual trouble from the taxpayers. That's not a prediction, just an observation of the historical record.

GOVERNMENT ADMINISTRATION

Because of the discipline and educational requirements of modern armed forces, the military is frequently one of the largest concentrations of administrative and technical talent in a nation. This is particularly true in the Third World, where military officers possessing management and technical skills have a lot of impact on government administration even if they haven't taken over the government. Industrialized nations have a more or less similar situation, although it works to their benefit, as the career soldiers retire while still young and add their experience to governmental and commercial organizations. In many nations, veterans are even given preference in civil-service jobs. While this is done largely for political purposes, it does keep the soldier's skills within the government. Third World nations also like to keep their career soldiers in government work after retirement. The soldiers prefer this too, largely because there are likely to be few legal employment opportunities for them outside the military or civil government.

Some nations, particularly the more sophisticated Third World ones, even take advantage of the special skills of their troops before they retire. In a number of countries, military personnel are assigned to civil administrative posts. Not a few countries, such as Mexico, use their troops on rural development projects, building schools, roads, water-supply systems, and the like, as do some of the developed countries. The United States Army Corps of Engineers has a long record of service on major civil engineering projects, while U.S. troops on maneuvers in Third World countries regularly engage in rural-development projects or run clinics. This sort of activity has several benefits. Many difficult but necessary projects get done. In addition, the troops gain experience in performing their wartime duties under more realistic conditions than normal training exercises. And the public-relations payoff may be politically valuable.

DEFENSE

In too many instances, the armed forces of a country not only are incapable of providing much defense, but make matters worse by creating the impression that the nation has some useful combat capability. Even major powers have difficulty assessing the readiness of their forces. Though the leaders themselves may have been in the military, they are not likely to be up on what constitutes combat readiness, given the latest developments in military art and science and the pathologies that affect armed forces at peace. As a result, they must rely heavily on the views of the military professionals who are actually running the armed forces. If these officers are competent and honest, the troops—and the nation—will be well served. But the professional leadership itself is not always certain what constitutes readiness, particularly after a long period of peace, or in an environment in which new technologies and techniques are coming along faster than they can be digested. Nor is a military dictator likely to be any better off in this regard, given that combat readiness is normally incompatible with a heavily politicized military. Indeed, the record on this score is pretty clear: Military dictatorships generally lose wars.

THE POSITIVE ASPECTS OF THE ARMS RACE

There are some beneficial aspects to maintaining a certain degree of international military tension. For one thing, if it doesn't get too out of hand, it helps prevent war. Though everyone agrees that it may be necessary to resort to arms at times, given reasonably rational leadership—that is, in the absence of an Adolf Hitler, Idi Amin, or Saddam Hussein—no one really wants war. As a result, a certain degree of international military tension keeps everyone on his toes. A few little wars going on here and there in which the major powers compete with each other through minor-power surrogates are also useful, as they allow the horrors of war to be demonstrated and deplored. Nuclear weapons make it too dangerous for the major powers to go at each other. So they fight their wars through third parties, which gives all concerned good examples of what everyone would suffer from if a general war broke out.

It is worth recalling that when World War I broke out in 1914, it had been over forty years since there had been a war between two of the European great powers and nearly a century since there had been a general war in Europe. Few people remembered how bad war was. Today, the wide availability of television and film helps insure that citizens inclined to a military solution are vividly reminded about the likely gruesome results. Thus an arms race can also be of some value in preserving the peace. So long as one of the competing powers does not fall behind, or *think* it has fallen behind, the mutual orgy of military expenditures keeps the soldiers amused, the patriots proud, and the politicians happy, while helping to advance technology. Despite momentary hysterics, whatever advantage one side may gain over the other through the introduction of a new technology or technique will never be sufficiently great to be a more than temporary edge, soon to be wiped out by the opposition's newest gimmick. As a result, getting ready for war becomes an ongoing process that never quite leads to war. Thus the intensive arms race between the United States and Russia has made "the Big One" so literally unthinkable that each of the Superpowers is less concerned that its opponent may start a war than that some minor power might trick it into one.

The principal shortcoming of an arms race is the incredible

amount of waste. Any arms spending is essentially waste, but given human nature and the history of international relations, a nation cannot exist long if it is unarmed. Fortunately, nuclear weapons make it possible to actually halt an arms race without losing the absolute ability to vaporize your heavily armed opponents. Given their present mutual inclinations toward disarmament, the East/West arms race will wind down during the 1990s so that the participants can make their economies more competitive and their citizens less restive and unruly.

EXAMPLES OF THE PROBLEMS OF CIVIL-MILITARY RELATIONS

Due to historical and cultural factors, different societies are prone to seek somewhat unique solutions to their problems with civil-military relations. National differences will show up in the character of their armed forces, the strategies that will be followed, and to civil-military relations and so on. Although many nations may develop similar patterns, there are as many solutions to these problems as there are countries, as can be seen from the accompanying sampler.

THAILAND

The military controls the media in Thailand, providing a novel and effective means of influencing the politicians and businessmen. This arrangement shows how military power can be translated into unusual civil powers and then leveraged into more lucrative activities. This also points out the fact that the military, as an institution, can own a wide variety of operations ranging from supermarkets (in the United States) to consumer goods factories (Russia).

ARGENTINA

Argentina has always had a relatively modern military force patterned on the latest European models. But the political immaturity of the Argentine armed forces, and of the populace as a whole, has resulted in an ongoing series of military coups, such that in the entire 150-year history of the country few democratically elected presidents have completed a full term of office. The armed forces have been politically active throughout the history of the country, and believe themselves the special guardians of what might be termed the nation's "soul." In the past, their desire to preserve their special status has led to considerable bloodshed. So any civilian regime in Argentina had best pay attention to what the officers are saying, and thinking.

UNITED STATES

Despite almost continuous fears of military dictatorship by a hysterical fringe of citizens on both the left and the right—even at times when the military was virtually a corporal's guard—the U.S. armed forces have played a very minor role in American political life, being effectively subservient to the political leadership, in the form of the president and Congress. There are a number of reasons for this. Even professional officers have been nurtured on the tradition of the "citizen-soldier," and the fundamental principles of democratic society run deep. Being in the service confers no particular social or political advantage, and certainly no economic one, as is often the case in the Third World. One becomes an officer much as one becomes a doctor, lawyer, or engineer; it's an occupation, perhaps one that makes greater demands on one's patriotism than most but still a trade, and one that society ideologically believes can be fulfilled by almost anyone. To be sure, American military professionals have political opinions, and are periodically at odds with the military and political leadership. But surprisingly few of them choose to express their views in public. Historically, many—Eisenhower, Patton—have deliberately chosen not to vote, as expressing a political preference could conflict with their obligation to obey the orders of the civilian command authority. The existence of a vigorous independent press, a viable two-party political system, and a demanding civilian economy all help to keep the troops under control and politically honest.

BRITAIN

During the mid-1600s, following a period of revolutionary excess that saw a king lose his head, the army overthrew the lawful government of England and installed a decadelong military dictatorship. A one-time only event, which clearly did not set a precedent, the Cromwellian military dictatorship was the result of a civil war in the 1640s, which necessitated the creation of a large, professional standing army. This was an anomaly, as an army is not essential to the defense of Britain. That function was for centuries the duty of the navy, and more recently the navy in conjunction with the Royal Air Force. Thus these services have always been the more prestigious in Britain, while at the same time being the least threatening to civilian and democratic political institutions. It is not for nothing that both the navy and the air force are "Royal" while the army is merely the army. In addition, British officers have always been well integrated into the social fabric of the country. Long recruited from among the younger sons of the aristocracy and gentry, they were hardly inclined to overthrow the existing political order. The fact that the future leaders of the armed forces have usually been educated in the very same institutions that have trained the political, scientific, literary, and religious elite of the nation—the "public school"—has also served to enhance the sense of identification of the officer corps with the establishment.

THE GERMANYS

Prior to reunification in October 1990, the military policies of both Germanys were strongly influenced by their need to cope with the problem of militarism and military politics that caused two world wars. East Germany attempted to preserve the forms of the old Imperial Army, which was a useful tool of the government, while denying any connection with militarism or Pan-Germanism or Naziism. West Germany was more open about accepting responsibility for the clouded past. In addition, it was more original in developing its armed forces, drawing upon some of the traditions and forms of the past—even of World War II in some instances—while instituting a number of innovative democratizing practices as well. Interestingly, both Germanys readily recruited officers from traditional military families. The two armies apparently had outgrown the interventionist tendencies that were characteristic of the German Army in the past, and became acceptably apolitical, highly professional, and very proficient. Indeed, arguably each was the best in its respective alliance. In both countries, the military was regarded with respect, though no longer the awe that prevailed in earlier generations. Politically, both Germanys were dedicated to the notion of eventual reunification of the nation, though each would only allow this program to be carried out under its own auspices. Fear of Germany runs deep in Europe, and it is worth recalling that the original nucleus of NATO, the Treaty of Dunkirk, between Britain and France in 1947, was specifically directed at the possibility of a resurgent Germany. German reunification in 1990 was as surprising as it was disturbing for Germany's neighbors.

EASTERN EUROPE

Save for Czechoslovakia, the countries of Eastern Europe also have had a militaristic tradition, and were essentially military dictatorships before World War II. The armies of Czechoslovakia and Poland were destroyed before that war really got under way, the former as a result of the Munich Pact and the latter as a result of the German and Russian invasions of 1939. In consequence, after World War II these armies had to be rebuilt. The new armies were based on forces raised during the war by the Russians to fight against Germany, those raised in the West being largely excluded. This experience was different from that of the other three Eastern European powers, Bulgaria, Hungary, and Romania. These nations had been active allies of the Axis during the war. As each chose a propitious moment to switch sides and adhere to the anti-German coalition, their armed forces retained a continuous existence. Although their forces were purged of "unreliable" elements, they maintained stronger ties to their past than did the Czech and Polish ones. Despite some similarities, all five armies draw heavily on their own national military tradition, rather than merely imitating that of Russia. Their use of Russian military equipment gives the appearance of uniformity, but there is a lot of diversity in all other areas. Like Germany, East European countries recruit officers from traditional military families, drawing even upon the former nobility. While respect for the armed forces runs high, they have been kept firmly under the control of the civil government, except in Poland. There internal political turmoil in the late 1970s and early 1980s brought the threat of Russian intervention. To forestall this, the army staged a coup that installed a military government headed by a former nobleman, Wojciech Jaruzelski, to bring the nation closer to the more orthodox Marxist line being preached by Moscow.

Despite rhetoric about "socialist brothers," the Eastern European nations had a low regard for each other. Ethnic tensions run deep, and there are numerous territorial disputes in the region. All have a history of hostility to each other: Shortly before the fall of the Ceaucescu regime in Romania, tensions between that country and Hungary were so bad there was talk of war. Several also have quarrels with their non–Warsaw Pact neighbors, notably Greece, Turkey, and Yugoslavia, who all more or less benefit from the protection of the United States. And most of them also have historic bones to pick with Russia. Thus, as with Germany, the probability of a Superpower withdrawal could be politically more dangerous than its continued presence.

RUSSIA

Russia has been described, for centuries, as an army with a nation attached. This is in recognition of the huge land forces that the Russian state has maintained since it emerged from Tatar domination in the 1400s. Centered around Moscow and territories to the northeast, Russia was always surrounded by hostile enemies. The next four centuries were ones of unremitting war and conquest. With no natural borders on the flat Eurasian plains, Russia had to conquer or be conquered. The czars were a crafty lot, and mostly managed to stay one step ahead of potential military takeovers. While many of the czars were successful warriors, more of them were adroit politicians. Mikhail Gorbachev is merely another in a long line of civil leaders who has managed to keep the troops content while getting them to do his bidding. This tradition of civilian rule is one most Russians cling to with a fervor that discourages any coup-minded generals. This is not a painless process. For it to work, the generals are allowed into the highest councils of the land, and their needs and aspirations are given consideration, if not always granted. Until the 1917 Revolution, there was a Troika in power, split among government officials, military leaders, and the Orthodox Church, all of which were theoretically subject to the czar. After the Revolution, the Communist party replaced the church (in more ways than most Communists would like to admit), and business went on as usual. Even the old secret police, the Okhrana, was essentially retained, evolving eventually into the KGB, which is basically a semi-independent organ of the Communist party. With this history and tradition in mind, Russia is one of the nations least likely to suffer a military takeover.

CHINA

China is a nation that went from feudal empire to modern police state in only a few decades. The transition has not been easy, and many disquieting feudal habits remain. For several thousand years, China has been a collection of different regions united by race and, to a lesser extent, language. For most of this period, an emperor (not always Chinese, but at least Asian) united the provinces by force of arms and political acumen. There has rarely been a national army. Instead, there were a number of regional ones that could be combined into a formidable force. But most of China has yet to go through an industrial revolution, so the idea of large armies equipped with modern weapons and transported long distances by railroad or ship does not exist. The "warlord" concept of armed forces raised and stationed in their home province, and owing primary loyalty to their local leader, is still strong. The most recent demonstration of this was in June of 1989, when the Chinese government had to shop around among the various regional armies to find one that would be willing to clear the pro-democracy mobs out of Beijing. Civil war was avoided only through a lot of astute politicking. No doubt reference was made to all the bad things that happened to China during the last period of warlord strife in the 1920s and 1930s. But old habits die hard, and the Chinese have good reason to look over their shoulders.

ISRAEL

Having an ever-present threat is an excellent spur to the development of efficient, politically reliable armed forces. A genuine "nation-in-arms," the Israeli armed forces consist of a very small regular cadre, supplemented by a very large pool of reservists who do regular stints of active duty. The Israeli armed forces are also one of the most democratically based in the world. All personnel enter the service through conscription, and no one can become an NCO without a tour in the ranks, or an officer without having first served as an NCO. In addition, Israeli officers lead from the front, and have very high casualty rates. These factors make for exceptionally close ties between officers and enlisted personnel. Aside from some religious extremists, the average Israeli, cognizant of the apparent odds and of the historical tribulations of the Jewish people, regards military service as a necessary and useful, if dangerous and occasionally unpleasant, duty. As almost everyone has done his, and her, time in the ranks, there is a broad understanding of military affairs. The armed forces are well regarded, but at the same time the subject of heated debate in the free-wheeling politics that characterize Israeli life.

THIRD WORLD NATIONS

In many Third World countries, the army is the most ethnically integrated element in the society. This is because most Third World armed forces are heirs to a colonial military or police force. While in some colonies this police force was recruited from only one tribal group or class, in most it was recruited broadly across tribal and class lines. Independence usually brought with it a service obligation for all citizens, at least in theory. Thus, in many such countries—particularly those independent in the last half-century—the army is frequently the only truly national institution, open to talented people regardless of tribal, social, or regional origins. These armies also probably represent the largest block of comparatively educated managerial people in the country. In those countries where a "revolution" has taken place—even if only in the form of a coup against an immediate post-independence leader—the army may consider itself possessed of a special mission to preserve national unity: This is common in Latin America. The result is a strong inclination for the army to intervene in politics, leading to numerous coups, whether because the troops believe they can run the show better, or to eliminate tribal conflict, or to elevate one tribe to primacy. Or because the leader of the army happens to be ambitious.

Most of these armies are not very professional. Few Third World armies, even those of Latin America, which mostly have long histories, have had much experience of foreign war. Although they wax rhetorical about potential foreign threats, their principal focus is internal, emphasizing defense of the regime against persons interested in overthrowing it, when not occupied overthrowing it themselves. This political activity tends to be injurious to military professionalism. In many Third World countries, the armed forces, most of which consist primarily of an army, actually have fewer men than the national police, which may be a well-armed, well-trained paramilitary force. This serves two purposes. The national police can be a useful counterweight to the political ambitions of the army. Indeed, so important is this role in some nations that there are two or even more such paramilitary forces, each technically responsible for a different aspect of internal security, but primarily available for use by the political leadership in a pinch or a putsch. Even Saudi Arabia, usually thought of as quite "stable," uses this technique. The second role for the paramilitary forces is to relieve the army of certain unpleasant duties. Thus, while the army remains the power behind the throne, the national police gets to do the dirty work, like slaughtering peasants or revolutionaries. This policy pays excellent dividends, and has largely been the experience in the Philippines, where the national police formed the principal instrument of repression during the Marcos years. It has also been the case in Chile, where, despite nearly two decades of a sometimes brutal military dictatorship, the reputation of the armed forces remains fairly high, because the national police did most of the beatings, torturings, and killings. In contrast, next door in Argentina, the intimate involvement of the armed forces in the murder of at least nine thousand people from 1977 to 1982 has had serious repercussions since the reestablishment of a democratic regime.

Each nation develops its own unique pattern of civil-military relations. While developed democratic and totalitarian societies keep their armed forces under tight rein, less developed societies have considerable problems in this regard. Though those of us living in an advanced democratic society may find this deplorable, it is important to understand that there is no "perfect" model for civil-military relations. Those that seem to work best, such as in the United States or Britain, have had centuries in which to evolve.

THE POLITICS OF DEFENSE SPENDING

The table takes a look at the relationship between defense spending and congressional politics on a district-by-district basis. All 435 congressional districts are represented. (Note that some procurement dollars are spent in Puerto Rico, Guam, and other U.S. territories that do not have a voting representative in Congress.)

$ RANGE—"Range" indicates the amount of DoD contract dollars—in millions—that districts receive: A district grouped in the "0–1" range benefited from contracts worth one million or fewer dollars per fiscal year. All figures are an average based on statistics covering the last few years of the 1980s.

CDs—Number of Congressional Districts that fall into each range of DoD contracts.

Avg DVI—Average Defense Voting Index for all districts in that range. DVI is the percentage by which the representatives from these districts cast so-called "pro-defense" votes. Higher DVIs indicate more pro-defense votes.

Avg DoD$—Average DoD contract dollars (in millions) each district in the range receives annually.

Tot DoD$—Total DoD contract dollars (in millions) received by all districts in the range.

Dems.—Number of Democrat party–controlled districts in that range.

Reps.—Republican party–controlled districts in that range.

The United States Department of Defense (DoD) makes sure that it spreads its contracts around to insure that the maximum number of legislators in Congress will vote positively on defense matters. Only a small number (8 percent) of districts are left out of DoD's list, perhaps because their record of pro-defense votes is 37 percent less than the average.

DEPARTMENT OF DEFENSE PROCUREMENT SPENDING IN
CONGRESSIONAL DISTRICTS AND DISTRICT REPRESENTATIVE
VOTING RECORDS ON MILITARY ISSUES

$ RANGE	CDs	AVG DVI	AVG DoD$	TOT DoD$	DEMS.	REPS.
0–1	36	33.4	3.4	124	28	8
10–19	24	62.9	15.8	380	13	11
20–49	85	54.1	34.6	2,941	50	35
50–99	86	51.2	73.9	6,352	56	30
100–199	64	60.5	143.6	9,187	33	31
200–299	39	53.6	241.5	9,419	27	12
300–499	35	62.1	379.4	13,278	20	15
500–999	38	51.8	695.9	26,445	21	17
1,000–3,999	26	55.1	1,865.4	48,500	14	12
4,000+	2	47.0	4,588.4	9,177	1	1
All	435	53.7	289.2	125,804	263	172
Dems.	263	33.8	266.6	70,125	263	0
Reps.	172	84.1	323.7	55,679	0	172

Source: Congressional Records Service, *Congress & Defense* series

Interestingly, the DVI of a district is not greatly influenced by the presence of military personnel, at least until base closings are announced. What does influence the DVI is the dollar value of defense procurement contracts let to local firms. Although there are exceptions, in general the trend is that the higher the DVI of a district, the more likely is it to be the beneficiary of big-bucks procurement contracts from the Department of Defense, or to be a relatively poor district in which even a small contract may have a significant impact on employment. The top ten districts in terms of procurement dollars have an average DVI of about 50, while the bottom ten, which get no procurement dollars whatsoever, have an average DVI of about 10. Note that the table does not reflect the influence of such contracts on the voting pattern of representatives from adjacent districts. A good case in point is on New York's Long Island, where Grumman has a plant in one district but draws employees from the surrounding five, whose representatives regularly vote en bloc to preserve the company's contracts, most recently in the matter of continuing production of the F-14.

The Merchants of Vaporware: The Problem of Procurement

·8·

Whet weapons do we need? How do we buy our weapons? Can we be certain we are getting the best military equipment? Why does corruption seem intertwined with military procurement?

One of the major components of shooting blanks is technology that doesn't work in combat the way it was theorized to work during its peacetime development. For example, as early as the American Civil War, military professionals discovered that their new single-shot rifled muskets were far more effective than they had expected. The longer range and greater accuracy of the rifled musket soon forced changes in battle tactics. This development does not seem to have impressed anyone on the other side of the Atlantic overly much, even though the Europeans had already used these new muskets in combat. Nonetheless, the carnage caused by the combination of new rifles and old tactics in the Italian War of 1859 was so great as to inspire Henri Dunant to propose the foundation of the Red Cross.

Europeans were equally unimpressed over a similar Russian experience in their 1877–78 war with the Turks, who were using American lever-action repeating rifles. In 1899, the British were surprised to discover that new rapid-firing magazine rifles and semiautomatic cannon in the hands of South African Boer farmers were extraordinarily deadly, but again most folks proved to be slow learners. The firepower lesson was reiterated several years later when Japanese rifles and machine guns mowed down Russian infantry—and vice versa—in Manchuria in 1904 and 1905. The Russians lost that war largely because the Japanese shot blanks less often overall than they did. A few years later, during the Balkan Wars (1912–13), the machine gun once again proved unusually deadly. But most European military theorists continued to maintain that the machine gun would not be a decisive weapon in a "major" war. Meanwhile, for over a third of a century, machine guns had seen wide use in colonial warfare, where they had proven eminently effective in shattering massed infantry charges. But those attacks had been delivered by "savages," and the troops of a first-class European power were hardly to be considered in the same league.

It took several years of sustained machine-gun slaughter during World War I to convince most military professionals not to underrate new weapons. This might have been a healthy trend, but instead military professionals swung the other way and began to overrate the new weaponry. To be sure, this didn't happen all at once, but it did take place gradually as the century wore on.

World War I had already provided an example of a high-tech weapons system that had not only been oversold but had also underperformed, setting a pattern that persists to this day. Consider the modern battleship. Shortly after the beginning of the century, Britain's Royal Navy introduced an innovative new battleship, HMS *Dreadnought*. This well-armored vessel, carrying ten heavy twelve-inch caliber guns and steaming at comparatively high speeds, immediately rendered all existing battleships obsolete. Shortly thereafter, every major power, and most middle-sized ones, began to invest in enormous fleets of such battleships, in what became the first modern arms race. Then came World War I, by which time there were in commission nearly sixty such battleships, some with guns of fifteen-inch caliber, plus over a dozen equally heavily armed, much faster, but lightly armored battle cruisers, with scores more abuilding. The British, who had dominated the seas for over two centuries, were one of the high-tech leaders of the age, along with the Germans and the Americans. Ironically, the United States had actually designed the first modern battleship, but dawdled over its construction, allowing the British to get theirs into service first. For this reason, battleships are called *dreadnoughts,* after Britain's first modern battleship, and not *michigans,* after the first U.S. modern battleship.

Their technical expertise and maritime experience made the British confident that they would emerge victorious from any fleet action against their German rivals. Even before World War I, British shipbuilders were surprised to discover that the Americans had been the first to start building the new-type ships and had the capacity to build more at one time than Britain. Articles in technical journals also indicated that the Germans were ahead in battleship technology. The British were still certain that their dreadnoughts were the equal of anyone's. Surprisingly, the new ships didn't get a chance at a real workout in combat until the war was nearly two years old, when, in mid-1916, over fifty battleships and battle cruisers of the British and German fleets clashed in the Battle of Jutland. The results were disappointing. The British admirals were rather dismayed to find that their ships took an inordinate amount of damage from German shell hits. It turned out that many aspects of the technology that went into the British ships were flawed. But there was more. The admirals on both sides at Jutland, and at any of the half-dozen other, less spectacular battleship engagements of the war, demonstrated a considerable degree of discretion, so that none of these encounters could be called a "decisive" action. This was due to another flaw in the new technology: The ships had become so expensive, their commanders were loath to take them "in harm's way." So victory, which was the only thing that could justify all that expense, proved elusive. The flawed nature of the new ships, and particularly the battle cruisers, did not turn fatal until the guns were fired in anger. There were several other unpleasant technological surprises during World War I, which also began a trend that has continued down to the present.

THE MILITARY-INDUSTRIAL COMPLEX

The cause of these technological surprises is a combination of the military believing what they want to believe about untried weapons and the convincing sales pitches of the arms manufacturers. Welcome to the military-industrial complex.

The military-industrial complex in the United States is a fairly new phenomenon. It has existed in other nations and at other times, whenever there were large peacetime armed forces and substantial arms-manufacturing institutions to support them. The problems this combination creates vary little from nation to nation. You basically have a lot of corruption and inefficiency in military procurement no matter what the nation or era. In democratic America, as we have seen, you also have a serious warping of the legislative process because the military-industrial complex distributes its contracts among select congressional districts so as to secure the votes needed to maintain large defense allocations in future budgets.

The purveyors of hardware to the military have added another layer of deception and confusion to military affairs. There's a saying common to many cultures through the ages, "No one ever went broke supplying the army." The problem is a classic one of the military buying many items in peacetime that would be revealed as shoddy only in wartime. And the wars were not as frequent as the shoddy weapons and equipment purchases. Even in relatively corruption-free cultures, there was the knowledge that suppliers were not being scrutinized as closely by the military as by civilian customers for similar items. For example, farmers buying tractors are going to demand far more performance per dollar than soldiers buying tanks. The reason is simple: Farmers put their tractors to work straight away, soldiers can only practice, there being so few wars.

So it has become something of an unspoken, and unacknowledged, tradition that the military is a great customer for lower quality, and higher profit, goods. The military always faces a difficult situation in peacetime because it must train for something in which it may never have a chance to participate: combat. Worse yet, weapons and equipment that have changed since the last war create changes in the way the next war will be conducted. The big problem is that there is no way of knowing exactly what impact new technology will have on the next war. Obviously, the defense manufacturers are also caught up in this uncertainty. But the manufacturers further complicate the situation by trying to sell what is most effective for their balance sheet. This is only natural, as they are in business primarily to keep their firms going. If they weren't, they would be quickly replaced by companies with a more realistic attitude. This pattern is not confined to the capitalist world, and is perhaps even more pronounced in the so-called "socialist states," where inefficient enterprises continued manufacturing inferior equipment primarily so that production quotas could be maintained, thus preserving bureaucratic careers and comfortable lifestyles among politically connected managers.

Ostensibly, these merchants provide equipment needed by the armed forces. In reality, the hardware is periodically unsuitable, unworkable, or simply not there when it's needed.

PROBLEMS AND CAUSES

First, the good news. Sort of. The military history of the last century is littered with weapons that were more like vaporware than hardware. So many new weapons have been produced that many are replaced before they ever have a chance to succeed, or fail, in combat. The primary cause of all this failed weaponry is the difficulty of figuring out how future wars will be fought. The precise characteristics of any future war are not easy to work out from the comfortable, and complacent, world of peacetime soldiering. As a result, when war comes, many of the unsuitable weapons, the wrong weapons, the unworkable weapons, are with us in abundance, while the right ones haven't been built. There are quite a few reasons for this.

THE UNSUITABLE WEAPONS

Some weapons are good in theory but bad in execution. These are the unsuitable weapons, systems that do have a useful role in combat, but one that may not be understood as the weapon moves from the laboratory to the battlefield. This is the most common problem during long periods of peace or in times of rapid technological change. Both of these conditions have applied since World War II. A weapon's effectiveness on the battlefield is always discovered under combat conditions. Without any combat for testing, weapons developers must guess, although they don't call it that. It's much more elegant and lucrative to call it research and development. All those scientists, engineers, and consultants are eventually upstaged by the first troops to hit the combat zone with the new weapons in hand. When reports come back that the weapons don't work the way they're supposed to, as in the case of U.S. tank destroyers or torpedoes in the early part of World War II, the weapons developers assert that the troops are using them improperly, or failing to maintain them, or some other useful excuse. Eventually, the views of the men on the line prevail, but in the meantime a lot of them may get killed. Two premier examples in this century of basically sound weapons systems suffering from unrealistic prewar expectations are the tank and the aircraft carrier.

The tank was first developed during wartime, World War I. The need was for a weapon that could accompany advancing troops across very broken ground and destroy defending machine guns. The first tanks did just that. They were lightly armored, just enough to protect against machine-gun bullets, used the recently developed modern caterpillar tread (like a bulldozer) to overcome obstacles, and were armed with a machine gun or light cannon to deliver fire. Mistakes were made in the design and use of these early tanks, but combat was an unambiguous way to see what worked and what didn't.

The first large-scale use of tanks, at Cambrai in late 1917, was something of a mixed success: Although the tanks gained ground, their mechanical unreliability proved a considerable handicap. Moreover, at the time, no one quite knew how to exploit what success there was, so that at best the outcome was a draw. But half a year later there were thousands of more capable machines in action, and techniques were developed to support them with infantry, which proved decisive in breaking the hitherto virtually impregnable trench lines. Then came twenty years of peace and plenty of time for design and doctrine to go astray. Going into World War II (1939–45), there were a lot more tanks available, and a lot more ideas about how they should be used. Not everyone could be right, and after the first tank battles, it become apparent that most peacetime tank designers and tacticians had been wrong. The errors varied as much as the imagination that went into them. The French made many design errors, for instance, building tanks with turrets too small and cramped for their crews to operate effectively, and with poor endurance due to a limited fuel capacity, and in any case assumed that tanks were a secondary weapon. The British built two different specialized types of tanks, one for fighting tanks and one for supporting infantry, which insured that there were never enough vehicles for either task. Britain also advocated using tanks in large, homogeneous masses, a common error ever since. Russia built thousands of tanks, but didn't replace them with more up-to-date designs quickly enough or train its troops to maintain or operate them effectively. Germany made the fewest errors, building too many light tanks early in the war and too many heavy ones later. German tactics were better too, largely as a result of extensive experimentation and realistic, large-scale peacetime maneuvers, and they eventually taught the British and Russians and everyone else to mix their tanks up with motorized infantry and coordinate them with motorized artillery and aircraft. The Italians came up with very similar notions about the use of tanks, but were unable to produce adequate tanks to implement their ideas. Americans were lucky with tanks, as they entered World War II late, and were able to copy what seemed best in German practice. This, and quantity production, helped offset the disadvantage of having a tank (the M-4 Sherman) that was in many ways obsolescent.

Despite the lessons of World War II, afterward the tendency to have unsuitable tank designs and tactics reasserted itself. Russia, which had produced one of the finest tanks of the war, the T-34, subsequently built tens of thousands of tanks with numerous design flaws, some of which didn't show up for years. Their 1950s T-55 series was too flammable because of the way the fuel system was laid out, and the 1960s U.S. M-60 had a similar problem because of a flammable hydraulic fluid. The T-55's successor (T-62) had so many flaws that its production run was cut short. The next Russian tanks, the T-64/72/80 series, were cursed with an unreliable automatic loader and one less crewman. Nonetheless, the Russians persist in trying to get this arrangement to work and ignore the constant reports of problems when these tanks have been used in combat, mostly by various Arab countries. This attitude toward unsuitable tanks is nothing new with Russia. When the Germans invaded in 1941, over 95 percent of Russia's 21,000 tanks were obsolete, early 1930s designs. Aside from being easily disposed of by German infantry, the inadequate tanks were quite demoralizing to the Russian troops. Then, as now, the Russians kept building obsolete designs in peacetime because their industry is organized to keep producing a fixed design, not rapidly adapting new designs as is the case in the West. Note that the new designs that were on hand in 1941 (the T-34 and KV series) quickly went into mass production and were frequently updated during the war, becoming key factors in the eventual Russian victory. But without the incentive provided by a war, Russian defense industries traditionally aim for quantity over quality or innovation.

To compound the unsuitability problems with tanks, World War II also saw the development of APCs (Armored Personnel Carriers). Initially, these were armored trucks with their rear wheels replaced by tracks, or obsolete tanks converted to carry troops. Supposedly, APCs permit infantry to keep up with the tanks, carrying the foot-sloggers into action where they are needed with a minimum of fuss. But there's always been a bit more uncertainty about what to do with APCs than with tanks. The infantry like APCs because they cut down on the walking, provide some protection from shell fragments and bullets, and give them someplace to live besides a hole in the ground. Moreover, from the beginning APCs began to carry heavy weapons, usually a heavy machine gun, which was a welcome addition to infantry platoon firepower. But combat soon demonstrated that APCs were easily chewed up by tanks and artillery, and while they were a bit less prone to mechanical breakdowns than tanks, their noise and size tended to attract enemy fire. The APCs did protect the infantry from small-arms fire and artillery fragments, but not to the extent their designers envisioned. During World War II, once the troops learned their limitations, APCs earned their keep largely by moving the infantry around fast enough so they could protect friendly tanks from enemy infantry and antitank artillery.

After World War II, most APCs began to resemble small tanks, as they became fully tracked and acquired thicker armor. Similarly, in the 1960s and 1970s the Germans and Russians developed APCs that mounted light artillery in their turrets.

These were called Infantry Fighting Vehicles (IFVs), because the infantry were supposed to fight from inside the moving vehicle. This has never worked in practice. The German IFV, the Marder, weighs as much as the standard medium tank of World War II and is more costly. Unlike those tanks, APCs have thinner armor, a lighter gun, and carry a squad of infantry. The Russian BMP, at half the weight of the Marder, is an engineering marvel, yet it is so cramped that the infantry are regularly rendered senseless after a few hours of bouncing around during off-road travel. In combat, its cramped turret contains an upgraded rocket launcher masquerading as a gun, an antitank guided-missile system, and several uncomfortable crew members. More crucial, the fuel tanks are in locations guaranteeing that the vehicle will quickly be incinerated when hit. Initial reports from Middle Eastern battlefields were not encouraging. The Russians blamed this bad news on the Arab operators of the BMPs and continued upgrading (30-mm cannon, etc.) and manufacturing the vehicle as the BMP 2.

In the 1980s, the United States brought forth the M-2 Bradley IFV. As yet untried in serious combat, it carries a formidable array of weapons, including an automatic 25-mm cannon, a TOW antitank missile launcher, and an infantry squad of only seven troops versus ten in the older M-113 APC. Though the Bradley has been criticized as being too expensive and too vulnerable, these unkind reviews would quickly be turned around if it performs well in sustained combat. The problem is, no one will know until the vehicle is used in heavy combat, and that may never happen. Testing, even testing "with extreme prejudice" (to the point of destruction), which is rare in military research and development, can only reveal the most obvious flaws. Many weapons developed since World War II came and went without ever being in combat.

The aircraft carrier, although born, like the tank, in World War I, really began to develop in peacetime. Most admirals were not very keen on having it, but in the 1920s the leaders of the major naval powers decided to avoid another warship-building arms race. The admirals were given a choice of scrapping some battleships or converting them to aircraft carriers. No one understood how powerful carriers would become, but the admirals figured any ship was better than a pile of scrap. The

Japanese, who were as battleship-minded as anyone else, went for the deal because, as everyone dismissed the value of air power, the 1922 naval disarmament treaty gave them a somewhat more favorable ratio in aircraft carriers compared with Britain and the United States while forcing them to accept a smaller battleship fleet. Throughout the 1920s and 1930s, the battleship still reigned as the premier naval weapon. The carriers were seen as scouting forces that could, if the opportunity presented itself, unleash their tiny aircraft against the mighty dreadnoughts, in the expectation that they might inflict some damage before the floating fortresses got down to trading one-ton shells. After the battle, the carriers might again go into action, sending their planes to harass a defeated enemy or to help cover the retirement of friendly forces.

Certainly, few people saw carrier aviation as an arm of decision. Several developments in the 1930s provided aircraft carriers with the edge they needed and few expected they would ever get. On the technical side, advances in aircraft design greatly increased the range, speed, and weapons load of carrier aircraft. More important, several U.S. Navy admirals were quite taken by the aircraft-carrier concept, which they saw as *the* principal combat ship. Despite the skepticism and derision of their battleship-smitten brethren, these visionaries persisted to the point of having a huge carrier-building plan approved before World War II began. Their expectations paid off, as during four days in December of 1941 the battleship ceased to be the principal warship. First, on December 7, 1941, 360 Japanese carrier aircraft attacked the American fleet anchorage at Pearl Harbor, sinking or severely damaging all eight battleships with this attack. The U.S. Pacific battleship fleet effectively ceased to exist. The second event occurred on December 10. Two British battleships, searching for a Japanese invasion fleet off Singapore, were set upon by Japanese land-based aircraft. Within an hour, the two dreadnoughts were sunk. As a result, the only major warships the Allies had left in the Pacific were three carriers that happened to be at sea when Pearl Harbor was hit. This gave the carrier admirals their chance. And they took it with commendable results, changing naval warfare as much as British gunners in the 1500s did, when they replaced ramming and boarding with cannon fire as the preferred method of fighting ships.

One would think that the Japanese would have learned from

their victories in December 1941. After all, it was one of their admirals, Isoruku Yamamoto, who had conceived the daring air strike on Pearl Harbor. But the Japanese admirals—even Yamamoto—were essentially battleship admirals, and viewed Pearl Harbor more as a lucky break resulting from a stroke of genius than as the fanfare signaling a fundamental change in naval warfare. So in June of 1942, while making an attack on Midway Island, the Japanese left their carriers unprotected and exposed to attack by the U.S. carrier aircraft: In effect, the Japanese carriers were being used as a screen for their battleships, instead of the other way around. The United States, which had got a few battleships into the Pacific by this time, didn't even bother bringing them along for the fight: After those terrible days in December of 1941, the United States—and Britain—saw clearly that the battleship stood little chance against aircraft, whether land- or carrier-based. The Japanese never recovered from the loss of four carriers—and hundreds of veteran pilots—at Midway. It was a clear case of unsuitable tactics. And as a result, American carrier aviation ultimately swept the Japanese fleet from the seas.

Since World War II, many major weapons systems have been developed and deployed that have not yet been tested in combat. The historical record indicates that most of these systems will, to one degree or another, be found unsuitable in combat, or at least unsuitable in terms of their original purpose. There is a "silver lining" to this cloud, because, as with both the tank and the aircraft carrier, at least the things are on hand and can be used once a suitable role for them has been developed.

But there is a worse situation than finding a weapon unsuitable, and that's finding that one is unworkable.

THE UNWORKABLE WEAPONS

Some weapons will never work in combat, no matter how flawless their development and testing. We don't normally hear about the weapons that will never work because the military isn't too keen on trumpeting that kind of failure. In wartime, you can afford to be adventurous. You find out real quick what works and what doesn't. And there's always a chance of finding something unexpectedly effective.

Unworkability is mostly a matter of degree. No matter how badly conceived a weapon is, you can throw enough of them into combat to have some effect. Unfortunately, the effect may be so piddling as to be counterproductive. To demonstrate this, let us consider some examples of the unworkable.

• In the 1950s, the U.S. Army thought it would be a great idea to have a missile system for taking out small, hard-to-hit targets, an idea that arose from World War II experience attacking German and Japanese bunkers. Thus was the Lacrosse system born. It never worked. Lacrosse was deployed, but in live-fire exercises it failed consistently. Finally, even the army procurement people got tired of subsidizing failure and killed the system. The reasons for the failure were hardly novel. Basically, the technology was not able to support the concept. Lacrosse was a fairly large missile fired from the back of a truck. A forward observer used a special designator to place a beam on the target, and the missile would ride the beam. In practice, the beam was disrupted by a wide variety of climactic conditions, and even on a clear day the missile's tracking systems were not always able to find their target.

• The Davy Crockett was a short-range nuclear weapon for use by the infantry. Basically, it was a mortar, with the oversize nuclear warhead sitting outside the end of the tube. Surprisingly, upon deployment it was discovered that the range of the mortar was too short to prevent the crew, and nearby friendly troops, from being injured by the effects of the blast and radiation. This effect was not clearly understood when the weapon was being developed. But during the 1950s, there were a number of outdoor nuclear tests involving infantry dug in close by to determine the effects of nuclear explosions on friendly troops. At first, it was believed that dug-in troops would be unharmed even if quite close to the detonations. Later, it was found that radiation contamination had been seriously underestimated, and inordinate numbers of men who had been involved in those tests began to die from various cancers in the 1970s. It was too late to help them, but at least the Davy Crockett system had been withdrawn.

• Radar homing air-to-air missiles were developed in the

1950s to give aircraft the ability to hit enemy planes that could not be seen, or identified, visually. Several thousand aircraft have since been brought down by such missiles, but only a handful of these were not first identified visually. Pilots are not convinced that they won't be shooting at friendly aircraft with these missiles. While the missiles themselves are fairly temperamental and unreliable, the biggest problem remains convincing the pilot that the unseen target is not friendly. This is a known problem with Western pilots and may not be as much of a difficulty with pilots trained in Russian methods, which stress doing what you are told and not thinking about it.

• Late in World War II, the United States deployed an elaborate stabilization system for its M-4 tank. This device would enable the tank to fire its gun accurately while on the move, but in practice the system proved too complex and troublesome for the crews. It also was a heavy drain on the tank's batteries, which were difficult to replace on the battlefield, and so the stabilization device was rarely used. In this case, the problem was that contemporary technology was not up to the task, at least not at a price the users were willing to pay. Three decades later, it was, and a workable stabilization system is used on the current M-1 tank.

• After World War II, one of the new technologies that caught on in a big way was supersonic bombers. One of these, the U.S. F-105, became immensely popular during the Vietnam War. The F-105 was 1950s technology, and the heaviest single-seat bomber in use. Yet its supersonic capabilities were rarely used, for two reasons. First, supersonic speed depended on an elaborate system of ductwork and flaps at the engine air intake. This difficult-to-maintain gear was only needed for supersonic flight, and there was never enough time to keep everything else on the aircraft operational. So it was common to ignore the extra equipment and just forgo supersonic flight. The other reason for doing without supersonic flight was that it was not really needed for most bombing missions. In fact, the much higher fuel consumption of supersonic flight provided pilots with less safety margin on the long-distance bombing missions the F-105s performed over North Vietnam. Clearly, supersonic speed for the F-105 was unworkable in combat for both maintenance and tactical reasons.

The unworkable is frequently also the highly debatable. True-blue air-force types will give you a hard time about radar-guided missiles today, just as they once did concerning strategic bombing during Word War II and subsequent campaigns of a similar nature. It was an article of faith going into World War II that masses of heavy bombers could bring any opponent to his knees. Well, it didn't work out that way. Although the bombers over Europe did a lot of damage, they didn't have a decisive effect on German war production. In fact, German production peaked in December of 1944, after more than four years of increasingly massive bomber raids. German output began to decline only as Allied ground forces overran the major German manufacturing areas. The bombers contributed by concentrating on the German railroads, which was a target system the Operations Research crowd and ground generals forced on the bomber generals to directly support the ground war. In the Pacific, it was not the bombing raids but the submarines that first slowed Japanese production, and then naval mines that finally brought it to a halt, by reducing the importation of raw materials. Again, the bomber advocates were forced to cooperate, by dropping naval mines, which they considered a waste of their efforts. After World War II, the bombers were again frustrated in Korea and Vietnam. One reason the air force fervently embraced bombers carrying nuclear weapons was because this was one way to assure that the enemy would be bombed into submission. But the nuclear option proved so frightening, as well as being a two-way street, that no country is likely to use it unless it has national suicide in mind.

How, then, did this bomber fixation get started, and keep going? First of all, aircraft are (or were) easy to build. This was especially true for the United States going into World War II. Warships took much longer, and organizing ground combat units was nearly as time-consuming. Aircraft were made from light metals and other items that America already produced in abundance. If you had a lot of money and not much time, aircraft were the weapon of choice. Until 1944, America had more airmen than infantry or sailors fighting the Germans. Similarly in the Pacific, land-based aircraft led the fight until sufficient aircraft carriers and other warships could be produced. Moreover, aircraft-carrier combat usually kept the carriers out of harm's way. The carriers' aircraft got chewed up at a prodigious rate, but they could be replaced much more quickly than the carriers themselves.

Being first into the fight also gave the fly-boys a certain edge in the propaganda department. Flyers were seen as more dashing than the plodding ground pounders. Best of all, the air force could make outrageous claims of damage done to the enemy by long-range bombers without fear of contradiction until the war was safely over, by which time no one would really be interested. Because most of the air combat was over enemy territory, one had to rely on deceptive air photographs and other tentative evidence of air-force effectiveness.

To further bolster its case, the air force did provide spectacularly effective close support of the ground troops. By 1944, swarms of U.S. fighter bombers would come to the aid of beleaguered ground troops. All those GIs, and the war correspondents with them, could see how effective air power really was. These fighter bombers also went after enemy units and supply convoys approaching the front line. Advancing troops came upon burned-out enemy columns and were further impressed by the job the air force was doing. The success of the "ground support" air force naturally led to an assumption that the "strategic bombardment" air force was equally successful, especially when one looked at all the rubble that the bombers had made of German cities. But after the war ended, teams of officers, engineers, and economists were sent to survey enemy cities and industrial areas hit by the heavy bombers. They found a lot of destruction, much of which had no lasting effect on war industry. They also found the enemy resourceful enough to work around the destruction when vital installations were hit in order to keep the factories working.

Long-range bombing also proved unworkable because between raids the defenders had time to repair damage and even move the targets, sometimes even siting plants in caves and mines. Output at some factories increased after a raid: The damage forced modernization of marginal plant. At times a bombing raid "immunized" a factory, as the Germans found that machinery was more durable than buildings. So they left the buildings wrecked, built shelters for the machines and workers among the ruins, and continued producing. Aerial re-connaissance showed a bombed-out plant, so it was not bombed again. The relative ineffectiveness of long-range bombers was noted, and acted upon, by all World War II participants except the United States. In fact, only America continues to maintain a large bomber force. Even today, despite the introduction of ICBMs, the United States spends more on bombers than missiles. Just because something doesn't work doesn't mean someone won't keep trying.

Occasionally, unworkable weapons are found to be of value. From time to time, the troops will take a weapon that doesn't work the way it's supposed to and find that it works perfectly in a totally different, and unanticipated, role. The U.S. LAW, which was supposed to permit infantrymen to knock out tanks, proved pretty useless in that role. But in Vietnam the grunts discovered it was quite handy as a bunker buster. This has happened a number of times, even with weapons that work fine in their original role. The marines, incidentally, noted the frequent use of antitank rockets for "bunker busting" and decided a rocket just for that purpose would be cheaper than an AT weapon, so they built one.

THE UNAVAILABLE WEAPONS

The high-tech disease has made unavailability of existing weapons a particularly vexing problem in the last twenty years. Before that, there were frequently problems with ammunition. This is still a problem. (See Chapter 3 discussion of the *Iowa* incident.) Ammunition is expensive, and it spoils over time, as the propellants and explosives are volatile chemicals that eventually decompose ("rot") and become unstable. This makes the cost of stockpiling it high. The usual "solution" is to underestimate wartime usage rates. When war comes, this can be rather tough on the troops, as no one is ever really sure how much ammunition is going to be needed in the first place. World War I ground to a virtual halt two months after it began largely because all the participants ran out of artillery ammunition. Actually, this was not due to lack of foresight. All armies had based their ammunition-consumption estimates on experience, adding what they considered a generous margin for error, and had established reserve industrial capacity to produce more ammunition once the shooting started. The problem was that all previous wars had seen days of intense combat followed by long periods of relative inactivity: During the Civil War, U.S. artillery ammunition expenditure averaged only about four rounds per gun per day; five years later, in the Franco-Prussian War, Prussian guns averaged even less, only two rounds per day. Once the troops came in contact in 1914, they didn't stop fighting until 1918. And those generous prewar ammunition stockpiles—some 800–1,200 shells per gun—and production lines proved inadequate.

This happened again during World War II, although not on so massive a scale. To a certain extent, the lesson had been learned. In the case of the United States, part of the reason for the shell shortage that developed in late 1944 was due to congressional meddling in production. Surprisingly, the army had actually overestimated its shell requirements during mobilization. As a result, there was considerable overproduction during 1943, prompting a congressional investigation aimed at reducing "waste," which resulted in a sharp cut in shell production. However, the United States was not heavily engaged in ground fighting from 1942 into mid-1944, so shell consumption was relatively low. Then came the massive campaigns in France following D-Day, which sent shell consumption skyrocketing. Fortunately, the shell shortage didn't seriously interfere with field operations, but it was fairly close. And even now, in every sizable conflict since World War II, there have been serious ammunition shortages. We still have problems in this area. Current U.S. ammunition stocks are apparently only sufficient for about sixty days of heavy combat, during which period production would increase only marginally. Nothing discourages the fighting troops more than to be told they have to ration artillery ammunition. The result is that more of the troops get killed, as artillery is used more to prevent friendly casualties than to cause enemy ones. Nothing deters the other fellow from attacking more than frequent and prodigious use of artillery. Somehow, the peacetime planners lose sight of how human nature works in wartime. Perhaps this is because human nature can't be cost-accounted, while shell consumption can.

As the weapons themselves have got more expensive, nations can afford fewer of them. This is nothing new. As recently as World War II, the United States found itself holding off the Japanese onslaught in the Pacific in 1942–43 with two or three operational aircraft carriers. One or two ships made a difference. This is even more the case today. The navy has worked hard to maintain a peacetime force of at least fourteen large carriers over the last twenty years in the face of growing costs and calls for budget cuts. There is an allegedly logical explanation for this. Officially, the operational minimum number of carriers necessary to maintain sufficient forces for the purpose of carrying out national policy is fifteen, considering the need for some carriers to be deployed abroad and some to be held as a central reserve, while some are in training or undergoing overhaul. That number is curiously similar to the fifteen battleships that were considered the operational minimum back in the 1920s and 1930s by both the United States and Britain. Old habits die hard. But just how many carriers do we *really* need?

Another expensive weapon that illustrates the point is the photo reconnaissance satellite. When the American space-shuttle program was shut down in 1986 after the *Challenger* accident, the United States had but one such satellite remaining. Had there been a military emergency in the next two years, satellite-recon operations would have been severely constrained. Satellites are expensive to build and launch. They also burn fuel while being moved around in orbit; but when the fuel is gone, the bird is nearly useless. After *Challenger*, the one satellite up was running low on fuel. This is an extreme case of unavailability, but it is an example of what is happening with nearly all modern combat systems.

In the past, when weapons ran short, the troops improvised, while the folks back home geared up production. This is what will happen in the future, but it's also somewhat of a good news/bad news situation. The bad news is that some technologies don't allow much improvisation. Many weapons can no longer be turned out as quickly as in World War II, when a fighter or a tank could be assembled in a week or so. The problem is tools. Unlike the metal stamping and assembly-line methods of World War II, modern fighter and tank production requires special machinery able to fold or forge superalloys: There are only a handful of these in the country, and most are already operating at 50 percent capacity or more. The current peacetime construction time for fighter aircraft is about a year per plane. In wartime, this could be speeded up quite a bit, but would still take up to six months. The weapons the aircraft use are equally complex and time-consuming to produce, and their cost makes it prohibitive to stockpile the missiles. In wartime, there would be considerable chaos as the lack of peacetime foresight forced manufacturers to improvise. Unlike World War II, the key material is not metal but silicon, and other, more exotic materials that go into electronic components. Factories for these electronic items have a long lead time.

The advantage here is that the improvising will be electronic. New and simpler electronic weapons can be built or improvised quickly. They will have to be. Existing peacetime stocks of weapons are certainly quite lethal. If the opposition has comparable weapons, the attrition will be rapid, as was seen during the 1973 Arab-Israeli war, the first in which large quantities of modern aircraft and missiles were used. Russia and the United States had to resupply their respective clients quickly, or the fighting would have petered out due to lack of armaments. Similarly, in 1982, the United States had to lend Britain stocks of missiles earmarked for NATO so that the Royal Navy could carry on the Falklands War. If the Superpowers, who build most modern weaponry, go at it, there will be no generous patron capable of dipping into weapons stockpiles to bail them out. This is where you improvise or die.

Actually, you are just as likely to die of boredom because, with no weapons, there may not be a lot to do at the front. Yet people are resourceful in desperate situations, and this is where the electronic improvisation comes in. Increasingly, armed forces use software (computer programs) to make their weapons work. Many weapons and other combat systems can have their software quickly changed. Improvements in software make weapons more effective. When you are down to your last few hundred aircraft, you want to maximize their survival in combat. Better software can do that. The same drill works for weapons, as well as sensors and fire-control equipment. Even if production shortages mean fewer guided missiles, we can make "iron bombs" (old-fashioned high-explosive bombs with no electronics) more accurate if the computers on the aircraft are tweaked in the right direction. A typical improvisation is the addition of fins and a guidance system to iron bombs to make them into somewhat-guided missiles. Limited supplies of such kits already exist. Under wartime conditions, these easily manufactured kits could easily become all that's available.

Since small arms and conventional-artillery ammunition production is fairly easy to step up, some of the troops may find themselves back in static positions with the war degenerating into a sort of World War I redux, with nuclear-reconnaissance satellites, until the medium-tech improvisations become available.

In the case of the United States, industrial mobilizations from the Civil War through World War II took place when the nation had vigorous and growing basic manufacturing industries. This has changed, as the Untied States has shifted to a service economy during the last thirty years. For example, any manufacturing requiring bending or cutting metal must use machine tools, devices that are now largely manufactured in Germany and Japan. The United States would have to secure air and sea access to these two nations in order to obtain additional machine tools quickly. If one or both of these nations were overrun, American industrial mobilization would be hampered. Then too, there's the problem of "loss" of certain domestic industrial installations, such as steel mills. In the face of stiff foreign competition, the United States has closed numerous older, less efficient plants. On mobilization, these plants would have to be hastily reopened and refurbished, assuming they haven't been torn down. Similar problems exist in the shipbuilding industry, the automotive industry, and even the shoe industry. Note also that though America began mobilizing its industry for World War II several years before the Japanese struck in December 1941, it still required a couple of years more before supplies of equipment, weapons, ammunition, and everything else became adequate.

QUALITY, QUANTITY, AND MONOPOLY

Peacetime arms production tends toward national monopolies. This leads to higher quality (or at least more expensive) weapons, and fewer of them. For example, when combat aircraft first came into use during World War I, some major nations had as many as a score of firms manufacturing fighters and bombers. The lean years of peace that followed the war saw many of these firms close. World War II kept the survivors in business, but the decades of peace after 1945 laid waste to the rest. By the 1980s, France had only one major player left, the United States but four, and there was not enough business to go around. In actual fact, there are no independent combat-aircraft builders left anywhere. The principal French aircraft firm, Dassault, is essentially an inefficient enterprise supported by a generous government for reasons of prestige. The U.S. firms—Grumman, Lockheed, McDonnell Douglas, Northrop—are all now really subcontractors, sharing contracts with each other as a means of mutual survival. The main reason for this is the vastly increased cost of individual aircraft and the subsequent reduction in the number of each model produced. In 1990, for example, there were sixty-one major types of fixed-wing and helicopter combat aircraft in use worldwide. The total number of aircraft is 55,000, or about 900 copies of each type. There are wide variations, as a handful of types have 2,000–5,000 copies in use. But even this is much less than the World War II period, when it was common to have over 10,000 copies of some aircraft types in use. While the number of aircraft has declined, and continues to do so, the cost of individual aircraft climbs ever higher. World War II fighters cost $500,000–$1,000,000 in 1990 dollars. Current fighters average $20 million each on the same basis, including R&D, and really "hot" ones more than twice that.

Current aircraft, on the other hand, *are* much more efficient, and, surprisingly, more reliable and safer, and would probably defeat a much larger force equipped with many more of the cheaper World War II planes. Note that a comparison should not be based just on the aircraft cost. Each plane needs a ground crew and other support. The actual cost ratio is something like ten World War II aircraft to one current jet fighter. Among other things, the World War II aircraft were more prone to noncombat losses from accidents and equipment failure. So despite the seeming ridiculous increase in cost, no one has any incentive to go back to cheaper Spitfires or Mustangs. There is an optimal balance between high tech and low price, although it's not an easy balance to find in peacetime. The United States learned this the hard way during the Vietnam War when its frontline aircraft were not able to establish a kill ratio comparable to that achieved during the Korean War, or even World

War II. Much of this was due to deficiencies in training, but a lot of it had to do with building the wrong technology, or too much technology.

Another example of the enormous cost escalation can be seen in a comparison between current and Vietnam era weapons (all prices in 1990 dollars). In 1970, the UH-1 ("Huey") helicopter cost $820,000. By the early 1980s, this same machine was costing $1.3 million, and its replacement model currently costs over $9 million. Even more striking increases can be seen in the cost of helicopter gunships, with the cost figures for the same three periods being $1.7 million, $4.5 million, and $19 million. The electronics for new weapons systems is the largest contributor to all this cost escalation, and it hasn't just affected aircraft. The comparable cost data for tanks are $830,000, $1.5 million, $3.3 million. For armored personnel carriers, it's $200,000, $260,000, $2 million. Warfare has not changed so dramatically in twenty years to justify such cost escalation. What is at work here is something more mundane, the ancient tendency of weapons manufacturers to jack up the cost of their goods when there's no war around to expose which costly improvement is worth it and which is not. To put it another way, the firms that offer the technology that appears the most impressive get the contracts. Without being able to really test the technology in peacetime, the next best thing is to make it expensive.

Peacetime military technology, however, tends to have a lot of bells and whistles that vastly increase the cost and often turn out to be a liability in combat. By "bells and whistles," we mean extra little doodads that may add a smidgen to the "effectiveness" of the weapon, at a price. Commonly a considerable price. Developing this spectacular new technology costs a lot of money, and in the capitalist West this has meant fewer and fewer firms, as the companies merge into larger entities able to more efficiently generate the vast sums needed to develop the new, high-tech weapons. With only a handful of companies, there is less chance for real innovation, and always, there is the paradox anyway of trying to invent new technology you can't always adequately test. And although there are a number of companies, if you count all the firms in the non-Superpower industrialized nations, most countries, especially the Superpowers, are reluctant to buy from foreign sources weapons that they could manufacture, even if these weapons are superior. Only the United States does this to some extent, and usually with great reluctance plus resistance from domestic arms suppliers. So there is some variety and sources of new ideas, but a nationalistic resistance to taking advantage of it.

Russia does not avoid any of these quality and quantity problems. In fact, Russia must contend with some additional burdens. Unlike the West, there are no arms manufacturing companies as such, although there are distinct industrial entities performing design, research, testing, and manufacturing. Each of these organizations jealously guards its independence and power, which is largely measured by the number of people employed. The Russian economy until recently was centrally planned, and all orders came from what is actually called "the Center." This began to change in the late eighties as initiative at lower levels was stressed in an attempt to eliminate shortages and improve product quality. Yet "the Center" still maintained an iron grip on key resource-allocation decisions. More changes in this system are predicted, but may take a while. Hitherto, planning has been—and is still being—done five, ten, even twenty years ahead, depending on the item. It is always assumed that a new weapon will be built in large quantities. To prevent obsolescence, systems are kept current with incremental improvements. New engines, new electronics, improved weapons, all contribute to keeping systems survivable on the battlefield. But it doesn't always work, for the Russians have an even worse problem than the West testing weapons in peacetime. As mentioned earlier, Russian forces don't use their equipment as vigorously in peacetime as do Western ones. The philosophy of Russian training is, above all, the preservation of equipment. Russian doctrine maintains the need to have a maximum amount of working hardware when a war starts. Wearing the stuff out during training is a no-no. With this in mind, Russian weapons designers go for maximum combat power and not a lot of durability. This creates equipment that cannot take the hard training Western gear regularly undergoes. One result of this is that many design flaws in Russian equipment are not revealed until a lot of it has been in combat, or used in training long enough for the troops to uncover the problems. Nonetheless, Russian designers are a capable bunch. Their weapons are lethal-looking and packed with clever features that enhance their effectiveness and overcome other problems unique to Russian manufacturing such as questionable quality control in the factories and haphazard maintenance and operation by the troops. Russian commanders are aware of these problems, although they are much less well known in the West. NATO, Israel, and other Western forces train very hard, and this produces results on the battlefield. This has not gone unnoticed in Russia during all those "small" wars that have taken place since 1945 in which Western and Russian weapons were pitted against each other. Starting in the 1970s, Russia began working on developing Western-style technology, but it didn't work. There were successes, but the Russians did not have sufficient manufacturing technology or military-training resources to pull it off. This became painfully obvious in Afghanistan, Iraq, and in hundreds of training areas in Russia.

One thing that forced the Russian military to agree to the current great restructuring and sharp cutbacks in the armed forces was the realization that the Russian economy was becoming increasingly incapable of matching the Western style high-tech gear that modern weapons needed. This has hit the Russian military particularly hard. For example, because most of their troops are short-term conscripts, complex equipment must be automated as much as possible. Otherwise, the ill-trained troops will not only have a difficult time getting the stuff to work properly, but will not be able to maintain it adequately either. Russian nuclear submarines, for example, lack trained enlisted men to such an extent that they go to sea with crews consisting of over two-thirds officers. Complex Russian weapons systems have a much lower readiness rate than comparable Western equipment. The troops and their officers know this as, increasingly, do Western intelligence officers. Without better technology, this automation approach becomes less and less viable. An optimal solution is to shrink the armed forces by weeding out the less capable conscripts and career personnel while beefing up the economy so that more automated equipment can be produced. The result would be a smaller, better-equipped, better-trained, and far more effective force. All troops are not equal, and the Russians know from their own wartime experience that one German, or Israeli, soldier can be worth several less capable opponents.

MERCHANTS' DIRECTORY

In the United States, the biggest chunk of the defense budget goes to personnel, about 27 percent, depending on how you count fringe benefits. A roughly equal sum, about $80 billion, is expended on procurement each year. The United States purchases weapons and munitions from dozens of major, and thousands of minor, suppliers, concluding, in a "normal" year, more than 15 million defense procurement contracts for hundreds of thousands of different kinds of items. These include everything from aircraft carriers, tanks, and bullets to toothpicks, feminine-hygiene products, and apples. The overwhelming majority of these contracts—upward of 90 percent—are for sums of less than $25,000. The balance is for the "big ticket" items.

Procurement contracts also go to thousands of firms. Eliminating those whose products are essentially "civilian"—the toothpick, personal-hygiene products, and apple suppliers—there are about 29,000 prime defense contractors, who in turn deal with some 10,000 subcontractors and suppliers, as well as with each other. This is an enormous number of firms, but there used to be even more: From 1982 to 1987, defense procurement spending went from $55 billion to $87 billion, yet the number of suppliers fell from 118,000 firms. Not all of this decrease can be assigned to consolidation; many firms stopped bidding because of the low profitability of most defense contracts. About one hundred firms account for about 75 percent of the defense procurement budget, and just ten firms account for nearly 60 percent of it.

For the 1987–88 fiscal year, a fairly typical one, the ten largest U.S. defense contractors were:

THE TOP TEN U.S. DEFENSE MANUFACTURERS

FIRM	DEPARTMENT OF DEFENSE CONTRACTS	% OF SALES
McDonnell Douglas	$7.7 billion	c. 20.6
General Dynamics	$7.0 billion	75.3
General Electric	$5.8 billion	24.8

THE TOP TEN U.S. DEFENSE MANUFACTURERS (*cont.*)

FIRM	DEPARTMENT OF DEFENSE CONTRACTS	% OF SALES
Lockheed	$5.6 billion	49.6
General Motors	$4.1 billion	4.0
Raytheon	$3.8 billion	49.4
Martin Marietta	$3.7 billion	65.4
United Technologies	$3.6 billion	20.9
Boeing	$3.5 billion	22.7
Grumman	$3.4 billion	97.1

These concerns together account for $47.4 billion, or about 16.3 percent, of the defense budget, and nearly 60 percent of the procurement budget. Note that percentages of corporate gross sales are based on figures for calendar year 1987, while the defense budget in question was that for fiscal year 1987, which begins late in that year and runs into 1988, so that the figures do not correspond exactly. Moreover, rounding has introduced an additional degree of inaccuracy.

These big-ticket outfits supply some of the most expensive single items. McDonnell Douglas, Boeing, Lockheed, and Grumann build aircraft. General Dynamics builds ships—in particular, nuclear submarines. Nearly all of these top suppliers are involved in missile or electronics production. While all major U.S. corporations have some business with the military, you will note that several of these top firms depend on the armed forces for most of their sales (Grumman, Martin Marietta, General Dynamics). This produces a certain air of desperation, as the loss of one or two major programs can do major damage to the firms' viability. It should come as no surprise, then, that these corporations will put up a spirited, and effective, fight when the Congress or the Defense Department tries to cut any of these huge projects.

Perhaps it is fortunate, however, that a number of firms supply equipment not only to the U.S. armed forces, but also to various foreign powers.

The principal defense exporters are more or less the same as the principal domestic suppliers: All the firms listed are among the top twenty domestic defense contractors. More interesting, there are relatively few "big ticket" sales to foreign powers by American defense firms.

THE TOP TEN U.S. DEFENSE EXPORTERS

FIRM	FOREIGN SALES	% OF SALES
General Dynamics	$1.4 billion	c. 15.0
General Electric	.6 billion	.4
Raytheon	.6 billion	7.8
Northrop	.6 billion	10.7
United Technologies	.2 billion	1.2
General Motors	.2 billion	.2
Boeing	.2 billion	1.3
Westinghouse	.2 billion	1.9
Hughes Aircraft	.2 billion	3.4
McDonnell Douglas	.1 billion	.3

The companies listed do most of their foreign business in the form of missiles, spare parts, and electronics, although a few do sell some combat aircraft (Northrop) and helicopters (United Technologies, McDonnell Douglas). One result of this is that foreign sales are much less important to the balance sheets of virtually all these firms. This is not uncommon in the defense industry worldwide. Although foreign sales may be of consequence in terms of helping to reduce production costs of a particular item, such as a fighter, all defense manufacturers, whether in the West, in the Soviet bloc, or among the neutrals and Third World nations, rely heavily upon domestic contracts for their survival.

Foreign military sales have significant foreign-policy implications. After all, you don't want to sell arms to an "unfriendly" regime. You also want to be certain that the equipment doesn't fall into the wrong hands, particularly if it represents advanced technology that your foes would love to get a look at. In addition, you want to be certain that the stuff is used only for purposes of which you approve. And you may have to send technicians to help the buyer use and maintain his new trinkets, thereby possibly putting citizens at some risk. As a result, the United States and most other countries require government approval of foreign military sales. About 80 percent of U.S. foreign military sales are sponsored by the government under various programs, and the remaining 20 percent—so-called 'private' sales—must have government licenses. All military matériel export agreements contain various restrictions on use and resale. Indeed, depending upon the regime doing the buying, sales of certain types of "civilian" equipment that might have military uses may also require U.S. approval, and have restrictions imposed. These attempts to control foreign-policy fallout from arms exports are not always successful. Israel, for example, ignored restrictions that had been placed on the offensive use of U.S.-supplied equipment when it invaded Lebanon in 1982. Similarly, Libya ignored contractual restrictions on its use of certain heavy-lift trucks and converted them into tank transporters. An even clearer illustration of the foreign-policy implications of arms exports can be seen in the case of Iran, which had purchased a huge quantity of advanced American equipment during the 1970s. Shortly after the Iran-Iraq War broke out in 1980, the Iranians sold a Phoenix missile to the Russians for a lot of more desperately needed low-tech arms. And one reason for the circumspection with which the United States acted during the 1979–81 hostage crisis was the fact that on the fall of the shah there were 24,000 American technicians in the country, helping to maintain all that hardware: Although most of them left in the months after the ayatollah took power, there were still several thousand present into 1980.

DOMESTIC SUPPLIERS

Many countries manufacture a lot of military equipment on their own. There are a number of reasons for this, but national pride and economic self-interest are paramount among them. Most of these enterprises are essentially inefficient. Canada, for example, produces a lot of simple stuff, at a cost 30 percent over what it could be bought for on the open market from larger and more efficient foreign firms, and uses a lot of World War II era plant to achieve this inefficiency. Japan also manufactures much of its own military equipment, mostly derivatives of U.S. designs, but with a respectable number of domestic ones as well. While Japan's plant is quite modern and the equipment very good, limited production runs lead to a considerably higher cost per unit. This is also the case with France, which recently decided to manufacture a domestically designed carrier fighter rather than opt for an American or British one, despite the fact the homemade product will probably cost about 30 percent more than the foreign one. Israel also indulges in this practice, partially out of concern over the possible loss of foreign suppliers and partially as a demonstration of national sovereignty: In fact, not only is much of what Israel produces more expensive than what it could buy abroad, but much of it requires components and licensing from other powers, notably the United States.

STYLE OVER SUBSTANCE

An overlooked aspect of arms procurement is what might be called the "We Gotta Have It Syndrome." Over the last few decades, some new equipment has been procured largely because of fashion, not to fulfill any genuine need. This is especially true if "they" have it. Even if it doesn't work. The "Sergeant York" DIVAD—"Divisional Air Defense"—system is an excellent case in point. During the 1973 Arab-Israeli War, the Israelis captured a Russian fully automatic, radar-controlled self-propelled multiple barrel antiaircraft-gun system, the ZSU-23. This weapon was built to provide defense of mechanized columns against fast-moving ground-attack aircraft. The U.S. Army subjected the ZSU-23 to extensive tests and found that it didn't work very well. But it seemed like such a good idea, the army decided it needed something of the sort itself. Thus was the "Sergeant York" born. Despite years of development, and hundreds of millions of dollars, it never worked. Eventually, Congress decided to kill it, but there were few people in the army who were willing to concede that this was a good move. The "Sergeant York" was not a bad idea, but it was poorly designed, badly developed, and excessively protected.

Similar events occur in Russian procurement. One of the better examples is the Russian version of swing-wing design military aircraft. The first such example was the 1960s U.S. F. 111. The swing wing, if properly implemented, gives the aircraft better performance over a wider range of maneuvers by allowing the wings to swing back or forward. On the downside, the swing-wing equipment adds substantial weight, cost, and complexity to the design. For example, the swing-wing F-14 fighter requires ninety-eight man-hours of maintenance per sortie while the similar, but fixed-wing, F-15 requires only thirty-four man-hours. Not wanting to fall behind, the Russians quickly worked to implement swing-wing technology in many of their new, and existing, aircraft. They found, as U.S. pilots did, that the swing wing was not really worth it. Their lower level of technology caused Russian aircraft so equipped to be much less effective than their Western counterparts. Western pilots like to joke that the best thing to come out of swing-wing technology was the damage done to Russian aircraft performance when the Russians adopted the technique on a larger scale than in the West. The swing wing is no longer considered a widely useful technology.

Interservice rivalry plays a role there as well. To be sure, there is some interservice cooperation in procurement. After all, everyone does use the same rifles and helmets. But there is actually not as much of this sort of cooperation as one would think. For example, it would seem natural that the air force and the navy should work together on aircraft development, or the army and navy on helicopter projects, but this has not proven to be the case. Occasional attempts to force the services to cooperate in this way have sometimes led to disastrous results, such as the F-111 fiasco, in which the aircraft became so big and complex that it proved totally unsuitable for use by the navy. On the other hand, the F-4, originally designed for the navy, proved eminently successful in the air force. The latest Navy SLBM (Sea-Launched Ballistic Missile) matches the Air Force MX (Peacekeeper) in all crucial characteristics, yet both are now in production, at enormous additional expense. The navy and army each develop and build their own SAMs (Surface-to-Air Missiles), even though one basic system could serve on land and sea with some modification. While some interservice effort would be required to resolve differing requirements, the army and navy find it easier (although more expensive) to develop separate systems. Likewise, the Marine Corps doesn't always use the same weapons and equipment as the army, even in cases where standardization would save great sums with negligible loss of functionality.

It must also be said that some new procurement occurs not because the existing equipment is obsolete, but merely because it's old, and perhaps doesn't fit the image of the "New Action Army/Navy/etc." A good example of this is the old reliable .45 caliber (11.4-mm) automatic pistol, which is to be replaced by a Beretta 9 mm, partially because the former is very heavy and not very accurate, while the Beretta is much handier and a bit more accurate, and doesn't kick quite so badly. These are certainly valid points, although the troops have found the .45 satisfactory for more than seventy-five years. Much is also made of the issue of "commonality" of ammunition with our NATO allies, who all use 9-mm pistols. However, the armed forces fail to make the same case with regard to the lack of "commonality" in most other forms of equipment, like tanks, aircraft, and spare parts, which are likely to be needed in far greater amounts than ammunition for the .45, which brings up another aspect of "fashion" in arms procurement, the "NIH factor." A major element in some of the debate over the Beretta decision had to do less with the relative merits of the .45 over the Beretta and more with the fact that Beretta is a foreign concern. Not only did this mean that "our tax dollars" would be going overseas, but also that the weapon in question was NIH or "Not Invented Here," the implication being that it was not likely to be as good as a domestic product. Many times over the last few decades, many countries, including the United States, have preferred to procure domestically produced equipment rather than perfectly satisfactory weapons produced by foreign manufacturers. This was partially motivated by a natural desire to support domestic industry. But it also has something to do with the belief that foreigners don't produce equipment quite as good as our own. Thus, in the 1950s and 1960s, when most NATO nations adopted an Italian 105-mm howitzer, the United States opted to produce one of its own. And when, almost a decade ago, Israel demonstrated the effectiveness of its remotely piloted reconnaissance drones, the U.S. Army, instead of buying the Israeli one, decided to go its own way. The resulting aircraft, the "Aquila"—Latin for "eagle"—has not proven very successful.

There are exceptions to this rule, as when the United States opted to procure a British-designed 105-mm tank cannon, and later a German 120-mm one, but the basic pattern is fairly unshakable. And all of these seemingly irrational reasons for procuring weapons play an important part in driving up costs.

CONTRACTING FOR CORRUPTION

Despite depressing headlines, which have led to a great deal of cynicism about defense contracts, the overwhelming majority of defense procurement programs are fulfilled without a hitch. Various investigators have concluded that "irregularities" occur in only about one of every 10,000 defense contracts. That's still a lot of irregularities, about 1,500 a year. Some of this is due to the apparent corruption in defense contracts. The real culprit, what actually causes the cynical spectacle of the Defense Department paying hundreds of dollars for ordinary items, is the enormous amount of paperwork that accompanies defense contracts. Most of this is mandated by Congress, whether with the intention of forestalling corruption or to insure compliance with various social, political, and economic goals. This form of corruption accompanies bigness in institutions. Organizations, whether they be commercial or institutional, have a tendency to reach a size where they become less, rather than more, efficient. This rot is not immediately apparent, but eventually accumulates and either causes a major overhaul in the organization, or a collapse, which is why, every few years, a truly huge company comes crashing down, seemingly without warning. In hindsight, there always are warnings, but the right people don't notice, or act upon, them.

Let us give you a personal example of how the contracts themselves contribute to corruption. Some years ago, the authors of this volume were both on the staff of a military historical journal. By chance, a library affiliated with the air force sent in a purchase order for a subscription. Among other things, this required the supplier, that is the magazine, to: confirm that no member of the staff was in any way related to the persons letting the contract for a subscription; to indicate whether the company was a "minority firm," and thereby eligible for certain "set asides"; to affirm the company's commitment to nondiscriminatory practices in matters of race, sex, age, and so forth; to certify that the principals were not the agents of a foreign power; and to declare the company's compliance with certain embargoes, such as those on the sale of arms to South Africa, North Korea, Cuba, and various other unpleasant regimes. (As the journal had subscribers all over the world, including a couple in some of the nations on the list, we were tempted to forgo the air-force subscription lest our editor end up in legal trouble for not observing this embargo. A lawyer familiar with such matters advised that it was doubtful that the U.S. Attorney's Office would prosecute a history magazine. But one can never tell.)

There was more. And there was also information about the

various forms that had to be submitted if it was necessary to explain a particular answer. The point is that a subscription that an ordinary citizen could take out by writing his name and address on a postcard required the magazine to complete a five- or six-page form. The last item on the purchase order was the most interesting. This permitted the contractor to charge the air force for the staff time required to complete the purchase order, at certain fixed, and very favorable, rates. On this basis, a $6 subscription could easily have cost the air force over $100 (largely in time required by various company staff in finding answers), a "cost overrun" of more than 1,600 percent. In this case, patriotism won out over greed, and the air force only paid the same as everyone else. But not everyone can afford to be so noble, particularly if the paperwork weighs in at four or five tons, as is by no means unusual in the case of some procurement projects. Your writers' bout with military procurement took place some twenty years ago. Contemporary contract procedures are even more complex, leading to widely heralded abuses that only complicate the already difficult task of procuring suitable weapons and equipment for the armed forces.

Such contract procedures are one aspect of the "cost overruns" that plague defense procurement projects. Budgetary machinations are also an important factor in driving costs up. Congress frequently mandates "stretch-outs" in purchase orders, procuring the same number of items but over a longer period of time, or cuts the total number of items to be produced. This will mean less expenditure now, which may please the taxpayers but will result in higher costs over the long term due to uneconomical production runs. The current record holder in this department is the B-2 bomber, which ran up a $25 billion tab for R&D before the first one was built. On a production run of 132 planes, this comes out to $180 million each for R&D, plus $340 million apiece to actually build each one. If the production run were cut in half, each remaining bomber would cost at least $360 million apiece for R&D, plus $340 million to build. If the production period were stretched out, the cost would also rise as it costs several billion a year just to keep the production organization in business.

THE BLEEDING EDGE OF TECHNOLOGY

Another important factor promoting the spiraling cost of defense procurement is technology. Many weapons-development projects push the limits of technology to an extraordinary degree. Often we aren't sure what we want new equipment to do, and may have highly unrealistic notions as to what new technologies are practical. For example, in the early 1960s the United States Army asked for a new tank to replace the M-60 in the 1970s. A lot was expected for the new vehicle, including a gas-turbine engine, a computer-stabilized gun that could fire either missiles or cannon shells accurately while on the move, better accommodations for the crew, superior protection, laser fire control, and so forth. In 1963, Congress approved the MBT-70 project, which was to be a joint venture with West Germany. By the late sixties, the project was in trouble, and the Germans decided to pull out and go with an upgraded version of their Leopard tank. Then, in 1970, Congress killed the MBT-70. But the army still needed a new tank, so a less ambitious project was approved, the MX-803. This ran into problems very quickly, and was canceled in 1971. So the army once more went looking for a new tank. In 1972, Congress approved the M-1 project. By 1976, when the MBT-70 was supposed to have been in the hands of the troops, the army had spent $540 million since 1963 and had only a handful of miscellaneous prototypes to show for it. Not until the early 1980s, twenty years after it had decided it needed a new tank, did the army get one. And the M-1 still had teething problems that were not fully worked out for another few years. Most of the problems with the MBT-70/MX-803/M-1 projects had been the result of unrealistic technological expectations. Some of these expectations eventually proved workable, like the gas-turbine engine, while others, such as the combined missile launcher/cannon, never worked. Meanwhile costs kept rising, so that the M-1 runs in the neighborhood of $3 million, nearly three times what it was originally expected to cost.

Technology is actually not at fault here. Our expectations of technology are the problem. When you push the limits of technology, you have to understand that costs are likely to spiral totally out of proportion to your original estimates. This is especially true in the United States, where the armed forces and Congress constantly redefine projects, adding requirements, capabilities, and parameters that were not in the original contract. These "bells and whistles" will not only increase cost, usually all out of proportion to the added capability, but will also delay completion of the project and create further opportunities for corrupt practices, and may actually degrade overall performance of the finished product. In short, the basis of this problem is the inability of anyone to say "enough!" Features are added until (nearly) everyone is happy. Except the taxpayer.

OVERRUNNING THE TAXPAYER

As a result of our essentially irrational procurement policies, overall defense projects run an average of nearly 50 percent more than their initial estimates. Over the last couple of decades, the capabilities of new weapons have risen an average of about 5 percent per year (on paper, anyway), while costs have gone up about 7 percent a year (for real). This is mostly due to pushing the limits of technology, plus "bells and whistles," and increasing paperwork. This is a lot of unexpected expense.

Actually, cost overruns in defense are far less than those in many other government contracts. The Rayburn House Office Building ran more than 50 percent above the original estimate, as did the Myerson Symphony Center in Dallas, while the New Orleans Superdome was more than 200 percent over budget, and the Central Park ice-skating rink more than 700 percent, and all four, as well as many other such projects, were completed far behind schedule, to boot. Whether in civil engineering or in military procurement, these cost overruns are as much the result of burdensome paperwork, bureaucratic interference, highly peculiar contract provisions, and technological ambition as of outright corruption. The abuses in nonmilitary governmental contracting lead to momentary flaps in the press and are soon forgotten. Those in defense contracts are more visible than those in other areas of government procurement, largely because they are subsumed under the heading of "defense," involve truly enormous sums of money to begin with, and are concentrated in a relatively small number of firms.

All this seemingly uncontrollable expenditure and corruption in defense procurement not only creates a very bad taste in the public's mouth, but it tends to make the taxpayers ever more cynical about defense, and ever more reluctant to dip into their pockets for worthy projects. There's got to be a better way.

CHANGES IN PROJECTED COSTS OF SELECTED DEFENSE PROCUREMENT PROJECTS

As can be seen from the following table, some projects end up in "overruns," while others do not. Commonly, overruns occur in projects that are highly innovative. Proven technologies usually experience "underruns," coming in at less cost than originally projected. A good example of this is the SSN-21 project, the prototype of which cost about twice what the production models are likely to cost.

Below are listed eighteen different "big ticket" defense procurement projects. Some explanation is necessary in order to make reading it easier. The item in question is listed under "Project," followed by the branch of the service and year of the original contract. In some cases, the original contracts were let nearly two decades ago, but the equipment is still being procured. In several other cases, the contracts were let very recently, and delivery has not actually begun. "Original Estimate, Project" is the projected cost of the project at the time the contract was let. Figures are in billions of dollars for "Original Estimate" and millions for "Unit Cost" (so $1.2 means $1.2 billion in the first case, $1.2 million in the second; note that we have rounded off these figures). The "K" used in "No." (Number) indicates that the number is expressed in thousands. To account for inflation, about 300 percent since 1970, all figures have been converted into 1990 dollars.

"No." indicates how many copies of the item were contracted for, while "Unit Cost" is the price each copy was supposed to cost under the original contract.

Not shown in the chart is "Current Estimate," which is the projected cost of the program as it stood at the beginning of 1990, given all changes in costs and quantity since the original contract date. Likewise, the unseen "Current Number" represents the number now expected to be produced when the

CHANGES IN PROJECTED COSTS OF SELECTED DEFENSE PROCUREMENT PROJECTS

PROJECT	SERVICE	YR	ORIGINAL ESTIMATE			CHANGES IN CONTRACT		CHANGE RATIO
			PROJECT	NO.	UNIT COST	CHANGE NO.	UNIT COST	
Abrams M-1 Tank	Army	72	$4.8	3325	$1.4	5992	$1.4	1.97
AMRAAM Air-to-Air Missile	Air Force	78	$11.6	24K	$.47	-73	$.001	1.00
Apache Helicopter	Army	72	$3.8	545	$7	439	$7.116	2.02
B-1B Bomber	Air Force	81	$29.5	100	$295	0	-$21	0.93
Bradley Fighting Vehicle	Army	72	$.4	1205	$.4	7280	$1.058	3.92
CG-47 Aegis Cruisers	Navy	78	$14.1	16	$880	11	$11.3	1.01
Copperhead Artillery Round	Army	75	$1.2	133K	$.009	-130K	$.493	53.8
CVN-72/73 Aircraft Carrier	Navy	82	$7	2	$3,483	0	-$293	0.92
EA-6B Wild Weasel Aircraft	Navy	84	$2.8	38	$72	60	-$18.9	0.74
F-15 Fighter	Air Force	70	$7.4	749	$9.8	423	$18.8	2.91
GLCM Cruise Missile	Air Force	77	$1.5	702	$2.2	-137	$3.6	2.67
Harpoon Antiship Missile	Navy	70	$1	2922	$.35	1527	$.645	2.83
NAVSTAR User Sets	Air Force	79	$4.9	27K	$.18	-1760	-$.017	0.91
P-3C Patrol Aircraft	Navy	84	$5	80	$62.8	-48	-$17.7	0.72
SSN-21 Submarine	Navy	85	$3.9	1	$3,875	11	-$2,301	0.41
Stinger SAM Missile	Army	72	$5.6	23K	$.24	40076	-$.189	0.22
Titan IV Launch Vehicle	Air Force	85	$2.5	10	$253	47	-$38.9	0.85
TOW2 Antitank Missile	Army	84	$2.6	141K	$.019	33308	-$0.000	0.99

contract is completed, and the unseen "Current Unit" cost, how much each copy now costs given changes in cost and quantity. Using the "Original" and "Current" data, we show the calculated "Changes in Contract," which is how much more (or less) money the program now costs compared with the "Original Estimate." "Change in No." is how many more (or fewer) copies are to be produced compared with the original contract, and "Unit Cost" represents the difference in the cost of each copy from the original contract. "Change Ratio" gives the "Current Unit Cost" as a multiple of the "Original Unit Cost."

Although the numbers on this table look fairly straightforward, they are actually fairly deceptive. Several of the projects that appear to have had serious cost overruns are in fact the result of significant qualitative enhancements, such as in the case of the F-15. The original version of this fighter weighed about twenty-eight tons and carried about 1.5 tons of deliverable munitions. The current model, the F-15E, runs about forty tons and carries about twelve tons of deliverable munitions. These developments cannot readily be reflected in a table such as this. Likewise, the table cannot account for certain "hidden" costs. For example, the B-1B seems to have come in at a bit less than its original cost estimate, which is technically true. When the first production models rolled off the assembly line in 1983, the project was three months ahead of schedule and 2.7 percent under budget. But this was partially due to the fact that when the B-1B contracts were let, a clean slate was used. The B-1B contracts more or less ignored previous investment in the original supersonic version, the B-1A, which had been canceled by the Carter administration. So the B-1B started out with a considerable head start. And after the production run had been completed, it became evident that the plane needed additional work. Thus the F-15, which appears to have experienced a serious cost overrun, was actually more economical than the B-1B, which superficially appears to have come in under budget. Note that if defense-project budget managers tried to pull these stunts in the civilian sector, they would have the SEC, IRS, and irate investors (and their lawyers), plus the media after them with a vengeance. And so it goes in the fantasy world of defense spending.

The Same, but Different: World Patterns in Shooting Blanks

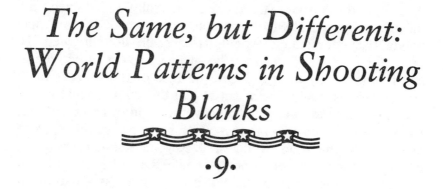

·9·

W hy do national military systems differ? What problems in military policy confront other nations? Why do various nations shoot blanks in different ways?

All nations have to cope with the problems of miscalculated, and sometimes wayward, military power. You don't have to be a Superpower to have serious problems with the appearance, or reality, of your military capabilities. Smaller nations have less to fear about unleashing their forces unsuccessfully in a war since they are habitually too poor to engage in wars with their neighbors, who are in turn themselves too poor to pose much of a threat. In such countries, the armed forces are useful for keeping the population in check, and for this they must have some degree of skill. It's one thing to go off to fight a neighbor, and have the troops get into trouble. It's much more upsetting if you must rely on the troops to keep irate citizens from getting at you, only to find the troops screwing up in this vital task, which may have a more serious personal impact on you than defeat in war.

Just as every nation is different, so too are their variations on these calculation and perception problems and how they deal with them. Large nations, for example, have large armed forces. Among all these troops, there are a few really well trained units, mostly composed of eager volunteers. For small military operations, these commando-type units generally do quite well. The rest of the armed forces may be of much lower effectiveness, and this fact may be ignored in the face of the success of the special troops. Only a war can reveal this to its fullest extent, and wars do tend to lead to improvements in training and readiness. We can see this process at work in Russia now, as the lessons of Afghanistan are digested. Regular Russian Army units in Afghanistan did very poorly, while the airborne and commando units did much better. Of course, there is a natural human tendency to play up success and play down failure, and it will be interesting to see how the Russian senior military leadership deals with this situation. Curiously, America had no similar problem in Vietnam, where most combat troops performed about the same, due partially to comparatively better, or at least more, uniform troops and lengthy training, and partially to cultural factors. There were morale problems toward the end of the Vietnam War, but even then the troops usually did well by then current standards. Similar morale problems were encountered in Afghanistan, but Russia found that its regular troops also had numerous serious and persistent operational problems in combat. This is not unusual, as Russia's armed forces have traditionally had a bad time during the opening stages of a war. This is usual with most nations; it's just a bit worse with Russia.

The various national differences are instructive, as well as entertaining. In this chapter, we discuss the basic pattern prevailing in several different nations in terms of the five major causes of shooting blanks. To review, these are:

- *Intelligence Confusion*—The ability of a nation's intelligence services to maintain an accurate picture of what potential opponents are up to.
- *Amateurism*—The military's ability to do what it says it can do.

• *Media Muddle*—How well the national media keeps the government and population informed about what is going on in military affairs.
• *Procurement Puzzle*—How effective is the nation at producing, or obtaining overseas, weapons, supplies, and equipment for the military: as they put it in the navy, supplying "Bullets, Beans, and Black Oil."
• *Wrong-War Syndrome*—How effective is the military, and the nation, in preparing for the next war they may have to fight.

UNITED STATES

Intelligence Confusion

The United States has the most powerful intelligence capabilities in the world. Despite frequent unfavorable comparisons to Russia's KGB, American intelligence agencies are well equipped to uncover any nation's secrets. The primary bottleneck is analysis.

America's wartime record has been mixed, with several outstanding achievements and a large number of mediocre performances. In World War II, and quite possibly in subsequent conflicts, the United States managed to break enemy codes, allowing American analysts to read many secret enemy communications. Particularly in the Pacific, this code-breaking was decisive several times. In Europe, where much of the code-breaking was done by the British, the unveiled German secrets were repeatedly ignored or misinterpreted (although this was less the case during the war against German submarines in the North Atlantic). In other areas, the intelligence work was thorough and efficient and above average, but not exceptional, in effectiveness.

After World War II, there were a string of intelligence disasters. First there was the failure to discover the North Korean preparations to invade South Korea in 1950. A few months later, there was another disastrous failure to predict Chinese intervention. Before Vietnam, there were a string of misinterpretations and wrong calls on the nature and intentions of Russian ground forces and strategic weapons. A combination of conservative analysis and bending to political demands produced a number of illusory "gaps." There was the bomber gap of the late 1950s and the missile gap of the early 1960s, based on the then-assumption that Russia had a superiority in these weapons when they were actually inferior. During the 1950s and 1960s, a "gap" was claimed for ground forces in Europe, which was later found to be incorrect. Vietnam produced what amounted to a running battle between military and CIA analysts as to the nature and composition of the enemy forces. The military crew, under more political pressure to put an optimistic veneer on the seemingly endless fighting in Vietnam, tended to come up with smaller numbers than the more detached, and thus more accurate, CIA.

After Vietnam, attention shifted to Europe and the Middle East. In Europe, there was a plethora of often-conflicting analyses from the various experienced intelligence organizations in France, Britain, and West Germany. The primary advantage the U.S. analysts had was a sky full of high-tech reconnaissance satellites. All these disagreements were mooted by a Russian arms buildup that began in the late 1960s and kept going into the early 1980s, which in turn caused a similar increase in arms spending by the United States from the late 1970s. The great intelligence failure here was missing the damage the Russian buildup had done to their economy. Again, the CIA was in the forefront of trying to unscramble the convoluted Russian economy. Eventually, the Russians admitted that they themselves were not sure what all the numbers were. In the West, the basic belief was that the Russians were well organized and coming on strong, an attitude that was grounded more in political beliefs than reality, but this is nothing new in the intelligence business.

Amateurism

Few nations train their troops more intensively than does the United States. This is particularly true of the technical services, like aviation, navy, and armor. Where all this effort frequently breaks down is in the coordination of the multiplicity of units and systems as evidenced by the 1980 Iran rescue mission and, to a lesser extent, the Persian Gulf operations in the late 1980s and early 1990s. The drill is always the same, everyone wants in on the action, whether they're needed or not. Even when cooler heads prevail, it is discovered that each of the services have great difficulty understanding how the others operate. And although the Panama and Iraq operations went far more smoothly than most recent American military endeavors, the problem perhaps still persists.

The United States achieved a very high degree of interservice coordination during World War II, but this rapidly fell apart after the war. Each subsequent war exposed the need to set things right, and to a certain extent this was done. But after the wars, the different services went their separate ways again. The problem today arises largely from duplication of effort. The navy has ships, infantry, and fighter bombers, and integrates these in a way that is at odds with how the army would like to do it. The army has its own attack aircraft (helicopters) that work with the infantry. Despite strenuous efforts, the army helicopters always seem to work better with the infantry than the ground-attack aircraft from the air force. The greatest amount of duplication occurs in the area of commando operations: Everyone wants in on this, and each service has its own special units trained and equipped to do the deed a slightly different way.

All nations have some problems with the various branches of the armed services not working together. It's just worse in America, due primarily to uncommonly strong interservice rivalries and to a lack of a genuine centralized military command hierarchy. This is a serious problem that can be traced back to geography. The United States has little need for a large standing army, as there is no neighbor, hostile or otherwise, with substantial land forces. The only thing that sustains army strength in peacetime is overseas garrisons and commitments. A similar fate holds true for the air force, which should be hardly more than an adjunct to the ground forces. Yet in order to justify its separate existence, the air force has tried to make strategic warfare its major activity.

Both the army and air force look warily at the navy, which, in addition to its monopoly on ships, has a more efficient overseas infantry force (the marines) than the army and a more effective strategic-weapons capability (missile submarines, cruise missiles, and carrier aircraft) than the air force. This is the nub of the high-level "right stuff" problem in America. If logic ruled, the navy would control most of the defense budget and all overseas operations short of major war. The army would be largely a reserve force, to be mobilized when the nation is threatened. The air force would be smaller than it is now, focused on ground support, and operate as part of the army. But logic does not rule in these matters, politics does. The navy had a head start in military matters because it was the only service that had to maintain large forces in peacetime. The army traditionally had a minuscule force of regulars that was augmented in wartime by masses of draftees, volunteers, and militiamen. Partially because of this, the navy developed its Marine Corps into more than the small force most navies maintained. Indeed, before World War II the marines were known as "the State Department's infantry" because of their frequent use to settle foreign entanglements when a bit of muscle was needed. The thinking was, "If the marines go in, it's an incident; if the army goes in, it's a war." When aviation came along, the U.S. Navy embraced it more enthusiastically than most others. The result of all this was that by 1945 the navy was a complete armed force unto itself with large land, air, and sea forces operating under a unified command. The army soon had its air arm spun off into a separate air force, leaving the navy still intact and even more powerful. This caused an ongoing period of vicious interservice politics.

This infighting is usually avoided in other nations by the use of a General Staff, which is basically a separate "service" whose sole purpose is planning and commanding all military operations. No such luck in the United States, which merely has a "Joint Chiefs of Staff," essentially a committee of all the service chiefs. Curiously, this arrangement recognizes the superior status of the navy in that the Marine Corps commandant, who is subordinate to the chief of Naval Operations, is one of the four "chiefs." The navy holds all the cards, as the United States is essentially a maritime power and must have a strong fleet.

Meanwhile the army and air force also are at odds over how much air-force strength should be dedicated to army support. The navy and air force constantly skirmish over who should control how much of the nation's strategic weapons. The army has from time to time had its eye on the elimination of the Marine Corps. These problems existed even during World War II, and in subsequent wars the coordination problems only got worse. It can thus be expected that in future conflicts, large or small, interservice rivalries, and just plain shoddy interservice planning, will continue to weaken U.S. military power, as most recently demonstrated in Grenada and Panama. However, operations in the Gulf War showed considerable improvement.

Media Muddle

The United States is the media capital of the world. In a nation possessed of a vigorous free press, a huge publishing industry, a pervasive video presence, and an energetic film industry, the American military is kept in high profile. But because the U.S. media are geared more toward entertainment than analysis, there is a distinct warping of reality when it comes to military matters. Celluloid heroics in war movies have long inspired young men, and caused drill sergeants to make prodigious efforts to wean recruits from stunts that work on the screen but are usually fatal on the battlefield. As recently as the 1983 Grenada operation, well-trained troops were seen with belts of machine-gun ammunition draped across their chests. This may look great in a film, but in practice allows the bullets to become soiled or damaged and more easily jam during firing, which can be fatal to the machine-gunner. Movies such as *Top Gun* increased applications for naval aviation, but because the movie did not show the downside of naval aviation, there is likely to be an increase in disillusioned naval aviators. Films such as *Platoon* give a more realistic view of combat, although like all movies, they cannot convey the most typical aspect of the grunt's life: boredom, routine, and fatigue. By comparison, a more useful branch of the U.S. media is the press, which constantly exposes the quite normal waste, ineptitude, and politics common to peacetime procurement. Other Western journalists do the same with their military, but U.S. society is much more open than even those of our NATO allies, and the U.S. military-industrial complex is larger, and is perhaps capable of more deplorable and newsworthy activity. In the West, soldiers are always looking over their shoulders at the press. The media are treated with respect, as their paper bullets can do real damage to a promising career.

Procurement Puzzle

It was the former general and U.S. president Dwight D. Eisenhower who coined the phrase "military-industrial complex." He knew what he was talking about, but neither he nor his successors were able to do much about it. Russia may indeed have a larger MIC, but in the open society of America, more is known of the U.S. version. This has been a mixed blessing. On the one hand, the United States has been able to provide lavishly for the care, feeding, and equipping of the troops. On the other hand, the cost of much of the matériel is astronomical, a lot of it doesn't always work as it's expected to, and the political influence of the defense industry has had a corrupting effect on government. The United States leads the world in having more military technologies than any other nation, but at the cost of failing to maintain the lead in many civilian technologies, which increasingly threatens the very basis of its robust economy. While the advanced military technologies are impressive, by their nature, military technologies are more expensive to develop than civilian ones. The lack of market pressure has a lot to do with this, and there's no way around it unless there's a war going on.

Wrong-War Syndrome

The U.S. military has persistent difficulties in trying to figure out what constitutes proper preparation for the next war. Its preference seems to be for a World War II clone, with full-scale mobilization of the nation's industrial and human resources. At the same time, in the forty-five years since World War II the armed forces have been called upon to perform only limited war operations. Some of these have been handled quite adequately, such as the 1948 Berlin Airlift, the 1958 Lebanese operation, and particularly in the Gulf War. After a rocky start, due largely to the lethargies of peace, they also performed well in Korea. But the armed forces were less effective in Vietnam, where the military leadership kept thinking in terms of a conventional Continental war and may well have brought too much firepower to the task. In several even more limited operations, such as the Mayaguez affair, the Iran rescue mission, Grenada, and the 1983 Lebanese operation, the public (through the eyes of the media) saw the performance of the armed forces as seriously flawed due to interservice rivalryand inadequate preparations. Many in the military disagree with this assessment, but with the exception of Grenada, all these operations were failures. Yet it might be said that history, and the public, look at combat the same way Vince Lombardi looked at professional football: "Winning isn't the most important thing, it's the only thing." Had Grenada come at the end of a string of victories in other operations, the media (and public) wouldn't have jumped on the flaws of that successful operation.

To some extent, the failures of the American armed forces have been due to the fact that they find themselves required to perform a dual role, having simultaneously to prepare for both a nonnuclear World War III and for more limited undertakings. One result of this has been that their successes in limited wars have been greatest in situations which most closely resemble "the Big One." Entering the 1990s, the United States is placing more effort on "low-intensity war." Nevertheless, the basic attitudes look toward "the Big One." Old habits die hard.

RUSSIA

Intelligence Confusion

Despite their enormous intelligence-gathering and analysis resources, the Russians suffer to a crippling degree from paranoia. Seven decades of worshiping the struggle against the "Reactionary Capitalist Forces" attempting to destroy the "Socialist Revolution" have reinforced traditional Russian suspicion of foreigners, and it's been difficult for even the most clearheaded KGB officer to escape the effects of this atmosphere.

The KGB and GRU intelligence personnel are a privileged caste within Russian society. Opinion surveys indicate that the average Russian respects, envies, and fears the KGB. As part of their security procedures, the KGB employees live a separate existence to a greater extent than do intelligence personnel in Western countries. There are a greater number of special laws protecting KGB operatives and even preventing interference by the regular police. In this environment, all manner of strange ideas can take root and flourish. Although some individual KGB operatives have a pretty good idea of what's going on in the West, the institutional perspective is more clouded. While it is unlikely that an error as gross as Stalin's failure to believe intelligence reports of an imminent German invasion in 1941 will be repeated, something similar is still possible. As recently as November of 1983, for example, the KGB sent out a worldwide alert to its operatives to check out what it believed was the imminent possibility of an attack by a coalition of Western nations.

Russia also has a problem with the enormous access it has to information in the West. While Russia is a closed society, in the West things are much more open, and so Russian agents gain much of their data simply by wandering around picking up documents. Some have even been caught walking into U.S. Congressional offices and asking for the items they wanted. (Sometimes they got what they were looking for, sometimes not.) Their problem is in figuring out what to believe and what to discount. Historically, Russian intelligence operations have never been notable for their efficiency: Most of the Russians' efforts have gone into keeping tabs on their own citizens, an area where there has always been some degree of efficiency. After the 1917 Revolution, external espionage became much more effective because a large number of ideologically sympathetic foreigners willingly lent a hand. Lagging behind America in satellite technology, Russia depends more on spies. The Russians also have problems with paranoia and political guidance affecting intelligence analysis, and while they are less forthcoming about their intelligence failures, judging from the number of problems they've had in the Third World, they are coming up short with their spies, diplomats, or both. Afghanistan was no bright spot of intelligence work, but indications are that political desires overruled the analysts' frank appraisal of the dismal situation. The *glasnost* movement of the late 1980s has cleared away much of the political fog that previously blinded the use of good intelligence.

Amateurism

For more than a century, Russia has several times gone into wars with units well prepared on paper but wretchedly unready in practice. The haphazard performance of regular Russian troops in recent operations indicates that this tendency has not changed. All military organizations tend toward bureaucratic inertia, and the huge Russian military is a somewhat extreme example of this. Change comes slowly. Although there is a cadre of intelligent, well-educated, and well-meaning officers, too many career officers are just along for the ride. The majority of the troops are short-term conscripts who would rather be somewhere else, and mostly are after their two or three years in uniform. Historically, however, the Russian army gets the "right stuff" after a few months of combat. Before that, they have abundant quantities of the wrong stuff.

Media Muddle

The media in Russia are state-owned and Communist party–controlled. As in the capitalist world, the media operate on the principle that the owner calls the shots. As a result, the military was for so long presented in such a worshipful light that no one paid much attention to the coverage. Since the late 1980s, *glasnost* has enabled the press to be more probing and frank about the military, and the result has been a stream of negative articles on it. Thus, the nation with a tradition of nothing but media illusions about the military is now undergoing a traumatic process of discovery as actual conditions are openly discussed. While this will probably lead to a few of the reforms that the Russian military has long been discussing, in some instances for many decades, before that happens, the population will have a lively time sorting out the past lies, the inventive rumors that grew up in response to these lies, and the current openness.

Procurement Puzzle

The largest and most corrupt military-industrial complex (MIC) the world has ever known has developed in Russia. Up until the 1960s, the Russian MIC wasn't all that perverse. The periods before, during, and immediately after World War II were notable for relative efficiency and the development of many cost-effective weapons. But in the 1960s, when the arms race with the West began in earnest, the MIC had a virtual blank check, and took full advantage of it. This led to tremendous abuses, some of which are only now coming to light. There are, for example, several research institutes that have not produced any new technologies in decades, while there are factories that continue to produce arms and equipment that were obsolete twenty years ago. Many more disasters remain hidden under layers of secrecy. Increasing problems with the economy during the 1990s will squeeze military budgets, and there will be a big scramble as the various MIC bureaucracies struggle for survival. It will be an interesting process, and not necessarily beneficial to the troops.

Wrong-War Syndrome

Russia prepares for the only type of war that counts, the defense of the motherland from invasion. Strategically, such a policy requires massive ground forces to be deployed along the numerous and lengthy borders of Russia, the world's largest nation. Yet this considerably diminishes the actual strength of these ground forces, because it is unlikely that a sizable proportion of them could be concentrated in any one place quickly. In previous centuries, Russia did have another type of army to supplement the regular forces, a mobile force used to conquer the sparsely populated areas in the eastern part of the country. The Cossacks were the most famous of these troops. While the light forces were used in the 1920s to reconquer the Central Asian provinces, since then Russia did not see a need for such units until Afghanistan. The lack of success there did not encourage the reinstitution of light forces, although helicopter-borne infantry and commandos were used extensively and have been much written about since. As the Russians do not have many new frontiers to conquer, at least no sparsely populated and wide-open ones, they are not preparing their armed forces for such activities.

There is, however, one other form of war that they are encountering and are not prepared for, and this is civil disorder. There were several major incidents in Eastern Europe since

World War II (East Germany, Poland, Hungary, Czechoslovakia), and in each case while the Russian Army successfully asserted the authority of Moscow's local political utensils, the operations were all handled with considerable clumsiness and unnecessary bloodshed. Civil disorders within Russia are handled by the special MVD internal-security troops. These are organized like regular infantry divisions, though more lightly equipped, and are composed of personnel chosen for their potential loyalty when confronting angry Russian civilians. As recent incidents in Lithuania, Georgia, Armenia, Azerbaijan, and elsewhere have shown, they are not notably good at effecting minimally violent crowd control.

THIRD WORLD

Intelligence Confusion

Only a handful of Third World countries, such as India and several of the Arab states, possess a real capacity to collect and evaluate intelligence likely to be of diplomatic or military value. This severely handicaps their ability to make effective policy decisions. Since many Third World nations are ruled by dictators, having an efficient intelligence system would not necessarily be of any particular help in any case, as such leaders are much more concerned with domestic politics than foreign affairs. Thus most Third World nations have more effective internal intelligence systems, designed to help the current "president-for-life" stay that way. So, given the principal political objective of most Third World governments, their intelligence establishment is sufficient unto the need.

Amateurism

Although several Third World armies—India, Egypt, Nigeria—are quite good within their environments, most exist primarily to look impressive on the parade grounds and to keep the local citizens in line. Since most Third World armed forces are descended from colonial military or paramilitary forces that existed to maintain local order, one would think that they would have few problems in this regard. While this is frequently the case, there are a number of Third World armies—Uganda,

Burma, Sri Lanka, Sudan—that are not very good at it, and usually resort to casual massacre. The result is often an ongoing state of low-level insurrection.

Media Muddle

Since virtually all Third World nations impose varying degrees of censorship on the press, there is not much open debate about the character and abilities of the armed forces. The public hears what the army—or the dictator—wishes it to hear. As a result, the citizens—not to mention the military leaders and the dictator—may have an inflated notion of what their boys can do. In consequence, there have been a number of very ill advised foreign adventures by overconfident dictators—Idi Amin, Muammar Qaddafi, Sukarno—caught up in the euphoria of their own press releases.

Procurement Puzzle

No Third World nation is capable of meeting all the material needs of its armed forces. A few—Egypt, Brazil, India—can produce a variety of equipment sufficient to meet peacetime demand, but not even these economically advanced countries could support a modestly long war from domestic resources. As a result, all Third World nations are more or less dependent upon imports of arms, ammunition, and even food to keep their military forces going. This is one reason international wars have been so rare in the Third World, as the developed nations of the capitalist "First" and Communist "Second" worlds have been known to dry up the supply of ammunition and equipment if they disapprove of how it is being used, as in the Burkina Faso–Mali War of 1985, the Honduran-Salvadoran War of 1969, and many others. Procurement corruption is also a factor, as it is in most nations, only more so. Control of the military is commonly a form of patronage in Third World nations. It gives those in power a license to steal, and a better chance to get away with it as military spending is less likely to be audited by those hard-nosed accountants from the World Bank.

Wrong-War Syndrome

Most Third World nations do not have much of a problem preparing for the wrong war. Few of them have any reasonably likely foreign foes, and as a result most of them never bother preparing for war at all, save for internal-security problems. The more developed Third World nations all have fairly predictable "enemies," and so have all tended to tailor their armed forces to meet these particular threats. This has not always proven helpful. India, which has been preparing for another "Big One" with Pakistan or China for nearly two decades now, was surprised to discover that its excellent army was not very effective at dealing with Tamil guerrillas in Sri Lanka. Likewise, Morocco's fine armed forces had been preparing for a confrontation with Algeria for a generation when they found themselves in difficulty when confronted by the Polisario insurrection in the Western Sahara in the late seventies.

ARGENTINA

Intelligence Confusion

To the extent that Argentina's leadership has largely been concerned with domestic "subversion" and the "dangers" posed by Brazil and Chile—with whom Argentina has been having an arms race for about a century and a half—Argentina has a reasonably efficient intelligence apparatus. This enables the country's leaders to keep the "revolutionaries" under control and to maintain the "balance of power" with their neighbors. But Argentine intelligence proved totally incapable of assessing what was a fairly assured international reaction to the 1982 invasion of the Falkland Islands, which resulted in a disastrous defeat.

Amateurism

The Argentine military has a long record of success at fulfilling its primary mission, keeping domestic affairs under control. It may also be said to have been successful in its secondary role, preparing for a conventional war with neighboring coun-

tries, as this has never happened. The military's success at its
none-too-difficult tasks inflated its notions about its abilities to
engage in more serious military undertakings, which led directly to the overconfident attack on Britain in 1982. Significantly, the air force, the most professional of the armed forces,
the one least involved in internal politics, and one that most
adamantly opposed the war with Britain, was the only service
to distinguish itself in action.

Media Muddle

Criticism of the military was a severe offense under Argentine law, with formal penalties involving heavy fines, and infor-
mally ranging up to death. As the armed forces effectively
controlled the media, they promoted the image of a tough, combat-ready force. This illusion was so pervasive that even the
leaders of the armed forces fell for it.

Procurement Puzzle

Although Argentina is quite industrialized by Third World
standards, and produces some excellent military equipment, its
capacity to produce this matériel in amounts and types sufficient to meet the needs of its armed forces is severely limited.
Since a great deal of matériel is thus procured abroad, in any
sustained conflict this would prove a handicap. The 1982 Falklands War ended at just about the time the Argentine Air Force,
which was carrying on the struggle virtually single-handedly,
began to run out of aircraft. Argentina's chronic economic
problems prevent it from rising above a Third World level of
industrialization.

Wrong-War Syndrome

Argentina is perhaps one of the best examples of "wrong-
war" preparations in recent decades. Armed forces that primarily existed as a police force to maintain themselves in power
against domestic political opponents not only found themselves
involved in a conventional war against a well-organized, properly trained, and thoroughly professional foreign foe, but had
actually sought the confrontation. The results were predictable,

given that Britain's paratroopers, marines, guardsmen, and Gurkhas were considerably more serious opponents than unarmed men, women, and children, particularly as the Argentine Army kept its best-prepared troops watching the Chilean frontier, just in case their "Latin brothers" decided to jump them while their attention was fixed on the Falklands.

THE MIDDLE EAST

There are three ongoing confrontations in the Middle East that provide excellent examples of shooting blanks, the Iran-Iraq conflict, the Arab-Israeli one, and the 1990–91 Persian Gulf crises.

Iran-Iraq

The Iran-Iraq War of 1980–88 was one of those rare conflicts where both sides took turns trying to outdo each other in shooting blanks.

Intelligence Confusion

It may be some time before Iraq reveals what its intelligence people were doing in 1980, but apparently they were obtaining more of their information from newspapers than from agents inside Iran. Although Iraqi Arabs had been living next to Persian Iranians for thousands of years, all this past experience went right out the window when Iraqi military and political leaders assumed that the revolution in Iran (not a rare event) would so disrupt its armed forces as to allow Iraq to march in and rearrange the border. It may well be that Iraq's dictator, Saddam Hussein, personally forced the issue; but like most dictators, Hussein was not about to risk his rule, and well-being, by endangering his armed forces. As a dictator without a loyal and effective army is either an exile or a corpse, Hussein had the agreement of some of his senior commanders, which made it easier to spread the blame around when the invasion blew up in their faces. The intelligence failures during the Iran-Iraq War spotlight the difficult time intelligence officers have under any conditions. Neither Iran nor Iraq had the intelligence resources of a Superpower, or even most European nations. In many cases, the rumor mill is the most common source of information, and discussions among the senior leaders are what pass for analysis. Once the fighting got under way, intelligence work became considerably more professional, but the lack of peacetime preparation made progress difficult. Iran was less concerned about this because of the divine nature of its motives. Since the leadership believed it had a direct line to God, who is all-seeing and does not require an intelligence department, they neglected this function. Unfortunately, the troops did need sound military intelligence, and suffered for the lack of it. Iraq eventually began receiving satellite and electronic intelligence from U.S. and other Western sources. As with most competitions in warfare, Iraq was not better at intelligence, just less inept.

Amateurism

Until the 1920s, there had been no independent Iraqi armed forces for several centuries as Iraq had been little more than a battleground for Persian (Iranian) and Turkish armies. Individuals had served in the army of the Turkish rulers that controlled Iraq for most of this period. After World War I, the British trained Iraqis for military service. But the Iraqis had not been in a war, except a brief attempt to aid Nazi Germany in 1941, which led to the virtual dissolution of their army by the British. Later a few units did acquire some experience while in the process of being savaged by the Israelis in the 1948, 1967, and 1973 wars.

Historically, the Iraqis were not noted for their military prowess; the Iranians were. This point was apparently lost on the Iraqi officers. The Iranians were better students of history, and better soldiers. Nevertheless, the Islamic Revolution in Iran crippled the regular military: Many of these highly trained troops were considered "tainted" by Western influences; and thus the religious leaders responded by forming a parallel army of "Revolutionary Guards." While these troops were enthusiastic and had God on their side, they were not bullet-proof and were quite crude in their tactics. The less militant and enthusiastic Iraqis took advantage of this. The fervent young Iranian volunteers learned too late that the despised Iraqi soldiers facing them were not shooting blanks. Iran did better once the professional soldiers were let out of jail, but they were never given full control of organization, training, or planning, so Iran was never able to make effective use of what resources it had.

Media Muddle

There's no such thing as a free press in wartime, but even in peace there's not much of it in the Middle East. The Iraqi press was largely responsible for sustaining the morale of the population through the war, which until the very end was seen as a desperate situation. There were few Iraqi victories and many bloody Iranian offensives. The Iranian press was not much better, but since the 1979 revolution had the benefit of different voices, as each faction in the revolutionary movement ran its own piece of the press. In Iran, the press became more strident in favor of the war as the Iranian casualties mounted. Yet after the war ended, the press did not preach any "Era of Peace" message but began to prepare their readers for a renewal of hostilities. This, at least, was in sync with reality, as both nations continued to spend on armaments at wartime rates.

Procurement Puzzle

In both nations, the arms-purchasing and manufacturing bureaucracies became the dominant economic forces during the course of the war. Each nation took a different approach to procurement. Iraq basically demanded that its oil-wealthy Arab neighbors provide billions in "loans" to assist in the defense against the common Persian enemy. These loans and grants were provided, with most of Iraq's oil wealth going to keeping up the morale of the civilian population. Iraq spent nearly $200 billion on weapons and even more in support, plus generous compensation to the survivors of war dead. In Iran, no loans or credits were sought or received, and only about $6 billion worth of weapons were purchased. For religious and nationalistic reasons, Iran paid in cash while building up its domestic arms manufacturing (employing about 60,000 workers and producing over 150 items). It has yet to be revealed how much Iran's able traders and merchants made out in all this horse-trading over arms. Iranian merchants are known for their ability to sniff out a commercial opportunity and make the most of it. Considering how successful Iran was in scrounging up weapons on the world markets, despite most major sources being closed to it for political reasons, its arms dealers certainly made something for themselves. In both nations, normal government spending on infrastructure (roads, schools, etc.) declined in order to support the war effort, and yet the cease-fire has not caused much diversion of funds to civilian uses. Thus these nations will pay the price for their war for decades to come as they reap the penalties of a nation with a run-down infrastructure.

Wrong-War Syndrome

Since the late 1960s, Iran and Iraq had been skirmishing on the border area where the 1980 war eventually took place. Each nation realized that the other was its biggest military threat, although Iraq also had to worry about a hostile Syria while the Iranians had to consider the possibility, albeit remote, of land grabs by the Russians. Both nations also had rebellious ethnic minorities. Iran had about half a dozen of these, but all were relatively small and weak compared with the large Kurdish minority Iraq had to cope with. Ever since Iraq was formed in the 1920s, it has been beset by rebellions by the Kurds. To make matters worse, there are also small Kurdish populations across the border in Turkey and Iran. The Kurds fight guerrilla style, and cross the border for sanctuary when it suits their needs. The Iraqis thus need an army for both guerrilla and conventional war, but have opted to keep the organization and training largely conventional.

In 1975, there was a formal agreement between Iran and Iraq that settled the border disputes largely in Iran's favor. In return, Iran withdrew support for the Iraqi Kurds. This caused Iraq to concentrate even more diligently on conventional war. Of course, Iraq was receiving most of its military aid from Russia at the time, and this included training for officers and troops. While this may do wonders for Russian troops, the rigid drills and doctrine did not do the Iraqis much good. Perhaps the training wasn't thorough enough. Whatever the case, after crossing the Iranian border in 1980, Iraqi units fell apart when they encountered significant Iranian resistance. This gave the impression that the Iranians had better troops, which was actually true. In 1980, the Iranians had the advantage of defending, and the psychological edge that comes from protecting one's homeland. Moreover, Iran actually had two armies. One was the U.S.-trained force, even though it was in the process of being purged by Iranian religious fanatics. The other, newer Revolutionary Guards, were young and untrained, but filled with religious and nationalist fervor. These troops proved a match for the conventionally minded Iraqis, as they were cohesive and not afraid to take casualties. This was just the opposite of what Iraqi commanders had expected. Their understanding of the religious revolution in Iran led them to believe that the purged regular army would not be in any shape to fight, and nothing else would be available to put up an effective defense. On the other hand, the Iranians soon found that their enthusiastic Revolutionary Guards had some drawbacks. Once the Iraqis had been forced on the defensive, the guards launched head-on attacks that mostly resulted in lots of dead guards and not much else. The leaders of the guards were largely untrained in military matters and proceeded to reinvent the basics that the regular Iranian Army troops already knew. This learning process took several years and never managed to catch up with Iraqi efforts to improve defensive tactics. Ultimately, this inability to perfect offensive tactics and implement adequate training for the young guard volunteers cost the Iranians victory in the war. Both nations were prepared for the wrong war, but Iraq won the conflict by rectifying its lack of preparation before Iran could.

Israel and Its Neighbors

Israel, a small nation surrounded by larger, more populous, and hostile neighbors, has managed to avoid extermination by making far fewer errors in the realm of shooting blanks.

Intelligence Confusion

From the very beginning, Israel built up a sizable advantage in this area. Many Israelis were migrants from neighboring Arab states, providing a ready supply of potential agents. Israel's close ties with the United States provided access to Superpower-grade intelligence, and Israel continues to drive a hard bargain when trading its local information for whatever the United States has to offer. Curiously, the only time Israel was in trouble on the battlefield was because of an intelligence failure, in 1973, when Egypt successfully deceived Israel on the timing and nature of the assault across the Suez Canal. The Arab countries confronting Israel are much less stable and devote most of their intelligence efforts to internal affairs. The Arabs also have less access to Superpower-grade intelligence. Although most Arab nations are cozy with Russia, the Russians are tightfisted about data. In truth, most of what the Superpowers have to offer is satellite photos and electronic intelligence. And although the Superpowers have comparatively small and vulnerable networks of agents in Middle Eastern nations, they are not willing to risk them by handing over information from these sources to Middle Eastern governments. Russia does not have as efficient a satellite-reconnaissance capability as the United States, and thus has less to offer its clients. Yet even without U.S. intelligence aid, Israel would be way ahead of its Arab adversaries: Although outnumbered in manpower and weapons, Israel has turned it information superiority into a lethal advantage.

Amateurism

Israeli military skill is rightly considered among the highest in the world, and this battlefield prowess springs from two dissimilar sources. The oldest is the guerrilla/terrorist/irregular military groups that preceded independence in 1948. There was something of a Wild West quality to life in pre-1948 Palestine, and Jewish inhabitants had to arm, train, and sometimes fight to survive. Many of the future senior military and political leaders came out of these clandestine combat units. The other, more numerous source of combat experience came from veterans of many World War II European armies, such as Britain's, which had even organized a Jewish brigade for combat duty in North Africa and Italy. The first Israeli combat units comprised these British Army veterans as well as veterans of U.S., Russian, French, Italian, and other forces. The *Wehrmacht* was not represented, for obvious reasons, but German blitzkrieg tactics were in large measure adopted.

With this core of combat veterans, and with their backs to the wall, the Israelis faced Arab units that were mostly well trained, but lacked adequate equipment and combat experience, led by officers equally without experience. Moreover, the average Arab officer was not as diligent as his Israeli opposite number. As always, the value of the troops is equal to (and multiplied by) the value of the officers. The Israelis were aware of their advantage, and the Arabs were not aware of their disadvantage until it was too late. This pattern persisted through several wars. It's not that the Arabs weren't trying to improve; they simply used less effective leadership techniques. Among the many "German" techniques the Israelis adopted or reinvented was the insistence on high-quality officers. This meant officers who got to know their job and their troops very well and led from out front. Most Arab nations adopted Russian methods, which were more bureaucratic and tended to be successful only when the troops spent long periods in combat. Because the Arab-Israeli wars were all brief affairs, the Arabs never caught up, and in loss after loss developed a feeling of inferiority that the Israelis would exploit.

Media Muddle

Most Arab media are state-controlled. If the powers that be decide that the armed forces are doing just fine, that's all anyone will hear about it from the media. The Israeli media, despite a hard-eyed military censor, are wide open and don't hesitate to debate military matters publicly. Moreover, the Israeli forces are basically a militia with most adult males belonging. This includes many members of the media. It's a raucous system, but it keeps everyone on his toes.

Procurement Puzzle

Most Arab arms are imported by way of diplomatic agreements with one of the Superpowers or a Superpower ally. Israel operates under the same conditions, with one important difference: Israel also has its own world-class industry. This, plus its more astute military leaders, provides Israel with a much more efficient mix of weapons and equipment. The Arab nations are more likely to get whatever they can rather than what they want or need. Israel's arms industry started out reconditioning weapons they were able to beg, buy, or capture in battle. These modified weapons were amazingly effective, especially since they were customized for the specific conditions Israeli forces faced against their Arab opponents. Today, the Israelis manufacture some types of weapons that are at the top of their class and sell them to just about anyone willing to pay cash. As a major part of the Israeli economy, the arms industries are protected by the government as a national asset. Some Arab nations also manufacture arms, but these are usually simpler items like infantry weapons and artillery. Israel builds everything up to aircraft, missiles, and electronics systems. The disparity in arms-acquisition capability gives the Israelis yet another battlefield advantage.

Wrong-War Syndrome

All sides in this confrontation are fully aware of who their principal enemy is likely to be. But Israel has always adapted better to probable changes in the types of battles it would have to fight. Arab nations were burdened with Russian doctrine that was more appropriate for the European plains and forests than the Middle Eastern deserts.

Persian Gulf, 1990–91

This was another one of those crises where there are abundant examples of how not to do things right.

Intelligence Confusion

First, Kuwait and Saudi Arabia misread Iraq's intentions. They were aided by bumbling U.S. diplomacy. Iraq was the biggest sinner of all, believing that it could seize Kuwait and get away with it. Everyone should have known better, as this situation had been simmering for decades.

Amateurism

Neither Kuwait nor Saudi Arabia put its heart into building a professional military force. These nations have a combined population at least equal to Iraq's, yet maintained armed forces less than a tenth as large. All that oil wealth had blunted the ancient warrior tradition among the Bedouin Kuwaitis and Saudis. The Iraqis were also putting themselves at great risk, their armed forces being no match for Western forces in the air and at sea. Morever, the Iraqis had never fought a mobile war in the desert. The Iran-Iraq war of 1980–88 had been a largely static affair and most of the action took place in marshland.

Media Muddle

The local press (Iraq and Saudi Arabia) was, and is, controlled by the government. The only independent reporting came from the Western reporters who poured into the area after August. Although Iraq and, to a lesser extent, Saudi Arabia, put controls on the reporters, there was still much to dig up and misinterpret. Experienced military reporters were in a minority and the editors and anchors called the shots as they thought best. As a result, there was a constant buzz of undigested analysis. Predictions of what would (or could) happen and when changed seemingly at whim. All of this did little to encourage the folks, and political leaders, back home.

Procurement Puzzle

Iraq found itself equipped for the wrong war. Most of its tanks were obsolete and fit only for fighting Iranian infantry. Iraq's air force had been optimized for firing missiles at tankers in the Gulf, not defending itself or attacking defended targets. The Saudis, while not building up their armed forces, had overbuilt support facilities, particularly for aircraft. As a result, U.S. Air Force planes found well protected and equipped airbases waiting for them. The United States also came up a winner, as it had been equipping and training to fight in the desert ever since the 1973 oil embargo. It isn't always bad news in the procurement department.

Wrong-War Syndrome

Kuwait and Saudi Arabia never seriously prepared to effectively fight any of their rapacious neighbors. Fortunately, Saudi Arabia did not hesitate to do what it could not previously admit to its fellow Arabs it would do: call in U.S. troops. Iraq was prepared to fight its neighbors, but not large Western armed forces.

The Problems Are Alive and Well: Wars, Real and Potential

·10·

Who is fighting whom? How are nations shooting blanks in current wars? What potential wars loom in the future? How can shooting blanks touch off these future wars?

While shooting blanks may not be the right thing to do, it certainly remains one of the more popular ways to employ armed forces. In this chapter, we describe several dozen past, current, and potential wars and how shooting blanks played, plays, or is likely to play a part in the conflict. There are lots of examples from which to draw. In the last decades alone, there have been hundreds of wars. Depending upon how you count these things, what with occasional two-, three-, four-, and even five-way conflicts, and a number of sporadic ones, there are at present between fifty and one hundred wars going on, most small, virtually all internal. Moreover, there are literally hundreds of potential wars, some having pedigrees going back centuries and some due to quite recent tensions. And no one can predict the actions of the numerous petty despots who rule more than a third of the world's nations.

Most past and current wars involve an aggressor who came to grief, leaving the survivors with little to show for their efforts save one more vivid example of shooting blanks. Often the victorious defender also did some shooting blanks of its own, but victory has a tendency to wash away any memory of such transgressions. The types of shooting blanks that are likely to take place in several of the prospective conflicts to be considered are somewhat unclear, but, given the track record of various nations, they are predictable within certain limits.

It is remarkable how frequently wars get started because a national leader ended up shooting blanks. Examination of even apparently successful military operations, such as the U.S. invasions of Grenada and Panama, reveal that a fair amount of shooting blanks was involved. In combat operations, things rarely work out as planned. Victories are dangerous because they remove a good incentive to correct problem areas. Overwhelming force hides deficiencies, which then continue to fester until they can get you into real trouble.

Many of the wars are internal: civil wars and rebellions. These conflicts nonetheless present the same opportunities for shooting blanks as the more conventional combat between nations. Civil wars and rebellions also become the cause of wars between nations, and most of our current wars fall into this category. The last Iran-Iraq war began because Iraq misinterpreted the extent to which the revolution in Iran had weakened Iranian combat power. The Falklands War was a direct result of the civil unrest within Argentina and the military government's misguided attempt to quiet the unruly civilians with a military victory against Britain.

ANGOLA: BRIAR PATCH IN ACTION

Everybody involved in the ongoing Angolan civil war is shooting blanks. It's all that ever seems to be predictable in that strife-torn nation. Long a Portuguese colony, over a decade of increasingly violent revolution caused Portugal to decamp in 1975. Among the several vaguely Marxist revolutionary groups, largely split along tribal lines, the one to reach the capital first, was FAPLA (yet another "peoples' liberation" group), which took charge of the government and immediately called upon the "International Socialist Community" for aid. Russia sent help, and the other revolutionary groups (which represented a majority of the population) objected. The losers soon coalesced around a group calling itself UNITA. Since the official government already had aid from Russia, UNITA had to look elsewhere. It didn't have to look far. The United States was interested, especially since the Russians seemed determined to make Angola an African Cuba. In addition, there was also oil in Angola, being pumped by American oil companies, as well as "American" coffee plantations. To complicate matters even more, South Africa got into the act. Aside from Angola's loud, and substantive, efforts to aid revolution within South Africa, Angola also bordered Southwest Africa (Namibia), which was illegally controlled by South Africa. A rebel group, SWAPO, was fighting South African forces in Namibia, and Angola provided sanctuary and material aid to the rebels. South Africa decided to up the ante by supporting the UNITA group of Angolan rebels.

The upshot of all these alliances was that the Angolan government troops found themselves shooting blanks as UNITA rebels proceeded to overrun large portions of the country. Russia did not want to back a loser, but the situation required more than advisers and weapons. Russia was not about to commit its own troops, but it was able to strike a deal with Cuba, which was beholden to Russia for billions of dollars a year in economic and military aid. So Cuba began exporting one item it produced in large quantity: troops. Eventually, over 55,000 Cuban soldiers ended up in Angola, a greater per capita manpower commitment than that made by the United States in Vietnam. Russia sent some advisers and technicians, and East German and Bulgarian technicians showed up too. Despite these efforts, UNITA held on to its territory and grabbed even more. But it was able to do this only because the South Africans were willing to commit troops whenever the massive annual government offensive came too close to overrunning UNITA base areas.

While these attacks were planned and run by Russian staff officers led by a senior Russian general, the most intensive fighting was frequently between South African and Cuban troops, with the government and UNITA forces cheering their champions on from the sidelines. One result was that as the South

Africans began taking casualties, they faced a politically embarrassing situation back home. South Africa wasn't shooting blanks on the battlefield, but it was on the home front, where the people were unwilling to suffer losses fighting Cubans. Apparently, even Cuba began to feel the pinch, though domestic opposition was necessarily muted. Besides, the Cubans resented all the press releases that ignored their role while inflating that of the Angolan government forces. And the Angolan government began to become concerned over the increasing influence of Cuba in its internal affairs. Meanwhile, the United States and Russia, who were more or less bankrolling the whole business, began to realize that the game may not have been worth the candle. Finally, in 1988, all concerned agreed to back off: Cuba would get out of Angola, and South Africa would get out of Angola and Namibia. The Angolan government would continue to get material aid from Russia, while UNITA would keep getting supplies from America, but both agreed to negotiate their differences, maybe. In effect, everyone agreed to allow the Angolans to sort things out themselves around the conference table, or, more likely, on the battlefield, a solution that could have been adopted many years, and many lives, ago.

ETHIOPIA: DYNASTIC POLITICS

Ethiopia is the only nation in Africa that has been almost continuously independent for most of its history, which goes back several thousand years. A primitive nation, in an out-of-the-way part of the world, it survived with an essentially intact feudal system for all these centuries. But in the 1970s, this changed when the emperor was overthrown by Communist-inspired army officers. Moving the country into the twentieth century proved to be a daunting task. Some regions inhabited by ethnic and religious minorities had long demanded independence. Many people openly opposed the Marxist government; some favored a more liberal form of government; some wanted an emperor back; some fought for an even more doctrinaire form of Marxism. The military junta had one immediate problem: foreign aid. Russia was the obvious choice, but the Russians were backing neighboring Somalia, which was fighting a low-key war with Ethiopia over a territorial dispute. Deciding that Ethiopia was the bigger prize, the Russians coldly dumped

Somalia and flooded Ethiopia with aid and advisers. But this was not enough, so the ever-willing Cuban mercenaries were called in, plus the usual Eastern European advisers and technicians and even a few South Yemenites, and soon the situation stabilized. But nothing that the Russians did could bring victory for the Ethiopian government, nor would the government accept their advice to negotiate a political settlement. Through the 1980s, the wars and revolutions went on, with the government forces getting the worst of it, while famine stalked the land and the Ethiopian Army began to grow unhappy with a government that refused to see the war as unwinnable. This decades-long bloodletting began to come to an end only in 1991 when Russian pressure, plus outright mutiny in the army, forced the government to agree to negotiations with the principal resistance movements. An unusually severe case of shooting blanks.

MOZAMBIQUE: THE OTHER ANGOLA

Mozambique, like Angola, was a Portuguese colony. It too gained its independence in the 1970s and then lapsed into civil war. The rebels were given aid and encouragement by South Africa. Unlike Angola, Russian assistance was more limited, and Cuban troops were not committed. In a rare gesture of solidarity among African nations, several neighboring states committed troops to assist the quasi-Marxist government. And, in an even more unusual development, both the United States and Britain pitched in on the same side as Russia with economic and technical assistance, and less formal military advice. Unlike the Angolan situation, the rebels in Mozambique were not very well organized and, in fact, many of the rebels were basically bandits. The difference has not meant much to the millions of civilians who have suffered during this armed chaos. The government forces have not been up to the task of suppressing the rebels, although this has a lot to do with South Africa stepping up aid to the rebels whenever it appeared government troops might be making progress. In the late 1980s, Mozambique agreed to cut its aid to South African rebels if South Africa would do the same for Mozambique's rebels. This seemed to be a reasonable compromise, but it never really took hold, as neither set of rebels was actually under the control of their ostensible patrons, and the violence, particularly in Mozambique, had become a way of life. So chaotic did the situation become that by late 1989 the South Africans had begun sending "nonlethal" military aid to the government of Mozambique in order to help protect the installations that supply them with much of their electrical power from the rebels whom they were formerly bankrolling. A case of everyone shooting blanks all around.

AFGHANISTAN: THE FOREVER WAR

There is probably no place on earth where there has been more shooting blanks than Afghanistan. For thousands of years, Afghanistan has lain astride the trade routes between China, India, the Middle East, and Europe, making it a desirable piece of real estate. But no one has been able to control Afghanistan for very long. The population has always been warlike, patient, and hostile to outsiders, to a degree only slightly more ferocious than their hostility toward each other. Rarely has anyone managed to rule the country in relative peace. The people are indeed so independent that one ruler called the country "Yaghistan" ("land of the unruly"). In addition to its strategic position, the country has a rugged territory and is itself very poor. It was no easy thing to march a large army into Afghanistan and expect to avoid starvation and disease, not to mention resistance. One would think the foreigners would stay out, but invasion has been common. The British tried several times, with poor results: Once they literally lost an entire army of 14,000 to Afghan tribesmen. Even the Russians, during their recent attempt at conquest, ran into these ancient limitations: There are simply not enough roads, or resources of any kind, to support large forces. And smaller numbers of troops are not adequate to suppress the hostile population. One would have thought that the Russians, who like to pay close attention to historical precedent, might have noticed the trend. But no, they went in anyway, trusting that their superior technology and ideology would be more than sufficient to overcome a bunch of ill-armed hill bandits. So Russia became the latest power to shoot blanks in Afghanistan.

GREECE AND TURKEY: ANCIENT ANIMOSITY AND POTENTIAL OIL

In the Aegean Sea, between Greece and Turkey, we find antagonisms simmering since the 1920s, rooted in centuries of hostility. In 1923, the Turks repulsed a Greek invasion. The Greeks had invaded because they thought the Turkish civil war then raging would enable Greece to permanently annex areas long inhabited by Greeks or to which Greece had an historic claim. As Iraq learned more recently when it marched into a revolution-racked Iran, civil disorder usually doesn't debilitate a neighbor enough to allow a foreign invasion. The argument is slightly different now, involving potential offshore oil deposits, as well as the usual ancient history, all wrapped up with a dispute over the status of Cyprus. Even though both Greece and Turkey belong to NATO, they each consider the other as the most likely opponent in a future war. All that either side is waiting for is that feeling of military superiority. Once you feel that way, you march, frequently to gain nothing but a lot of grief. The most impressive aspect of shooting blanks in this dispute is that both sides are doing so in very much the same fashion: adulation of the armed forces, trust in the "historic justice" of their cause, an almost barbarian pride in their national greatness, and belief that if things come to a fight, the other side will be a pushover. While Turkey, which has the larger, and arguably the stronger, armed forces, tends to be the quieter of the two in this dispute, Greece has proved highly aggressive, working on the assumption that either the West or the Russians will help out if things get out of hand. A disaster waiting to happen.

CHILE AND ARGENTINA: DISPUTED ISLANDS AT THE END OF THE WORLD

The Beagle Channel lies at the southern tip of South America, hard by Cape Horn. There are three tiny islands in the middle of this perpetually cold, roily, foggy waterway. Since 1902, Argentina and Chile have been at odds over this obscure real estate. The stakes never seemed high enough to risk major combat, although there have been some minor skirmishes. Both nations have realized that all their domestic posturing was a sham when it came to just how effective the armed forces really are. Although Argentina has a larger population (32 million versus 13 million), Chile has larger and, arguably, more effective armed forces. This is probably one reason that the Argentine junta backed off in a showdown with Chile in 1979, opting to take on the British three years later. While the dispute has been settled diplomatically in the wake of the Falklands War, the hostilities remain. The situation is a prime example of how shooting blanks brings nations to the brink of war. In this case, the line was not crossed, which can be attributed to the internal problems in both nations. But don't think the issue is dead: This sort of problem has a way of returning to life long after its "resolution," particularly if a national political leader needs some righteous cause to divert folks' attention from a corrupt or incompetent regime.

BELIZE: THE WAYWARD BOUNDARY IN THE JUNGLE

Belize—formerly British Honduras—is a recently independent Central American country that since 1972 has been the cause of armed confrontation between Britain and Guatemala. The latter claims Belize is a part of its national patrimony, stolen centuries ago by the British. Despite the fact that Belize is a member of the United Nations, and has pledges of security support from such diverse powers as the United States and Cuba, Guatemala insists the country has no legal right to exist. Occasional incidents and probes provoked by Guatemalan troops have forced Britain, the former colonial power, to bolster Belize's slender army by stationing troops there to prevent Guatemala from making a land grab. One battalion of infantry and some aircraft (under 1,000 troops altogether) have proven sufficient to deter the entire Guatemalan armed forces (over 30,000 men), plus, perhaps, the memory of Britain's willingness to mount a major effort to retake the Falklands in 1982. Guatemala is also caught up in civil disorder and the general unrest in Central America. But these situations could change. And then what?

THE FALKLAND/MALVINAS ISLANDS: WORTHLESS ROCKS AND NATIONAL PRIDE

The Falklands War between Argentina and Britain in 1982 had its origins in a dispute that began centuries ago, and essentially revolves around who first discovered the islands. The British have controlled the islands since 1831, when they moved in to suppress piracy. Leisurely negotiations over the status of the islands have been going on for decades, the principal obstacle to Britain turning them over being the fate of the 1,500 inhabitants, all English-speaking. More recently, the dispute over the islands has still not resolved itself, and Britain now maintains a large garrison there just to remind Argentina of who owns the place, despite the cost, which is many times more than what Britain ever invested in developing the islands, which are anyway virtually barren economically.

IRAN AND IRAQ: THE FIVE-THOUSAND-YEAR WAR

The Iran-Iraq War of 1980–88 is among the most recent examples of how expensive shooting blanks can be. This war began when Iraq decided to resolve an ancient border dispute by invading Iran. While revolution and confusion were the order of the day in Iran, thousands of Iraqi troops pouring across the border quickly generated widespread patriotic feelings among Iranians. What was odd about all this was that it was a situation that had been repeating itself for several thousand years. For that long, Iraq has frequently been at the center of one empire, and Iran (Persia) another. The waterway over which the war was ostensibly fought has been a focal point of contention between the two regions many times in the past. You'd think someone in Iraq would have opened a history book before ordering the troops out. In any event, the 1988 ceasefire was just that. Both sides (particularly Iraq) kept forces massed on the border. When Iraq invaded Kuwait in 1990, it did so with its strategic reserve (The Republican Guard), leaving behind its massive forces on the Iranian border. When the Kuwait invasion brought U.S. and allied forces pouring into Saudi Arabia, Iraq quickly abandoned what little Iranian territory it still held and finally settled the war on Iran's terms. It was all for nothing.

KUWAIT AND IRAQ AND THE REST OF THE WORLD

Having failed to solve one border dispute (with Iran) by armed force, Iraq turned on Kuwait in 1990 to clear up another territorial disagreement. If only to demonstrate that lightning does strike twice, Iraq again thought that success was only a short military operation away. This time, Iraq's trade was embargoed, its overseas assets frozen, and one anti-Iraq resolution after another rolled out of the UN. Then, within six months, half a million troops from thirty nations were sweeping into action. The only favorable thing that can be said of Iraq is that it is providing vivid examples of how not to use armed forces to solve diplomatic problems.

ARABS AND ISRAELIS: "GOD GAVE THIS LAND TO ME!"

The Arab-Israeli wars (1948–49, '56, '67, '73, '82) all provide excellent examples of shooting blanks. In 1948, the Arabs invaded the nascent Israeli state only to be beaten back. Twice ('56, '67), the Arab forces mobilized for an attack, but the Israelis saw it coming and got in the first blows. The fourth time the Arabs did succeed in making the first blow, but the Israelis managed to recover quickly and go on to win. That Israel won all of these wars simply demonstrates the extent to which the Arabs were shooting blanks. After making essentially the same mistakes four times, the Arab states are markedly reluctant to try it again. This has not lulled Israel into an urge to disarm. While peace has been made with Egypt, internal unrest there could change that. Syria is now the principal enemy, but Syria is at odds with its neighbor Iraq and is having financial difficulties maintaining its large military forces and its lengthy involvement in Lebanon. This last problem brought about the latest Arab-Israeli war, the Israeli invasion of Lebanon in 1982. The situation there was so chaotic that this was not even considered a proper war by many. Nonetheless, several battles were fought between Israeli and Syrian forces, and casualties on all sides numbered in the thousands before Israel withdrew its forces. Israel's most serious ongoing problem is unrest among its own Arab population. This unrest ties up a significant number of its troops and could eventually be seen as a pretext for Syria to attack. Iraq even tried to pull Israel into its Kuwait affair. Meanwhile extremism on both sides prevents even the suggestion of a peaceful solution from having much of a chance.

LEBANON VERSUS LEBANON: NATIONAL SUICIDE

Lebanon lurched into another of it frequent civil wars in 1975. This was only the most recent in a continuing series of internal wars stretching back over many centuries. In the nineteenth century, one such conflict took nearly thirty years to resolve. The basic problem is that the country is inhabited by numerous cohesive, and mutually antagonistic, religious, ethnic, tribal, clan, and family groups, who require little incentive to go to war with one another. None of these factions is sufficiently numerous to dominate all the others—which is the traditional way that a "nation" gets built—but each of them thinks a great deal of itself and becomes agitated when another group gains some real or imagined advantage. What kept the factions from each others' throats for so long was the presence of foreign troops. For most of its history, Lebanon has not been independent. For the last few centuries, it was a loosely held province of the Turkish Empire and, for a good deal of this century, a dependency of France. Things held together for a generation after full independence was attained after World War II. But by the early seventies, the postwar political arrangement began to fall apart, and sundry groups began to shoot blanks in earnest, each believing that its cause was just, and that it had the power to prove it. All these factions were unrestrained by various outsiders, such as Syria, Israel, and several NATO powers, including the United States, who have usually found themselves shooting blanks in Lebanon as well. The Lebanese situation is in many ways similar to that found in many former colonies, though with a greater degree of ferocity, as most of these newly emerging nations were artificial creations of the former imperial power. There are a lot of Third World countries with numerous mutually hostile minorities and no dominant majority. Which means there's a lot of potential for shooting blanks.

INDIA AND PAKISTAN: THE MARTIAL RACE VERSUS THE PACIFISTS

The Indo-Pakistan wars since 1947 were more than a rekindling of ancient animosities between Moslems and Hindus on the Indian subcontinent. When Britain gave up its Indian colonies in 1948, arrangements were made to set up two nations, one primarily Hindu (India) and the other heavily Moslem (Pakistan). The Hindus had much more territory and population (by four to one), but the Moslems had been the warrior conquerors for several centuries before the British showed up in the 1700s, and then rather faithful servants of the British during their two centuries of rule in the vast subcontinent. In fact, they were such loyal servants that the British invented the notion of the "martial races" of India. This tended to exclude Hindus, thus providing a convenient excuse for not arming the latter, Hindus being the more independent-minded folks in India, and many of them pacifists as well. Such details were not easily forgotten, and the two nations soon found themselves at odds over several territorial and other disputes. India won all these conflicts, despite Pakistani confidence in its "martial" people. The outcome should have surprised no one: Both nations built their armed forces from the British-trained units of the old Imperial Indian Army. Officers on both sides had gone to the same military schools and were frequently on good personal terms even when trying to defeat each other on the battlefield. Quality was not really a factor, but numbers were. And India had the numbers. Pakistan, which regularly behaved aggressively, was repeatedly shooting blanks.

IRAQ AND SYRIA: THE WAR OF WORDS

The Middle East has been the center of major empires for as long as there have been records of such things. In ancient times there were various manifestations of Egyptian, Persian (Iran), Anatolian (Turkey), Mesopotamian (Iraq), and Syrian empires, which, over the centuries, have waxed and waned. But all of these areas remain the focus of strong national ambitions. Most are content to mind their own affairs most of the time, but at any given moment at least two of them have tended to overlap to a large degree. This pattern continues, and provides the basis for several wars, some of them still unfought. The Iran-Iraq conflict, noted above, has been fought. The Syro-Iraqi one has not, yet. Syria and Iraq have a common border. They also share a number of other things. Both have been in the empire business before. But for centuries, Iraq was caught between more powerful Turkish, Persian, and Egyptian ambitions, and then subsumed in the British and French empires after World War I. It is only since the 1940s that these two nations have been free of foreign domination. Each sees itself as deprived of national territories. Syria yearns for Lebanon and Palestine (and parts of Turkey); Iraq feels it should be ruling all the Arabs to its south, or at the very least Kuwait. Iraq feels put upon because it is the chief bulwark against the dreaded Persians. Both Syria and Iraq also have the deep feeling that each should be ruling the other. These attitudes breed a certain amount of hostility. But because the Iraqis have had the Persians (and lately the United States–led United Nations army) to worry about, and Syria always has Israel on its border, they have had to defer working out Syrian-Iraqi differences on the battlefield. There is no reason to believe these two would not have a go at each other if things settled down on the other fronts.

RUSSIA AND THE UNITED STATES: THE REAL "BIG ONE"

World War III has not happened largely because of the way the Russian General Staff calculates who would win. While the Western armed forces use computerized war games, or map exercises, to calculate the possible outcomes of future wars, Russia uses a formulaic approach. The two key techniques in this concept are "Norms" and "Correlation of Forces." The Norms are standards for performing military activities, and cover everything from how long it takes a soldier to load a tank cannon or position a machine gun, all the way up to the time and resources needed to move a tank division or nuclear submarine a certain distance. Norms are calculated for potential opponents, and their expected effectiveness is worked out. This is all done with formulae and reduced to tables of numbers. The Norms for units from Russian and foreign forces are then compared to produce the Correlation of Forces, a mathematical statement of who's stronger, or more likely to prevail. While these techniques are known in the West, the exact Russian calculations are, reasonably enough, a state secret. What is known is that the Russian officers working on these calculations are a very intelligent and well-educated bunch. The Russians have a lot of historical combat experience, and the General Staff draws upon this in devising their formulas. But while the theory of this system is fairly credible, its successful execution is more of a problem. Most of the Russian combat experience was collected from operations by experienced units. Going into a war tomorrow, they would not have many combat-experienced troops, and no combat-experienced units. The Russians call this the "discipline problem": Conscript troops trained in peacetime simply don't have the edge of combat veterans. Based on their historical analysis, this could present them with an unfavorable Correlation of Forces in the crucial opening stages of a war. Their experience also shows them that they must win quickly, if at all. And if they were able to overcome these problems, there is the danger of nuclear weapons.

Over the past three decades, the Russians have wrestled with these problems. To help them along, they have had some proxy combat experience by way of battles mostly involving Arab units fighting with Russian weapons and tactics against Israelis. The results have not been encouraging. Then Afghanistan came along, and the Russian conscript troops did indeed perform erratically. Using elite airborne and commando units, Russia did score some battlefield successes in Afghanistan. But the bulk of the Russian armed forces consists of less well-prepared conscripts, and it is with these conscripts that any future war would have to be fought.

The Russian General Staff's job is to prepare for war should it come. But World War III has never occurred because there has been no reason for it. The arms buildup in Russia and the West was largely the result of paranoia, sometimes justified, on both sides. For example, the current Russian government was born in the Revolution after World War I. For many decades, the Russians were committed to carrying their revolution to the rest of the world, and after World War II, succeeded at least in part by taking over the governments of most Eastern European nations. Meanwhile China fell to a Communist faction following its civil war. Many citizens and leaders in the West thus saw

Russia as dedicated to achieving world conquest and felt there was substantial evidence supporting this attitude.

Russia was never so powerful as it appeared at the time, although this was only known in hindsight. Meanwhile the West armed, a very natural reaction that in turn fed Russia's own traditional paranoia. Western nations were never keen on invading Eastern Europe and Russia. But to Russia, the growing Western military strength created a Correlation of Forces that could eventually go against it. Russia was more aware of the shaky loyalty of its Eastern European allies than the leaders in the West. The Russian economy was also faltering. Russia never rebuilt all those sectors of the economy that were devastated by the various wars and internal unrest it endured from 1914 to the present; agriculture, for example, has never attained the productivity achieved before the Revolution. As the post–World War II generation came of age and noticed that its standard of living did not even measure up to that of its East European satellites, it became less enthusiastic about world revolution and military power. The Russian government has been shooting blanks for seventy years in order to justify the enormous personal and economic sacrifices of its people. Eventually, though, the people caught on, and are now rattling their chains so vigorously that even senior Communist officials fear that the "Reds" may return, in the form of the people clamoring for the rewards of the Revolution.

KOREA: DMZ POLITICS

A Demilitarized Zone (DMZ) has separated North and South Korea roughly along the 38th parallel since the end of World War II. On either side of this two-kilometer unpopulated zone are two of the world's largest, most heavily equipped, best-trained armies. The Korean War began in 1950 when Communist North Korean forces crossed the border separating the two portions of the country. This was a typical case of shooting blanks, as the United States and the United Nations objected to such a blatant case of aggression and met force with force. By 1953, both sides were frustrated by over a million dead and a static fighting line. Massive infusions of Chinese troops saved the North Koreans from defeat, but they were not able to push the UN forces out of South Korea. A cease-fire went into effect during 1953, but a peace treaty was never signed: Both Koreas insisted on reunification, each on its own terms. So for some four decades, nearly 2 million well-armed troops have glared at each other across the DMZ. The North Koreans made no secret of their receptiveness to try for another military solution, backing up their commitment with regular raids, tunnels under the DMZ, and assassination plots. Give the North Koreans credit, though. They shot blanks in 1950 and were unwilling to try again unless they had a better chance of success. The Chinese were impressed with the beating they took at the hands of American troops, were not eager to repeat the process anytime soon. Moreover, many current senior Chinese officials lost sons in the fighting, and China has problems of its own to attend to. Russia had provided most of the hardware and equipment for the fighting, as well as fighter pilots and technical specialists. But Stalin died in 1953, and by the late fifties Chinese-Russian relations were becoming strained. North Korea has not shown any willingness to go it alone.

LIBYA AND EGYPT: PEOPLE, SAND, AND OIL

Egypt and Libya are not friendly neighbors. Part of this has to do with Muammar Qaddafi, Libya's eccentric dictator. Most of it has to do with the changes in the historical relationship between the ancient nation of Egypt and the fairly recent entity known as Libya. Egypt has been a nation for thousands of years, although during many centuries it was a province of a larger empire. Its neighbor, Libya, has rarely been independent, and for the most part has been a location, not a nation. Within Libya, there are several self-sufficient city-states and a lot of wild tribes wandering around the interior. It has been this way for several thousand years. Then Italy conquered the territory in the early 1900s and unified it as a colony. A kingdom was established after World War II; then oil was discovered. A lot of oil. And there were never many people in Libya to share in all this new wealth. Egypt has a lot more people, and a lot less oil. Egypt would like to annex Libya, which was done a few times in the past, but never to lasting effect as there was then no point in controlling poor and sparsely populated Libya. Now that there's oil and wealth in Libya, and the same small population, the prospect of annexation is more appealing. But as odd as Libya's leader may be, he's not crazy enough to do anything that would give Egypt justification to come in. Egypt needs some kind of serious provocation, as the rest of the world, and particularly other Arab nations, not to mention Israel, would not be amused by an unprovoked Egyptian conquest of Libya and its oil. So there the situation stands waiting for someone to shoot blanks.

NIGERIAN CIVIL WAR: THE PAINS OF NATION BUILDING

When the British took over the area that now comprises Nigeria, the territory was occupied by hundreds of sovereign, or at least mutually hostile, tribes, cities, and states. A century of colonial administration did not erase the differences among these numerous independent-minded groups. The post–colonial government of the 1960s inherited a functioning civil service, a credible army, and a lot of oil wells. The civil servants had learned well from their British mentors, and for a time they did an admirable job in reconciling the well-organized Moslems in the north with the Christian and animist groups in the rest of the country. But one group, the coastal Ibos, chafed under this arrangement. The Ibos, who were more adept at adopting European ways, particularly in education and commerce, were seen as a bit too eager (commercially) by many other Nigerians, who discriminated against them, harassed them, and ultimately massacred them. It was thus not surprising that the Ibos declared their independence as Biafra in 1969. Although Biafra had a qualitative advantage, the rest of the country had the numbers. Biafra's other problem was outside assistance, both material and diplomatic, which was never as much as was expected, or needed. The Biafrans allowed their nationalistic zeal to overcome their judgment. They shot blanks. They lost their war for independence in 1970, with enormous suffering.

THE SOUTH CHINA SEA: ISLANDS AND OIL

Since the 1800s, several powers have claimed possession of a large number of forlorn islands and reefs in the South China Sea. But it wasn't until the Vietnam War was over, and oil was suspected to be present under these islands, that any serious moves were made to enforce the claims. There is a large list of contenders including China, Vietnam, the Philippines, Malaysia, and Indonesia. Some of the islands are occupied by token garrisons from the various contending nations, which has led to several small-scale armed clashes among the rivals, notably China and Vietnam. Things settled down in the 1980s, when any moves to enforce claims were stalled by the fortuitous combination of a Russian naval base in Vietnam and a long-standing mutual-defense treaty between the Philippines and the United States. China was not about to take on the Superpowers over the possibility of oil. But if the Superpowers weaken their support for their allies, the Chinese would be encouraged to reassert their historic role as the local imperial power. Whether this would result in shooting blanks is uncertain. It could, and similar situations in the past have.

CHINA AND RUSSIA: THE EAST IS RED

In the 1860s, Russia's centuries of eastward expansion ran into China, or rather, overran Chinese territory. The Russians had reached the Pacific via the northern Siberian wilderness in the 1600s. While China was not a formidable military force at that time, it was a long way back to Moscow and the centers of Russian population and power, so a secure Russian presence wasn't established until the mid-1800s. Within a generation, Japan was also grabbing Chinese territory. By 1905, the Japanese had beaten the Russians and gained some of the choicer portions. China was a victimized bystander in all this, being in the midst of civil war and revolution. When the dust settled in 1949, the Communist faction had won the civil wars, and Russia welcomed the now–Red Chinese into the international Communist community. But this fraternalism did not include returning all that former Chinese territory, now occupied by millions of Russians, and including the major port of Vladivostok as well as an increasing array of air and naval bases. More vexing was Russia's attitude of superiority over Orientals. Aside from its long antipathy to Oriental nomad invaders, Russians saw themselves as the vanguard of European civilization. The Chinese were not Oriental nomads, but the heirs of one of the most ancient, and highly developed, civilizations on the planet, who, in turn, had some prejudices of their own. They might now profess to follow Marx, but they were still Chinese. And the Chinese took second place to no one. There was also the matter of Europeans having had their way with China for the last century or so: While the Russians might welcome the Chinese with open arms, they still had Chinese blood on their hands and Chinese territory within their borders.

So within ten years, the alliance began to unravel. It might have happened even sooner had it not been for the Korean War, in which China needed all the material and technical assistance it could get from Russia. And that might not have happened were it not for the United States seeing Reds instead of Chinese when it looked at China. But in any case, by 1960 China and Russia were shooting at each other across their borders. This situation died down as both nations mobilized to assist the North Vietnamese in the Vietnamese Civil War. But even before that was over, China was trying to establish diplomatic relations with the United States while Russia was politely asking the Americans if they would mind terribly much if Russia nuked Chinese missile and nuclear installations. America said yes to the Chinese and no to the Russians. Meanwhile centuries of animosity between Chinese and Vietnamese resulted in some border fighting. When the Vietnamese turned to the Russians, handing over a large naval base built by the Americans, China now felt surrounded by the Russians. But the Chinese think in the long term. Instead of arming to the teeth, they cut their armed forces and focused on building their economy. China always had the people advantage, and believed that if they could leapfrog their economy ahead of Russia, which has its own internal problems, the lost territories would be easier to reclaim. Besides, beyond the former Chinese territory on the Pacific coast, there is Siberia and its natural resources. Until recently, no one bothered with this wilderness because there were more exploitable lands closer to home. Now there are a lot more people, especially Chinese, and a lot fewer unoccupied lands closer to home, particularly in China. Russia took Chinese territory when China was weak. China would not hesitate to return the favor. There is a lot of shooting-blanks potential on the Russian-Chinese border.

TAIWAN: THE OTHER CHINA

In 1949, the losing side in the Chinese Civil War fled to Taiwan, the large island a few miles off China's coast. There, with the help of the United States fleet, the Nationalists withstood Communist Chinese attempts to push them off. Although with only 2 percent of mainland China's population, Taiwan rapidly developed into an economic powerhouse, which by the late 1980s had a GNP one quarter the size of Communist mainland China. And while the United States and Communist China were by the late 1970s on speaking terms once more, despite Communist Chinese protests, the United States continued to maintain economic and diplomatic relationship with Taiwan. The Communists wanted to reincorporate Taiwan into China, but during the 1980s the Communists changed their attitude toward running their economy. It became more capitalist and less socialist. Taiwan's economy was always unabashedly capitalist and undeniably successful. Taking Taiwan by force would likely ruin that economy and could also cause a confrontation with the United States. Nonetheless, before the 1970s, when Taiwan's economy really got into high gear and relations with the United States improved, China built up a marine infantry force and quantities of amphibious shipping opposite Taiwan. Part of the reason for this was to prevent Taiwan, which still insisted it was the only legitimate government for all of China, from invading the mainland. As unlikely as that seemed, there were still many Chinese who would welcome a non-Communist Chinese government. But this force of marines was largely trained to attack, not defend. For three decades, then, nearly a million Chinese troops stood ready to conquer Taiwan. Aside from Taiwan's own formidable forces and the U.S. fleet, these plans were also interrupted by armed confrontations with Russia in the 1960s, the turmoil of the Cultural Revolution in the late 1960s, and assistance to North Vietnam during the Vietnam War.

There was also an ethnic factor at work on Taiwan itself. For centuries, Chinese have been going to live and work in foreign nations. These "overseas Chinese" usually maintained close relationships with their language and culture, and the folks back home. These Chinese didn't assimilate very well, and were willing to support China's foreign policy in various ways. As a result, the Chinese attitude is that eventually they'll get Taiwan back if only because the island is full of homesick Chinese. Meanwhile these homesick Chinese are a minority on an island full of ethnic Chinese who have lived there for centuries and consider themselves Taiwanese and who would prefer to be an independent nation with no links to China: The Taiwanese Chinese speak the Amoy dialect of Chinese while the Nationalists who fled there in 1949 speak Mandarin. A civil war on Taiwan, or severe civil unrest, might tempt China to liberate the island. The Nationalist Chinese minority on Taiwan began introducing democracy during the late 1980s to placate the native Taiwanese majority. This may head off civil unrest. But there's still a lot of shooting-blanks potential surrounding Taiwan.

THE SUDAN: ALLAH LAUGHED

An old Sudanese saying has it that "When Allah created the Sudan, Allah laughed." It is a poor, parched land, the largest country in Africa, fully one-fourth the size of the United States. Just south of Egypt, it's more of a place than a country, the one place where Arab and African have met and mingled in great numbers. The population of 25 million is mostly Moslem, with about a third being animist or Christian. These ethnic and religious divisions have made the nation largely ungovernable. It's sort of the Afghanistan of Africa, except that the invaders eventually quit the place in disgust after conquering it, instead of being run out by the locals. For millennia this was the invading Egyptians' experience. Then Arabs moved down from the north, mixed with the Africans moving up from the south, and that is when most of the population became Moslem. Like Afghanistan, the social structure relied heavily on tribes, and the tribes normally warred on one another. The Arab tribes were the worst offenders, raiding each other and particularly the Africans. The goal, aside from some excitement, was livestock and slaves. A central government is at a big disadvantage in this type of situation. The constant rebellions, civil wars, and general unrest arise from all the many groups shooting blanks at once. It's a common situation in countries that are not quite nations. Such endemic and unfocused violence is the ultimate in shooting blanks.

COLOMBIA: LA VIOLENCIA

Lebanon is not the only nation to go to war with itself, shooting blanks in the process. Colombia, occupying the north-western shoulder of South America, has seen four decades of bloody internal strife. The country has numerous vaguely leftist revolutionary groups, plus many antileftist groups, and not a few very well-organized criminal gangs. A hundred thousand deaths and injuries are suffered each year because of this vio-lence, which cannot easily be attributed to any specific political or economic causes. Attempts to explain the situation fall back on references to "national character" and "lack of civil re-sponsibility." Colombians just call it *"la Violencia"* (the Vio-lence) and take it in stride as best they can. Up close, you see a gun culture and a readiness to keep blood feuds going from generation to generation. In the last two decades, trafficking in cocaine and other drugs has created still more large, well-armed groups ready to gun down real or imagined opponents, who are also effectively at war with the state. The victims have in-creasingly been diligent police, prosecutors, judges, journal-ists, and politicians. This has made individual violence even more common, and more difficult to stop. After some particu-larly egregious crimes, including the murder of a prominent presidential candidate in mid-1989, the government began to become more aggressive in its approach to the problem, with an initial degree of success that suggests it knew who was do-ing what all along. The government's counteroffensive has re-sulted in a still higher rate of violence, and a quasi-war situation that promises to endure for some time. As if all this shooting blanks were not enough, the United States, which is helping to finance the government's efforts, has vaguely offered to com-mit troops to lend a hand, which reminds some folks of the almost casual way in which the United States became involved in Vietnam.

CYPRUS: HISTORIC ANTAGONISM

Cyprus, a large island strategically located in the eastern Mediterranean, has been an important factor in the politics of that region for thousands of years, most often as a pawn and rarely as a player. Anciently settled by Greeks, the island gained an infusion of Turkish inhabitants during several centuries of Ottoman rule, which ended in the 1880s when Britain took over. Although the Greeks in Greece, independent since the 1820s, demanded that their Cypriot brothers be "reunited" with them, their pleas went unheeded. But with the waning of empire, Greek Cypriot demands for reunification began to take a violent form. This not only upset the British, but also the Turks, concerned for their brethren, who constitute about a third of the population of the island. When Cyprus finally gained its independence in 1960, a complex formula was adopted that required that the president be a Greek Cypriot and the vice president a Turkish one, along with a 70/30 split in legislative representation between the two communities. The settlement was guaranteed by Britain, Greece, and Turkey, who were each, in turn, granted residual military rights on the island. Unfortunately, few Greek Cypriots, and none of their cousins back in Greece, were inclined to accept these terms. The result was a series of armed clashes between Greek Cypriots, supported by Greek troops secretly landed by the Greek Navy, and Turkish Cypriots. Things finally came to a head in 1974, when the Greek-dominated Cypriot Army, backed by a large contingent of Greek troops, attempted a coup preparatory to "reunification" with Greece. The ensuing massacres, mostly of Turks by Greeks but occasionally of Greeks by Turks, found various UN and British peacekeeping forces unable to do anything, and prompted a massive invasion from Turkey, which was technically permitted under the agreements that created an independent Cyprus. This resulted in the partitioning of the island, and the creation of a quasi-independent Turkish Cypriot republic that Turkey insists is part of a Cypriot confederation that no one else recognizes. And there the situation rests. It was a massive case of shooting blanks on all sides, and has great potential for more, particularly given long-standing tensions between Greece and Turkey elsewhere.

SOUTH AFRICA: THE APARTHEID STATE

Surely one of the more bizarre potential war situations in the world, as well as one of the oddest ethnic imbroglios in a continent noted for odd ethnic combinations, South Africa is ruled by a white minority, some of whose members have occupied the nation longer than several of the black groups who are in the majority. Although afflicted by much civil disorder and unrest, the situation has fallen far short of the wartime conditions common in many other African nations. This is no accident. The white minority has the most effective armed forces on the continent, a fact they work constantly to sustain and do not hide from potential internal or external opponents. The South Africans also have a highly efficient intelligence service and a semi-free press that gets cut short mostly when the subject turns to large-scale violence. Officially barred from dealing with most major arms suppliers, South Africa has built a large domestic arms industry and still manages to trade overseas for anything else. The armed forces have long stood ready to deal with low-level conflicts in neighboring countries as well as with various forms of internal unrest. All this would be for naught were it not that the government is also moving toward eliminating the causes of some of the nation's internal unrest and its conflicts with neighbors.

Meanwhile the opponents of the South African establishment consist mostly of various black ethnic groups who may be as mutually hostile toward each other as toward the white South Africans, plus a minority of the white minority who are of more progressive bent, and happen to be of English, rather than Boer, ancestry. One result of this is that some black groups more or less collaborate, though usually not too openly, with the whites, while formally joining in the demands for drastic change in the social and political structures of the country. Several of these groups are really asking that the social and political structures of the country be turned over to themselves. And there are constant suggestions that one of the largest ethnic groups, the Zulu, would be more than happy to cut a deal with the ruling white ethnic group, the Afrikaaners (Boers), a deal that many Boers believe would be the best of a bad bargain.

On top of that, there are the foreign powers who are putting in their oars as well. Many of the African states who are formally on record as opposing South Africa, and regularly condemn various Western powers for their continued dealings with the South African regime, are themselves more or less dependent upon (covert) commercial, military, and political ties with South Africa: There's even an airline that *only* flies between South Africa and countries that regularly condemn it in the United Nations. Meanwhile the Russians, the most vociferous of foreign critics of South Africa, have their own covert links to the apartheid regime due to a mutual interest in keeping up the price of gold and diamonds on the international market. And the United States, which formally opposes certain policies of the current regime but prefers diplomatic solutions, some years ago found several of its diplomats in South Africa expelled for espionage. Although of late there has been considerable movement toward dismantling apartheid, the potential for shooting blanks is enormous.

WESTERN SAHARA: DESERT MADNESS

The Western Sahara is an enormous, arid region on the northwest coast of Africa, just south of Morocco. For ages, this resourceless, virtually uninhabited area was an appendage of whatever local empire was in the ascendancy. Going into the twentieth century, this was Morocco. But then Morocco was itself partitioned between France, which got the choice parts, and Spain, which got the rest, including Western Sahara. By the 1970s, however, various powers began to pressure Spain to leave, which was due less to altruism and anti-imperialism than to the discovery that the vast wastes of the region hid a fortune in phosphates. Spain pulled out in 1975—just a few weeks after Francisco Franco died—leaving the area to be divided up between Morocco and Mauritania.

But Algeria, which claims some parts of Morocco, objected, and very shortly after a Saharan national liberation front (Polisario) became active from bases in Algeria. Pressure from Polisario soon forced underpopulated and impoverished Mauritania to pull out, which left the whole territory to populous, moderately wealthy, and well-armed Morocco. Although initially fairly inept, by the mid-eighties the Moroccans had succeeded in securing control of all the useful parts of the country by virtue of building a series of huge dunes that prevented the free movement of the truck-borne rebels. But the Moroccan economy was beginning to show the strains of the war, while Algeria was finding the cost of supporting Polisario much higher than anticipated, particularly as it sought to distance itself from a reputation for extremism (a situation not helped by Polisario's inclination to take potshots at Spanish fishing boats off the coast). As a result, in 1988 all parties sat down to negotiate. Over feeble protests from Polisario concerning the details, a plebiscite was scheduled, a solution that could have been tried many years, many lives, and many dollars sooner. Yet the fighting continues, causing unrest in Morocco and Algeria.

THE PERSIAN GULF, KUWAIT AND IRAQ

When Britain sorted out this area in the wake of the Turkish Empire's collapse, it did a fairly good job. Saudi Arabia and Kuwait were never under the complete control of the Turks, and Britain had been building good relationships with these two gulf states for over a century. Iraq was reconstructed around the ancient Arab Baghdad province and a part of Turkey (Mosul) and a sometime part of Persia (Basra). Someone no doubt thought that Iran (Persia) and the Turks would keep the Iraqis busy. This is generally true, but in 1990 Iran was busy rebuilding after a revolution and war while Turkey was preening itself for eventual entry into the Common Market. This gave Iraq a chance to take a reckless lunge south at the historically worthless, thinly populated but now oil-soaked Bedouin lands. This was not unexpected, as the Bedouins are still few and they now have much wealth. If not the Iraqis, then the Iranians were expected to make a lunge. Consider the 1990–91 war just the first chapter in a long train of events that won't be played out until the last drop of oil is extracted from Arabia.

NATIONAL FAVORITES: A SAMPLER OF NATIONAL PREFERENCES IN SHOOTING BLANKS

Shooting blanks is something of a universal pastime. Most of the wars and potential wars in the world demonstrate this to different degrees; and in every instance at least one side, and frequently both, are deeply involved in shooting blanks. To demonstrate this, we have looked at some of the world's bigger players to determine their respective proclivities and preferences in terms of the five factors we've identified as contributing to shooting blanks.

Each of the sample nations on the following list is rated on the basis of "A" (deals with it very well) to "D" (poor) on how they handle each of these items. The ratings merely show relative standing. In some categories, no one is really outstanding (as with intelligence) or completely out of it (as in the impact of media). Ratings are relative, as each power is judged within its own limitations and environment. Thus, a Vietnamese "A" in Procurement Puzzle does not mean that Vietnam has better equipment than the United States, which has a "C" in this category, but only that given their respective economic capabilities and military requirements, Vietnam does a better job of securing what it needs than does the United States. Each rating, then, is predicated upon an evaluation of the following:

- Intelligence Confusion (Intel): How good is the country in obtaining and analyzing information on potential opponents? "A" means the intelligence services are efficient and effective.
- Amateurism (Amateur): How effective are the armed forces and how aware are their leaders, both political and military, of their abilities? "A" indicates that the troops are well prepared and that the leadership has a good sense of what its troops can get away with.
- Media Muddle (Media): How effective are the media in keeping all concerned informed about military capabilities and situations? "A" means the media provide most people with an accurate picture.
- Procurement Puzzle (Procure): To what extent is the nation able to obtain effectively and economically the weapons and equipment its troops need? "A" indicates that, within the limitations of the national economy, the most suitable equipment is being obtained at reasonable cost.
- Wrong-War Syndrome (Wrong War): Are the armed forces getting ready for the types of wars in which they are most likely to become involved? An "A" in this category means

that they have a realistic notion of whom they are most likely to fight and how to go about doing so.

NATIONAL FAVORITES: A SAMPLER OF NATIONAL
PREFERENCES IN SHOOTING BLANKS

	INTEL	AMATEUR	MEDIA	PROCURE	WRONG WAR
Britain	A	A	A	C	B
China	B	C	C	B	B
Egypt	B	B	B	A	A
France	B	B	B	C	B
Germany	A	A	A	B	A
India	C	B	C	C	B
Iran	C	C	C	B	B
Iraq	B	C	C	B	C
Israel	A	A	A	A	A
Japan	B	A	B	A	B
North Korea	B	B	D	B	B
Russia	A	C	C	B	B
South Korea	A	B	B	A	A
Syria	B	C	D	B	B
United States	A	B	B	C	B
Vietnam	B	A	C	B	A

Britain

Over the centuries, the British have made just about every military mistake possible. To their credit, they have got through most of this century making fewer errors overall than most other nations. The only current weak spot is procurement, where a reluctance to recognize their shrinking position as a world-class arms manufacturer frequently causes the British to forego the best weapons so as to "buy British."

China

China has serious problems taking an accurate measure of its troops' abilities, as was demonstrated in 1979 when large-scale border battles with Vietnam ended in disaster for Chinese troops. The Chinese media is state-controlled and ordinarily leaves the military alone, meaning that the media become a means to cover up military shortcomings. Procurement has been poor since the 1950s because China lacks industry capable of producing modern weapons or allies willing to supply them, but they do manage to produce most of what they need, albeit of less than state-of-the-art quality. As in Russia, a separate network of military factories exists to produce military goods. During the 1980s, the armed forces were simultaneously cut back and modernized, but because modernization of the economy was given a higher priority, there was more cutting than modernizing in the armed forces. The modernization plan was intended to transform the troops from a quasi-guerrilla force to a modern conventional-combat force. The guerrilla-war concept was a leftover from revolutionary and radical doctrines pursued during the 1950s and 1960s. Current doctrine calls for fighting a conventional mechanized war although the troops are still largely equipped and trained in the style of fifty years ago. Moreover, no Chinese army has ever fought as a mechanized army, so it is problematic just how well the Chinese military will adapt to these new forms of combat. The political upheavals of 1989, and the army participation in restoring order, will be a setback. That many units refused to attack civilians shows that command and control are not absolute. The media also demonstrated an ability to influence troop attitude. Yet the troops can't train or reequip while keeping the peace in the cities. The outcome of all this is going to be interesting.

Egypt

As the only Arab country to have beaten Israeli troops in battle, Egypt has demonstrated it has learned something about dealing with the causes of shooting blanks. Despite relative isolation from other Arab nations since their peace treaty with Israel, the Egyptians have maintained a good intelligence system. Troop quality has slipped somewhat since its 1970s peak, but most of this change has been recognized and adjusted for. The media is comparatively free, but is reluctant to harry the armed forces too closely. Egypt's strong point has been procurement, which has included a lot of domestic industry and generous donations from the United States. Likely opponents in a future war are Libya, internal dissidents and, finally, Israel. The structure of the armed forces has been balanced to yield the best prospects against any of these.

France

Relatively isolated from any foreign threat and inclined to do things differently than its neighbors and allies, France has built up a mediocre record in all categories of shooting blanks. Although possessed of an exceptional diplomatic intelligence service, France's military intelligence lacks the resources to match the Superpowers' and is also prone to involvement in domestic political matters. Although her elite units are world class, France's military abilities are generally overestimated by her leaders, and these attitudes are reinforced by a partisan press. Procurement is even more insular and inefficient than Britain's, although France has been more successful in exporting weapons, even those for which its own forces have little use. Again, the efficient diplomatic service assists the exports, and the powerful arms industries. Over the last decade, France has become more realistic about what types of wars it is likely to fight and how to go about it. This has been aided by increased cooperation with Germany and NATO in general, after decades of trying to go it alone.

India

A country that comprises dozens of distinct ethnic and linguistic groups, India has no real rivals in the region. Although bordering China, a serious potential enemy, most of the Indian frontier runs through the Himalayas; moreover, the adjacent Chinese territory is Tibet, a troublesome region for China. The only significant opposition in the area is from Pakistan, which is much smaller but may soon have nuclear weapons. Overall, this lack of viable opponents has allowed India to lapse into dangerous attitudes regarding shooting blanks: One result is that the Indian Army has proven surprisingly inept in Sri Lanka. This may become a serious and tragic problem if Pakistan does reach nuclear capability and tensions again rise between the two nations. Note that India's procurement situation is one where much equipment is bought or licensed from western firms and from Russia (the Russians want to keep the Indians suitably anti-Chinese), but India also builds much equipment of its own design. The quality of much of this domestically built material varies, and procurement in general is something of a political football.

Iran

Religious fervor and revolutionary zeal have blindsided Iran's efforts to avoid shooting blanks since the 1979 revolution and 1980–88 war with Iraq. Extreme political attitudes have limited the effectiveness of the Iranians' intelligence agencies, once among the more effective in the region. These same attitudes have made it difficult to maintain accurate appraisals of their own military abilities, this even after nine years of war, a situation aided and abetted by the Iranian media. Sheer survival instincts have led Iran to adopt more pragmatic attitudes in procurement and preparation for war, with a "rehabilitation" of former imperial officers, and to develop an extensive domestic arms industry. Iran continues to purchase arms at the same rate as during the war and plans to do so through the mid-nineties. Relations with Russia have been improved, largely because Russia is normally a trading partner and always a source of inexpensive weapons. As the only likely enemies are Iraq and internal dissidents, preparations for the future are likely to be well focused.

Iraq

Being the underdog in the Iran-Iraq War, Iraq was forced to be more effective in order to survive. This took some doing. Its intelligence service overestimated the degree to which the Iranian revolution had weakened that nation's armed forces, but once the war got started it proved fairly adequate to the task of figuring out what Iran was going to do next. Iraqi troops were not too good at the onset, nor was their equipment well maintained or well used. Fortunately for them, the Iranians were in worse shape, and the Iraqis got better more quickly, while solving their equipment problems through massive foreign procurement. The biggest weak spot is a state-controlled media, which amplify whatever the dictator (Saddam Hussein) wants to believe instead of offering more rational and less disastrous alternatives. This eventually became a major problem when Iraq invaded Kuwait in 1990. Despite the Iraqi propaganda blitz, numerous Iraqi army officers resisted the idea of invading an Arab neighbor (and many were shot for such treason). Up to August 1990, the Iraqi armed forces had accumulated a respectable amount of combat experience and were reasonably well organized and led for a war with the likes of Iran. But that war had been fought in a nondesert environment (largely marshlands) against an ill-trained, mainly static, and unimaginative opponent. Iraq never demonstrated any capacity for maintaining high-quality armed forces. Loyalty is always a problem and maintaining huge quantities of equipment has proven difficult, given the shortage of technically competent personnel.

Israel

Being on a constant war footing since its very inception, Israel has learned to avoid the causes of shooting blanks. Under these conditions, you either adapt or perish. So far, Israel has survived, accumulating excellent "marks" in all categories in the process.

Japan

Limited resources hobble Japanese intelligence efforts, although close links with the United States help in this area. The government appears to have a firm notion of the capabilities of its armed forces, which are widely regarded as thoroughly professional. The media usually promote economic imperatives at the expense of legitimate military requirements, particularly in procurement, where a desire to "buy Japanese" results in excellent but highly expensive equipment. While the post–World War II constitutional limits on the extent and nature of military preparations hamper Japan's attempts to prepare for war against a particular opponent, the armed forces appear well prepared to defend national territory and secure the sea lanes surrounding the home islands, but they would still have to rely on the United States to sustain the flow of raw materials from more distant areas.

North Korea

The single-minded goal of the government of North Korea remains the conquest of South Korea. Intelligence appears to be adequate, at least insofar as South Korea is concerned. The armed forces have an optimistic notion of their abilities, but by no means an inflated one. The most dangerous aspect of the situation is the state-controlled media, which could better be described as a Ministry of Propaganda, and could cause a potential disaster should the leaders begin to believe their own press releases. There is a satisfactory domestic-arms industry, which is supplemented by purchase from abroad. The fact that the entire energies of the North Korean armed forces are directed toward the ultimate struggle to "reunify" the country could prove embarrassing in the event of a conflict with a third party.

Russia

Although Russia is possessed of a formidable intelligence establishment, this is outweighed by serious problems in perceiving the actual abilities of its combat troops. Russia's combat history in the last 150 years has been mixed. In addition to losing in World War I, the Russians were beaten by the Japanese in 1905. Before that, they suffered a humiliating, and costly, defeat at the hands of Britain and France during the 1850s Crimean War and did poorly against the Turks in 1877–78. This is why their victory in World War II looms so large in their minds. The media are another problem, as they tend to prevent any meaningful discussion or to ask any embarrassing questions. *Glasnost* has changed this quite a bit, but it is difficult to expect any effective change at the troop level for quite some time. The military is not accustomed to taking advice: Although voices are being heard from junior officers, the old guard of generals is likely to resist. All this commotion will not do much for military readiness.

South Korea

South Korea has been successful in controlling the causes of shooting blanks, largely due to the very real threat posed by North Korea. Intelligence is good, although due to its rigid style of top-down command, the military has had a problem in accurately evaluating its own abilities, as bad news has a difficult time moving up the line. Until recently, the military dominated the government, but with military control gone, the media now go a bit overboard in criticizing the armed forces. A strong and growing industrial economy is adequate to supply the armed forces with excellent equipment, whether from domestic production or foreign purchase. As South Korea borders only one country, North Korea, there is nothing to divert attention from the principal military problem likely to confront the armed forces.

Syria

Because it has one of the more brutal dictatorships in the Middle East, it has been difficult for Syria to cope with the causes of shooting blanks. One positive element of the situation is the excellent intelligence service, which has a close and rewarding relationship with Russia's KGB. Syrian military intelligence's biggest handicap is that its primary opponent, Israel, has an outstanding counterintelligence capability. Like all tightly controlled dictatorships, Syria has iron control over the media, which print only what the government wants printed. There are serious doubts about just how competent Syrian forces are. Officers must be chosen more for political than military ability. Procurement is constrained by dependence on Russia for both financing and arms, and the Syrians have to take what is offered. There are several different wars the Syrians may be called on to fight, including one with the superior Israeli forces and another with a battered but more politically threatening Iraq. There is also constant involvement with irregular forces in Lebanon, and the Syrian Army must always be ready to move once more against dissident Syrians.

United States

Perhaps because of Pearl Harbor, Tet (and Vietnam in general), and the many world hot spots it must watch, the United States has put a relatively large amount of resources into intelligence-gathering and analysis. What hobbles this effort is the sheer size of the military and political communities that the intelligence services must support. The right information is there, but the organizations are so huge it's difficult for the right people to find out what is real and what is lobbying. The large and aggressive media help keep the political and military leadership on their toes, though how effective they are at informing the citizens as to the abilities, readiness, and problems of the armed forces is debatable. The weakest area for the United States is procurement. This is largely because the process has been highly politicized, with political considerations carrying more weight than military ones. Another weakness is trying to figure out who the troops may have to fight, and under what circumstances, a problem that is to some extent inescapable, given the country's numerous diplomatic and strategic commitments.

Vietnam

Over four decades of constant warfare have taught the Vietnamese a lot about shooting blanks and how to avoid it. Considering their limited resources, they do a very good job. Their biggest problem, as with most dictatorships, is their state-controlled media. The press can easily amplify any odd war-making ideas the leadership conjures up and this may get to the point where an unwanted war is difficult to avoid.

Germany

Intense involvement with military matters over the last century has given the Germans a sober attitude toward the causes of shooting blanks. The only rough spot is intelligence, where extraordinary efforts by Russian and, in the recent past, by the former East German intelligence agencies have made it very difficult to keep military secrets in Germany. This has compromised many of Germany's otherwise sterling intelligence achievements. Otherwise, the German record is excellent.

Negotiating Away the Arms Race: Peace in Our Time?

·11·

Wh   hat can we do about war? Will war ever be eliminated? Can it even be controlled? What has been done to promote peace? Why is disarmament so difficult? What drives the peace process?

War has been around for a long time. And so have efforts to in some way "limit" the worst effects of the business. "Rules" for warfare go back to antiquity. Originally, these were essentially religious taboos: One did not make war at certain times of the year, for instance, or on certain days, for fear of offending one deity or another. There was a certain practicality about these rules, such as those that, in many early cultures, granted priests, heralds, and physicians a degree of immunity; after all, they might come in handy. As literacy came about, so did treaties. Initially, these agreements defined the terms for ending a war, but these later sometimes developed into agreements on how to avoid it. During medieval times in Europe, the Roman

Catholic Church went a few steps further and drew up a list of prohibitions on when one could fight, against whom, and with what. This last item, "with what," was the first real attempt to limit weapons. Usually, these were new, "more horrible" weapons, such as the crossbow, and the prohibition only extended to use against fellow Christians: Nasty new weapons were normally considered fine for use against non-Christians ("infidels"). Although well intentioned, these rules—and the simultaneously evolving customs of "honorable" conduct—had only a modest effect on the frequency, intensity, and inhumanity of war. Nevertheless, they made many people feel slightly better about the whole unfortunate business.

Aside from providing spiritual guidance, it's been a long time since the clergy played so large a role in trying to regulate warfare. But the politicians who have taken over the task appear to be no more successful than were the popes and bishops.

The last hundred years or so has been something of a golden age of conferences and agreements on arms reduction and regulation. This same period has also seen more people killed in war than in any previous era. But these arms-control efforts have not been useless, and are motivated by the realization that modern weapons are more destructive than anything in the past. Nuclear weapons have spurred the negotiations process along.

ARMS RACES AND ARMS NEGOTIATIONS

Most previous arms races ended in wars, not negotiated reductions in armaments. Nuclear weapons seem to have reversed that trend. This has been the experience since World War II, and particularly since the late 1960s, when two things happened. First, the two Superpowers each achieved the capacity to launch unstoppable strategic nuclear-armed missiles at each other. Second, two decades of nuclear tests were leaving noticeable radioactive contamination in the atmosphere. It was time to talk.

But the history of earlier attempts at negotiating arms limitations was not an encouraging one. Before and after World War I, there were some apparently substantial agreements. But the pre-1914 accords did not stop World War I, or things like poison gas, massacres of war prisoners, and the aerial bombardment of defenseless civilians, all of which had been "prohibited" in the generation before the war. Nor did the even more extensive 1920s agreements (limiting naval forces and banning poison gas) stop the wars they were intended to thwart. Though these treaties did postpone matters for nearly a decade, World War II came along anyway, and was worse for the waiting. It wasn't until the 1960s that another serious round of arms-limitation talks were held. Their usefulness is still being debated, but at least there hasn't been a World War III. The major problem has always been agreeing on basic issues of what weapons are worth. Other issues are always dragged into the negotiations, but everything eventually comes back to this one.

For our purposes, we want to know what effect these treaties have had on nations' abilities to avoid shooting blanks. All of these treaties either involved items none of the participants were overly concerned about, or were the result of some hard bargaining that produced agreements some participants would henceforth be under pressure to cheat on. For example, while many of these agreements went by the wayside during major conflicts, they have had considerable effect on the minor wars. In the latter case, the agreements can be used as a propaganda tool. Nations are not as emotionally involved in minor wars, and arms-limitation agreements retain more clout. In effect, the growing web of arms restricting treaties retard the march toward war. You might say that the more you negotiate in peacetime, the less everyone bleeds in wartime.

WHAT AM I BID FOR . . . ?

You can get a good idea of what people really think about their armed forces' capabilities by examining the weapons they try to limit or eliminate through negotiation. Even more telling are the troop units and weapons systems that actually *are* eliminated by negotiation.

Any arms-limitation negotiations, regardless of the matter at issue, must sooner or later address the question of the relative value of all the armaments covered by the negotiations. This is always an extremely tricky business because:

1. All nations have different yardsticks for measuring their own and others' military power.

A nation's geographic situation helps to determine the value it places on various components of its armed forces. All nations are subject to this, of course, and a good example is the different situations faced by Russia and the United States. Russia is the largest nation in the world and is surrounded by a larger collection of former, current, and potential enemies than any other state. There are few natural barriers that might impede an invasion of Russia by any of her neighbors. Thus Russia has—requires—the world's largest army. In contrast, the United States, while not nearly so large as Russia, is also an extensive bit of real estate. But the United States is surrounded by oceans and two friendly (and much weaker) nations. Because of its insularity, the United States has the world's largest navy and marine corps. If anyone wishes to invade it, they will first have to cross an ocean, getting past the U.S. fleet. America's situation is more favorable than Russia's, as the United States is the only nation in this century to launch successful transoceanic invasions. Moreover, the United States now has a worldwide network of land, naval, and air bases. As a consequence, America can strike anywhere with considerable military force, while itself remaining relatively immune from attack.

Russia's defense scorecard is less encouraging. The country has repeatedly been subject to foreign invasion, mostly to devastating effect. In this century, Russia has been invaded twice. The World War I German invasion was settled by an unfavorable peace treaty, and only Allied victory in the West saved Russia from losing large portions of its western provinces. The World War II German invasion ended in a Russian victory, but at the cost of over 20 million dead. These experiences have left indelible scars. Russian defense planning is haunted by the prospect of another invasion. Worse, they also have a serious internal-security problem. Russia is one of the last old-fashioned empires, with half the population non-Russian and not entirely happy with how the Russians run things. This is another justification for the large ground forces, as they can be—and have been—deployed against restive citizens.

Because of their situations, the United States and Russia have significantly different attitudes toward land and naval forces. The United States considers naval forces primary, ground forces secondary, while Russia's attitude is just the opposite. As a consequence, Russia is unwilling to trade away too many ground forces and the United States reluctant to reduce the size of its fleet.

However, plans currently do exist for reductions in U.S. naval and Russian ground forces. Because of the emphasis each nation places on these forces, they have tended to overbuild in the past thirty years. Going into the 1990s, Russia must shrink its ground forces and the United States its fleet because neither can afford to maintain them at their present size. This has happened before. Economics was a major driving factor in the naval-reduction agreements of the 1920s. Yet twenty years later, the fleets were larger than ever and locked in a gigantic naval war.

The military policy of all nations is vitally influenced by geography. Britain still maintains a navy comparatively larger than its army; this is natural, as the sea provides Britain with a defensive moat, though one across which most of the country's food and raw materials must flow. The British Royal Air Force is also fairly large. During World War II, Britain discovered that the English Channel might keep ground forces out, but not aircraft, which is one of the reasons for the size of the RAF. France shows another aspect of force planning. Geography makes France vulnerable to both naval and land attack, so she must have both a strong army and an adequate navy. Moreover, believing that the judicious application of military force in peacetime is beneficial, France has large intervention forces as well, since the country has many overseas commitments. The Foreign Legion is frequently sent to hot spots in Africa, and several divisions of paratroops and light infantry also stand ready for duty outside the country. In contrast, Germany until recently faced the massed might of the Warsaw Pact (now defunct) and thus deployed the most powerful ground forces in Western Europe. Seen in this light, these differences in fundamental military policy all are perfectly rational. There are, however, further complications.

Geography aside, there are a number of other reasons why different countries adopt differing military structures. Each nation's military experience and history differs, as does its degree of industrial and technological sophistication. These differences lead to variant perspectives on how to build a force structure. Western nations place greater emphasis on air power than on masses of tanks. The West also has far more electronic equipment deployed with their troops. In contrast, the Russians stress large masses of tanks supported by considerable parks of artillery, with much less reliance on air power and electronics. Similarly, Russia and Western nations use submarines differently: In the event of war, Russia will use its subs to defend against Western carriers and amphibious forces, while the West will use its subs to hunt Russian ones. Now sit down at the negotiating table and try to figure out mutually acceptable reductions in forces. How do you balance the relative value of a computer-controlled artillery-spotting radar against a battalion of artillery? How do you compare the very effective U.S. SOSUS system, an extensive network of underwater sensors for detecting submarines and surface ships, against Russia's enormous numbers of submarines? In the end, this comes down to a question of how you compare apples to oranges.

What usually occurs in such situations is that a nation convinces itself that a reduction is necessary, desirable, possible, or permissible, or any combination of these. Russia's currently announced "unilateral" reductions are primarily prompted by economic concerns. The country's economy is collapsing under the burden of what essentially has been full, continuous wartime industrial mobilization dating back to the 1930s. The Russian decision in this regard is by no means unique. The costs of the Vietnam War prompted the United States to allow its land, sea, and air forces in Europe to degrade substantially. As much as half the combat strength of these forces was drained away to support the Southeast Asian war. Nevertheless, then as now, Europe was far more important to American security and prosperity than Vietnam. Moreover, at that time Russia was actually building up its forces in Europe. So we had a situation in which the United States was practicing disarmament in Europe for no better reason than to support a war in a region of dubious importance to American national interests. After the United States left Vietnam, its forces in Europe were again rebuilt. Recently the United States has again been talking about—and in some instances implementing—various cuts in defense, also more or less "unilaterally." But now it's the ruinous cost of modern weapons that is replacing the expense of the Vietnam War as a reason for disarmament.

Despite both the Russian and the American cuts, there will still be plenty of weapons left over with which to negotiate.

Nonetheless, this poverty-induced self-disarmament will indicate which weapons each side feels it can most readily do without, and will also make it much easier to spotlight what each side considers essential weapons. There are likely to be three major developments in the 1990s.

WHO NEEDS NUKES?

Both Superpowers have already shown a willingness to get rid of many of their nuclear weapons. No one wants to use them, and there are more than enough (over 50,000) to destroy civilization many times over. The biggest problem facing both Russia and the United States are the "nuclear unions," the bureaucracies and military organizations that build and train to use nuclear weapons. This problem is complex because each nation has several different types of nuclear weapons, each represented by an organization keen on not getting negotiated out of existence in some disarmament scheme. The United States has three air force "unions," one for bombers, one for land-based intercontinental missiles, and one for tactical aircraft. The army has nuclear artillery and short-range missiles. The U.S. Navy has its powerful submarine ballistic missile (SSBN) union, while its carrier aircraft deploy thousands of nuclear weapons that Russia considers nearly as dangerous as ICBMs. The navy has also introduced cruise missiles for its surface ships and subs. This makes a total of seven interest groups in the U.S. military. Note that not all these groups are happy with their nukes, as the handling of these weapons requires onerous precautions. Those "unions" that also have conventional weapons would favor fewer nuclear weapons.

In Russia, the situation is similar. The land-based missiles belong to a separate service, the Strategic Rocket Forces. The artillerymen of the Russian Army control a lot of nuclear weapons as well, and have a lot more influence than artillerymen in the U.S. Army. Frontal Aviation—the tactical air force—has a nuclear capability too. While Russia has no nuclear-carrier lobby—yet—there are two groups of submarine systems with nuclear weapons, ballistic missiles for strategic targets, and cruise missiles for tactical attacks on ships and other targets, plus cruise-missile-armed surface ships. In addition, a larger portion of the Russian economy develops and manufactures nuclear weapons than in the United States, giving the Russian leadership another formidable special-interest group to worry about. Try to negotiate away one group's weapons and you'll get pressured by that group. To avoid this problem, the 1988 INF treaty was negotiated with no input from the U.S. military. The brass screamed and moaned after the deed was done—there appears to have been similar opposition in Russia—but by then it was too late and their protests and doomsaying were an annoyance rather than an obstacle. Thus in both countries these interest groups are on alert now because of the INF treaty, so future negotiations will get more opposition from the various nuclear fiefdoms.

Poverty may also help to promote partial nuclear disarmament. Due to technical problems with pollution, mismanagement, waste disposal, and aging equipment, operations of the U.S.'s heavy water and nuclear-weapons plants have been severely restricted, and the cost of refitting them, or building new ones, is considered prohibitive. The Russians appear to be having even more severe problems with their nuclear-weapons plants. Both powers will have to spend money on new installatons. Given that they are both inclined to reduce certain types of delivery systems, they may settle for more modest stockpiles, which would need smaller, less costly production and maintenance facilities.

RETURN OF THE TRADITIONAL RUSSIAN ARMY

Recently, Russia went back to its history books and decided it could restructure its ground forces. There are several trends coming together, largely due to the tremendous equipment bloat the Russian ground forces have after four decades of buildup. The basic problem is that the Russians do not retire old equipment very readily, and this is especially true with armored vehicles. The result is that while more sophisticated vehicles were introduced during the 1980s, tens of thousands of vehicles built in the 1950s and 1960s continue in service. Additionally, the pool of well-educated conscripts is not growing as quickly as the masses of complex equipment that they must maintain. Doctrine and tactics are also becoming more complex. And increasingly, things in general just aren't working. Currently, many officers are calling for a professional army, on the Western model, using volunteers in the ranks. Others want to revive the ancient Russian militia. Currently under consideration is a possible compromise, one tried from time to time in the past, most recently in the late 1920s, which would be a little bit of both: a smaller, largely volunteer professional force supplemented by a large, part-time conscript militia.

THE U.S. LEGIONS COME HOME

The United States is also thinking about restructuring its armed forces, after the largest peacetime buildup in its history. There is some pressure to withdraw American ground forces overseas, as the United States now deploys a quarter of its troops abroad. This is expensive and causes increasing foreign and domestic political problems. At home, taxpayers chafing under growing trade and budget deficits see billions being spent to defend nations who appear to be growing rich at our expense in world export markets. Meanwhile the populations of those nations are also showing increasing reluctance to play host to large contingents of American troops. Already Spain has forced removal of a major U.S. air unit, and several other nations are considering similar moves. And while bringing the troops home would obviously save Americans a lot of money, such a move might not be easily accomplished, as the U.S. armed forces are likely to be reluctant to see their missions and strength reduced. Many of the returning troops would not be needed at home, and there would be reductions in current force levels. There is also the prospect of interservice squabbles because the navy would most likely suffer proportionally smaller cuts than either the army or the air force. At the very least, the accompanying debate will be informative and entertaining.

2. No nation wants to admit that its forces are inferior to someone else's.

This has a corollary: No nation wants to lose a negotiating edge by making a big thing about its forces being superior.

There is actually not much dispute over numbers of troops and weapons, except where these data are highly secret and there are arguments over whose estimate is more accurate. There are also disagreements on how to classify weapons. But in this age of satellite reconnaissance, everyone has a pretty accurate count on the major items of equipment.

There is also little dispute about operational capabilities of weapons and equipment, except where the data are closely held. The major problem with assessing the operational capabilities of weapons is that most of the new ones are not thoroughly tested: It takes combat or years of peacetime use to get an accurate idea of what new weapons can actually do. And while all nations have this problem, what results is the almost comic situation of each side trying to create the impression that the other is stronger, though not too much stronger. Naturally, neither will admit it's the stronger, as that would imply that aggression is planned. And neither side will admit to debilitating weakness, as this would imply that all those billions spent on defense had somehow gone for nothing.

History provides a way out of this paradox. Throughout the ages, it has been demonstrated that raw numbers imply neither inferiority nor superiority. It's not the numbers that count, but the intangibles like leadership, training, and the will to fight. In peacetime, few admit to any deficiencies in these categories. When the shooting starts, one side—sometimes both—will invariably be found to be catastrophically deficient in these areas. As we enter the 1990s, we hear curiously different messages from the two European adversaries. NATO forces proclaim that they have never been better-equipped and better-trained. From the East, we hear a different tune, as the Warsaw Pact armies prepare to unilaterally disband dozens of divisions and discard thousands of major weapons. While Russia has led the arms race in Europe since the 1960s, it now admits to serious morale, training, leadership, and readiness problems. Reports from witnesses in Afghanistan indicate that the Russians weren't making this up. So if they now admit that long-brewing problems are boiling over, why are they unilaterally cutting force levels? The usual answer from Moscow is that the situation is so serious that drastic measures are needed. While Lenin constantly proclaimed the virtues of quantity, quality is now in favor. The reasoning seems to be that it's better to have smaller good forces than larger mediocre ones. The Russians are not admitting to being inferior, they are simply trying to do better with fewer troops and smaller budgets. This will complicate any disarmament talks because, at the moment, whatever estimate the Russians had of their own military strength is undergoing revision. For a while, no one will have any firm idea what a Russian soldier is worth.

Attempting to measure, or even to discuss, the question of troop quality inevitably leads to major disputes. Throughout history, this quality has been the crucial factor in battle. But giving a quantitative value to morale, leadership, and training is shunned by most nations, especially during peacetime. Even those that do develop techniques for assessing such values try to keep them secret. Nations that don't have an official policy of quantifying combat power still use a form of such techniques. In effect, they tend to consider each of their troops equal to their counterparts in other nations, a folly that can prove very costly in wartime.

And then there is the pumpkins-and-potatoes question. Quantification and evaluation of troop capability are a particularly insidious problem. It springs from a number of causes, the first of which is national pride. Troops are raised and trained with the idea they will succeed in battle. This is an old tradition, and it becomes a national point of honor to think that one's own troops are better than one's neighbor's. Never mind that the historical track record says otherwise, these details can always be explained away. Some of the explanations are perversely convincing, however. For example, Russia has taken more casualties than its opponents in most of the wars it has fought against Western powers, but ultimately won a lot of those wars. It's the final score that counts. When Russia inculcates the troops, the emphasis is on the outcome of the wars, not the much less attractive events that led up to the victory.

Next we have political expediency. Defense budgets are a problem in all countries. Large amounts of money must be extracted from the citizenry and put into nonproductive use to support the military. The military leaders secure these funds by alternately stressing the power of their potential opponents and pointing out how remarkably well the forces in their care have been built up. Forecasts of the "threat" always loom larger around budget time, while one's own forces are displayed to good effect the rest of the year. Historically, this has been the pattern in the U.S.-Russian arms race, as Eisenhower and Khrushchev both observed when they commiserated over the common problem of how to deal with military leaders who kept pointing out how strong the other guy was. One's defense establishment does not want to be pinned down to any one particular formula for calculating what its own forces are capable of versus the capabilities of its potential opponents. If this is done and one's potential opponents decline in relative capability, your military leaders will have a hard time maintaining current defense spending, much less securing any increases. Going into the 1990s, this is what NATO nations are faced with. The Russians are cutting back, and admitting that their forces are not necessarily all they're cracked up to be. Where does this leave NATO military leaders come next year's budget?

Then there is the problem of secrecy. Military command staffs do calculate a quality factor, at least some do, but for reasons of military security, and national pride, they keep this secret. Russia is one of the major practitioners of this quantification. Combat officers carry a small book of "norms" with them when they go into action. For example, these norms give the number of artillery shells needed to destroy an enemy position. While this quantity of munitions is initially based on experience and experimentation, it is modified depending on the nationality of the target. A German unit might need 50 percent more shells on its position than a Dutch one in order to achieve the same effect. One reason the Russians try to keep these data secret is that they imply that Russian forces are not man-for-man comparable with likely opponents.

Finally, there is indecision, usually accompanied by a lack of objectivity. This is the American disease, though one widely shared by many other NATO nations. All NATO countries use war games and models to work out the details of potential wars. To do this, you have to quantify, there's no way around it. Unfortunately, precision can also be elusive, and accuracy nettlesome. An accurate model might suggest that the troops of one NATO power are superior to those of another. Objectively, this is a very reasonable conclusion. But the sensibilities of the various allies have to be taken into account. As a result, given the potentially embarrassing implications of these quantifications, they are likely to be done in a haphazard fashion. Each different model—and there are dozens of major ones—uses a different quantification scheme. As a result, rarely are two models more than roughly comparable. Moreover, most of these models are essentially baseline quantifications, rooted in a hodgepodge of often superficial technical data from various sources. Ultimately, the premise of them all is that the Russians are essentially comparable to NATO troops on a one-for-one basis. Historically, this is not true: It's not even true among the troops of the various NATO nations. Some scholarly research, particularly by Trevor N. Dupuy, the retired United States Army colonel and author, has demonstrated that traditionally there have been significant national differences, not merely between Russian and Western European troops, but among the troops of the Western European powers as well. But the historical approach gets elbowed aside by the numerous makeshift methods. The end result is basically to ignore qualitative differences.

3. All nations are willing to negotiate away weapons that they consider obsolete, impractical, or counterproductive, or that help potential enemies more than themselves.

For over a century, arms-reduction and disarmament talks have been seen by most powers as a means of reducing the other fellow's military power. At London in 1854 the two principal naval powers, Britain and France, promoted a ban on certain types of commerce raiding naval forces—privateers—which had traditionally been the means by which nations with weak navies had contended with the major maritime powers in war. The United States, a seasoned privateering nation from way back, chose not to sign. This they regretted less than ten years later, as Confederate privateers devastated Union shipping. Three generations later, Britain, the premier maritime power, attempted to get submarines banned at the naval-disarmament conferences in the 1920s: After all, submarines detracted more from Britain's maritime position than they added. Two generations later, in the late 1970s, Leonid Brezhnev got a good deal of propaganda mileage out of his "No First Use of Nuclear Weapons" pledge and his campaign to ban the so-called "neutron bomb," measures likely to have helped Russia a lot more than the West, which believed it needed the threat of such weapons to keep Russia's enormous fleets of tanks in check. Russia's recent proposal to mothball a large number of submarines if the United States does likewise with several aircraft carriers is a similar idea: If needed, subs can put to sea with partially trained crews, but carriers cannot operate with partially trained air groups. The United States has institutionalized this approach with its "Competitive Strategies" program, which attempts to take advantage of Western strengths instead of trying to compete directly with Russia in quantity production. This technique identifies areas where Russia is weak and develops weapons or tactics that will exploit these weak spots. A good example is the cruise missile, which takes advantage of Russia's relatively poor antiaircraft-missile technology and vast areas to be defended. Another area being exploited is "smart" mines that use microprocessor-driven sensors to seek out Russian armored vehicles without human intervention. These weapons have an easy time going after armored vehicles, and the mine technology is difficult for Russia to duplicate in quantity.

Another traditional game played at disarmament conferences is to ban weapons that one expects will not work anyway. This gives everyone a warm feeling of having accomplished something while costing them nothing. Thus, at The Hague in 1899 and again in 1907, every nation in the world agreed that bombarding cities from the air was anathema. At that time, the only means by which this could be done was from the highly unreliable airship; the airplane, invented in 1903, would change the equation, but not for many years. Bans on weapons that are potentially as dangerous to the users as to their victims, such as poison gas and biological agents, are also popular. These patterns continue.

Another area favored in arms reduction is the elimination of weapons that don't work very well anyway. In 1989, Russia announced that it would withdraw thousands of tanks and artillery pieces from its Warsaw Pact allies. Westerners expected that these would largely be older equipment, such as towed artillery and 1950s-vintage T-55 tanks, but this was not entirely the case. While all of the artillery pulled out was older, towed models, some recent tanks were also withdrawn. In order to understand the reasoning behind this, you must follow the intense debates in the Russian military literature. After decades of worshiping masses of tanks and towed artillery operated by ill-trained conscripts, the Russians came to realize that what they have essentially produced is a large number of very expensive targets. Many of their latest tanks have not performed as expected, being more complex and less reliable than earlier models. These tanks also have three-man crews, unlike the four commonly found in the tanks of most other nations. The automatic gun loader, which eliminated the fourth man, actually requires more maintenance than three men can provide. In consequence, the system breaks down a lot, and the gunner has to manually load the gun, as well as run the fire-control system. This reduces the rate of fire to unacceptable levels. Hence, this apparent "unilateral disarmament" move on the part of the Russians may actually result in a strengthening of their forces in Europe.

Russia's recent decision to destroy large quantities of military equipment was welcomed as a first step in Superpower disarmament. But disarmament was only of secondary concern in this decision: The primary impetus was economic. The Russian economy, the source of its military power, was in decline, and resources had to be diverted from the armed forces. It's not enough to stop building complex systems like tanks. Russia is estimated to build about 3,000 tanks annually, though possibly as few as the 1,500 they officially claim to produce. Each of these vehicles is in service for fifteen to twenty years. Each year the tank is in service consumes additional resources. Tank components wear out quickly and are expensive to replace. For disarmament to have a noticeable economic effect, many vehicles must be retired quickly.

DEFENDER VERSUS DEFENDER

Arms reductions usually don't occur until both sides agree that neither can overcome the other in a war, or that there really isn't much grounds for having a war to begin with. At that point, it becomes obvious, and mutually beneficial, to cut back on arms spending so long as it doesn't alter the military balance. The situation in Europe from the late 1940s to the present is a curious example of two forces that cannot overcome each other, and won't admit it. The Russian-dominated Warsaw Pact had, on paper, superiority in numbers. Yet the Russians constantly proclaim that their forces are defensive. Despite the raw numbers, historically, their position has some validity. There are four areas that worry the Russians but get little attention in the West.

First, there were Russia's restive East European allies. The thirty Russian divisions in East Europe were seen as an occupation force by both the Russians and the East Europeans. At least once in every decade since World War II there had been a serious uprising or disturbance in Eastern Europe. Without those thirty divisions, it's doubtful most of these nations would have been Russia's "allies." If current trends continue, all of those occupation troops will be withdrawn, further loosening Russia's influence in the area, and also further reducing the apparent threat to Western Europe.

Second, closer to home, because Russia knows from harsh experience that her troops perform poorly in the opening stages of a war, the thirty divisions in East Europe are expected to buy time for the hundreds of less well-prepared divisions in the homeland to mobilize.

The third fear is the threat posed by Western technology and German troops. The Russians have a lot more respect for Western technology than does the West. And after two World Wars they also have a lot of respect for the capabilities of German troops. Official propaganda aside, the Russian General Staff does not see NATO forces as being easy to stop if they were to advance into Eastern Europe.

And then there is the German Problem. Russians see themselves as "Elder Brother" to the other Slavic peoples. Germans, who have been marauding into Slavic territories for over a thousand years, are historically the enemy the Russian "Elder Brother" must deal with. World War II was actually the first time in centuries—since 1414 to be precise—that Slavs, led by Russia, actually won a decisive war against Germans. Germany was divided from 1945 to 1990, much to the relief of the Russians, as well as other Eastern Europeans—not to mention many Western Europeans. Fear of renewed German militarism still exists in the region. While a united Germany can mobilize only about twenty divisions, they are German divisions. In this century those same Germans have twice cut Russian armies to ribbons and advanced on Moscow. More than anything else, Russia wants to keep the German genie bottled up. Any Russian with a memory of World War II does not relish going to war with Germans again. Many in the West ignore or discount all these Russian fears. Although one pre-1990 Russian war plan calls for a lightning strike across the border to disrupt NATO forces before they can get organized, such a (successful) large surprise operation in peacetime is alien to Russian military history. So the Western NATO alliance prepared for an invasion from Russian forces that are actually preoccupied with keeping Eastern Europe under control and holding the line against a NATO invasion. This might have been considered amusing were it not an officially sanctioned state of affairs and the cause of one of the most expensive and ruinous arms races in history.

Negotiations for really deep cuts in European-based arms have been going on for some time. In the last three years there has been quite a lot of progress. The INF treaty was the start, although it covered only a very small portion of the nuclear weaponry in question. What put these negotiations into high gear? Perhaps the most important point to consider is that while arms races may fuel ill will among nations, they begin because of preexisting ill will. So disarmament negotiations can succeed only if everyone feels better about everyone else. We are now in a period of extraordinary good relations among the major powers. The Treaty of Paris in 1990 effectively dismantled the armies and arms race plaguing Europe since the 1950s. Yet we should remember that a similar spate of goodwill occurred in the 1920s, and led to some moderately successful disarmament agreements. But then the militarists took power in Japan, and Hitler arose in Germany. These developments led to World War II, and are a ghostly memory haunting all disarmament conferences: We may trust you now, but what about ten years from now?

LOOKING AT THE RECORD

The disarmament and arms-control efforts over the last century or so fall into three distinct periods. Each period, whether that preceeding World War I, or that between the world wars, or that of the Cold War era, has had a different focus, as the nations involved attempted to cope with differing sets of problems.

PRE–WORLD WAR I DISARMAMENT NEGOTIATIONS

Disarmament, in the modern sense, was not possible until we had massive armaments, in the modern sense. All of this began to happen only about a century ago, with the development of mass-produced weaponry and "high tech" armaments and huge conscript armies. The major agreements reached before World War I dealt with the regulation of conduct in combat, that is, the standards for treatment of prisoners of war, medical personnel, and civilians; the prohibition of certain weapons, including poison gases, the aerial bombardment of cities, and hollow-point bullets; and the rights of neutrals, that is, the regulation of neutral shipping in wartime. Nevertheless, most of these agreements were ignored by the major powers when a war broke out between them, although there was some enthusiasm for enforcing these agreements in wars among lesser powers. Whatever the case, precedents were set and some good was done.

POST–WORLD WAR I DISARMAMENT MOVEMENT

In the wake of the ruinous cost of World War I, the arms race that led up to it, and the incipient arms race that began to develop after it, several major nations held serious talks regarding ways to prevent a repetition of the 1914–18 bloodbath. There were a number of important problems with this. The primary one was that two of the major military powers—Germany and Russia—were not a part of these discussions. As a result of defeat and the Treaty of Versailles, Germany was officially disarmed, although even during the 1920s the German General Staff was planning the massive rearmament that would take place a decade later. Meanwhile, defeat, the Revolution, civil war, and insurrection, coupled with efforts to "build communism," removed Russia as a player until the 1930s: nor was anyone really talking to revolution-minded Russia until then anyway. The French made matters difficult by remaining largely aloof from disarmament discussions, feeling that they had to follow their own program in order to prevent a third ruinous war with the Germans, in the tradition of those of 1870–71 and 1914–18. But France was a major player only in the European area, and even there only on the ground. There were really only two global powers, Britain and the United States, plus Japan, which was enormously powerful in the Pacific. The United States had, as was its custom, demobilized its ground forces with almost indecent haste after 1918. Britain did the same, not being overly fond of large armies. Japan had not mobilized large ground forces for World War I and was far from Europe. But the three nations were all strong in naval forces. This led to the one notable disarmament episode between the World Wars, the Naval Disarmament Treaties of 1922 and 1930.

The first of these, the Washington Naval Arms Limitation Agreements of 1921–22 among Britain, Japan, and the United States, and their extension, the London Agreement of 1930, were hammered out as a means of avoiding another naval arms race like the one that preceded World War I. The treaties were remarkable in that capital ships were actually scrapped or converted to other uses. Ships under construction were canceled, limits were established on the building of replacements for those capital ships allowed to each of the parties, and design restrictions were established for future construction. More significantly, the three powers agreed that the United States and Britain, each of which had interests in both the Atlantic and the Pacific, "needed" about 60 percent more capital ships than did Japan, which had interests only in the Pacific. The Japanese accepted this deal when the other powers sweetened it by barring new fortifications in Western Pacific islands controlled by the United States and Europeans. Although Britain failed to get submarines banned, these were agreements that did make a difference, as fleets actually were reduced. The treaty had some unintended results. One was that Japanese militarists would later use it to argue that the Japanese Empire had been insulted by relegation to a state of inferiority. Another was that some battleships under construction were converted to aircraft carriers, which were not thought worth covering in the treaty. Although subsequent agreements were reached on these and other classes of warships, efforts at achieving further significant reductions in naval armaments, which were made well into the 1930s, came to grief due to demands for "parity" by a militarized Japan and a resurgent Nazi Germany. Thus a treaty aimed at reducing tensions and armaments actually eventually increased both. Disarmament doesn't always work out the way you think it will.

In contrast to the naval-arms limitation agreements of the period 1921–30, the other agreements between the World Wars were actually "feel good" agreements, of more political then practical consequence. For example, the League of Nations, a sort of predecessor to the UN, was created by the Treaty of

Versailles in 1919. The League successfully dealt with a number of tense, albeit minor, international situations, despite the fact that the organization was inherently flawed by the reluctance of the United States to become a member. The 1929 Geneva Convention also made a number of important revisions to the existing "rules of war." And then there was the Kellogg-Briand Pact, in which the United States did participate. Signed in 1928, this was a widely touted bit of fluff in which all nations renounced the use of force and declared that war was no longer an acceptable way to settle international disputes, except, naturally, for purposes of "self-defense." Kellogg-Briand made everyone applaud, but did nothing for the cause of peace. Too many nations were intent on continuing to use force to sort out the problems that preceded, and followed, World War I. As a result, by the late-1930s a new and massive arms race was on again, and World War II was a few short years away. Perversely, Kellogg-Briand had helped create this new war, for the pact stood as a psychological obstacle to the use of force when they still had the power to act by France and Britain against the rising might of Nazi Germany in the mid-1930s.

World War II put an end to all disarmament talks until the fighting was over and the Cold War had begun.

COLD WAR NEGOTIATIONS

World War II was followed by massive demobilization. In the United States, where demobilization forthwith was in keeping with traditional American practice at the end of a war, 9 million troops were sent home in just one year. In Europe and Russia, on the other hand, demobilization was prompted largely by economic necessity. Despite the peace, despair, hunger, and revolution were in the air. Russia, which had already virtually annexed much of Eastern Europe in its desire to establish a defensive "moat" against future German aggression, threw itself behind all this unrest. And soon the Cold War was on. World War II left only two nations with significant military power, Russia and the United States. By the late 1940s, both Superpowers were rebuilding their forces, which continued into the 1950s. But in the late fifties economic considerations caused Russia to substantially reduce its armed forces. Curiously, at about the same time, the United States was also going through a significant reduction in force levels, prompted partially by economic reasons but mostly by the adoption of a policy of "massive retaliation" with nuclear forces in the event of any military confrontation. These reductions were not negotiated, and due to the Russian penchant for secrecy, most people in the West were unaware of the extent of the Russian cuts. Meanwhile, both Superpowers had rapidly growing nuclear arsenals. And both were conducting extensive atmospheric nuclear weapons tests.

By the early 1960s, attention began to focus on the significant buildup of radioactivity in the atmosphere as a result of these tests. Partially out of concern for the atmosphere and partially out of a growing sense of the enormous danger posed by nuclear arms that grew out of a series of increasingly tense crises in the early 1960s, and under enormous pressure from public opinion on both sides of the "Iron Curtain" as well as among neutrals, this led to a series of treaties designed to limit nuclear arms in various ways. These were the first real arms-limitation agreements of the Cold War era. A surprising number of additional agreements followed, and fall more or less into three categories:

1. Neutralization Agreements. These impose limitations on the deployment of weapons, and particularly nuclear weapons, in various regions, including Antarctica, Outer Space, the ocean floor, and several specific geopolitical areas.

2. Confidence-Building Agreements. Such treaties are designed to improve the degree of cooperation and trust between the Superpowers; examples would include the Hot Line Treaty, verification of military maneuvers, notification of accidents, and respect for human rights.

3. Disarmament Agreements. These treaties limited or eliminated certain classes of weapons, or banned the development of certain new weapons, and curbed testing of nuclear arms. Salt I or the INF Treaty, banning medium-range nuclear missiles, would fall into this category.

WORK IN PROGRESS

In recent years there are always a number of treaties under negotiation, while many existing ones are being renegotiated. Several of those presently in the works are even more far-reaching than the numerous agreements that have already been concluded. This is one reason why the negotiations for these proposed treaties have been so protracted. Recently, the two most important such negotiations, dealing with the military balance in Europe, have finally borne fruit.

MBFR

The Mutually Balanced Force Reduction talks began in the late 1970s, with the idea of negotiating cuts in conventional forces by NATO and the Warsaw Pact. They dribbled off into insignificance because no agreement could be reached on whose forces were worth what, or even who had what. The Warsaw Pact had a considerable superiority in numbers, and offered one-for-one reductions. NATO saw this as a means of making the imbalance even worse because one-for-one would have made the ratio of forces even less favorable for NATO.

CAFE

Conventional Armed Forces in Europe talks are related to the MBFR talks. In September of 1989, NATO proposed cuts in air forces that would leave each side with 5,700 combat airplanes and 1,900 combat helicopters in the area between the Atlantic and the Urals. The Warsaw Pact wanted to exclude interceptors from the 5,700 ceiling for fixed-wing aircraft. This was in the tradition of giving away things that would harm you less than your opponent, as the Pact needs interceptors to counter NATO's more effective ground-attack aircraft. Meanwhile, at least all parties seemed to agree that stringent verification measures will be needed.

With the increasing openness in Russia and the democratization of Eastern Europe in late 1989, both the MBFR and CAFE talks took on a new character. On November 20, 1990, a major and wide-reaching agreement was achieved which mandates reductions in virtually all categories of troops and equipment in Europe, so that by 1994 NATO and the Warsaw Pact will have reduced their armed forces in Europe to a level of equality. Germany has granted several billion dollars to Russia to provide housing for troops to be withdrawn to the Soviet Union. The United States, meanwhile, has drawn upon its forces in Germany to bolster its efforts in the Persian Gulf. What is more interesting is that the signatories have already expressed, or implied, a desire for still further reductions. In addition, the rapid disintegration of the erstwhile Soviet bloc suggests that genuine European disarmament may not be far off.

Despite this resounding success, there are a number of other important bits of "unfinished business" still remaining.

START *(Strategic Arms Reduction Treaty)*

In the afterglow of the INF Treaty, and the increasing strength of the Gorbachev government in Russia, discussions were begun to make similar cuts in strategic weapons. Aside from the MIRV—multiple warhead—counting problem, the United States has deployed over a thousand sea-based cruise missiles (SLCMs). The SLCMs are even more difficult to count than MIRV warheads, as an almost identical missile is used to carry conventional warheads. The U.S. Navy plans to deploy several thousand SLCMs with both conventional and nuclear warheads. What is probably going to happen is an agreement to monitor missile-assembly plants, as under INF, as well as ships and submarines.

Strategic Defense

With SDI (the Strategic Defense Initiative, or "Star Wars"), the United States attempted to move into research areas in which Russia had been active for over a decade. This scared the hell out of the Russians because it might work, and even if it didn't, the "spin-off" from all those dollars invested in esoteric anti-satellite technologies could lead to unpredictable advances in other defense electronics and hardware. Interestingly, Russia's own research into antisatellite weapons was an outgrowth of their 1960s ABM (Antiballistic Missile) systems. While the United States had given up ABM work after the 1972 ABM treaty, Russia kept the few ABM systems allowed in the treaty and increased R&D on advanced systems. The current American SDI program, despite misgivings about its ability to completely protect against nuclear attack, soon made rapid progress in technical areas that had stumped the Russians. A strategic defense treaty would limit work in this area and save both nations from financial distress.

Chemical Weapons

After the first widespread use of chemical weapons, during World War I, no one relished the idea of using these substances again, at least against powers capable of retaliating in kind. The problem with chemical weapons is that they are indiscriminate and cause the troops to lose their ardor for combat even sooner than is normally the case. The idea of severely reducing holdings of chemical weapons, or banning them completely, has been building for several generations. Negotiations have been going on for some time, and Superpower enthusiasm for such an agreement appears to be growing, particularly given the actual, and anticipated, procurement of poison gas by unstable Third World regimes. North Korea has been working in the area for over a decade, Iraq and Iran have been at it since the mid-1980s, and Libya seems to be trying to get into the act as well. Much the same is likely to happen in the case of biological weapons.

Confidence Building

There's been a lot of this in recent years, mostly involving agreements that make the Superpowers feel better about each other. Assuming the current trend toward ever-friendlier relations continues, we can expect a good deal more of this sort of thing. Among likely bets are regular port calls by warships, joint space ventures, and increased overflight privileges, as well as contacts between World War II veterans organizations, and perhaps even exchanges of military cadets or academy professors. Some Russian test pilots, showing off their new MiG-29 and Su-27 fighters at Western air shows, have also suggested competitions between Russian and Western combat aircraft. Who knows, perhaps the Russians will even allow Western researchers access to their military historical archives?

THE MINISTRY OF FINANCE AND DISARMAMENT

After World War II, nuclear weapons discouraged the major powers from fighting one another directly. Instead, they fought each other by manipulating and subsidizing smaller powers. Meanwhile, ruinous sums were spent to build up conventional and nuclear arsenals on the off chance there would be another world war. Over four decades of this has had debilitating effects on all concerned, but especially on Russia's economy. In the past century, economic ruin has not stopped any arms race, although today, the real and potential economic damage from excessive arms spending is more widely recognized.

Because current national economies are much more tightly integrated with each other than was the case in the past, countries that harm their national economies with their defense-spending policies are more quickly put upon by nations that don't. For this reason, it's likely that disarmament will spread. The reason is simple: In an increasingly technological military environment, a nation's economic strength is a far greater factor in military power than at any time previously. In times past, you could stockpile armaments with the reasonable expectation that they would last for generations. Such is no longer the case. Warships can no longer be maintained ready for service for a century or more, and small arms and artillery are no longer useful for more than one generation. Weapons now not only become obsolete more quickly, but cost much more to replace. A World War II tank cost less than $400,000 in 1990 dollars. The average cost for a modern tank is nearly $3,000,000. While the performance of the modern tank is superior to its 1945 ancestor, the opposing tanks are equally improved, and the work of a tank has not changed, nor the enormous number of them required to get the job done.

Military budgets have, in fact, have not grown nearly as much as costs. National wealth has grown enormously since World War II and while there has been enough money to fund tremendous increases in defense spending, there are limits. In response to these formidable prices, nations have reduced the number of expensive weapons they buy. Air forces have fewer fighters, and navies fewer ships. Armies have not shrunk as dramatically because their weapons and equipment costs have not escalated as much as aircraft and ships. The major powers have also added new classes of equipment, such as strategic nuclear weapons, reconnaissance satellites, and computers, expensive items that did not exist fifty years ago. Indeed, since the early 1960s, over a trillion dollars has been spent on strategic nuclear forces alone, and in the United States and Russia, over 10 percent of defense spending has been for the nukes and their delivery systems.

All components of strategic systems are expensive, and escalating in cost right along with ships and aircraft in general. Up through the 1970s, the primary builders of strategic weapons, the United States and Russia, had no pressing economic problems. The United States came out of World War II with the world's largest industrial economy, easily generating about 50 percent of gross world product. While Russia was devastated by the war, her people were accustomed to hardship and willing to work diligently for several decades to rebuild. By the 1970s, Japan and Germany had rebuilt their industries and were pushing American products out of many markets. The U.S. economy was losing its competitive edge, and living standards were no longer increasing as they had every year since 1945, while in Russia there were growing rumbles of discontent as weapons piled up and all the people had to show for it was continuing shortages of consumer goods. By the 1980s, the solution to these problems was clear: Resources had to be diverted from arms to nondefense industry or there would be serious political problems on both sides of the Iron Curtain. The disarmament movement appears to be led by the Ministry of Finance.

MAJOR DISARMAMENT CONFERENCES

What follows is a summary listing of all "successful" disarmament, arms control, and peace-promoting attempts since the middle of the last century. Read 'em and weep, or laugh (depending on your sense of humor).

MAJOR DISARMAMENT CONFERENCES

YEAR-CONFERENCE	PARTICIPANTS	OUTCOME
1854—London	Great Powers	Ban on Privateers
1854—Washington	All Powers	Rights of Neutrals
1856—Paris	Great Powers	Rules of Blockade
1864—Geneva	All Powers	Rights of Noncombatants
1899—Hague	All Powers	Codification of Rules of War, Peaceful Settlement of Disputes

YEAR-CONFERENCE	PARTICIPANTS	OUTCOME
1904—Geneva	All Powers	Status of Hospital Ships
1907—Hague	All Powers	International Court
1919—Versailles	Allied Powers	Disarmament of WW I Losers, League of Nations Created
1922—Washington	Naval Powers	Successful Naval Disarmament
1925—Locarno	European Powers	Agreement on the Integrity of Frontiers set at Versailles
1925—Geneva	All Powers	Ban on Poison Gas
1928—Havana	All Powers	Status of Neutrals at Sea
1928—Paris	All Powers	Renunciation of War, the Kellogg-Briand Pact
1929—Geneva	All Powers	Rules of War Modifications
1930—London	Naval Powers	Modifications to Washington Pact of 1922. Modifications to Law of War
1932—Geneva	All Powers	League of Nations World Disarmament Conference: Collapses in 1934
1935—AGNA	Britain, Germany	Anglo-German Naval Agreement
1935—London	Naval Powers	Japan Scuttles New Naval Agreement
1949—Geneva	All Powers	Modifications to Rules of War, Status of Civilians in Wartime, Status of Red Cross
1955—Vienna	Big Four	Austrian State Treaty
1959—Washington	Great Powers	Antarctic Neutralization Treaty
1961—New York	All Powers	Arbitration Treaty
1962—Geneva	Superpowers	Tentative Ban on Nuclear Arms in Space
1963—Geneva	Superpowers	U.S.-Russia Hot Line Established
1963—Moscow	Superpowers	Nuclear Test-Ban Treaty
1967—Geneva	Superpowers	Ban on Nuclear Arms in Space
1967—Tlatelolco	Latin Americans	Latin American Nuclear-Free Zone
1968—W-L-M	All Powers	Nuclear Nonproliferation Treaty
1971—W-L-M	Superpowers	Nuclear-Free Seabed Treaty
1971—Geneva	Superpowers	Agreement on Avoiding Accidental War
1972—Geneva	Superpowers	SALT I
1972—Geneva	Superpowers	ABM Treaty
1972—Geneva	Superpowers	Incidents at Sea Treaty
1972—W-L-M	All Powers	Biological and Toxic Weapons Treaty
1973—PNW	Great Powers	Agreement on Prevention of Nuclear War
1974—TTB	Superpowers	Threshold Test-Ban Treaty
1974—ABMA	Superpowers	Amendment to ABM Treaty
1975—Helsinki	European Powers	European Security Agreement
1976—PNE	Great Powers	Peaceful Nuclear Explosions Treaty
1977—Geneva	All Powers	Modifications to the Geneva Convention
1977—W-L-M	All Powers	Environmental Modification Treaty
1979—Vienna	Great Powers	Security of Nuclear Materials Treaty
1979—SALT II	Superpowers	SALT II
1980—Geneva	All Powers	Draft Protocol Concerning Nondetectable Fragments

YEAR-CONFERENCE	PARTICIPANTS	OUTCOME
1980—NMC	Nuclear Powers	Nuclear Materials Convention
1984—Stockholm	European Powers	European Security Conference
1987—Geneva	Superpowers	INF Treaty
1987—Geneva	Superpowers	Nuclear Risk Reduction Centers Treaty
1988—Geneva	Superpowers	Ballistic Missile Notification Treaty
1989—Paris	All Powers	Abolition of Chemical Weapons
1989—Moscow	Superpowers	Prevention of Dangerous Military Activities
1990—Moscow/Bonn	Germany, Russia	Treaty on Soviet Forces in Germany
1990—Paris	European Powers	MBFR/CAFE Treaty

"All Powers" refers to a majority of the nations existing at the time.

"European Powers" refers to Britain, France, Germany, Italy, and the smaller Western European powers prior to World War II, and to the thirty-odd nations in the European area, plus the United States and Canada, since then.

"Great Powers" include the United States, Britain, France, Russia, Germany, Italy, plus Austria-Hungary to 1918, Japan from about 1900, China from World War II.

"Naval Powers" refers to the United States, Britain, Japan, France, and Italy in the interwar period.

"Nuclear Powers" refers to those nations possessing nuclear weapons.

"Superpowers" refers to the United States and the USSR.

In every case, other powers may have participated but were peripheral to the indicated nations.

"W-L-M" indicates treaty was signed in Washington, London, and Moscow simultaneously: Negotiations were usually at Geneva. Other abbreviations simply reflect that the negotiations took place at various locations and were known by the title of the agreement.

NEGOTIATION NOTES

1854: At London, Britain, somewhat reluctantly supported by France, forced a ban on the use of privateers (a kind of pirate who was given a license by a belligerent power to prey on some other power's ships) in naval warfare and codified the rules of naval attacks on merchant ships.

1854: The Washington Conference formulated an agreement on the status of neutrals at sea in time of war. This was essentially an extension of the London conference.

1856: The Pact of Paris defined the conditions that had to be met in order to have nonbelligerent nations respect a naval blockade. The United States found these rules quite handy during the Civil War, as Britain, which had championed their adoption, had to go along with them. The three treaties concluded in 1854–56 were the first real arms-control agreements in history. They also helped bring about America's entry into World War I more than a half-century later, for international law failed to keep up with technology: Submarines were not covered by these pacts.

1864: At Geneva the powers agreed on the noncombatant status of the Red Cross, medical personnel, and the wounded.

1899: This Hague conference did make some difference. It spelled out what were to become the modern "rules of war." While these rules can go by the board in the heat of combat, they have been invoked in many a war-criminal trial and have given some troops pause before committing what could be deemed a war atrocity. This was one "disarmament treaty" that can be said to have saved lives. It also included bans on things like poison gas, aerial bombardment of cities, and various other weapons that no one thought were practical. The instigator of this conference was the czar of Russia.

1904: This agreement extended the terms of the 1864 agreement to maritime warfare, and called for immunity from attack for clearly marked hospital ships.

1907: This Hague conference reaffirmed the basic provisions of the earlier ones and by setting up an International Court, tried to eliminate a loophole in all these agreements of how you settle disputes over the rules. As the International Court, which, in one form or another, has persisted to this day, had no police capability to back up its decisions, its rulings depended on the goodwill of the participants to be enforced. Sometimes this works, sometimes it doesn't. Even if, and frequently particularly if, the court's rulings cannot be enforced, they have great propaganda value that cannot be totally ignored by the offending party.

1919: The Versailles Treaty demonstrated how not to do it. If you're going to disarm, it's got to be voluntary. This treaty forcibly disarmed Germany and the other defeated powers, on paper anyway. Fifteen years later, Germany was well on its way toward building up the world's most powerful armed forces and loudly calling for the treaty's repudiation. Versailles is an example of "peace negotiations" so flawed that they became a cause of a major war. A similar "peace" was forced on France after its defeat by Germany in 1871, which in part led to World War I, which led to World War II: In 1940, Germany insisted the French surrender in the same rail coach used for the 1918 German surrender. These things can easily get out of hand and should be avoided.

1922: Naval Limitation Treaty. This was, at that time, the biggest and most successful disarmament agreement in history. The United States, Britain, and Japan, with Italy and France in support, agreed to, and executed, massive reductions in the size of their navies, and accepted—the Japanese reluctantly—limitations on the size of their fleets in the future. Two major naval powers (Germany, with the second-largest fleet in 1914, and Russia, the fifth) were left out of the negotiations but tacitly acceded to the limitations, neither being in a position to rejoin the arms race anyway.

1925: The Locarno Pact was a "feel good" agreement, in which the principal Western European powers all swore that the frontiers established by the Treaty of Versailles were "permanent," with Germany (then prostrate economically and militarily) even accepting the "legitimacy" of the Rhineland demilitarized zone. Hitler denounced this in 1936, after Germany began rearming.

1925: At this Geneva conference, virtually all the nations in the world agreed to adopt a policy of "no first use" of poison gas, reserving the right to produce and maintain such weapons for retaliatory use should someone break the agreement. A lot had changed since the 1899 ban on what was then considered an impractical weapon: World War I had given the great powers plenty of practical experience on what chemical weapons could do. And although the ban has largely held up during wars between major powers, chemical weapons are still produced and stockpiled in large quantities, which goes to show you how much faith nations put in these agreements. Moreover, most powers have not been reluctant to use chemical weapons against nations or groups that cannot respond in kind. In these cases, the offending power loses much international prestige, which was something and thus a rare example of arms control more or less working. The United States didn't get around to ratifying this until 1977.

1928: The Havana Agreement reinforced the terms of the existing treaties and customs on the status of neutrals with regard to maritime warfare, with particular reference to submarines. Germany, now forbidden to have submarines, was not consulted.

1928: The Kellogg-Briand pact was pure public relations. It was a classic "feel good" agreement in which everyone concurred that war was no good and no one should do it. Please. Six years later, the Nazis were seizing power in Germany. Within another two years, Germany was rearming. Three years later, World War II broke out, the most destructive war in human history.

1929: This is what soldiers mean when they refer to the "Geneva Convention" and the "rules of war." The 1929 conference updated and reaffirmed much of the work done at The Hague in 1899. It has held up remarkably well, particularly with regard to prisoners of war. Even when nations violated the prisoner provisions, they nervously looked over their shoulders. For good reason: Several German and Japanese leaders who allowed or tolerated violation of the convention during World War II were hanged for it. This treaty can be said to have saved lives and alleviated suffering.

1930: This London conference confirmed the terms of the 1922 Washington Naval Agreement, further cut battleship numbers, and imposed limits on smaller warships. The acrimony that attended this conference, particularly from the Japanese, was the first sign that the historic inclination toward cooperation among the principal powers was coming apart.

1932: The World Disarmament Conference had been called for by the Covenant of the League of Nations in 1919, to supplement the disarmament of the World War I losers by the Versailles settlement. At first some progress was made in accepting the idea that all powers should cut their forces. But with the rise of Hitler, the whole thing collapsed when Britain proved unable to entice France into conceding a revision to the Versailles limitations on German military power. In 1934, Hitler denounced the conference, and withdrew from the League. The following year he denounced Versailles. No one did anything.

1935: The Anglo-German Naval Agreement was prompted by Hitler's denunciation of the disarmament clauses of the Treaty of Versailles. The British, rather than see him embark upon a massive naval arms program, conceded him the right to build a navy equal to 35 percent of their own tonnage, annoying in the process France, the United States, and Japan, which had not been consulted. Nor did it do much to impede Hitler's ambitious construction plans. In any event, the Germans were never able to reach the generous tonnage limits of this agreement.

1935: The end of the 1922 Naval Disarmament agreement. The second London conference was necessitated by Japan's 1934 declaration that she would not be bound by the 1922 Naval Arms Limitation treaty after 1936. Japan was miffed because Britain and the United States were each allowed 60 percent more capital ships. While this figure had been arrived at in recognition of the two nations' worldwide naval responsibilities, Japan was now in the hands of militarists who were easily offended and basically threw the naval treaty out as of this conference. Although the United States, Britain, and France attempted to cobble together a new agreement, their efforts were worthless without Japan. Most serious arms-limitation treaties don't last this long: By 1937, the naval shipyards of the world were experiencing a boom in construction like that which preceded World War I.

1949: During World War II, the Geneva "rules of war" were more or less adhered to, save for frequent lapses on the Eastern Front and to a lesser extent in the Pacific. During the war, the German armed forces, which largely ignored many of the rules on the Eastern Front, commissioned a study to determine whether a complete abandonment of the rules—including use of poison gas and biological agents—would be militarily useful. The conclusion was that such a move would be counterproductive, even on the Eastern Front, where most of the fighting was going on and where their military situation was increasingly desperate. So the rules more or less worked, at least well enough to make it worthwhile to tidy up the rule book a bit and ratify it all over again, with additional provisions concerning the safety of civilians and a reaffirmation of the status of the Red Cross. The United States didn't ratify this one until 1956.

1955: Austrian State Treaty. Provided for the withdrawal

of U.S., British, French, and Russian forces from Austria, and the restoration and permanent neutralization of an independent Austria. This was the first troop reduction agreement of the post–World War II era.

1959: The Antarctic Treaty was designed to put territorial claims in the area on hold, and to keep weapons and military operations out. This was a no-lose proposition, as there was nothing militarily significant about Antarctica, and everyone could pat himself on the back for being such a peace-loving fellow. It was a first step, and provided a precedent for Cold War participants to start talking about weapons issues.

1961: Formally established a mechanism for the submission of disputes to arbitration under the auspices of the International Court of Justice or similar bodies. Another example of the incremental effects of peace agreements. This arbitration process was first worked out in the 1907 agreements and continually updated and refined over the years. It has been used quite a lot. While the results have not been breathtaking, they have made a difference and saved lives. Not until 1970 did the United States ratify this agreement, and many other nations have yet to do so.

1962: The Tentative Ban on Nuclear Weapons in Space was an agreement to negotiate for a treaty banning such weapons in space. In 1962, both sides had grand plans for space-based weapons, and it seemed like a good idea to talk about the question.

1963: The Hot Line Treaty. The introduction of ballistic missiles had made everyone nervous about accidents and misunderstandings that could lead to an unintentional war. Then came the Cuban Missile Crisis of 1962, when for a time it looked like the unthinkable was going to happen. It was a sobering experience, never since repeated, and led directly to this agreement, which set up open communications links between senior leaders in Washington and Moscow beginning in 1962. Used several times during various crises, this link continues to the present, with much-improved technology: Fax machines have replaced teletypes. Although not a disarmament agreement, it has made conflict less likely and is significant as the first of many practical nuts-and-bolts agreements that recognized the complex factors that lead to and sustain modern warfare. Pragmatic agreements like this don't make a decisive difference, but they do have some tangible impact. In contrast, too many arms agreements and peace treaties are little more than paper-shuffling exercises.

1963: The Nuclear Test-Ban Treaty was the first negotiated arms-limitation treaty in over thirty years. It barred nuclear-weapons testing in the open air, under water, or in space. The treaty was forced on the participants by the realization that atmospheric—open air—nuclear-weapons tests were creating an increasingly dangerous level of radiation. Although premised on the understanding that testing was crucial to the development of new nuclear weapons, from this point on, nuclear tests could only be conducted underground, where the harmful radiation would be contained. It wasn't so much a matter of if these weapons would work, or indeed should exist, but how powerful the new designs would be and how much radiation they would create. France and China did not sign the treaty, but their atmospheric tests were not numerous enough to increase atmospheric radiation to dangerous levels. India, and possibly South Africa, exploded small devices that had no noticeable global radiation effect, and the existence of this treaty discouraged further testing. Israel has nuclear weapons and is suspected of testing them underground, which has the added advantage of making the test difficult to detect.

1967: Outer-Space Treaty. As both the United States and Russian man-in-space programs advanced, Russia readily agreed to ban nuclear weapons on the moon and in outer space. This latter item was a concession on Russia's part, as they had shown great interest in placing nuclear warheads in satellites, a technique that would have allowed them a better chance at launching a nuclear surprise attack. But there would have also been a high probability of radioactive accidents when one of these satellites got into trouble and came down accidentally. Russia would later invoke the "spirit" of this agreement to protest U.S. work on the SDI missile-defense system; the United States likewise invoked this treaty to protest Russian tests of antisatellite systems. In the spirit of the exercise, Russia insisted that it had no antisatellite systems. Meanwhile both sides use nuclear-powered radar satellites. Some of these have accidentally come down, although none over populated areas. Yet.

1967: The Latin-American Nuclear-Free Zone was another one of those goodwill, no-risk treaties. Latin America is the

United States' backyard, and is well-isolated from any of the other nuclear powers. The important thing about this agreement was that it was the first tangible step in the Superpowers' program to prevent other nations from obtaining nuclear weapons. But recent activities by Argentina and Brazil indicate that these nations may be thinking of developing some; hence, this treaty would then become a valuable tool in deterring them from following through with such programs.

1968: Four months after the Latin-American Nuclear-Free Zone treaty was signed, the Nonproliferation Treaty went into effect. Three of the nuclear powers—the United States, Russia, and Britain—agreed not to help any nonnuclear power obtain technology for atomic weapons. Although France and China did not sign, they did more or less adhere to its provisions. The big loophole in this was the proliferation of nuclear-power plants. Consequently, there was a lot of nuclear material moving around, and the technology for building nuclear weapons was becoming widely known. By the early seventies, India had the bomb, by the late 1970s, Israel and South Africa had it as well. Nations like Pakistan and Iraq are not far behind. This treaty did not stop nuclear proliferation, but it did slow it down.

1971: The Nuclear-Free Seabed Treaty was another of the "we better do something now before something terrible happens" agreements. Plans were afoot to use nuclear mines against submarines and merchant shipping. Use of these mines in wartime would have been bad enough, but all those nukes sitting on the ocean floor in peacetime were another cause for possible radioactive contamination when the inevitable accidents occurred. This was also a period of great optimism in efforts to limit nuclear weapons.

1971: With the Agreement on Avoiding Accidental War, the Superpowers pledged themselves to take various measures to ensure that they wouldn't go to war "by mistake." The pact includes provisions for notification in the event of troops being sent into action, of accidents at sea, and, particularly, of accidental launches of nuclear missiles. The treaty was also an admission by the Superpowers that their "fail safe" systems were not necessarily so.

1972: SALT I. The Strategic Arms Limitation Treaty (SALT) between the United States and Russia was a major breakthrough, as it curbed the growth of nuclear weapons. It did not stop that growth, but simply set some limits on how far it could go. The limits were on individual missiles and missile-carrying submarines. There was much suspicion and distrust on both sides, but the treaty went through and was generally obeyed. Both sides dismantled older missiles and subs as new ones increased the number owned to the treaty limits.

1972: ABM Treaty. Along with SALT and the Seabed Treaty, there was agreement to cease deployment of Antiballistic Missile defense. This was a pragmatic deal, as neither the United States nor Russia appeared to be having much success in making these systems work anytime soon. When SDI (Star Wars) came along ten years later, this treaty was essentially broken, at least in principle.

1972: Incidents at Sea Treaty. The Superpowers agreed to observe good manners at, and over, the seas. This was necessary since their ships and aircraft were in the habit of cutting through each other's formations, often leading to dangerous situations, such as collisions.

1972: The Biological and Toxic Weapons Agreement reaffirmed and strengthened the existing ban on such weapons. The agreement does not prevent research into biological and toxic weapons, on the grounds that this is necessary to help develop countermeasures, should someone else use them.

1973: The Agreement on Prevention of Nuclear War was basically a pious gesture that made everyone involved appear devoted to the cause of peace. Its practical effect was as a "confidence building" measure.

1974: The Threshold Test-Ban Treaty was an extension of the Limited Test-Ban Treaty, again between the United States and Russia. Underground explosions were limited to 150 kilotons. Much technical information was to be exchanged to enable compliance on both sides to be monitored, but the information was not exchanged until 1988, leaving the treaty to be upheld on the honor system. Both sides apparently did observe the bans, although technically the treaty has never been properly ratified.

1974: The amendment to the 1972 ABM Treaty extended certain provisions of the original agreement.

1975: The Helsinki Accords were a major watershed in the reduction of tensions and disarmament in Europe, and were the first agreement in which the European neutrals took part. There are essentially three elements: a general agreement on the status of frontiers, an agreement on what constitutes basic human rights, including provision for monitoring compliance, and a complex agreement on advanced notification of military maneuvers and large-scale troop movements, including provision for observers to monitor such activities. Until recently, compliance with the human-rights provisions has been spotty in the Warsaw Pact, but other aspects of the treaty have been meticulously followed by all parties. This has produced an ongoing stream of news stories showing Western officers, and sometimes journalists, wandering around in the midst of Russian and East European military maneuvers. Russian officers were now likewise present at a large number of Western maneuvers. While both sides have previously had satellite photos of these maneuvers and had (in the West) later debriefed defector participants, the presence of observers went a long way toward dispelling the fear of surprise attack. Thus Russian forces became less intimidating as the rigidity and ineptness of Russia's conscript troops were revealed. Also noticeable was the greater efficiency of the East European conscript units. Officers on each side got to know each other, and in general lowered the anxiety and paranoia level.

1976: The Treaty on Peaceful Nuclear Explosions was technically designed to limit the power of nuclear devices used in civil-engineering projects to no more than 150 kilotons. There had been much speculation about using nuclear explosions for port construction, canal building, and the like during the 1950s and 1960s, when the long-term dangers of radiation were not well known. By the seventies, the idea of using nuclear devices for such excavation projects had been dropped. This treaty was really about closing a loophole in the Threshold Test-Ban Treaty. Like that agreement, it has never been ratified, but has been adhered to.

1977: Modifications to the Geneva Convention have occurred with some frequency over the last twenty-five years. Among the provisions concluded in 1977 were one that prohibited children under fifteen from being recruited as soldiers (a proposal to raise the minimum age to eighteen has been under consideration since early 1989). But both Russia and the United

States dawdled over ratifying this treaty, as it also concedes belligerent rights to "freedom fighters." Russia finally gave its assent in mid-1989; the United States has yet to do so.

1977: The Environmental Modification Treaty was intended to prevent deliberate modification of the ecosystem as a military measure, and to improve international awareness of the fragility of the ecosystem. This was another "feel good" treaty, as it is unlikely to change anything that the world's armed forces already plan to do. Environmental modification as a military weapon is largely a science-fiction concept. It has been done on a small scale in the form of deforestation for thousands of years. Ancient armies were known to burn areas covering hundreds of square miles, or divert rivers to flood huge areas; The Americans' use of Agent Orange to destroy vegetation in Vietnam is only the most recent example. This treaty has larger modifications in mind, although it may be used to beat any combatant over the head for the least form of environmental modification. The U.S.—and Iraq—haven't ratified this yet.

1979: The Security of Nuclear Materials Treaty was necessitated by increasing incidents of theft and "loss" of nuclear materials, including weapons-grade plutonium. Despite the agreement, the problem persists, particularly in the West. This treaty provided a basis for international cooperation in tracking down and stopping illegal transfers of nuclear materials. Thus far, there has not been much action in halting this trade. Like drugs, where there's a market, there are money and suppliers.

1979: SALT II, a follow-on to SALT I, had been in the works since the earlier treaty. But the era of good feeling which had existed in the early seventies was over, largely as a result of a Russian buildup in conventional arms during the mid-seventies. What made SALT II particularly tricky was that it attempted to cover missiles that had multiple warheads (MIRVed missiles). While you could count missiles by seeing their silos or submarine carriers, such was not the case with MIRVs. The United States was ahead in MIRV technology, so Russia saw MIRV restraint in their best interest. The United States knew that Russia was working furiously trying to catch up in the MIRV area and was not about to trust their promises about which missiles had MIRVs and how many warheads were in each missile. While the treaty was signed, the U.S. Congress was not willing to ratify it, particularly after the Russian invasion of Afghanistan in 1980. Although not ratifying SALT II, the Superpowers have more or less adhered to its terms.

1980: The Draft Protocol Concerning Nondetectable Fragments bans wounding agents—bullets and such—that cannot be located by X rays. Only a draft, this is not technically in force, and so has technically not been violated by Russia, which used plastic fragmentation devices in Afghanistan.

1980: In the Nuclear Materials Convention, the Superpowers agreed to take better care of potentially dangerous materials, a definition that was extended to include certain technologies that could be used to produce weapons-grade nuclear materials.

1984: The Stockholm European Security Conference was essentially a reaffirmation of the terms of the 1976 Helsinki Accords, with some modifications and extensions of the military provisions.

1987: The INF Treaty was a breakthrough agreement between the United States and Russia. The Intermediate Nuclear Forces affected (medium-range nuclear missiles) were actually eliminated. Another breakthrough was the implementation of extensive on-site inspection to ensure compliance. The inspection periods extend to the turn of the century. These inspection procedures provided a precedent for a similar approach on MIRVed missiles. This gave life to the START (Strategic Arms Limitation Treaty, or "SALT III") talks.

1987: Nuclear Risk Reduction Centers Treaty. Each Superpower agreed to establish a unified national center to handle all notification requirements mandated under the various existing agreements. This was one example of how disarmament can actually increase bureaucracy and expenses.

1988: The Ballistic Missile Notification Agreement requires the Superpowers to inform each other of test firings of ballistic missiles.

1989: The Declaration of Paris put 149 nations on record as being committed to the definitive abolition of chemical weapons. The problem is that no one is really certain how to go about it.

1989: The Treaty on Prevention of Dangerous Military Activities was sparked partially by incidents such as the Soviet downing of a Korean airliner in the early 1980s. Under its terms, each side agrees to refrain from the use of force in case of accidental border incursion by the other's forces, to refrain from using potentially blinding laser devices to scan the other's forces, and to establish special procedures when the forces of both are operating in potentially explosive areas, such as the Persian Gulf in recent years. In addition, the powers agree not to jam or otherwise interfere with each other's military communications in peacetime. This was a unique treaty in several ways, not least because it was negotiated directly by the top U.S. and Russian military brass. A month after it was signed, the pact was put to the test. A Russian MiG-23 took off from a Polish base and ran into engine trouble; the pilot ejected. But the aircraft's engine problem cleared up and it continued flying for 500 miles until it ran out of fuel and crashed in Belgium. The pilotless MiG was spotted by NATO radar and intercepted and escorted for most of its flight path by a pair of F-15s. There was never any notification from Russia that one of their MiG-23s was missing and headed west. Apparently the Russians lost track of the plane, thinking it had veered off and crashed into the Baltic. Gives one pause about the efficacy of Russian defenses. The Russians agreed to pay damages, and apologized to boot.

1990: In the Treaty on Soviet Forces in Germany, the Russians agreed to evacuate all their forces from German soil, while the then West German government undertook to underwrite the expenses of relocating and rehousing the troops. This was a follow-on agreement to a pact among the former occupying powers (United States, Russia, Britain, and France), not to oppose German reunification.

1990: MBFR/CAFE Treaty. Provided for major reductions of conventional forces in Europe.

NOTABLE DISARMAMENT EFFORTS THAT FAILED

While many ambitious disarmament agreements fail in their purpose, let us not forget all those major disarmament proposals that failed even before they got to the negotiating table. One of the more notable in this genre was the Baruch Plan, offered by the United States in 1946, when it had a monopoly on nuclear weapons. This initiative proposed to entrust all nuclear weapons to the UN, as well as all the technology required to build them. The UN would henceforth control nuclear-weapons technology. Russia proposed a similar plan, but refused to allow any inspections within its borders. The Baruch Plan was passed by the UN, but was killed by a Russian veto. A similar fate befell President Eisenhower's "Open Skies" proposal, which would have permitted Soviet overflight of U.S. territory, in exchange for the same privilege over Russia, so that each country could assure itself that the other wasn't planning anything untoward. The Russians called it a cover for "espionage," and the matter died, though recently, in the light of the increasingly friendly relations between the United States and Russia there has been talk of actually implementing Eisenhower's nearly forty-year-old proposal. In the meantime, satellite reconnaissance has largely achieved what Eisenhower proposed. Current negotiations are working toward expanding the INF Treaty provisions that put human observers in each other nation's weapons factories. Ike would be pleased.

An unusual failure in disarmament took place in 1927, when a second naval-disarmament conference met at Geneva. This came a cropper on the question of the limits that should be placed on the number of cruisers that the United States and Britain should be allowed to have. Britain held out for seventy. The United States felt that this number was excessive, due mostly to budgetary considerations: The higher figure would compel her to spend money on new construction. Although this conference was a failure, negotiations continued, which resulted in the more successful 1930 London Conference.

Among less significant disarmament efforts that have failed, we may note the 1974 Ayachucho Conference, in which the principal South American powers attempted to end their 150-year-old arms race by a "freeze" of forces at their current levels: The effort clashed with nearly everyone's ambition to have "sufficient" military power to meet any possible "threat."

Living with the Problem: What Can Be Done, Item by Item

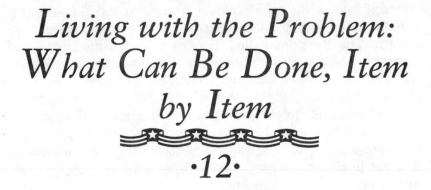

·12·

"**S**hooting blanks" will not disappear anytime soon. At least we ought to recognize the problem for what it is. However, armed with the knowledge of what the problems are and how they work, there are steps we can take to minimize their effects.

What follows offers some choices, some encouragement, and some possible views of a more realistic future. Some of these suggestions may seem simplistic. Many are likely to appear to be little more than common sense. And a few may seem outlandish. Most have been found to work in someone's defense establishment, while those that have not been tried seem worthy of consideration. Suggestions are listed in order of the five causes of shooting blanks we have used throughout the book.

INTELLIGENCE CONFUSION

Having the wrong information, or misinterpreting good data, is the most common cause of wars, and is an especially important factor in losing wars. Overcoming these problems requires one to go straight to the primary causes of this confusion. Intelligence agencies have to make some changes.

1. Open Up.

If they want to build user confidence in what they do, intelligence services can't operate in the dark all the time. Opening up is a tricky business that intelligence people would prefer to avoid, but in a democracy you have to put a lot of your cards on the table if you want to stay out of trouble. Even Communist intelligence and security organizations are beginning to take a lot of heat domestically. Being more open about what they are doing, how they are doing it, and what the results are would make the work of intelligence agencies more reliable and useful to dubious citizens and decision makers.

In October of 1962, some intelligence officers tried to dissuade President John F. Kennedy from publishing reconnaissance photos of the Russian missile sites under construction in Cuba, fearing that this would reveal the sophistication of our reconnaissance operations. Kennedy overruled them, and the photos proved immensely useful in securing support from our Allies, who were concerned that the whole affair was merely a ploy to find an excuse for ousting Castro. In contrast, few people were convinced when the Reagan administration accused Libya of sending death squads after various American officials in the early eighties, largely because the president's "We know" didn't constitute very reliable evidence. The trick is to reveal information without endangering the source, particularly human sources who can easily be put at risk, which may have been the problem in the case of the Libyan "hit men." But we must recognize that in order for our information to be useful we must at times reveal it. Indeed, in many ways there are too many secrets, most of which need not be. Edward Teller, "the Father of the H-Bomb," once remarked, "I wish I could tell you about this. The Russians know it, we know it, and they know we know it. About the only ones who don't know it are the American people."

A lot of secrets don't really do very much good, like the timing of spy satellite launchings, and some are downright silly, like the occasional barring of the public from space-shuttle landings. Excessive secrecy only leads to disbelief, and frequently corruption. Oddly enough, there are already a lot of secret and sensitive data being released, although it is done to further partisan political goals. Rarely is anyone punished for this, unless they do it for strictly financial gain. Note also the enormous difference between the amount of intelligence released in the West versus the piddling amounts revealed in the Eastern bloc nations. Western intelligence capabilities have not disappeared as a result, although many argue that they have been damaged. The trend, over the last few decades, has been toward more openness. This has not put the intelligence people out of business and has kept them out of a lot of trouble. There should be more openness.

2. Sympathy for the Devil.

The intelligence agencies themselves can do a lot of public-relations work to make the public (and many intelligence users) aware of the tricky conditions under which they operate and the many limitations of the data they produce. The James Bond and "dirty tricks" image has not helped, particularly when most intelligence operatives have more in common with university academics than libidinous assassins. Intelligence agencies might consider encouraging their analysts to write more frequently for the popular press. While this will cause more work for the internal-review people (censors), the gains in public respect should far outweigh this cost.

3. Depoliticize Intelligence.

Because politicians approve budgets and control careers, intelligence has become a bloody partisan battlefield. Intelligence agencies are regularly caught up in domestic political machinations. We expect this in totalitarian nations, where most intelligence assets are used against domestic opponents. But democracies are incapable of avoiding the temptation either.

The great secrecy that pervades intelligence operations enables government officials and politicians, including the president, to extract confidential information from the intelligence agencies and use it to further highly partisan political goals, such as promoting pet projects or killing someone else's, or merely getting reelected. J. Edgar Hoover, the longtime head of the FBI, the United States' principal internal-security service, routinely traded information with politicians to maintain his, and the FBI's, power. Some of this information was used for extortion and blackmail. Money was rarely involved, but political favors were.

Most of the information passed and used for political purposes is low-powered stuff. The occasional high-powered use of secret information in politics tends to bring the house down and send all concerned scurrying for cover. Yet even before the dust settles, the low-powered trade in secrets is back in operation. The intelligence agencies cannot afford to offend the people who appropriate their budget and approve their promotions. As a result, they do not operate at peak efficiency. An autonomous oversight system, with Congress and the president exercising indirect, instead of direct, control over promotions and the like might greatly improve the intelligence service's ability to get across unpleasant realities. Consider the Federal Reserve System as a possible model, with a "board of directors" composed of retired senior political leaders, academics, diplomats, and military personnel, and perhaps even presidents and Supreme Court justices.

4. Get Organized.

Senior American military and civilian intelligence users increasingly complain of the duplication of effort and unreliability of the output of the enormous U.S. intelligence establishment. Part of the problem is that there are so many organizations, and too many of them serve one master a bit too slavishly. For example, the different branches of the armed forces each have considerable intelligence operations. The army, navy, and air force all require many bits of intelligence that are, in theory, common to them all as each service needs up-to-date appraisals of foreign armed forces and national capabilities. Yet as each of these separate intelligence organizations produces its own studies on these subjects, they don't all come to the same conclusion. Many of these studies appear to be quite different. Curiously, the army studies all seem to indicate that more U.S. ground forces are needed to deal with the situation. The air force concludes that more aircraft are needed, and naval intelligence tends to see the situation as one that could be best handled with additional U.S. warships. One doesn't have to see too many of these studies to conclude that someone, perhaps everyone, is off base. Compounding the problem is a lack of attention to areas that do require investigation. For example, for many decades the threat of a major war with Russia concentrated a disproportionate amount of intelligence on the NATO/Warsaw Pact and Superpower confrontation. Yet most of the wars, including Vietnam, Iraq, Afghanistan, and Korea, were the products of political and economic developments that received inadequate attention from the major intelligence agencies. The effectiveness of intelligence agencies would be vastly improved if their parochial blinders could be removed.

AMATEURISM AND THE RIGHT STUFF

For some reason, the ancient admonition "Know thyself" is very difficult advice to follow. There are some seemingly simple methods that may help improve our capabilities and our understanding of them, as well as of those of our potential opponents.

1. Look at the Record.

Nations, like individuals, have personalities and habits. This is particularly true in warfare. Never mind the win/lose ratio, look at the way people fight their wars. Get down to the details and plot the trends. You will find that nations are remarkably consistent from decade to decade and even century to century. Taking a close look at the historical record will reveal much about a nation's future prospects on the battlefield. Just remember to maintain a healthy respect for the possibility of unexpected, but perfectly normal, changes in the basic pattern. Studying the past will show you a pattern of performance, not a timetable of future events. The United States Civil War or World War II are more important guides to American determination and endurance in a crisis than is Vietnam; Stalingrad is more useful in assessing Russian resilience than is Afghanistan. The results of this study will not always be flattering to the subjects: We tend to forget disasters and play up the glorious triumphs. Any future wars will contain plenty of both.

2. Don't Let the Old Soldiers Fade Away.

Combat experience is highly perishable. There aren't that many wars. When the fighting stops, most of the troops flee back to civilian life, eager to forget the horrors of combat. Those combat veterans who stay in uniform are a valuable resource. They know what it's like to be shot at, and they know what the current armed forces are like. These old soldiers are one of the few links peacetime troops have to the realities of the battlefield. Unfortunately, the combat-experienced officers rise in the hierarchy to a position far removed from the one they occupied in combat. A wartime platoon leader has a hard time applying that experience years later as a peacetime battalion or division commander. NCOs don't rise too far from their wartime posts. Your combat private will, twenty years later, be a platoon sergeant or company first sergeant. These guys are still close to the action. Yet it is the officers who are considered the experts. Some senior officers do maintain a useful perspective on the battlefield. But far more of the combat experienced NCOs will know what it's all about.

This raises an interesting proposition. What if officers and NCOs were brought together regularly with veterans who commanded at the same level as that in which they are themselves serving? The "old warriors" could tell the peacetime troops quite a lot about what really goes on in combat, and they would do it from the same perspective. It's true that a World War II–era squad leader would now be seventy years old, but he would find much in common with today's twenty-two-year-old squad leader. This is done, to a limited extent, in some nations with good results. Russia, in particular, considers its Afghanistan combat veterans a precious resource. The Russians also routinely trot out their World War II vets for bull sessions with the troops. The British paratroopers do much the same thing. Lieutenant General Sir John Frost, who led the 2nd Parachute Battalion in its heroic defense of the "Bridge Too Far" at Arnhem in September of 1944, regularly descends on his old outfit to tell it like it was, and was there at dockside when the Paras sailed for the Falklands. The U.S. Army does this to a limited extent, organizing conferences in which German and Russian veterans of World War II participate, but curiously neglects its American counterparts.

Another useful device might be to organize seminars among junior officers in which the memoirs of their counterparts in previous conflicts are read and discussed. World War II was very rich in company-officer writings, many of which contain invaluable tips and suggestions, lessons that lieutenants and captains have had to relearn in every war. Nor should fiction be neglected, since such classics as Ernest Hemingway's *A Farewell to Arms,* Erich Maria Remarque's *All Quiet on the Western Front,* Henri Barbusse's *Under Fire,* and Norman Mailer's *The Naked and the Dead* were written by veterans who had something to say about men in war.

3. Keep the Historians Busy.

History is one way to keep the experience of war fresh. Heavy doses of analytic and narrative history, both the "classic" and the contemporary, should be a required part of the education of all officers, at all levels, to keep alive the "flavor" of combat and develop an understanding of the creative thinking that is so important a factor in military success. The Marine Corps already does this, with a "recommended reading list" for officers and NCOs. That's a step in the right direction, even though it wasn't instituted until 1989.

In addition, distinguished military historians should be recognized, utilized, and rewarded. To some extent, this is being done, and the American armed forces now have special chairs for visiting professors of military history at many institutions. But this is not enough. Younger historians, including officers, should be encouraged to specialize in the field. And while more recent conflicts have been the object of a revival in military history, many periods in the long and sorry history of war are generally neglected in the education of officers. Some of this is due to the assumption that technology has so altered the conduct of war that nothing can be learned from studying the Scipios or Marlborough, but they were among the most successful soldiers of all time, brilliantly creative strategists and tacticians. Not a little of this neglect of the past is due to a kind of arrogance that assumes nothing can be learned from the operations of, for example, Serbia's Radomir Putnik during his campaigns of 1912–15, because although he won spectacular victories, his army was small, and the campaigns insignificant and conducted against ineffective foes. Yet these were daring operations, skillfully executed in the face of greatly superior numbers. This attitude is common among U.S. officers, less so in other Western nations and quite different from the intensive historical studies Russian officers are exposed to. As Napoleon said, "Study the campaigns."

4. The Medium Is the Message.

Recognize a vital factor of modern life, the TV generation. It's not enough to stress history, it should be "packaged" in a format that contemporary troops will readily absorb. The use of film should be promoted. Such noted documentaries as *The Battle of San Pietro* and the German training films *Engineers to the Front* and *Men Against Tanks* give a brutally realistic picture of war. Film archives should be combed for the sort of footage that cannot be shown publicly for fear of offending someone's sensibilities, such as the grisly sequence of a French regiment stacking its dead after an abortive assault in 1915. There are also many commercial films that can make essential points about war and leadership, such as *Gallipoli, The Battle of Culloden, Paths of Glory, Das Boot, Platoon, Glory, The Bridge,* and even *Henry V.*

5. Resort to Technology.

The introduction of large-scale "laser tag" training techniques for U.S. combat units in the early 1980s is a step in the right direction. This system, which uses lasers in place of weapons and an array of sensors on men and equipment, accurately re-created the effects of enemy fire and impressed the troops enough to change their approach to training and combat. Ironically, this more realistic training also exposed defects in officer training and selection. Many officers were found to be unable to cope with combat conditions, while others were so intent on being successful in these "battles" that they cheated by ignoring the electronic alarms that went off when they were "hit" by a laser beam. Ironically, the laser-tag experience, particularly the large-scale exercises at the U.S. National Training Center (NTC), have had a more significant effect on the troops, who see all too clearly that their officers are often not up to the task of leading them in combat. Moreover, the hundreds of battalion engagements at NTC during the past decade have not made U.S. officers noticeably more proficient (at least according to the won-lost record). But the results of the NTC experience are percolating upward in the army hierarchy. Similar exercises in the navy and air force are also having their effect at the Pentagon. The senior commanders cannot ignore the fact that their officers and troops are not as well-prepared for combat as was previously thought. Change is in the wind, and this is a unique event for a peacetime armed forces.

Other Western nations are adopting the laser-tag technology, and some have even made interesting improvements in it. The Russians, who are aware of serious deficiencies in their training techniques, are trying to assemble their own scattered laser-tag gear in one place for large-scale exercises, but are having trouble with senior brass who are resisting more realistic training. (It's expensive and could be embarrassing.) Use of "laser tag" maneuvers, computerized models, and manual war games should be extended. Efforts are under way to deploy realistic interactive videos using multiple terminals with several players. Not surprisingly, America is leading the way in this area, but there is much more to be done.

6. Establish a General Services Staff Branch.

Many of the housekeeping functions of the armed forces should be unified. There is not much practical reason to maintain three separate Medical Corps, Nurses' Corps, Chaplains' Corps, Finance Corps, and so on. The Marine Corps, which is effectively a separate branch of the service, gets along fine with the navy supplying its administrative needs. Even the medics in marine units are actually sailors in marine uniforms. Genuine differences in the particular requirements of each service could be met by improved training, individual specialization, and the introduction of more uniform procedures. A General Services Staff branch would eliminate duplication of effort, lower costs, and reduce personnel somewhat due to centralization of administrative overhead. It should be noted, however, that this would be extremely difficult to implement, as the different services have two centuries of separateness and no desire to surrender any of this independence to an interservice General Staff. There is also the national antipathy toward centralized military control. Most Americans are descended from immigrants who fled nations terrorized by General Staffs and/or military dictatorships. Nevertheless, the General Staff idea is not completely dead, and something may eventually come of it.

7. Stress the Special Status of Combat Troops.

Currently, all troops get the same expensive benefits, particularly the twenty-year pension. This pension was originally instituted in recognition of the destructive physical effects of even peacetime soldiering in the combat arms. But today, only a small fraction of the troops are in the combat arms and exposed to these risks. With everyone getting the same benefits you are, in effect, discriminating against the combat troops, who expose themselves to much more discomfort and danger during the rigors of peacetime training. This causes a lot of experienced combat arms officers, and especially NCOs, to get into noncombat jobs later in their careers. The more older NCOs you have in combat units, the more effective those units will be. But after twenty years of hard soldiering in such units, many NCOs head for the easier life of a noncombat job, or get out on pension. The solution is to recognize the differences in some financial sense. Proposals have been made in the past that give the troops with the nastiest jobs more money, while making noncombat troops wait longer than twenty years before they are eligible for half-pay retirement. Aside from the financial fairness of such arrangements, the combat troops get a big morale boost by having their additional sacrifices recognized.

8. Stress the Quality of Military Leadership.

Leadership is the particular bane of peacetime armed forces. America has always found itself with a number of excellent military leaders when it goes to war, so that's not the problem. The problem is that there are always too many inept commanders when the shooting starts. These are the people who lose the early battles and get a lot of troops needlessly killed or maimed. There are several things that can be done to improve leader quality in peacetime:

- *Identify and Recognize the Leaders.* In this century, military operations have become much more noncombat activities than ever in the past. This has brought about an emphasis on management at the expense of leadership. While good managers are rare, they are easier to identify than those who can handle the chaos of combat, and easier to supervise too, since the efforts of these officers can be more readily seen in peacetime. Battlefield leaders are difficult to pinpoint without a battlefield experience to separate the real ones from those who wish they were. Moreover, real combat leaders are normally not the sort of people you might want to have around in peacetime, because they're unruly, or slovenly, or unpleasant: the Grants, the Pattons, and the Stonewall Jacksons. When the shooting starts, the side with the larger number of these leaders and warriors in place will carry the day. If you can't find good people to fight the war, bad ones will. The use of more realistic training (as in the laser-tag maneuvers) and profiles of successful combat leaders from previous wars provides opportunities to identify the good combat leaders.
- *Support Higher Pay for Officers and NCOs.* This will not ensure there won't be incompetents, but it will help keep the abler officers and NCOs around. Many things encourage the more capable people to leave the service, and the opportunity to get paid more for their talents is one of them. After all, you get what you pay for. When you lose too many good people, the mediocre types predominate and create a mediocre standard of performance.
- *Make Company Commanders Majors.* The British have been doing this for many years, with a captain as executive officer. This means that there is less need to transfer officers away from their units upon promotion, while providing a more experienced officer in charge. After all, combat is the most desperate, chaotic, and difficult task the military must handle. Company commanders are the highest-ranking officers who regularly get caught up in this end of

the business. You need all the experience and seasoning you can get in your company commanders.
• *Cross-Assign Officers.* At least once in their career, officers should be assigned to duty with one of the other services for a year or so, either in their own specialty or in a staff position. This does not mean an extension of the so-called "joint service" duty now mandatory for flag rank, which merely requires that a flag candidate must have served on a mixed-services staff. We mean put that naval aviator in an air-force cockpit or let an army infantry officer serve with a marine rifle company for a year. This would improve their understanding of the capabilities and limitations of the other services.
• *Encourage and Humor the Warriors.* The Vikings recognized that some men got high on combat. These individuals were called "Berserkers," and were put up front where they could do their fellows the most good, and were recognized for their fanatical skill in battle. These people were not good life-insurance risks, but neither is anyone else on the battlefield. Studies have shown that your modern Berserker actually survives longer on the battlefield than his more timid kin. Ask anyone who has been in combat, and he will tell you of at least one "natural" warrior he knew. Ace fighter pilots are of this breed, but all forms of combat have them. The basic problem is that these natural warriors are not easily recognized or identified in peacetime. Moreover, warriors are hard to handle in peacetime. Troops who are at home in battle are equally likely to brawl and raise hell in general during peacetime soldiering. This leads to many warriors being kicked out of the peacetime military. Many officers and NCOs maintain the fiction that "nice" troops are preferable no matter what the cost in combat effectiveness. Nevertheless, wartime studies show that there *are* warrior-type personalities out there, and all too frequently they are not discovered until the shooting starts. By then it is often too late to reorganize the combat units to best use the warriors. Those units that survive their first few battles largely intact (many are wiped out) reorganize themselves around the warriors. Many officers, in effect, turn operational control of their units over to the warrior type NCOs when in combat. When the shooting

stops, these same insightful officers take special care to keep their warriors from getting locked up because of rear-area mischief.

Many nations try to corral such enthusiasm into elite combat units like paratroopers and commandos, but this does not solve the problem of the warriors left in regular units. Special units also do not address all the problems with warrior officers, who may be smoother articles but still nonconformist and troublesome. The most vexing problem is actually identifying the battlefield warriors. It usually takes one to know one, so the longer you are at peace, the harder it is to even separate the warriors from the rest of the crowd.

• *Foster Greater Officer/Enlisted Cohesion.* New officers should go through basic training with new enlisted personnel, thus giving them a "worm's-eye view" of the business. In the past, some armed forces, such as the German Army, required a tour in the ranks for all officer candidates, a practice that Israel has adopted. The results have certainly been impressive, but even more could be done. The United States has, since the late 1980s, encouraged ROTC (college-based officer training) candidates to join a local reserve unit and go through basic and advanced infantry training with the enlisted troops. This will pay large dividends in combat.

In several armies, such as the British, officers and enlisted personnel opting for Special Forces, such as airborne or commandos, take training together regardless of rank. The Irish, British, and Australians encourage officers and enlisted men to engage in athletic competitions together, or to take part in special activities, such as mountain climbing, underwater archaeological explorations, or tropical expeditions, which forge strong personal bonds of respect and loyalty, while helping to promote unit cohesion. In contrast, the Russians, as part of a long-standing tradition, discourage too much familiarity between the officers and troops. While this tradition abated a lot during World War II, it came back and stayed after 1945.

9. Enhance Unit Cohesion.

Stop paying lip service to "unit cohesion" and start doing something about it. While individual talents and capabilities are important, how well the troops operate as a team makes the biggest difference in combat. Most nations with a military tradition recognize this. America, for most of this century, has not. But "unit integrity" is coming back into fashion and should be emphasized. These are several things that can be done to accomplish this:

• *Remember the Regiment.* The largely paper existence of institutional regiments in the U.S. Army should be exploited. Genuinely distinctive traditions, customs, anniversaries, and insignia should be established to link the several battalions of each regiment together and tie the troops in with the historical achievements of their predecessors, which could be enhanced by special honors to famous former members of the unit.

• *Keep Combat Units Together.* This is not easy, but can be done. Volunteer armies, like the British or American, lose about half their first-term enlistees after three or four years. But new recruits could be trained in special depots detailed to support the battalions of a particular parent regiment, so that early on they are imbued with the traditions and history of the regiment, while being trained by, and with, the men alongside whom they will serve, which would give them a closer identity with the unit to which they will eventually be assigned. In addition, enlisted men and officers are moved around too much, in order to attend various schools, to serve as recruiters, to work on staffs, or due to promotions. Instead, institute a number of changes that would keep these people with the same units for most of their careers. Somehow it has been forgotten that there have been some very capable armed forces that employed NCOs and officers who spent twenty years running an infantry company or an engine room on a ship. Here, the United States might well emulate the British. Rather than transfer personnel to schools and staff assignments, they should be "seconded" to such posts, temporarily detached from their unit, to which they will eventually return. This simple change enables the individual to identify with "his" (or "her") battalion, ship, or squadron no matter where they are or what they're doing. If rotation of personnel is necessary, send the troops to the other battalions of their regiment or to its training depot.

• *Institute Territorial Recruiting.* The British have been doing this for centuries, as has the United States National Guard. Establish recruiting areas for units and assign locally recruited personnel to them as much as possible. This may mean that in wartime you have to take the heat from politicians if the local boys suffer heavy casualties, but the advantages in morale, recruiting, and effectiveness would be worth it.

10. Maximize Personnel Utilization.

So-called "up or out" policies, which require officers who fail to be promoted to retire, should be reexamined. Many officers who may not qualify for higher rank may be perfectly competent in their present jobs. Also, there should be some flexibility about mandatory retirement provisions: In wartime, it has not been unknown for infantry companies to be ably led by fifty-five-year-old NCOs, but the rules as they are would not allow a captain or major to continue in the service at such an age, regardless of ability. This is one reason why good NCOs are so crucial. Whether in a volunteer or a conscript force, any first-term trooper who qualifies for reenlistment is probably NCO material and willing to stick with "his" unit for the rest of his career. So NCOs are the one class of leader who are most likely to settle down and do a good job at one thing for many years. Throughout history, many of the most successful armed forces promoted former enlisted personnel right up through battalion commander. In other words, a capable recruit would climb through a few NCO ranks, be made a junior officer, and eventually become a lieutenant colonel commanding the battalion. Battalion commanders of this type are priceless on the battlefield.

11. Pay for the Training.

Training is honored more as a desirable concept than an expensive reality. Training *is* expensive. Taking a division out for a week of field exercises can cost millions of dollars. Shooting off a lot of expensive weapons can cost millions more. Ships and aircraft are even more expensive to operate regularly enough to give the troops an edge. The big problem is political. The payoff of large training expenses only shows up in wartime. During peace, training expenses are simply expenses. Worse yet, troops are hurt and killed during training, making for even more political fallout. We must pay the cost, and reap large savings in lives on the battlefield.

12. Don't Forget SNAFU.

Soldiers have long recognized that war and combat arc chaotic and unpredictable businesses. During World War II, this phenomenon was given a name: SNAFU ("Situation Normal, All Fucked Up"). In a quite understandable desire to bring order out of chaos and do better next time, the role of SNAFU is played down in studying past wars and preparing for the next one. This is a grievous and expensive error. It goes against human nature to dwell on SNAFU and accept its inevitable presence in any future war. This is particularly true with organizations, as many of the troops (with or without combat experience) sense that things aren't going to proceed according to plan. SNAFU cannot be conquered, but you can be alert to its possibilities, and thus be better at coping with it than the other fellow. That alone is a significant battlefield advantage.

MEDIA MUDDLE

Although the media are, among other things, supposed to serve up the news, this function is submerged by entertainment in the democracies or propaganda in the dictatorships. Despite this substantial handicap, there are some positive steps that can be taken to lessen the damage the media version of the news does to world peace.

1. *Educate the Journalists.*

Most journalists assigned to cover the military have no specific preparation for this daunting task. Those who did serve have some knowledge of what's going on, at least as far as their experience in a specific branch went; but by and large, the reporters are on their own. This leads to a lot of misunderstanding and misinterpretation by the reporters, and a lot of misinformation gets passed on to their audience. Much of the confusion could be eliminated if the armed forces provided thorough and regular training courses on just what the military is all about. These sessions could not be very long, as the reporters' employers would not want their people tied up in nonproductive tasks, and could be modeled on the "familiarization" courses that the armed forces had for journalists in the Second World War, or that they presently hold for civilian professors assigned to teach military history in conjunction with ROTC programs. One important change would be to have the familiarization courses run by officers, NCOs, and troops from operational units. Using the public-affairs officers would not work, as these people also have an unsteady idea of what actually goes on in the "real" army (or navy or air force). A week or two of such familiarization would pay big dividends in terms of better understanding.

2. *Educate the Audience.*

This is tougher than educating the journalists. Keen interest in military affairs is a minority activity among the general population. The best that can be hoped for initially is more accurate reporting by the media, although the military itself would do well to provide accurate, clear publications defining the official position. Items like the Department of Defense's annual *Soviet Military Power* are a step in the right direction. However, publications like this are still prone to attempts at manipulating the issues in the face of contrary evidence. If the military is going to compete in the public market for ideas, it cannot afford to shoot blanks.

3. Be Up-Front.

A policy of being open and apolitical about things like the East-West military balance, procurement blunders, accidents, and everything else would serve the long-term interests of the military better than trying to slant the data at every opportunity to try to make the military look good (particularly when the facts are otherwise). And it would help if, from time to time, the armed forces reminded the public that they are not perfectly oiled, smooth-running war machines, that SNAFU is an ancient military tradition. The truth works, even when it hurts.

4. Encourage Military Journalists.

There are many good writers in the ranks. Although the military tends to keep a tight rein on troops who write for civilian publications, they could lighten up a bit and encourage this activity more. If civilian publications were able to make greater use of uniformed contributors, the quality and accuracy of military reporting would increase substantially.

THE PROCUREMENT PUZZLE

Problems in military procurement are ancient and intractable. We can't give you much hope other than to point out that there is a potential for progress.

1. Reform the Reforms.

For as far back as the historical records go, you find corruption and ineptitude in weapons procurement. Efforts to reform the process have an equally long pedigree, which has mostly led to more, or different kinds of, abuses, while in turn adding additional layers of bureaucracy and paperwork to the process, further driving up costs. Something new is needed. Reforming the military-procurement process is an ongoing activity in most nations. Many nations solve the problem, after a fashion, by making arms manufacturers state-owned enterprises. This creates operations that are less efficient than privately owned companies but subject to a lot less of the usual corruption. Other nations import most of their weapons. In fact, all nations, including Russia, import some weapons or weapons components. Unfortunately, this provides more opportunities for shady dealings. The major cause of all this is that, unlike commercial goods, weapons can't really be adequately tested in anything short of combat, and most military procurement reform efforts stumble over this issue. Part of the reason is intractable: There is no easy way to replicate the stress and unpredictability of combat. Even lesser solutions, such as shooting at new systems with live ammunition to see how robust they are, fall prey to cost problems. Increasingly, new and complex weapons systems are considered too expensive to expend in such tests. Yet as untried technology plays an increasingly vital role in a weapon's effectiveness, it becomes ever more essential to find ways of testing it adequately. This is not to say that effective weapons are not currently produced. But the current system achieves its eventual battlefield success by adding a numbing, and costly, array of features to the weapons. In wartime, the weapons designers can quickly learn what is needed and what is not. The breakthrough in procurement reform will thus come when a way is found to develop and test weapons possessing only what is needed. The past attempts at reform have been quite dismal at solving the problem. New solutions have to be devised and tried. Reformers have to keep at it until something is found that works.

2. Create a "Procurement Officer" Career Option.

Currently, in the U.S. armed forces, a new weapons project is assigned a "project manager," an officer who will oversee things for a year or two before moving on to another post. There are two problems here. The first is that with development projects taking as many as a dozen years to see fruition, this procedure does not provide for much continuity in project oversight. Every year or two there's another project manager who has to learn the ropes from the ground up. And what project manager, considering his career prospects, is likely to blow the whistle on "his" program? More likely, he will jolly his superiors along, talk about "technical difficulties," and pray reassigment comes before the whole project collapses. While military officers are selected and trained to be leaders and managers, procurement is a business, and this requires additional skills beyond mere leadership and management. Many military officers do retire and go on to successful business careers. Identifying these potential business types and offering them attractive careers in procurement would make the operation more effective. Many European nations use variations of this approach successfully. This system is particularly effective if you put these future procurement officers into combat units early in their careers where they can see what the troops are really up against.

3. Shrink the Pie.

Nations have long known that the simplest way to deal with procurement problems is to simply make less money available. Also, get Congress out of the minutiae of procurement, so it can concentrate on matters of policy and decide how much we can afford to spend. Then let the brass decide who gets what. This has worked in the past. As if by magic, previously "must have" spending levels disappear as generals and admirals quickly find out how to get by on a lot less. Necessity begets imagination, and solutions are found to the problems of building better weapons for less money. President Eisenhower used this technique for a time, basically telling the Joint Chiefs that he would allocate them a particular sum of money in his forthcoming budget and that they had to figure out how to share it among themselves. It worked pretty well, as the JCS had to apportion the money without being able to lobby various Cabinet members and legislators. This approach is tricky. After all, Eisenhower was a respected and experienced military man, and was thus less likely to be the victim of energetic lobbying by his admirals and generals. Most politicians don't have that insulation. So the brass tries to get around such proposals by hustling Congress and even the president. And sometimes a dispirited military will simply cut back across the board and go to seed. But it doesn't always happen that way, and because of this there is hope.

4. Stick to the Point.

Whatever the project, go for an appropriate technology, even if it isn't necessarily high tech. Promote systematic, incremental research-and-development projects over those that look for "breakthroughs," which are likely to prove elusive and expensive. Once a project has been defined, stick to it; don't add any new capabilities or requirements. Above all, avoid panic in procurement projects. Panic is easier to avoid in wartime procurement projects, when combat experience is available to settle disputes. Also, since there's a lot of urgency to get the damned stuff to the troops as quickly as possible, there's much less temptation to delay a new weapons project so that it can be made "even better." Only strong leadership can solve these problems in peacetime, and you can't legislate strong leadership.

5. Let the Market Decide.

Foster competition in procurement, and reward contracts on a genuinely competitive basis. In addition, manufacturers should be required to guarantee that their products work as specified, with real penalties for failure. This has been shown to work whenever it has been tried, even for exotic items. Defense suppliers nearly always become more expensive when they are the only source for an item. If there is competition, the item price comes down quite a ways, and very quickly too. As if by magic.

6. Really Reform Procurement Contracting.

Lots of major industrial firms, such as AT&T, seem to manage their procurement far more efficiently than does the Department of Defense. Exploit their expertise. Model DoD procurement contracts more closely on those used in private industry. Institute real penalties for failure to fulfill contractual provisions. Create a procurement oversight commission composed of successful executives, former members of Congress and government officials, retired military personnel, journalists, and professional muckrakers who have the authority, staff, and resources to investigate contract fulfillment.

7. Bar Retired Officer Employment by Defense Contractors.

Too many retired military personnel find a second career in the very defense firms with which they formerly had to deal as representatives of the armed forces. There has been more than a suggestion that favors were exchanged in a number of instances, and even where the jobs were offered and accepted in a wholly open and aboveboard fashion, the appearance of corruption is so great as to deepen public cynicism about defense procurement. Such a measure would close an important employment track for former officers, but alternative second-career tracks would open if several of the other proposals for the utilization of retired personnel are adopted.

8. Effective Internal Auditors.

Some form of independent oversight is needed. Among notable suggestions is that retired officers, or officers nearing retirement, be assigned, as civilian employees, to such oversight activities for the duration of the project. Without uniformed promotion pressures, such officers would have more incentive to get tough, while providing the necessary experience and continuity. It would also provide an alternative "career track" for high-ranking retirees not interested in working for a defense contractor. This could even be combined with the Defense Department's recent proposal to introduce a specific "procurement officer" career track in each of the services, so officers could specialize in this type of duty. An added benefit would be to allow procurement officers of one service to be cross-assigned to duty as inspectors general on projects of one of the other services: With no ax to grind, and no superiors threatening their promotion prospects, such officers would prove invaluable.

9. Pray for a Miracle.

It's easier to win a war than it is to produce cost-effective weapons in peacetime. The avalanche of new technology has tossed peacetime war planning into a black pit of uncertainty. For example, through the 1980s, the United States has been spending over $50 billion a year on electronics, the most complex of technologies. Every nation has the problem to one degree or another, thus no one has an advantage. The prospects of eliminating the various causes of peacetime procurement fiascoes are slim. One might say, it would take a miracle to do it.

WRONG-WAR SYNDROME

This one is easy to fix, until you take a close look at how difficult the easy solutions will be to implement.

1. Look at the Record.

The historical record is important here, but equally so is an unvarnished look at the contemporary scene. The United States has historically possessed an "intervention" style military. That is, mobile and lightly armed ground forces and a fairly large navy to transport the troops to where they are needed. Large, elaborate ground forces have been characteristic of the relatively short periods in which the nation has been involved in a major war. Even the Civil War was a contest between masses of lightly armed infantry (although that was largely attributable to current technology and practice). World War I saw the United States sending in masses of infantry, and raising large infantry units was one area in which America had a good track record. Only during World War II did America raise and operate technology-heavy units. Since World War II, most of the military problems the United States has faced were best met with lightly equipped infantry units. Yet the United States became fixated on the Russian threat in Europe to the exclusion of the more likely military threats elsewhere. Both Korea and Vietnam were light-infantry wars. Since 1945 only in the Gulf has America faced an actual military emergency that called for the type of ground forces it had built up. Voices were constantly raised in the United States, including from within the military, that preparations should be made for the more likely types of war, and starting in the early 1960s, these attempts became more concrete. But even the Special Forces of that era met continual opposition from mainline military leaders. This has persisted right into the 1980s. The air force sided with the mainstream army's "Big War" thinking while the navy, with its marines, was alone equipped, as historically has been the case, to go out and fight the "little" wars. The admirals were no less entranced by the prospect of a Big War, but the navy's war would consist of seizing islands and beachheads with fairly small numbers of marines. This just happened to be the same capability needed for the more common, post–World War II low-intensity war.

Russian military leaders share the basic U.S. attitude about the future preparation for the Big War. Afghanistan was not unexpected, as Russia had previously fought over equally rugged country populated by equally stubborn inhabitants. As recently as the 1920s, Russian troops subdued Central Asia and the Caucasus. Yet there was no preparation for that kind of irregular war in difficult terrain, which makes sense when you consider that in all previous cases of this kind of war, Russia had been able to use massive numbers of conventional troops to systematically reduce hostile populations; although Afghanistan proved to be the exception because there were no railroads and few roads over which supplies could be moved to support a large number of troops. The problem could have been overcome with a massive airlift and road-building program, but that would have required more resources than Russia was willing to commit to Afghanistan's pacification. Russia has a long history of invading and conquering neighbors, most of which was done by using small units operating in vast, thinly populated areas. This type of operation has largely been dropped from the Russian repertoire during the past century of mass armies and no more empty spaces to conquer. It's not known if the Russians tried to aid their Afghanistan forces by extracting wisdom out of their historical archives; nations that have been fighting for several centuries discover, usually too late, that the battles they have just lost were fought before, and that they just made the same mistakes all over again. Soldiers are well advised to look over their shoulders at where they've been before advancing into a seemingly "new" situation.

2. Work With the Diplomats.

Soldiers and diplomats have never got along all that well, as many from both camps see the envoys as starting wars and the troops trying to end them on favorable terms. Once in a while the roles may get reversed, with the military pushing for a battlefield solution and the diplomats urging a less violent approach. This situation came about due to a combination of class conflict and working habits. Diplomats are polished, poised, and prone to, well, more diplomatic behavior. Soldiers, by the nature of their trade, are blunter and rougher around the edges. Diplomatic efforts are generally long-term efforts, while combat is noted for its comparative brevity: Wars cannot last too long because they are so damned costly. Money matters too. Armies are expensive beasts, while the Diplomatic Corps of a nation spends a small fraction of what the armed forces get. Government bureaucrats keep score by the size of budgets and staffs. On both counts, the troops beat out the diplomats. This arrangement does not help a nation prepare for future wars. The diplomats are closer to potential opponents and are better equipped to sort out who will fight, why, and how. This is not to take anything away from the military-intelligence people, but war involves more than the combat units. Warfare is nation against nation, and countries are complex organisms that diplomats are trained to be sensitive to. Even major wars will have their texture and direction changed by aspects beyond the items commonly tracked by military intelligence. But once a war begins, unless it's a minor one, there isn't a lot the diplomats can do until the fighting dies down and one side or the other shows a willingness to negotiate. Until then, relatively minor tasks, like keeping after allies and neutrals, is about all the diplomats can contribute. It's not that either the diplomats or soldiers need more work, but both of them hobble their mutual efforts by not cooperating more in peacetime. To get more cooperation means changing long-standing customs and ways of looking at matters of war and peace. You don't fix old problems without changing old habits.

3. Beware the Easy Victory.

The most common error leaders make when committing military forces is underestimating how long the fighting will take. It's quite amazing how quickly people forget that military operations rarely finish quickly but usually grind on interminably. Take the American experience. When the Civil War began in 1861, most Union—and Confederate—leaders insisted that it would be over quickly. The one exception was the senior Union military man, Winfield Scott. He said the fighting would be hard and would go on for several years. Scott was forced into retirement, yet the war went on for four years at great cost. A few years later came calls to speed up the suppression of Indian raiders in the American West. Again, there were no quick fixes. Only years of constant campaigning finally wiped out the Native Americans' military power. Then came the Spanish-American War of 1898. More calls for a quick victory, which seemed to come true as Spanish forces largely rolled over when confronted with American military force. However, the Spanish colony of the Philippines was already involved in a national rebellion, which U.S. troops inherited. This went on for a few more years and several hundred thousand deaths. It became something of a preview of Vietnam, complete with vigorous debates in the States over whether the war should be stopped.

The United States missed the "Home before the leaves fall" euphoria at the onset of World War I in 1914, but by 1917, few people were talking about an instant victory. As it was, three years of hard fighting had made the introduction of large American forces the final straw for German hopes. Twenty-one years later, at the start of World War II, people were more sober-minded about how long the war would take. They were right, as the fighting dragged on from 1939 to 1945.

After World War II, old habits were revived. When North Korea invaded the South in 1950, U.S. troops went in expecting to set things aright and be home by Christmas. They were— Christmas of 1953, as the enemy proved tougher than expected, or maybe American forces were not as tough as thought. Meanwhile the French had got bogged down in several colonial wars, with the military protesting to the end that victory was just around the corner. The United States took over from them in Vietnam, and the phrase "Light at the end of the tunnel" entered the national vocabulary. The 1983 Grenada invasion and operations that same year in Beirut both required more time and resources than were first predicted. It is almost always this way. Don't ever let anyone tell you differently.

4. Get Our Priorities Straight.

Too often decisions of great strategic importance have been made in haste, as a "knee-jerk" reaction to developments, rather than on the basis of deliberate consideration. As a result, our real interests get neglected. Weakening the defense of Europe to sustain a war in Vietnam was a perfect example of this. Directly or indirectly, the United States has defense commitments to nearly half of the countries in the world. Surely not all are "vital" to our national interest. We must recognize that some places are essential to national security, and that there are lots of places that are wholly unimportant to it. It is also important to recognize that because someone is not with us does not mean he is necessarily against us. Lots of people have their own views, which may not be the same as ours and yet may not be damaging to us. In addition, we must understand that the game we are playing—global politics and national security—has no end. It can never be won, merely abided. We must be mindful of long-term goals, not short-term successes. The current shrinking of the U.S. defense budget will force us to reexamine our overseas defense commitments. Once we have our priorities firmly established, we can better prepare the sort of armed forces that are capable of securing them.

WILL ANYTHING BE DONE?

You cannot cure the shooting blanks syndrome; you can only reduce its extent and soften its impact. Yet we can no longer afford to shoot blanks as we have done in the past, for we can no longer accept the potential costs. In earlier times, shooting blanks might have meant that a few more people got killed, or a battle or two was lost, or a province was stolen. Nowadays a nuclear war could easily cost us civilization. So something must be done. As we, the citizens of the democracies, are part of the problem, having shaped our military institutions in the ways that we have, we are also the solution. There are ways to limit the danger. First, we must recognize that the problem exists, that military power, once unleashed, is not very predictable in its results and implications.

Second, we have to accept that there are going to be a lot more wars.

Third, going into the next century, less than ten years from now, many more nations will have nuclear weapons. More nations will have more nonnuclear weapons and increasingly capable ones at that.

Fourth, ballistic missiles will become increasingly common, and what was once a rich man's war of nuclear-tipped missiles will become an option available to a far wider range of countries.

While the four decades of nuclear stalemate have kept the major powers from each other's throats, there are a growing number of smaller wars between opponents with increasingly lethal weapons. Shooting blanks will become more common and more lethal, and the side effects much more far-reaching.

Nuclear terrorists are a long-feared horror that will eventually become a reality. And the reality will as likely be in your own backyard as in some far-off battlefield.

You now know what shooting blanks is, what causes it, and what can be done to lessen its effects. Do what you can to control shooting blanks, or else . . .

Recommended Reading

There isn't a lot of literature on the phenomenon of shooting blanks, but there are a number of works that touch upon its various aspects.

Norman R. Augustine. *Augustine's Laws*. New York: American Institute of Aeronautics and Astronautics, 1983. A biting, satirical, and highly critical look at the military procurement process in America by a former undersecretary of the army who currently runs a major defense contractor, Martin Marietta.

Correlli Barnett. *The Desert Generals*. 2nd edition. New York: Viking, 1982. A controversial but convincing look at the ways in which the British shot blanks in the North African Campaign during World War II.

Mark Clodfelter. *The Limits of Air Power: The American Bombing of North Vietnam*. New York: The Free Press, 1989. A critical look at the U.S. Air Force's continuing romance with "strategic bombardment," and how this affected the course of the Vietnam War.

Norman Dixon. *On the Psychology of Military Incompetence*. London: Jonathan Cape, 1976. An incisive and insightful examination of a broad subject. Has a chapter titled Bullshit, so you know the author is up on the subject.

Robert A. Doughty. *The Seeds of Disaster*. Hamden, CT: Archon, 1985. A detailed examination of how the French contributed more to their 1940 defeat than the Germans. Covers poor French planning, doctrine, and training.

James F. Dunnigan. *How to Make War*. 2nd edition. New York: William Morrow, 1988. A handbook on all aspects of modern war, except why it happens. One of the inspirations for this book.

Trevor N. Dupuy. *Numbers, Predictions, and War*. Indianapolis: Bobbs, Merrill, 1978. Dupuy analyzes over sixty engagements during World War II to demonstrate the critical differences in the character of various armies.

Charles M. Fair. *From the Jaws of Victory*. New York: Simon & Schuster, 1971. Dedicated to noted Civil War incompetent General Ambrose Burnside, this is an amusing but biting survey of military ineptitude in history. It's not perfect, but it's a place to start.

Paul L. Ferrari, Raul L. Madrid, and Jeff Knopf. *U.S. Arms Exports: Policies and Contractors*. Cambridge, MA: MIT Press, 1988. Lots of good data, and much food for thought.

Jacques S. Gansler. *Affording Defense*. Cambridge, MA: MIT Press, 1989. A look at some of the problems of the defense budget, with some surprising insights into why we often shoot blanks in procurement.

David H. Hackworth, with Julie Sherman. *About Face*. New York: Simon & Schuster, 1989. The memoirs of an American "Supersoldier" who eventually decided there was too much shooting blanks going on in Vietnam and got out of the army under controversial circumstances. "Hack" then emigrated to Australia and became a millionaire businessman. He was a natural warrior who could express himself well in print. His account of how he developed his battlefield skills in Korea and Vietnam is a classic.

David C. Hallin. *The Uncensored War*. New York: Oxford University Press, 1986. A study of the press and the Vietnam War.

Anthony Herbert. *Soldier*. New York: Holt, Rinehart, & Winston, 1973. The memoirs of one of America's "Supersoldiers," who takes a hard, critical look at some of the ways in which the U.S. Army shot blanks during the Vietnam War. Remarkably similar to Hackworth's book.

John Keegan. *The Face of Battle*. New York: Viking, 1989. A soldier's-eye view of what it's like to be in combat. His *Six Armies in Normandy* (London: Jonathan Cape, 1982), looks at the differences in performance among the Allied and German armed forces during the Normandy Campaign.

Phillip Knightley. *The First Casualty*. New York: Harcourt Brace Jovanovich, 1975. A frequently amusing history of war correspondents, how they got it right, how they got it wrong, and how they sometimes got involved.

A. J. Krepenevich. *The Army and Vietnam*. Baltimore: Johns Hopkins, 1986. An examination of the thesis that the U.S. Army lost the war in Vietnam largely because it came prepared to refight World War II.

Michael Mallet and Williamson Murray, ed., *Military Effectiveness*, 3 vols. London: Allen & Unwin, 1988. A telling analysis of the effectiveness of the principal armed forces of the world in the era of the world wars.

R. J. Overy. *The Air War, 1939–1945*. New York: Stein & Day, 1981. Rather than deal with the air war in meticulous operational detail, Overy handles it on the basis of broad themes and patterns, such as strategy, organization, and production. The conclusions, always reasonable but frequently surprising, are not always what the fly-boys would have them be.

John Prados. *The Soviet Estimate: U.S. Intelligence Analysis and Russian Military Strength*. New York: Dial, 1982. A thoughtful look at what we got right, what we got wrong, and why in our attempts to calculate Russian military power during the Cold War, thus providing a good notion of some of the reasons for one form of shooting blanks.

Gordon W. Prange, with Donald M. Goldstein and Katherine V. Dillon. *At Dawn We Slept*. New York: McGraw-Hill, 1981, and *Pearl Harbor: The Verdict of History*. New York: McGraw-Hill, 1986. This pair of volumes deals with the most disastrous instance of the United States' shooting blanks in World War II, the debacle at Pearl Harbor, about which the authors write, "There's enough blame for everyone." In their *Miracle at Midway* (New York: McGraw-Hill, 1982), the authors take a look at the other side's blunders that led to the Japanese defeat at Midway.

Gerhard Ritter. *The Schlieffen Plan: Critique of a Myth*. London: Oswald Wolff, 1958. The subtitle gives a pretty good notion of the conclusions of this meticulous evaluation of Germany's "Perfect Plan" for World War I.

William L. Shirer. *The Collapse of the Third Republic*. New York: Simon & Schuster, 1969. An oldie but a goodie when it comes to looking at what amounted to the national frenzy of shooting blanks on all levels—political, diplomatic, economic, and military—that afflicted France in the 1920s and 1930s. When you're finished, think about the United States in the recent past.

Barbara Tuchman. *The Guns of August*. New York: Macmillan, 1962. The best look at that most massive case of shooting blanks, 1914.

The United States Strategic Bombing Survey. Washington, D.C.: USSBS, 1945–49. A largely neglected guide to the ways in which U.S. strategic-bombardment policy in World War II was a massive and expensive case of shooting blanks. Perhaps at 200 volumes its length has something to do with why it's ignored. Or perhaps its conclusions are upsetting to some.

Martin van Creveld. *Fighting Power: German and U.S. Army*

Performance, 1939–1945. Westport, CT: Greenwood Press, 1982. The U.S. Army does not come out well is this detailed comparative study.

Cecil Woodham-Smith. *The Reason Why*. New York: McGraw-Hill, 1953. A marvelous account of that most wondrous instance of shooting blanks, the Charge of the Light Brigade.

INDEX